IARIA

ICSEA 2018

The Thirteenth International Conference on Software Engineering Advances

October 14 - 18, 2018

Nice, France

ICSEA 2018 Editors

Luigi Lavazza, Università dell'Insubria - Varese, Italy

Roy Oberhauser, Aalen University, Germany

Radek Koci, Brno University of Technology, Czech Republic

Printed from e-media with permission by:

Curran Associates, Inc.
57 Morehouse Lane
Red Hook, NY 12571

Some format issues inherent in the e-media version may also appear in this print version.

Printed by Curran Associates, Inc. (2018)

International Academy, Research, and Industry Association (IARIA)
412 Derby Way
Wilmington, DE 19810

Phone: (408) 893-6407
Fax: (408) 527-6351

petre@iaria.org

Additional copies of this publication are available from:

Curran Associates, Inc.
57 Morehouse Lane
Red Hook, NY 12571 USA
Phone: 845-758-0400
Fax: 845-758-2633
Email: curran@proceedings.com
Web: www.proceedings.com

Table of Contents

LSTM Recurrent Neural Networks for Cybersecurity Named Entity Recognition 1
Houssem Gasmi, Jannik Laval, and Abdelaziz Bouras

A Practical Way of Testing Security Patterns 7
Loukmen Regainia and Sebastien Salva

An Ontology-Driven Framework for Security and Resiliency in Cyber Physical Systems 13
Rohith Yanambaka Venkata, Patrick Kamongi, and Krishna Kavi

An Experimental Evaluation of ITL, TDD and BDD 20
Luis A. Cisneros, Marisa Maximiano, Catarina I. Reis, and Jose A. Quina

Reinforcement Learning for Reliability Optimisation 25
Prasuna Saka and Ansuman Banerjee

Concurrency Analysis of Build Systems 33
Vasil Tenev, Bo Zhang, and Martin Becker

Measuring Success in Agile Software Development Projects: a GQM Approach 38
Abdullah Aldahmash and Andy Gravell

A Method to Optimize Technical Debt Management in Timed-boxed Processes 45
Luigi Lavazza, Sandro Morasca, and Davide Tosi

Continuous Improvement and Validation with Customer Touchpoint Model in Software Development 52
Tanja Sauvola, Markus Kelanti, Jarkko Hyysalo, Pasi Kuvaja, and Kari Liukkunen

Measuring and Improving the Quality of Services Provided by Data Centers: a Case Study 61
Martin Zinner, Kim Feldhoff, Michael Kluge, Matthias Jurenz, Ulf Markwardt, Daniel Sprenger, Holger Mickler, Rui Song, Andreas Tschipang, Bjorn Gehlsen, and Wolfgang E. Nagel

The Various Challenges Faced by the Software Startup Industry in Saudi Arabia 72
Abdullah Alqahtani

Software Engineering Education: Sharing an Approach, Experiences, Survey and Lessons Learned 79
Jose Carlos Metrolho and Fernando Reinaldo Ribeiro

Multi-Clustering in Fast Collaborative Filtering Recommender Systems 85
Urszula Kuzelewska

So You Want to Build a Farm: An Approach to Resource and Time Consuming Testing of Mobile Applications 91
Evgeny Pyshkin and Maxim Mozgovoy

Considerations for Adapting Real-World Open Source Software Projects Within the Classroom 95
Hyunju Kim

Sentiment-aware Analysis of Mobile Apps User Reviews Regarding Particular Updates 99
Xiaozhou Li, Zheying Zhang, and Kostas Stefanidis

Database Model Visualization in Virtual Reality: A WebVR and Benediktine Space Approach 108
Roy Oberhauser

Redefining KPIs with Information Flow Visualisation – Practitioners' View 114
Jarkko Hyysalo, Markus Kelanti, and Jouni Markkula

Tracing and Reversing the Run of Software Systems Implemented by Petri Nets 122
Radek Koci and Vladimir Janousek

ADA Language for Software Engineering 128
Diana ElRabih

Supercomputer Calculation of Gas Flow in Metal Microchannel Using Multiscale QGD-MD Approach 132
Viktoriia Podryga and Sergey Polyakov

An Enumerative Variability Modelling Tool for Constructing Whole Software Product Families 138
Chen Qian and Kung-Kiu Lau

Feature-Oriented Component-Based Development of Software Product Families: A Case Study 144
Chen Qian and Kung-Kiu Lau

ICSEA 2018

Forward

The Thirteenth International Conference on Software Engineering Advances (ICSEA 2018), held on October 14 - 18, 2018- Nice, France, continued a series of events covering a broad spectrum of software-related topics.

The conference covered fundamentals on designing, implementing, testing, validating and maintaining various kinds of software. The tracks treated the topics from theory to practice, in terms of methodologies, design, implementation, testing, use cases, tools, and lessons learnt. The conference topics covered classical and advanced methodologies, open source, agile software, as well as software deployment and software economics and education.

The conference had the following tracks:

- Advances in fundamentals for software development
- Advanced mechanisms for software development
- Advanced design tools for developing software
- Software engineering for service computing (SOA and Cloud)
- Advanced facilities for accessing software
- Software performance
- Software security, privacy, safeness
- Advances in software testing
- Specialized software advanced applications
- Web Accessibility
- Open source software
- Agile and Lean approaches in software engineering
- Software deployment and maintenance
- Software engineering techniques, metrics, and formalisms
- Software economics, adoption, and education
- Business technology
- Improving productivity in research on software engineering
- Trends and achievements

Similar to the previous edition, this event continued to be very competitive in its selection process and very well perceived by the international software engineering community. As such, it is attracting excellent contributions and active participation from all over the world. We were very pleased to receive a large amount of top quality contributions.

We take here the opportunity to warmly thank all the members of the ICSEA 2018 technical program committee as well as the numerous reviewers. The creation of such a broad and high quality conference program would not have been possible without their involvement. We also kindly thank all the authors that dedicated much of their time and efforts to contribute to the ICSEA 2018. We truly believe that thanks to all these efforts, the final conference program consists of top quality contributions.

This event could also not have been a reality without the support of many individuals, organizations and sponsors. We also gratefully thank the members of the ICSEA 2018 organizing committee for their help in handling the logistics and for their work that is making this professional meeting a success.

We hope the ICSEA 2018 was a successful international forum for the exchange of ideas and results between academia and industry and to promote further progress in software engineering research. We also hope Nice provided a pleasant environment during the conference and everyone saved some time for exploring this beautiful city.

ICSEA 2018 Steering Committee

Herwig Mannaert, University of Antwerp, Belgium
Mira Kajko-Mattsson, Royal Institute of Technology, Sweden
Luigi Lavazza, Università dell'Insubria - Varese, Italy
Roy Oberhauser, Aalen University, Germany
Elena Troubitsyna, Abo Akademi University, Finland
Radek Koci, Brno University of Technology, Czech Republic
Stephen W. Clyde, Utah State University, USA
Sébastien Salva, University Clermont Auvergne (UCA), Limos, France
Christian Kop, Universitaet Klagenfurt, Austria
Luis Fernandez-Sanz, Universidad de Alcala, Spain
Bidyut Gupta, Southern Illinois University, USA

ICSEA 2018 Industry/Research Advisory Committee

Teemu Kanstrén, VTT Technical Research Centre of Finland - Oulu, Finland
J. Paul Gibson, Telecom Sud Paris, France
Adriana Martin, National University of Austral Patagonia (UNPA), Argentina
Muthu Ramachandran, Leeds Beckett University, UK
Michael Gebhart, iteratec GmbH, Germany

ICSEA 2018

Committee

ICSEA Steering Committee

Herwig Mannaert, University of Antwerp, Belgium
Mira Kajko-Mattsson, Royal Institute of Technology, Sweden
Luigi Lavazza, Università dell'Insubria - Varese, Italy
Roy Oberhauser, Aalen University, Germany
Elena Troubitsyna, Abo Akademi University, Finland
Radek Koci, Brno University of Technology, Czech Republic
Stephen W. Clyde, Utah State University, USA
Sébastien Salva, University Clermont Auvergne (UCA), Limos, France
Christian Kop, Universitaet Klagenfurt, Austria
Luis Fernandez-Sanz, Universidad de Alcala, Spain
Bidyut Gupta, Southern Illinois University, USA

ICSEA Industry/Research Advisory Committee

Teemu Kanstrén, VTT Technical Research Centre of Finland - Oulu, Finland
J. Paul Gibson, Telecom Sud Paris, France
Adriana Martin, National University of Austral Patagonia (UNPA), Argentina
Muthu Ramachandran, Leeds Beckett University, UK
Michael Gebhart, iteratec GmbH, Germany

ICSEA 2018 Technical Program Committee

Shahliza Abd Halim, Universiti of Technologi Malaysia (UTM), Malaysia
Erika Abraham, RWTH Aachen University, Germany
Muhammad Ovais Ahmad, University of Oulu, Finland
Jacky Akoka, CNAM & IMT, France
Saadia Binte Alam, Advanced Medical Engineering Center (AMEC) | University of Hyogo, Japan
Mohammad Alshayeb, King Fahd University of Petroleum and Minerals, Saudi Arabia
Zakarya Alzamil, King Saud University, Saudi Arabia
Daniel Andresen, Kansas State University, USA
Gilbert Babin, HEC Montréal, Canada
Doo-Hwan Bae, School of Computing - KAIST, Korea
Aleksander Bai, Norsk Regnesentral, Norway
Jorge Barreiros, ISEC (Instituto Superior de Engenharia de Coimbra) / NOVA-LINCS, Portugal
Bernhard Bauer, University of Augsburg, Germany
Ateet Bhalla, Independent Consultant, India
Kenneth Boness, University of Reading, UK
Mina Boström Nakicenovic, NetEnt, Stockholm, Sweden
Nadia Bouassida, Higher Institute of Multimedia and Informatics, Sfax, Tunisia
Hongyu Pei Breivold, ABB Corporate Research, Sweden
Fernando Brito e Abreu, Instituto Universitário de Lisboa (ISCTE-IUL), Portugal

Felipe Silva Ferraz, CESAR School, Brazil
Maria Spichkova, RMIT University, Australia
Fausto Spoto, University of Verona / JuliaSoft Srl, Italy
Sidra Sultana, National University of Sciences and Technology, Pakistan
Mahbubur Rahman Syed, Minnesota State University, Mankato, USA
Sahar Tahvili, RISE SICS Västerås AB, Sweden
Shigeaki Tanimoto, Chiba Institute of Technology, Japan
Sobhan Yassipour Tehrani, King's College London & Jaguar Land Rover, UK
Dhafer Thabet, University of Mannouba, Tunisia
Pierre F. Tiako, Tiako University, USA
Elena Troubitsyna, Abo Akademi University, Finland
Mariusz Trzaska, Polish-Japanese Academy of Information Technology, Poland
Masateru Tsunoda, Kindai University, Japan
Sylvain Vauttier, LGI2P - Ecole des Mines d'Alès, France
Colin Venters, University of Huddersfield, UK
Laszlo Vidacs, Hungarian Academy of Sciences / University of Szeged, Hungary
Vinay Vkulkarni, Tata Consultancy Services, India
Stefan Voget, Continental Automotive GmbH, Germany
Song Wang, University of Waterloo, Canada
Hironori Washizaki, Waseda University / National Institute of Informatics / SYSTEM INFORMATION, Japan
Bingyang Wei, Texas Christian University, USA
Xusheng Xiao, Case Western Reserve University, USA
Rihito Yaegashi, Kagawa University, Japan
Rohith Yanambaka Venkata, University of North Texas, USA
Guowei Yang, Texas State University, USA
Stoyan Yordanov Garbatov, OutSystems, Portugal
Haibo Yu, Shanghai Jiao Tong University, China
Saad Zafar, Riphah International University, Islamabad, Pakistan
Michal Žemlička, AŽD Praha / Charles University, Czech Republic
Qiang Zhu, The University of Michigan, Dearborn, USA
Martin Zinner, Technische Universität Dresden, Germany

Copyright Information

LSTM Recurrent Neural Networks for Cybersecurity Named Entity Recognition

Houssem Gasmi[1,2], Abdelaziz Bouras[1]
[1]Computer Science Department, College of Engineering, Qatar University
Doha, Qatar
[2]Université Lumière Lyon 2, Lyon, France
email:houssem.gasmi@qu.edu.qa
email:abdelaziz.bouras@qu.edu.qa

Jannik Laval
DISP Laboratory
Université Lumière Lyon 2
Lyon, France
email:jannik.laval@univ-lyon2.fr

Abstract— **The automated and timely conversion of cybersecurity information from unstructured online sources, such as blogs and articles to more formal representations has become a necessity for many applications in the domain nowadays. Named Entity Recognition (NER) is one of the early phases towards this goal. It involves the detection of the relevant domain entities, such as product, version, attack name, etc. in technical documents. Although generally considered a simple task in the information extraction field, it is quite challenging in some domains like cybersecurity because of the complex structure of its entities. The state of the art methods require time-consuming and labor intensive feature engineering that describes the properties of the entities, their context, domain knowledge, and linguistic characteristics. The model demonstrated in this paper is domain independent and does not rely on any features specific to the entities in the cybersecurity domain, hence does not require expert knowledge to perform feature engineering. The method used relies on a type of recurrent neural networks called Long Short-Term Memory (LSTM) and the Conditional Random Fields (CRFs) method. The results we obtained showed that this method outperforms the state of the art methods given an annotated corpus of a decent size.**

Keywords- Information Extraction; Named Entity Recognition; Cybersecurity; LSTM; CRF.

I. INTRODUCTION

Timely extraction of cybersecurity information from diverse online web sources, such as news, vendor bulletins, blogs, forums, and online databases is vital for many types of applications. One important application is the conversion of unstructured cybersecurity information to a more structured form like ontologies. Knowledge modeling of cyber-attacks for instance simplifies the work of auditors and analysts [1]. At the heart of the information extraction tasks is the recognition of named entities of the domain, such as vendors, products, versions, or programming languages. The current NER tools that give the best performance in the field are based on feature engineering. These tools rely on the specific characterizing features of the entities in the field, for example, a decimal number that follows a product is very likely to be the version of that product and not quantities of it. A sequence of words starting with capital letters is likely to be a product name rather than a company name and so on.

Feature engineering has many issues and limitations. Firstly, it relies heavily on the experience of the person and the lengthy trial and error process that accompanies that. Secondly, feature engineering relies on look-ups or dictionaries to identify known entities [2]. These dictionaries are hard to build and harder to maintain especially with highly dynamic fields, such as cybersecurity. These activities constitute the majority of the time needed to construct these NER tools. The results could be satisfactory despite requiring considerable maintenance efforts to keep them up to date as more products are released and written about online. However, these tools are domain specific and do not achieve good accuracy when applied to other domains. For instance, a tool that is designed to recognize entities in the biochemistry field will perform very poorly in the domain of cybersecurity [3].

CRFs emerged in recent years as the most successful and de facto standard method for entity extraction. In this paper, we show that a domain agnostic method that is based on the recent advances in the deep learning field and word embeddings outperforms traditional methods, such as the CRFs. The first advancement, which is the word2vec word embedding method was introduced by Mikolov et al. [4] . It represents each word in the corpora by a low dimensional vector. Besides the gain in space, one of the main advantages of this representation compared to the traditional one-hot vectors [5] is the ability of these vectors to reflect the semantic relationship between the words. For instance, the difference between the vectors representing the words 'king' and 'queen' is similar to the difference between the vectors representing the words 'man' and 'woman'. These relationships result in the clustering of semantically similar words in the vector space. For instance, the words 'IBM' and 'Microsoft' will be in the same cluster, while words of products like 'Ubuntu' and 'Web Sphere Server' appear together in a different cluster.

The second advancement is the recent breakthroughs in the deep learning field. It became feasible and practical because of the increase in the hardware processing power especially GPUs and the surge in the data available for training. Deep neural networks can automatically learn non-linear combinations of features with enough training data. Hence, they alleviate the user from the time-consuming feature engineering [6]. Besides requiring feature engineering, traditional methods such as CRFs can only learn linear combinations of the defined features. The specific deep learning method we used is LSTM, which is a type of Recurrent Neural Networks (RNNs) that are particularly suitable for processing sequences of data, such as time series and natural language text [7].

We applied the LSTM-CRF architecture suggested by Lampal et al. [8] to the domain of cybersecurity NER. This architecture combines LSTM, word2vec models, and CRFs. The main characteristic of this method is that it is domain and entity type agnostic and can be applied to any domain. All it needs as input is an annotated corpus in the same format as the CoNLL-2000 dataset [9]. We compared the performance of LSTM-CRF with one of the fastest and most accurate CRF implementations, which is CRFSuite [10]. Unlike domains such as the biomedical domain, annotated corpora in the field of cybersecurity are not widely available. The corpora used to train the model were generated as part of the work of Bridges et al [1]. LSTM-CRF achieved 2% better overall item accuracy than the CRF tool.

The paper is organized as follows: Section II reviews the related work in the field. Section III provides an overview of the LSTM-CRF model. The next Section describes our evaluation method and the data pre-processing steps. Section V outlines and discusses the results. Finally, Section VI concludes the paper.

II. Related Work

Approaches to NER are mainly either rule-based or machine learning/statistical-based [11], although quite often the two techniques are mixed [12]. Rule-based methods typically are a combination of Gazette-based lookups and pattern matching rules that are hand-coded by a domain expert. These rules use the contextual information of the entity to determine whether candidate entities from the Gazette are valid or not. Statistical based NER approaches use a variety of models, such as Maximum Entropy Models [13], Hidden Markov Models (HMMs) [14],Support Vector Machines (SVMs) [15], Perceptrons [16], Conditional Random Fields (CRFs) [17], or neural networks [18]. The most successful NER approaches include those based on CRFs. CRFs address the NER problem using a sequence-labeling model. In this model, the label of an entity is modeled as dependent on the labels of the preceding and following entities in a specified window. Examples of frameworks that are available for CRF-based NER are Stanford NER and CRFSuite.

More recently, deep neural networks have been considered as a potential alternative to the traditional statistical methods as they address many of their shortcomings [19]. One of the main obstacles that prevent the adoption of the methods mentioned above is feature engineering. Neural networks essentially allow the features to be learned automatically. In practice, this can significantly decrease the amount of human effort required in various applications. More importantly, empirical results across a broad set of domains have shown that the learned features in neural networks can give very significant improvements in accuracy over hand-engineered features. RNNs, a class of neural networks have been studied and proved that they can process input with variable lengths as they have a long time memory. This property resulted in notable successes with several NLP tasks like speech recognition and machine translation [20]. LSTM further improved the performance of RNNs and allowed the learning between arbitrary long-distance dependencies [21].

Various methods have been applied to extract entities and their relations in the cybersecurity domain. Jones et al. [22] implemented a bootstrapping algorithm that requires little input data to extract security entities and the relationship between them from the text. An SVM classifier has been used by Mulwad et al. [23] to separate cybersecurity vulnerability descriptions from non-relevant ones. The classifier uses Wikitology and a computer security taxonomy to identify and classify domain entities. The two previously mentioned works relied on standard NER tools to recognize the domain concepts. While these NER tools obtained satisfactory results in general texts, such as news, they performed poorly when applied to more technical domains, such as cybersecurity because these tools are not trained on domain-specific concept identification. For instance, the Stanford NER tool is trained using a training corpus consisting mainly of news documents that are largely annotated with general entity types, such as names of people, locations, organizations, etc.

To overcome the limitations of NER tools in technical domains and identify mentions of domain-specific entities, Goldberg [5] adopted an approach that trains the CRF classifier of the Stanford NER framework on a hand-labeled training data. He achieved acceptable results that are much better than the two previous efforts. Although they produced good results, the effort involved in painstakingly annotating even a small corpus prohibits the practical implementation of this approach. To address this problem, Joshi et al. [3] developed a method to automate the labeling of training data when there is no domain-specific training data available. The labeling process leverages several data sources by combining several related domain-specific structured data to infer entities in the text. Next, a Maximum Entropy Markov Model has been trained on a corpus of nearly 750,000 words and achieved precisions above 90%. This type of training relies on external sources for corpus annotation. These resources need to be regularly maintained and updated to maintain the quality and precision of the text labeling.

Given the benefits of neural networks, this paper aims to apply the LSTM method on the problem of NER in the cybersecurity domain using the corpora made available by

Joshi et al. [3]. We analyzed the results achieved and compared them with the CRF method.

III. LSTM-CRF MODEL

In this Section, we will provide an overview of the LSTM-CRF architecture as presented by Lample et al. [8].

A. LSTM-CRF Model

RNNs are neural networks that have the capability to detect and learn patterns in data sequences. These sequences could be natural language text, spoken words, genomes, stock market time series, etc. Recurrent networks combine the current input (e.g., current word) with the previous perceived input (earlier words in the text). However, RNNs are not good at handling long-term dependencies. When the previous input becomes large, RNNs suffer from the vanishing or exploding gradient problems. They can also be challenging to training and very unlikely to converge when the number of parameters becomes large.

LSTMs were first introduced by Hochreiter et al. [7] They are an improvement on RNNs and can learn arbitrary long-term dependencies, hence can be used for a variety of applications such as natural language processing and stock market analysis. LSTMs have a similar chain structure as RNNs, but the structure of the repeating nodes is different. LSTMs have multiple layers that communicate with each other in a particular way. A typical LSTM consists of an input gate, an output gate, a memory cell, and a forget gate. Briefly, these gates control which input to pass to the memory cell to remember it in the future and which earlier state to forget. The implementation used is as follows [8]:

$$\mathbf{i_t} = \sigma(\mathbf{W}_{xi}\mathbf{x}_t + \mathbf{W}_{hi}\mathbf{h}_{t-1} + \mathbf{W}_{ci}\mathbf{c}_{t-1} + \mathbf{b}_i)$$
$$\mathbf{c}_t = (1 - \mathbf{i}_t) \odot \mathbf{c}_{t-1} + \mathbf{i}_t \tanh(\mathbf{W}_{xc}\mathbf{x}_t + \mathbf{W}_{hc}\mathbf{h}_{t-1} + \mathbf{b}_c)$$
$$\mathbf{o}_t = \sigma(\mathbf{W}_{xo}\mathbf{x}_t + \mathbf{W}_{ho}\mathbf{h}_{t-1} + \mathbf{W}_{co}\mathbf{c}_t + \mathbf{b}_o)$$
$$\mathbf{h}_t = \mathbf{o}_t \odot \tanh(\mathbf{c}_t)$$

The sigma sign σ is the elementwise sigmoid function and $\odot$ is the elementwise product.

Assuming we have a sequence of n words $X = (x_1, x_2, \ldots, x_n)$ and each word is represented by a vector of dimension d. LSTM computes the left context lh_t which represents all the words that precede the word t. A right context rh_t is also computed using another LSTM that reads the same text sequence in reverse order by starting from the end and go backward. This technique proved very useful and the resulting architecture, which consists of a forward LSTM and a backward LSTM, is called a Bidirectional LSTM. The resulting representation of a word is obtained by concatenating the left and right contexts to get the representation $h_t = [lh_t;rh_t]$. This representation is useful for various tagging applications, such as the NER problem at hand in this paper.

Figure 1 shows the architecture of the Bidirectional LSTM-CRF model. It consists of three layers.

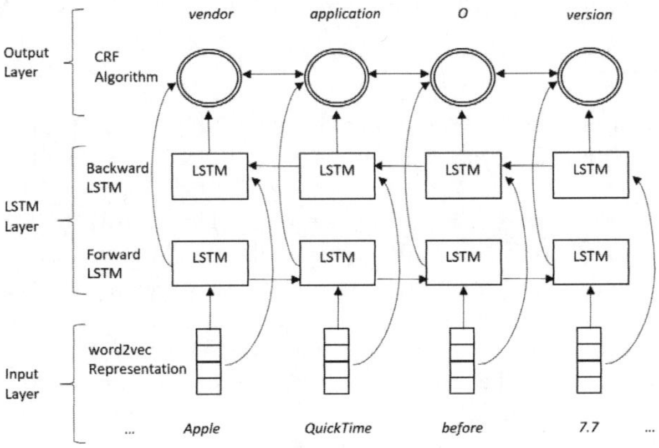

Figure 1. Bidirectional LSTM Architecture

From the bottom, the first layer is the embedding layer. This layer takes as input the sequence S of words $w_1, w_2, \ldots, w_t$. and emits a dense vector representation (embedding) x_t for each of the words in the sequence. The sequence of embeddings $x_1, x_2, \ldots, x_t$ is then passed to the bi-directional LSTM layer which refines the input and feeds it to the final CRF layer. In the last layer, the Viterbi algorithm is applied to generate the output of the neural network, which represents the most probable tag for the word.

IV. EVALUATION

In this section, we will introduce the benchmark tool, the preprocessing performed on the gold standard corpora, and the metrics we used for evaluation.

A. Competitor System

We compare the performance of the LSTM-CRF architecture against a CRF tool that uses a generic feature set for NER with word embeddings. These features were designed for domain-independent NER and defined by the tool writer. Using word embeddings in both systems will help us compare only the CRF method with the suggested LSTM-CRF architecture and negate the effect of word embeddings. We used the CRFSuite to train a CRF model using the default settings of the tool.

B. Gold standard corpora

We performed our evaluation on around 40 entity types defined in three corpora and also analyzed the performance of the model on a subset of the seven most significant entities of the domain. Each word in these corpora is auto-annotated with an entity type. The corpus is an auto-labeled cyber security domain text that was generated for use in the Stucco project. It includes all descriptions from CVE/NVD entries starting in 2010, in addition to entries from MS Bulletins and Metasploit. As stated in [1]: "While labelling these descriptions may be useful in itself, the intended purpose of this corpus is to serve as training data for a supervised learning algorithm that accurately labels other text documents in this domain, such as blogs, news articles, and tweets.".

C. Text Preprocessing

In its original form as provided by Bridges et al [1], all the corpora were stored in a single JSON file with each corpus represented by a high-level JSON element. To facilitate further processing, we converted the file to the CoNLL2000 format as the input for the LSTM-CRF model. In the newly single annotated corpus, we removed the separation between each of the three corpora and annotated every word in a separate line. Each line contains the word mentioned in the text and its entity type as show in the following example:

...
Apple B-vendor
QuickTime B-application
before B-version
7.7 I-version
allows B-relevant_term
remote B-relevant_term
attackers I-relevant_term
to O
...

As for the CRF model, the CRFSuite requires the training data to be in the CoNLL2003 format that includes the Part of Speech (POS) and chunking information with the NER tag appearing first as shown below:

...
B-vendor Apple NNP O
B-application QuickTime NNP O
B-version before IN O
I-version 7.7 CD O
B-relevant_term allows NNS O
B-relevant_term remote VBP O
I-relevant_term attackers NNS O
O to TO O
...

As the original corpus did not contain the POS and chunking information, the training corpus had to be reprocessed. We started by converting it to its original form (i.e., a set of paragraphs). Then, we used the python NLTK library to extract the necessary information for each word in the corpus. Finally, we converted the text back to the expected format shown above.

D. Evaluation Metrics

We divided the annotated corpus into 3 disjoint subsets. 70% was allocated for the training of the model, 10% for the holdout cross-validation set (or development), and 20% for the evaluation of the model. We compared the two models (LSTM-CRF and CRF) in terms of accuracy, precision, recall, and F1-score for the full set of tags and for a subset of the most relevant tags of the domain. In our experiments, the hyperparameters of the LSTM-CRF model were set to the default values used by Lample et al. [8].

V. Results and Discussion

We evaluated the performance of the NER method that is based on the LSTM-CRF architecture against a traditional state of the art CRF tool that uses standard NER features. The evaluation was performed on three different sets covering over 40 entity types from the cybersecurity domain. For evaluation purposes, we will analyze the average performance of models across all the entity types, then we will consider the most popular entities that appear frequently in the cybersecurity vulnerability descriptions and evaluate the performance on these entities only. The entities considered are *vendor, application, version, file, operating system (os), hardware,* and *edition*. The reason for this is that we are usually not interested in extracting all entity types but only a subset of them that are most relevant to the application at hand.

A. Performance of LSTM-CRF and CRF

Starting with the global item accuracy of both models, Figure 2 shows the accuracy values measured on the test set at each iteration of the training stage for 100 iterations. LSTM-CRF achieved an accuracy of 95.8% after the first iteration and increased gradually to reach values between 98.2% and 98.3% starting from iteration 23 until the end of the training. On the other hand, the CRF method started slowly at accuracies of 65% and increased rapidly to reach accuracies of 96% where it leveled off to reach eventually 96.35% at the end of the training.

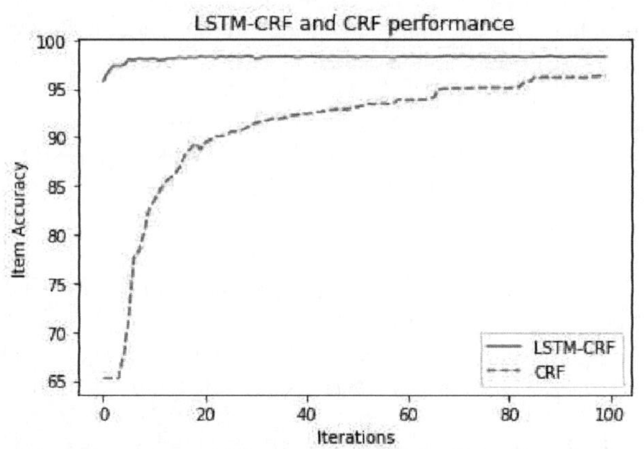

Figure 2. Item Accuracy for LSTM-CRF and CFR

The average performance of the two models across all the entity types in the training set is shown in the table below:

TABLE I. Average performance metrics for all entity types

	Precision (%)	Recall (%)	F1-score (%)
LSTM-CRF	85.16	80.70	83.37
CRF	80.26	73.55	75.97

As we can see, the performance metrics in terms of precision, recall, and F1-score show that the results for LSTM-CRF are better that their CRF counterparts.

We then compared the performance of LSTM-CRF and CRF on the most popular seven entity types in the domain. The results for each method for the different entities in terms of F1-score, precision, and recall are shown in Tables II, III, and IV. LSTM-CRF achieved the best performance for all the entities types with the exception of the *hardware*, and *edition* tags, which affected the average considerably. On average (macro average), F1-scores are 82.8% for the generic LSTM-CRF method and 84.4% for the generic CRF method. In terms of precision, the results are close at 87.2% and 89% respectively. As for the recall, it is 80.1% and 81.8% respectively.

TABLE II. F1-SCORES OF CRF AND LSTM-CRF FOR SEVEN ENTITY TAGS

Entity type	LSTM-CRF (%)		CRF (%)
	Development	*Test*	
Vendor	94	93	92
Application	90	89	87
Version	98	98	95
Edition	80	60	80
OS	95	95	93
Hardware	60	46	63
File	99	99	84
Average	**88**	**82.8**	**84.4**

TABLE III. PRECISION OF CRF AND LSTM-CRF FOR SEVEN ENTITY TAGS.

Entity type	LSTM-CRF (%)		CRF (%)
	Development	*Test*	
Vendor	95	94	94
Application	90	89	88
Version	98	98	95
Edition	80	76	87
OS	98	97	95
Hardware	69	57	79
File	99	1	85
Average	**89.8**	**87.2**	**89**

TABLE IV. RECALL OF CRF AND LSTM-CRF FOR SEVEN ENTITY TAGS

Entity type	LSTM-CRF (%)		CRF (%)
	Development	*Test*	
Vendor	93	92	90
Application	89	90	86
Version	98	98	95
Edition	79	50	75
OS	95	93	91
Hardware	54	39	52
File	100	99	84
Average	**86.8**	**80.1**	**81.8**

We can see that the overall item accuracy of the resulting LSTM-CRF model is higher by 2% than the CRF model. Likewise, the average precision, recall, and F1-score across all entity types are better by an average of 6.5%. As for the performance metrics per entity type, the LSTM-CRF model performed better on five entity types and poorly on the *hardware* and *edition* tags. The reason for this poor performance is related to the size of the training data. Deep learning algorithms such as LSTM, needs lots of data for better predictions. The more data we have, the better the prediction model can get. Upon analyzing the data set, it turned out that very few entities are tagged with these two tags compared to the other entities. There are 549 entities tagged as *hardware* and 565 tagged as *edition*. These numbers are relatively low compared to other tags, such as *application* (19093 tags) and *vendor* (10518 tags). Therefore, the first five tags overwhelmed the other poorly performing two tags. Increasing the size of the training data that contains more examples of these tags will improve the prediction of the model.

VI. CONCLUSION AND FUTURE WORK

As this paper showed, the results demonstrate that LSTM-CRF improved the accuracy of NER extraction over the state-of-art traditional pure statistical CRF method. What is impressive about the LSTM-CRF method is that it does not require any feature engineering and is entirely entity type agnostic. Even the format of the training corpus is much simpler, thus requiring less text pre-processing. This alleviates the need to develop domain-specific tools and dictionaries for NER. In the future, our research will concentrate on applying the LSTM-CRF method on entity Relations Extraction (RE). RE is concerned with attempting to find occurrences of relations among domain entities in text. This would provide a better understanding of product vulnerability descriptions. For example, RE could extract information from a vulnerability description that would help us distinguish between the product or tool that is the mean of an attack and the product being attacked. With information extraction becoming more accurate, more automated, and easier to achieve using recent neural networks advancements, there is a pressing need to turn this advancement into applications in the domain of cybersecurity. One such application is the conversion of the textual descriptions of cybersecurity vulnerabilities that are available in the web into a more formal representation like ontologies. This gives cybersecurity professionals the necessary tools that grant them rapid access to the information needed for decision-making.

ACKNOWLEDGEMENTS

This publication was made possible by NPRP grant # NPRP 7-1883-5-289 from the Qatar National Research Fund (a member of Qatar Foundation). The statements made herein are solely the responsibility of the authors.

REFERENCES

[1] R. A. Bridges, C. L. Jones, M. D. Iannacone, K. M. Testa, and J. R. Goodall, "Automatic labeling for entity extraction in cyber security," *arXiv preprint arXiv:1308.4941,* 2013.

[2] T. H. Nguyen and R. Grishman, "Event detection and domain adaptation with convolutional neural networks," in *Proceedings of the 53rd Annual Meeting of the Association for Computational Linguistics and the 7th International Joint*

Conference on Natural Language Processing (Volume 2: Short Papers), pp. 365–371, 2015.

[3] A. Joshi, R. Lal, T. Finin, and A. Joshi, "Extracting cybersecurity related linked data from text," in *Semantic Computing (ICSC), 2013 IEEE Seventh International Conference on*, pp. 252-259, 2013.

[4] T. Mikolov, I. Sutskever, K. Chen, G. S. Corrado, and J. Dean, "Distributed representations of words and phrases and their compositionality," in *Advances in neural information processing systems*, pp. 3111-3119, 2013.

[5] Y. Goldberg, "A primer on neural network models for natural language processing," *Journal of Artificial Intelligence Research,* vol. 57, pp. 345-420, 2016.

[6] J. Schmidhuber, "Deep learning in neural networks: An overview," *Neural networks,* vol. 61, pp. 85-117, 2015.

[7] S. Hochreiter and J. Schmidhuber, "Long short-term memory," *Neural computation,* vol. 9, pp. 1735-1780, 1997.

[8] G. Lample, M. Ballesteros, S. Subramanian, K. Kawakami, and C. Dyer, "Neural architectures for named entity recognition," *arXiv preprint arXiv:1603.01360,* 2016.

[9] E. F. Tjong Kim Sang and S. Buchholz, "Introduction to the CoNLL-2000 shared task: Chunking," in *Proceedings of the 2nd workshop on Learning language in logic and the 4th conference on Computational natural language learning-Volume 7*, pp. 127-132, 2000.

[10] N. Okazaki, *CRFsuite: a fast implementation of Conditional Random Fields (CRFs),* 2007.

[11] P. Cimiano, S. Handschuh, and S. Staab, "Towards the self-annotating web," in *Proceedings of the 13th international conference on World Wide Web*, pp. 462-471, 2004.

[12] P. Pantel and M. Pennacchiotti, "Automatically Harvesting and Ontologizing Semantic Relations," in Proceedings of the 2008 Conference on Ontology Learning and Population: Bridging the Gap Between Text and Knowledge, Amsterdam, The Netherlands, The Netherlands, pp. 171-195, 2008.

[13] H. L. Chieu and H. T. Ng, "Named entity recognition: a maximum entropy approach using global information," in *Proceedings of the 19th international conference on Computational linguistics-Volume 1*, pp. 190-196, 2002.

[14] A. McCallum, D. Freitag, and F. C. N. Pereira, "Maximum Entropy Markov Models for Information Extraction and Segmentation.," in *Icml*, pp. 591-598, 2000.

[15] H. Isozaki and H. Kazawa, "Efficient support vector classifiers for named entity recognition," in *Proceedings of the 19th international conference on Computational linguistics-Volume 1*, pp. 1-7, 2002.

[16] X. Carreras, L. Màrquez, and L. Padró, "Learning a perceptron-based named entity chunker via online recognition feedback" in *Proceedings of the seventh conference on Natural language learning at HLT-NAACL 2003-Volume 4*, pp. 156-159, 2003.

[17] A. McCallum and W. Li, "Early results for named entity recognition with conditional random fields, feature induction and web-enhanced lexicons," in *Proceedings of the seventh conference on Natural language learning at HLT-NAACL 2003-Volume 4*, pp. 188-191, 2003.

[18] R. Collobert, J. Weston, L. Bottou, M. Karlen, K. Kavukcuoglu, and P. Kuksa, "Natural language processing (almost) from scratch," *Journal of Machine Learning Research,* vol. 12, pp. 2493-2537, 2011.

[19] Y. Goldberg, "A Primer on Neural Network Models for Natural Language Processing.," *J. Artif. Intell. Res.(JAIR),* vol. 57, pp. 345-420, 2016.

[20] A. Graves, A. Mohamed, and G. Hinton, "Speech recognition with deep recurrent neural networks," in *Acoustics, speech and signal processing (icassp), ieee international conference on*, pp. 6645-6649, 2013.

[21] F. A. Gers, J. A. Schmidhuber and F. A. Cummins, "Learning to Forget: Continual Prediction with LSTM,", *Neural Compution*, vol. 12, pp. 2451-2471, 10 2000.

[22] L. Jones, R. A. Bridges, K. M. T. Huffer and J. R. Goodall, "Towards a relation extraction framework for cyber-security concepts," in *Proceedings of the 10th Annual Cyber and Information Security Research Conference*, pp. 11, 2015

[23] V. Mulwad, W. Li, A. Joshi, T. Finin and K. Viswanathan, "Extracting information about security vulnerabilities from web text," in *Web Intelligence and Intelligent Agent Technology (WI-IAT),* 2011 *IEEE/WIC/ACM International Conference on*, 2011.

A Practical Way of Testing Security Patterns

Loukmen Regainia and Sébastien Salva
LIMOS - UMR CNRS 6158
University Clermont Auvergne, France
email: loukmen.regainia@uca.fr, sebastien.salva@uca.fr

***Abstract*—We propose an approach for helping developers devise more secure applications from the threat modelling stage up to the testing one. This approach relies on a Knowledge base integrating varied security data to perform these tasks. It firstly assists developers in the design of Attack Defence Trees (ADTrees) expressing the attacker possibilities to compromise an application and the defences that may be implemented. These defences are expressed by means of security patterns, which are generic and re-usable solutions to design secure applications. ADTrees are then used to guide developers in the generation of test cases and Linear Temporal Logic (LTL) specifications. The latter encoding properties about security pattern behaviours. Test verdicts show whether an application is vulnerable to the attack scenarios and if the security pattern properties hold in the application traces.**

***Keywords*-Security pattern ; Security Testing ; Attack Defence Tree ; Test Case Generation.**

I. Introduction

Preventing attackers from exploiting software defects, in order to compromise the security of applications or to disclose and delete user data, may be considered as the main motivations for software security. It is well admitted that the choice of security solutions and the audit of these solutions are two tasks of the software life cycle requiring time, expertise and experience. Unfortunately, developers lack resources and guidance on how to design or implement secure applications and test them. Furthermore, different kinds of expertise are required, e.g., to represent threats, to choose the most appropriate security solutions w.r.t. an application context, or to ensure that the latter are implemented as expected.

Several digitalised security bases, documents and papers have been proposed to guide developers in these activities. For instance, the Common Attack Pattern Enumeration and Classification (CAPEC) base makes publicly available around 1000 attack descriptions, including their goals, steps, techniques, the targeted vulnerabilities, etc. In another context, security pattern catalogues, e.g., [1], list 176 re-usable solutions for helping developers design more secure applications. The security pattern, which is a topic of this paper, *intuitively relates countermeasures to threats and attacks in a given context* [2]. This profusion of documents makes developers drown in a sea of recommendations taking security with different viewpoints (attackers, defenders, etc.), abstraction levels (security principles, attack steps, exploits, etc.) or contexts (system, network, etc.). In this paper, we focus on this issue and propose an approach to assist developers devise more secure applications from the threat modelling stage up to the testing one. The originality of this approach resides in the facts that it relies on a Knowledge base to automate some steps and it does not require that developers have skills in (formal) modelling.

Brief review of related work, and contributions: Numerous papers proposed methods for generating test cases from models to check the security of systems, protocols or applications. Among them, several papers, e.g., [3], [4], focused on models not to describe the implementation behaviour but rather to express attacker goals or vulnerability causes of a system. These works take Threat models as inputs, which are manually written. If these lack of details (parameters, attack steps, etc.), the final test cases will be too abstract as well. Furthermore, these methods do not give any recommendation on how to write tests and on how to structure them. Hence, developers lack guidance to write tests and to reuse them.

We proposed in [5] a preliminary approach for helping developers devise more secure applications with a guided test case generation approach. It is based on a first Knowledge base integrating security data. The approach firstly queries the Knowledge base to help developers write an Attack Defense Tree (ADTree) encoding the attack scenarios that may be performed by an adversary and the defences, materialised with security patterns, which have to be integrated and implemented into the application. Thereafter, the approach helps generate security test cases to check whether the application is vulnerable to these attacks. However, it does not assist developers to ensure that security patterns have been correctly implemented in the application. This work supplements our early study by covering this part.

Few works dealt with the testing of security patterns, which is the main topic of this paper. Yoshizawa et al. introduced a method for testing whether behavioural and structural properties of patterns may be observed in application traces [6]. Given a security pattern, two test templates (Object Constrant Languauge (OCL) expressions) are manually written, one to specify the pattern structure and another to encode its behaviour. Then, developers have to make templates concrete by manually writing tests for experimenting the application. The latter returns traces on which the

OCL expressions are verified. Our approach requires neither complete models nor formal properties. It generates ADtrees to help developers choose security patterns. Furthermore, with our approach, developers do not need to have a good knowledge and skills on the writing of formal properties. Instead, we propose a practical way to generate them. Intuitively, after the choice of security patterns, our approach provides UML sequence diagrams, which can be modified by the developer. From these diagrams, we generate LTL properties, which capture the cause-effects relations among pairs of method calls. After the test case execution, we check if these properties hold in application traces. The developer is hence not aware of the LTL formula processing.

Paper Organisation: Section II introduces the Knowledge base used by our approach. Section III gives the first three steps of the approach, which aim at generating threat models, proposing security patterns and providing UML sequence diagrams. Section IV addresses the generation of test cases and LTL properties, which are used to return test verdicts. We finally conclude in Section V.

II. Knowledge Base Overview

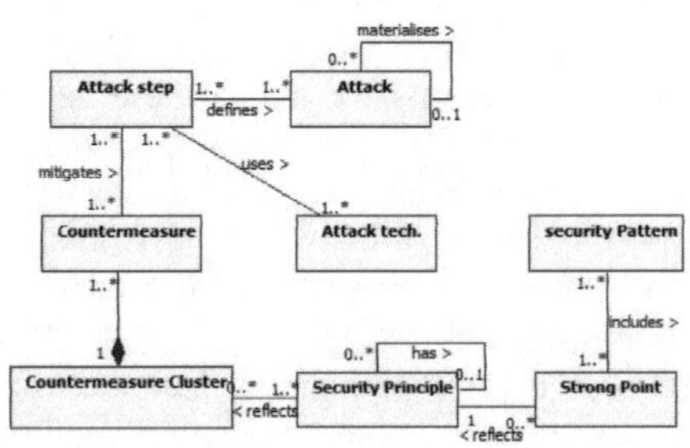

Figure 1. Knowledge Base meta-model part 1

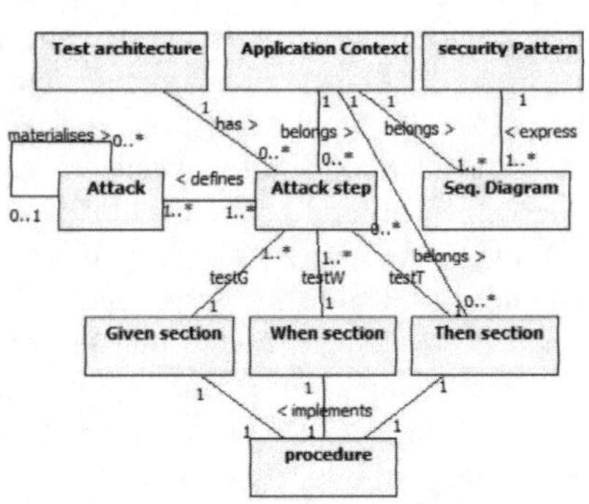

Figure 2. Knowledge Base meta-model part 2

Our approach relies on a Knowledge base to automate some of its steps. Its meta-model is depicted in Figures 1 and 2. We summarise its architecture in the following but we refer to [5] for a complete description and for the data integration. The meta-model associates attacks, techniques, security principles, security patterns, test cases and UML sequence diagrams. To increase the precision of the relations, we chose to decompose attacks into sub-attacks, and into attack steps. These steps are associated to countermeasures, allowing to prevent attack steps. We also decompose security patterns into strong points, which are sub-properties expressing pattern key design features. Relying on a hierarchical organisation of security principles, the method maps countermeasure clusters to principles and strong points to principles. As countermeasures usually are detailed properties, we gather them into clusters (groups) to reach about the same abstraction levels as those of the security principles.

In Figure 2, an attack step is also associated to one Application context and one Test architecture. The context refers to an application family, e.g., Web sites. The Test architecture entity refers to textual paragraphs explaining the points of observation and control, testers or tools required to execute the attack step on an application, which belongs to an Application context. Next, we map attack steps onto Given When Then (GWT) test case sections. For readability and re-usability purposes, we chose to consider the "Given When Then" pattern to break up test cases into several parts:

- the Given section aims at putting an application under test in a known state;
- the When section triggers some actions;
- the Then section is used to check whether the conditions of success of the test case are met (assertions). We suppose that a Then section returns the message "$Pass_{st}$" if an attack step st has been successfully executed, "$Inconclusive_{st}$" if some test case procedures have not been executed due to various problems (e.g., incomplete test architecture, network issues, etc.) or "$Fail_{st}$" otherwise.

A test case section is linked to one procedure stored in the Procedure table, which implements the section. These procedures may be completed with comments or with blocks of code to ease the test case development. But, they must remain generic, i.e., re-usable with any application in a precise context.

For this paper, we have updated the Knowledge base in such a way that a security pattern is also associated to UML sequence diagrams, themselves adapted to application contexts. Indeed, security pattern catalogues often provide UML sequence diagrams expressing the security pattern behaviours. These diagrams show how to implement a security pattern with regard to an Application context.

As a proof of concept, we generated a Knowledge base specialised to Web applications (The paper [5] details some data acquisition and integration steps). It includes information about 215 attacks (209 attack steps, 448 techniques), 26 security patterns, 66 security principles. We also generated 627 GWT test case sections (Given, When and Then sections) and 209 procedures. The latter are composed of comments explaining: which techniques can be used to execute an attack step and which observations reveal that the application is vulnerable. We manually completed 32 procedures, which cover 43 attack steps. We used the testing framework Selenium and the penetration testing tool ZAProxy [7], which covers varied Web vulnerabilities. This Knowledge base is available here [8].

III. Security and Security Pattern Testing

Figure 3 depicts an overview of the six steps of our approach, beginning by the construction of a threat model and ending with the generation of test verdicts expressing whether an Application Under Test (AUT) is vulnerable to the attack scenarios encoded in the threat model and whether security pattern behaviours hold in the AUT traces. Before describing these steps, we briefly recall some notions about the ADTree model.

A. Attack Defense Trees (ADTrees)

ADTrees *are graphical representations of possible measures an attacker might take in order to attack a system and the defenses that a defender can employ to protect the system* [9]. ADTrees have two kinds of nodes: attack nodes (red circles) and defense nodes (green squares). A node can be *refined* with child nodes and can have one child of the opposite type (linked with a dashed line). Node refinements can be disjunctive (as in Figure 4) or conjunctive. The latter is graphically distinguishable by connecting the edges between a root node and its children with an arc. We extend these two refinements with the sequential conjunctive refinement of attack nodes. This operator expresses the execution order of child attack nodes. Graphically, a sequential conjunctive refinement is illustrated by connecting the edges, going from a node to its children, with an arrow.

Alternatively, an ADTree T can be formulated with an algebraic expression called ADTerm and denoted $\iota(T)$. In short, the ADTerm syntax is composed of operators having types given as exponents in $\{o,p\}$ with o modelling an opponent and p a proponent. $\vee^s, \wedge^s, \overrightarrow{\wedge}^s$, with $s \in \{o,p\}$ respectively stand for the disjunctive refinement, the conjunctive refinement and the sequential conjunctive refinement of a node. A last operator c expresses counteractions (dashed lines in the graphical tree).

B. Model Generation, Security Pattern Choice (Step 1 to 3)

Step 1: Initial ADTree Design

The developer establishes an initial ADTree T whose root node represents the attacker's goal. This node may be refined with several layers of children to refine this goal. We suppose that T at least has leaves labelled by attacks available in the Knowledge base. Otherwise, a semantic alignment may be required to replace some attack labels.

An example is given in Figure 4: the goal, given in the root node of the ADTree, refers to the injection of malicious code into an application. This goal is disjunctively refined by two children expressing two more concrete attacks, described in

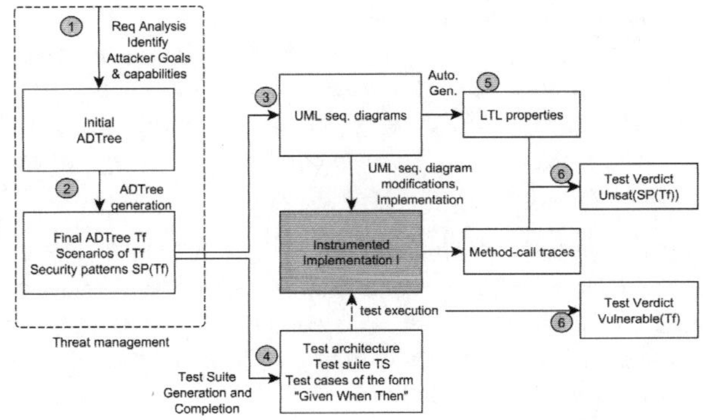

Figure 3. Overview of the 6 steps of the approach

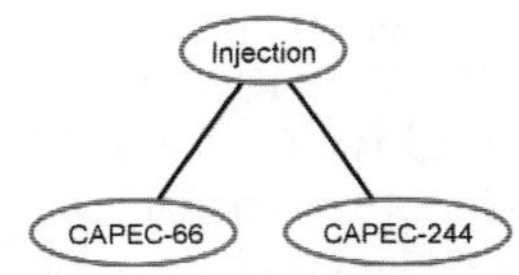

Figure 4. Initial ADTree example

the CAPEC base: CAPEC-66: SQL Injection and CAPEC-244: Cross-Site Scripting via Encoded URI Schemes.

Step 2: Detailed ADTree Generation

The Knowledge base is now queried to automatically complete T with more details about the attack proceeding and with defense nodes labelled by security patterns. We summarise this step in the following:

For every node labelled with an attack Att, the Knowledge base is called to automatically generate an ADTree denoted $T(Att)$. This ADTree has a specific form satisfying the meta-model of the Knowledge base. More precisely, the root of $T(Att)$ is labelled by Att. This node may have children expressing more concrete attacks and so forth. The most concrete attacks have step sequences (edges connected with an arrow). These steps are connected to techniques with a disjunctive refinement. The lowest attack steps in the ADTree are also linked to defense nodes, which may be the roots of sub-trees expressing security pattern combinations whose purposes are to counteract the attack steps. The developer can now edit the ADTrees $T(Att)$ to edit some attack steps w.r.t. the application context. He or she also has to choose the security patterns that have to be contextualised and implemented in the application. After this step, we assume that a defense node either is labelled by a security pattern (it does not have children) or has a conjunctive refinement of nodes labelled by security patterns. These generated ADTrees have a specific form, which are encoded by these ADTerms:

Proposition 1 *An ADTree $T(Att)$ achieved by the previous steps has an ADTerm $\iota(T(Att))$ having one of these forms:*

1) $\vee^p(t_1, \ldots, t_n)$ *with* $t_i (1 \leq i \leq n)$ *an ADTerm also having one of these forms:*
2) $\overrightarrow{\wedge}^p(t_1, \ldots, t_n)$ *with* $t_i (1 \leq i \leq n)$ *an ADTerm having the form given in 2) or 3);*
3) $c^p(st, sp)$*, with* st *an ADTerm expressing an attack step and* sp *an ADTerm modelling a security pattern combination.*

The first ADTerm expresses children nodes labelled by more concrete attacks. The second one represents sequences of attack steps. The last ADTerm is composed of an attack step st refined with techniques, which can be counteracted by a security pattern combination $sp = \wedge^o(sp_1, \ldots, sp_m)$. We call this ADTerm a Basic Attack Defence Step $c^p(st, sp)$, shortened BADStep. $BADStep(T_f)$ denotes the set of BADSteps of T_f (final ADTree).

Figure 5 depicts a part of the ADTree of the attack CAPEC-66. Each lowest attack step has a defense node expressing pattern combinations. Step 2.1, which identifies the possibilities to inject malicious code through the application inputs, requires more patterns than the other steps to filter these inputs. Some of them have relations: for instance the pattern "Application Firewall" can be replaced by "Intercepting Validator" or "Output Guard".

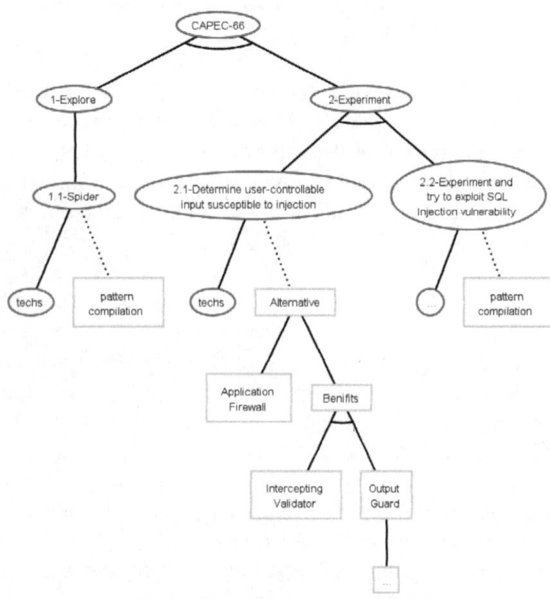

Figure 5. Part of the ADTree of the Attack CAPEC-66

In the initial ADTree T, each attack node labelled by Att is now automatically replaced with the ADTree $T(Att)$. This can be done by substituting every term Att in the ADTerm $\iota(T)$ by $\iota(T(Att))$. We denote T_f the resulting ADTree, and $SP(T_f)$ the security pattern set found in $\iota(T_f)$.

In this step, we finally extract from the Knowledge base a description of the test architecture required to run the attacks on the application under test and to observe its reactions.

Step 3: UML Sequence Diagram Extraction

For every security pattern found in T_f, we extract a list of UML sequence diagrams from the Knowledge base, each being related to the application context. These show the behavioural activities of the patterns. We now suppose that the developer implements every security pattern in the application. At the same time, he/she can choose to modify the generic class and method names labelled in the UML sequence diagrams. In this case, we assume that the sequence diagrams are annotated to point out these modifications.

As example, Figure 6 illustrates the UML sequence diagram of the security pattern "Intercepting Validator", whose purpose is to control the compliance of user requests with regard to a specification. The validation must be performed in the server side. For instance, while the pattern implementation, if the name of the method "process" has to be modified by "send", the new label must be of the form "process/send" to express the substitution.

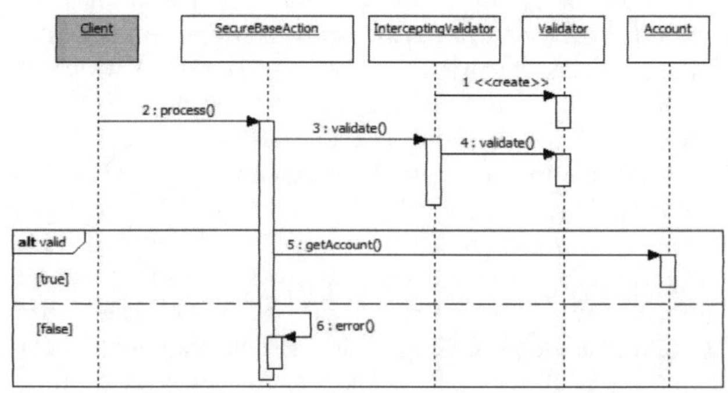

Figure 6. Intercepting Validator sequence diagram

IV. Attack and Security Pattern Testing

At this stage, an ADTree encodes the notion of attack scenarios over BADSteps, a scenario being is a minimal combination of events leading to the root attack.

Definition 2 (Attack scenarios) *Let* T_f *be an ADTree and* $\iota(T_f)$ *be its ADTerm. The set of Attack scenarios of* T_f*, denoted* $SC(T_f)$ *is the set of clauses of the disjunctive normal form of* $\iota(T_f)$ *over* $BADStep(T_f)$*.*

An attack scenario s is still an ADTerm over BADSteps. $BADStep(s)$ denotes the set of BADSteps of s.

Step 4: Test suite generation

Let us consider a security scenario $s \in SC(T_f)$. Given a BADStep $b = c^p(st, sp) \in BADStep(s)$, we generate the GWT test case $TC(b)$, which aims at checking whether the application under test AUT is vulnerable to the attack step st. $TC(b)$ is constructed by extracting from the Knowledge base, for the attack step st, one Given section, one When section and one Then section, each related to one procedure. The Then section aims to assert whether the application is vulnerable to the attack step st; these sections are assembled to make up the GWT test case stub $TC(b)$.

After having iteratively applied this test case construction on the scenarios of $SC(T_f)$, we obtain the test suite TS with $TS = \{TC(b) \mid b = c^p(st, sp) \in BADStep(s) \text{ and } s \in SC(T_f)\}$.

Step 5: Security Pattern LTL Property Generation

Our approach aims at checking whether security pattern behavioural properties hold in the AUT. Instead of asking the developer to write these properties, we automatically generate them from UML sequence diagrams. This step analyses sequence diagrams, recognises behavioural characteristics and translates them into LTL properties.

Given a security pattern sp and its UML sequence diagram, the latter is firstly transformed into a UML activity diagram. We propose 5 transformation rules whose three are depicted in Table I. Intuitively, these rules transform each method call in the sequence diagram by an action state in the activity diagram. We took inspiration from the transformations of UML sequence diagrams to state machines proposed in [10]. This transformation allows us to use the mapping of UML activity diagrams to LTL properties proposed by Muram et al. [11]. The transformation rules are based upon the Response Property Pattern [12], which describes the cause-effect relations among method calls. Three examples of transformations are given in Table I. At the end of this transformation sequence, we have a set of LTL properties $P(sp)$ for every security pattern $sp \in SP(T_f)$. Although the LTL properties of $P(sp)$ do not necessarily cover all the possible behavioural properties of a security pattern sp, this process offers the advantages to not require generic LTL properties modelling pattern behaviours, and to not ask developers to instantiate these generic LTL properties to match the application model or code.

TABLE I
TRANSFORMATION RULES

Sequence	Activity	LTL properties
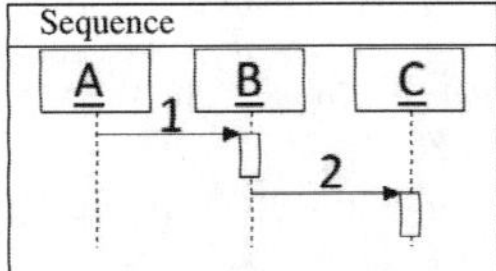	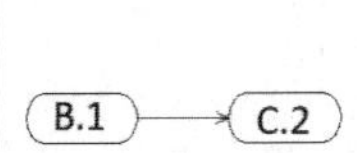	$\square(B.1 \longrightarrow \lozenge C.2)$
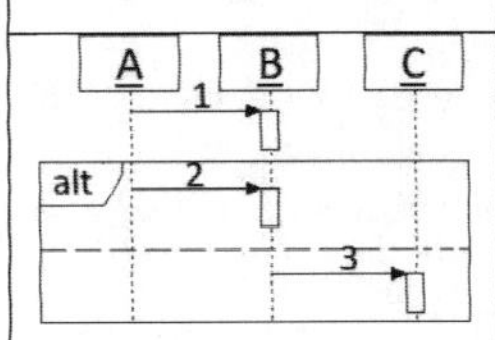	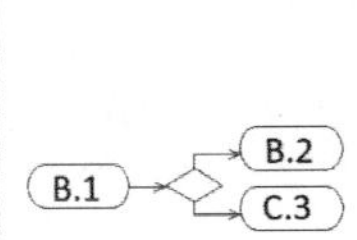	$\square(B.1 \longrightarrow (\lozenge B.2) xor (\lozenge C.3))$
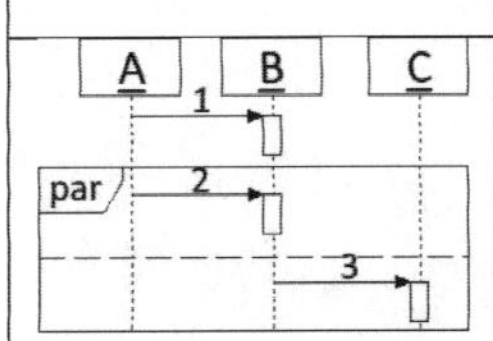	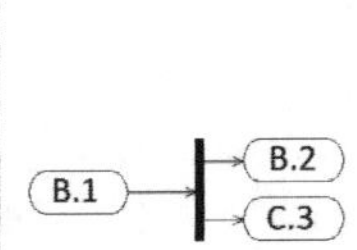	$\square(B.1 \longrightarrow (\lozenge B.2) and (\lozenge C.3))$

From the example of UML sequence diagram given in Figure 6, four LTL properties are generated. Table II lists them. These capture the cause-effect relations of every pair of methods found in the UML sequence diagram.

TABLE II
LTL PROPERTIES OF THE PATTERN INTERCEPTING VALIDATOR

p_1	$\square(Controller.SecureBaseAction.process \longrightarrow \lozenge InterceptingValidator.Validator.create)$
p_2	$\square(InterceptingValidator.Validator.create \longrightarrow \lozenge interceptingValidator.InterceptingValidator.validate)$
p_3	$\square(InterceptingValidator.InterceptingValidator.validate \longrightarrow \lozenge InterceptingValidator.Validator.validate)$
p_4	$\square(InterceptingValidator.Validator.validate \longrightarrow (\lozenge model.Account.getAccount) xor (\lozenge Controller.SecureBaseAction.error))$

Step 6: Test Verdict generation

Once the GWT test case stubs are completed by the developer, these are executed on AUT. The test architecture allowing the experimentation of AUT is described in the report provided by Step 2. The execution of a test case $TC(b)$ on AUT, leads to a local verdict denoted $\text{Verdict}(TC(b)||AUT)$, which takes as value a test case assertion message. Furthermore, we consider that the AUT is instrumented with a debugger or similar tool to collect the methods called in the application while the execution of the test cases of TS. After the test case execution, we hence have a set of method call traces of AUT denoted $Traces(AUT)$. With a model-checking tool, e.g., Declare2LTL [13], our approach can now detect the non-satisfiability of LTL properties of a security pattern sp on $Traces(AUT)$. The predicate $Unsat^b(sp)$ defines this detection:

Definition 3 (Local Test Verdicts) *Let AUT be an application under test, $b = c^p(st, sp) \in BADStep(T_f)$, sp_1 a security pattern in sp, $TC(b) \in TS$ be a test case.*

1) $\text{Verdict}(TC(b)||AUT) =$
   -$Fail_{st}$ (resp. $Pass_{st}$) means AUT is (resp. does not appear to be) vulnerable to the attack step st;
   -$Inconclusive_{st}$ means that various problems occurred while the test case execution.
2) $\text{Unsat}^b(sp_1) =_{def}$ *true if* $\exists p \in P(sp_1), \exists t \in Traces(AUT), t \nvDash p$; *otherwise,* $\text{Unsat}^b(sp_1) =_{def} false$;

Subsequently, we define the final test verdicts with regard to the ADTree T_f. These verdicts are given with the predicates $\text{Vulnerable}(T_f)$, $\text{Unsat}^b(SP(T_f))$ and $\text{Inconclusive}(T_f)$ returning boolean values. The predicate $\text{Vulnerable}(b)$ is also defined on a BADStep b to later apply a substitution $\sigma : BADStep(s) \rightarrow \{true, false\}$ on an attack-defense scenario s. A scenario s holds if the evaluation of the substitution σ to s (i.e., replacing every BADStep term b with the evaluation of $\text{Vulnerable}(b)$) returns true. When a scenario of T_f holds, then the threat

TABLE III
TEST VERDICT SUMMARY AND SOLUTIONS

Vulnerable(T_f)	Unsat^b($SP(T_f)$)	Incon (T_f)	Corrective actions
False	False	False	No issue detected
True	False	False	At least one scenario is successfully applied on AUT. Fix the pattern implementation. Or the chosen patterns are inconvenient.
False	True	False	Some pattern behavioural properties do not hold. Check the pattern implementations with the UML seq. diag. Or another pattern conceals the behaviour of the former.
True	True	False	The chosen security patterns are useless or incorrectly implemented. Review the ADTree, fix AUT.
T/F	T/F	True	The test case execution crashed or returned unexpected exceptions. Check the Test architecture and the test case codes.

modelled by T_f can be achieved on AUT. This is defined with the predicate Vulnerable(T_f). Unsat$^b(SP(T_f))$ is true as soon as a security pattern property does not hold on $Traces(AUT)$. Table III informally summarises the meaning of some test verdicts and some corrections that may be followed in case of failure.

Definition 4 (Final Test Verdicts) *Let AUT be an application under test, T_f be an ADTree, $s \in SC(T_f)$ and $b = c^p(st, sp) \in BADStep(T_f)$.*

1) Vulnerable$(b) =_{def}$ *true if* Verdict$(TC(b)||AUT) = Fail_{st}$*; otherwise,* Vulnerable$(b) =_{def}$ *false;*
2) $\sigma : BADStep(s) \rightarrow \{true, false\}$ *is a substitution* $\{b_1 \rightarrow \text{Vulnerable}(b_1), \ldots, b_n \rightarrow \text{Vulnerable}(b_n)\}$*;*
3) Vulnerable$(T_f) =_{def}$ *true if* $\exists s \in SC(T_f)$: $eval(s\sigma)$ *returns true; otherwise,* Vulnerable(T_f) $=_{def}$ *false;*
4) Inconclusive$(T_f) =_{def}$ *true if* $\exists s \in SC(T_f)$, $\exists b \in$ BADStep(s)*:* Verdict$(TC(b)||\ AUT) = Inconclusive_{st}$*; otherwise,* Inconclusive$(T_f) =_{def}$ *false.*
5) Unsat$^b(SP(T_f)) =_{def}$ *true if* $\exists sp \in SP(T_f)$, Unsat$^b(sp) = true$*; otherwise,* Unsat^c($SP(T_f)$) $=_{def}$ *false;*

V. CONCLUSION

This paper proposes an approach taking advantage of a Knowledge base to assist developers in the implementation of secure applications through six steps covering threat modelling, the choice of security patterns, security testing and the verification of security pattern behavioural properties. It guides developers in the generation of ADTrees and test cases. In addition, it automatically generates LTL properties, encoding security pattern behaviours. As a consequence, the approach does not require developers to have skills in (formal) modelling or in formal methods. We have implemented this approach in a tool prototype [8]. We briefly summarise its features in this paper: it generates ADTrees stored into XML files, which can be edited with *ADTool* [9]. Our tool also builds GWT test case compatible with the Cucumber framework [14], which supports a large number of languages. These test cases can be imported with the IDE Eclipse. The verification of LTL properties is performed with the Declare2LTL model checker. We started to perform some experiments on Web applications to assess the user benefits. An evaluation will be presented in a future work.

REFERENCES

[1] R. Slavin and J. Niu. (retrieved: 07, 2018) Security patterns repository. [Online]. Available: http://sefm.cs.utsa.edu/repository/

[2] M. Schumacher, *Security Engineering with Patterns: Origins, Theoretical Models, and New Applications.* Secaucus, NJ, USA: Springer-Verlag New York, Inc., 2003.

[3] A. Morais, E. Martins, A. Cavalli, and W. Jimenez, "Security protocol testing using attack trees," in *2009 International Conference on Computational Science and Engineering*, vol. 2, Aug 2009, pp. 690–697.

[4] N. Shahmehri et al., "An advanced approach for modeling and detecting software vulnerabilities," *Inf. Softw. Technol.*, vol. 54, no. 9, pp. 997–1013, Sep. 2012.

[5] S. Salva and L. Regainia, "Using data integration for security testing," in *Proceedings 29th International Conference, ICTSS 2017*, 10 2017, pp. 178–194.

[6] Y. Masatoshi et al., "Verifying implementation of security design patterns using a test template," in *2014 Ninth International Conference on Availability, Reliability and Security*, Sept 2014, pp. 178–183.

[7] OWASP. (retrieved: 07, 2018) Zap proxy project. [Online]. Available: https://www.owasp.org/index.php/OWASP_Zed_Attack_Proxy_Project

[8] R. Loukmen and S. Sbastien. (retrieved: 07, 2018) Zap proxy project. [Online]. Available: http://regainia.com/research/companion.html

[9] B. Kordy, S. Mauw, S. Radomirović, and P. Schweitzer, "Attack–defense trees," *Journal of Logic and Computation*, p. exs029, 2012.

[10] R. Grønmo and B. Møller-Pedersen, "From sequence diagrams to state machines by graph transformation," in *Theory and Practice of Model Transformations*, L. Tratt and M. Gogolla, Eds. Berlin, Heidelberg: Springer Berlin Heidelberg, 2010, pp. 93–107.

[11] F. U. Muram, H. Tran, and U. Zdun, "Automated mapping of UML activity diagrams to formal specifications for supporting containment checking," in *Proceedings FESCA 2014, Grenoble, France, 12th April 2014.*, 2014, pp. 93–107.

[12] L. Patterns. (retrieved: 07, 2018) response ltl pattern. [Online]. Available: http://patterns.projects.cs.ksu.edu/documentation/patterns/response.shtml

[13] M. M. Fabrizio et al. (retrieved: 07, 2018) Declare toolkit. [Online]. Available: http://www.win.tue.nl/declare/

[14] Cucumber. (retrieved: 07, 2018) Cucumber website. [Online]. Available: https://cucumber.io/

An Ontology-Driven Framework for Security and Resiliency in Cyber Physical Systems

Rohith Yanambaka Venkata, Patrick Kamongi and Krishna Kavi

University of North Texas
Denton, Texas-76203
Email: [ry0080, pk0158, krishna.kavi]@unt.edu

***Abstract*—Cyber-Physical Systems (CPS) can be described as an integration of computation and physical processes, where embedded systems monitor and control physical processes. Advances in technologies, such as networking and processors have enabled the adoption of CPS in safety-critical systems like smart grids and autonomous vehicles. Cyber-attacks, as the name suggests, target components in the cyber space with the intention of disrupting the functionality of the physical components. In this paper, we present an Ontology-driven framework that captures the relationship between cyber and physical systems to semantically reason about the impact of cyber-attacks on the physical systems. We demonstrate the idea using a reference Red-Light Violation Warning (RLVW) Vehicle to Infrastructure (V2I) network. Our proposed Ontology provides the ability to identify vulnerabilities in cyber systems that may impact a given physical system, enumerate potential mitigation steps and help design resilient physical systems that can meet their design specifications despite the occurrence of a cyber-attack.**

Keywords*–*Cyber Physical Systems; CPS; Security; Resiliency; Ontology.

I. INTRODUCTION

Cyber-Physical Systems (CPS) are systems that involve coordination between two components: cyber (or computational) and physical systems. Ashibani et al. [1] describe CPS as a combination of tightly integrated physical processes (such as actuation), networking and computation. The physical processes are monitored and controlled by cyber subsystems through network interconnects.

The proliferation of CPS has gained increased traction with the advances in networking and embedded system technologies like system-on-chip (SoC) and wireless transmitters. With the increased capability and complexity in CPS, they have found application in domains such as smart cities, transportation, and power grids. However, this growth has come at the cost of potential cyber-attacks [2]. Often, security and resiliency are either not paid the attention they deserve or are disregarded altogether. As a result, cyber-attacks on CPS are becoming increasingly prevalent, as evidenced by recent attacks targetting critical infrastructure:

- A cyber-attack in 2016 crippled a power grid in Ukraine, affecting at least 100,000 people. The attackers used software-based attacks to shut down the Remote Terminal Units (RTUs) that control circuit breakers, causing a power outage for about an hour [3].
- A German steel mill was the target of a cyber-physical attack in 2014, when malicious actors took control of the mill's production software and caused material damage to the mill [4].
- On 21 October 2016, an attack on DNS service provider Dyn caused issues for a list of well-known services such as Twitter, GitHub, Reddit, Spotify, Netflix, and PayPal. A Mirai botnet compromised tens of millions of IP addresses. All in all, about 100,000 devices were involved. This was the then largest attack ever recorded with network traffic volume reaching 1.2Tbps.
- Perhaps the most recognizable of all the attacks was the STUXNET worm that infected Iranian nuclear power plants [5]. The worm caused the centrifuges to spin too quickly and for too long, damaging or destroying the delicate equipment in the process. This is an excellent example of how cyber-attacks affect physical systems.

It is evident from these examples that an attack targetting the cyber domain (cyber-attacks) can adversely impact the normal operation of the physical systems that they control. The impact is especially acute in safety-critical systems.

One way to understand the impact of cyber-attacks on physical systems is by modeling CPS systems using Ontologies. An Ontology is a formal description of knowledge as a set of concepts within a domain and the relationships that hold between them [6]. To enable such a description, we need to formally specify components such as individuals (instances of objects), classes, attributes, and relations as well as restrictions, rules, and axioms. Ontologies not only introduce a shareable and reusable knowledge representation but, can also add new knowledge about a domain [6]. Ontologies provide numerous advantages.

- Ontologies enable automated reasoning about data [6].
- They provide the ability to represent data formats, including unstructured, semi-structured or structured data, enabling smooth data integration, easy concept and text mining, and data-driven analytics [6].
- Adding additional relationships, integrating multiple Ontologies and cross domain concept matching are also possible.

CPS enable technological advances in diverse critical domains such as healthcare, traffic flow management, and smart manufacturing. Design needs vary across the domains of operation. So, Ontologies may be able to capture complex dependencies and relationships between the cyber and physical components

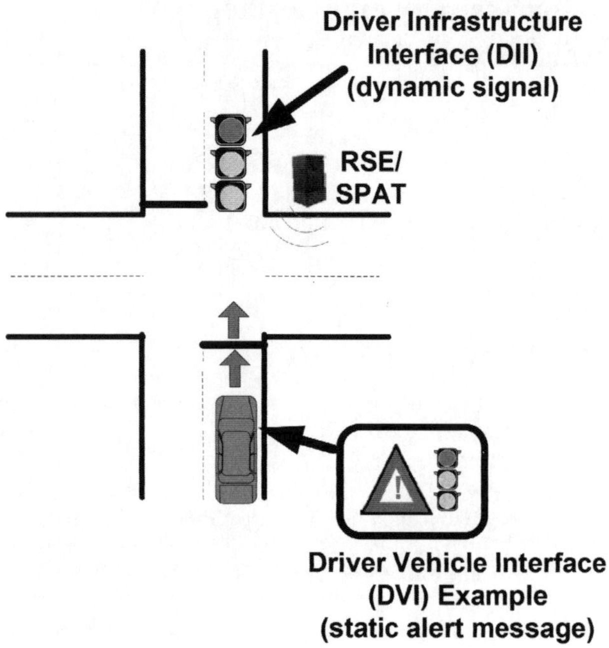

Figure 1. The Red Light Violation Warning system [8].

and potentially identify common design principles across multiple domains. Cyber-attacks may or may not affect the physical system of a CPS. To understand the impact of attacks on the functioning of physical components, the relationships captured by the Ontology can be used to semantically reason about security and resiliency of the physical components.

In this paper, we present our Ontology-driven framework that captures some of the physical and cyber components of a Vehicle-to-Infrastructure (V2I) reference architecture [7], including design goals and requirements specification from their design artifacts. This includes information such as functional, security and resiliency requirements. The objective is to understand the relationship between the cyber and physical components of the V2I CPS system to be able to reason about security and resiliency of the physical system. The Ontology will help understand the impact of cyber-attacks on the physical components. This information can then be used to identify mitigation techniques (in physical or cyber domains) and design changes that can help improve the security and resiliency of the physical system.

The paper is split into 6 sections. In section II, we briefly describe the reference architecture that is used to validate the Ontology. Section III outlines some of our previously-developed tools that perform vulnerability management. The CPS Ontology and the reasoning process are briefly described in section IV. A case study using the Red-Light Violation Warning (RLVW) and the CPS Ontology is presented in section V, followed by the conclusion in section VI.

II. REFERENCE ARCHITECTURE - RED LIGHT VIOLATION WARNING (RLVW)

The RLVW safety application involves providing a cooperative vehicle and infrastructure system that assists drivers in avoiding crashes at signalized intersections by first advising the driver of a signalized intersection, followed by a warning to the vehicle's driver if, based on their speeds and distance to the intersection, they may violate an upcoming red light. As a vehicle equipped with a Driver Vehicle Interface (DVI), a screen on the dash that displays alerts from the infrastructure as the vehicle approaches an intersection equipped with a Road Side Equipment (RSE)-controlled traffic light. It receives messages about the signal phase and timing (SPaT), intersection geometry, and position correction information [7]. SPaT, a traffic signal control information that conveys the current movement state of each active phase in the system can aid in safety, mobility and monitoring the environment [9]. The driver is alerted or warned if the RLVW application determines that given current operating conditions, the driver is predicted to violate the red light.

The RLVW system is one of six safety applications developed by the United States Department of Transportation [7]. The goal of the RLVW application is to improve roadway safety by reducing red-light running and collisions at signalized intersections [7]. The infrastructure and vehicle components include both cyber and physical components. Figure 1 shows various components of the RLVW application. We will evaluate our Ontology with this architecture as a baseline. This application contains:

1) Infrastructure component: The infrastructure component is responsible for warning drivers of an approaching intersection well in advance. In addition, drivers also need to be warned if their approach is likely to result in a red light violation.

2) Vehicle component: The vehicle component is responsible for sensing the world, conveying intent (to other vehicles and the infrastructure) and situational awareness. All of this information needs to be sent to the infrastructure.

- Sensing the world includes measuring speed, getting current Global Positioning System (GPS) coordinates and determining the lane currently being driven on.
- Conveying intent is vital in a connected vehicle environment (especially Vehicle to Vehicle network). The information exchanged may influence the behavior of other entities in the network.
- Situational awareness involves attributing context to the data collected by a physical component. For example, if a sensor measures the speed of the vehicle to be 60 miles per hour, the relevant cyber component needs to determine if this is a safe speed given the current context. This speed may be acceptable on a highway but, not within city limits.

3) Design goals: In this section, we look at some of the design goals and specifications of the RLVW application before we present a preliminary outline of our Ontology design in the subsequent sections.

Figure 2 outlines some of the important design goals of the communication model being considered. The three primary objectives of V2I is to prevent/minimize fatalities, injuries and property damage. One of the ways this can be achieved is by using the RLVW application, which attempts to satisfy the design goals by reducing red light running and traffic collisions. The various design specifications and their relationships are reflected in Figure 2.

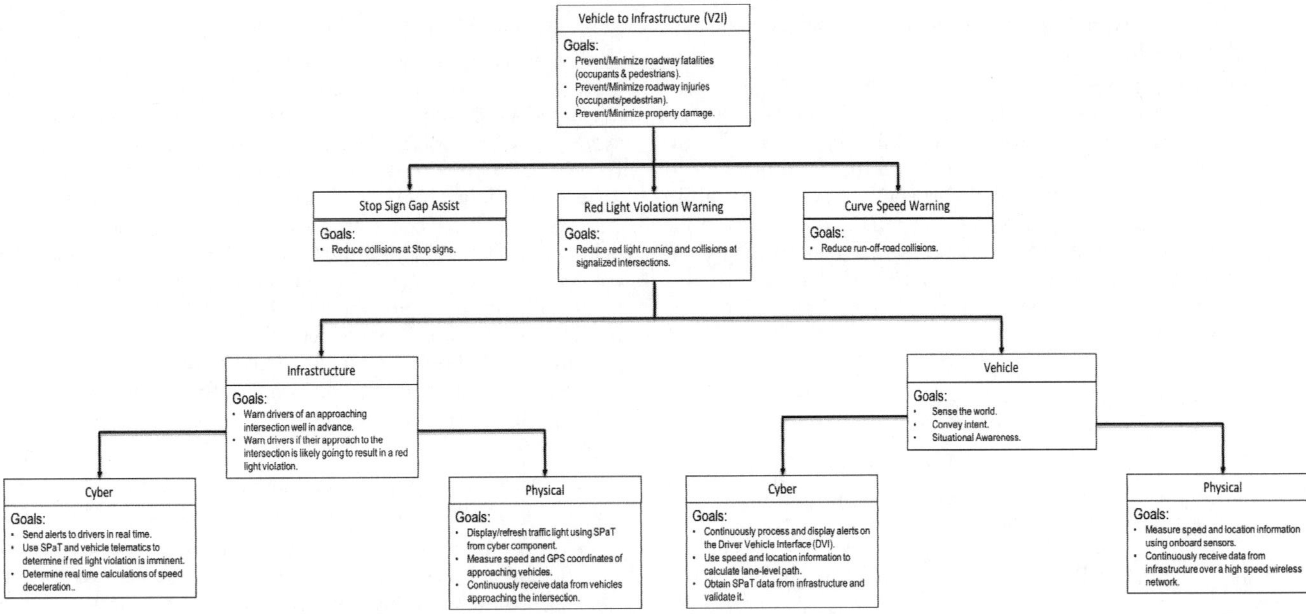

Figure 2. Design goals for RLVW.

The National Institute of Standards and Technology (NIST) has published a framework that provides guidance in designing, building, verifying, and analyzing complex CPS systems [10]. The CPS Framework captures the generic functionalities that CPS provide, and the activities and artifacts needed to support conceptualization, realization, and assurance of CPS [10]. The framework describes the following series of steps within a reference architecture.

- The domain of the CPS needs to be identified.
- Facets or views on CPS encompassing identified responsibilities in the system engineering process [10] need to be identified. These include conceptualization, realization, and assurance. They contain well-defined activities and artifacts (outputs) for addressing design goals (or concerns) [10].
- Aspects need to be consolidated. Aspects are high-level groupings of cross-cutting concerns. Concerns are interests in a system relevant to one or more stakeholders. These may include Functional, Business, Timing, Data, Trustworthiness, etc [10].

Our objective is to reason about security and resiliency so, we focus only on the trustworthy concerns. Trustworthiness is the demonstrable likelihood that the system performs according to designed behavior under any set of conditions as evidenced by characteristics including, but not limited to, safety, security, privacy, reliability and resilience [10]. In the next section, we briefly describe vulnerability assessment for cyber systems using some of our previous work.

III. Vulnerability-based Threats Assessment

Given a deployed Cyber-Physical System that leverages one or more IT (or cyber) components for normal operations, security evaluation of the IT system is a priority.

In our previous work, we have designed solutions (VULCAN [11], and NEMESIS [12]) to automate essential security management tasks to assist in identifying, assessing and mitigating the threats that may affect any given IT system (this apply to the Cyber components that power a Cyber-Physical System).

Let us consider an example of an IT component (that is part of a Cyber-Physical System) such as the "Qualcomm SD 820 Firmware". Our VULCAN Framework [11], enable us to model and represent such an IT component using a Common Platform Enumeration (CPE) standard [13].

An Ontology Knowledge Base (OKB), which is a populated Ontology, plays a central role within the VULCAN framework by capturing various critical public data feeds of IT products (e.g., Application/Software, Operating System, and Hardware) vulnerability, attack, and mitigation information using an evolving and semantically rich Ontology model.

The vulnerability index generated by VULCAN captures information about publicly known vulnerabilities (including their insightful information) that affect our assessed IT component. Figure 3 shows a simplified view of the generated vulnerability index to highlight a few vulnerabilities (including their vulnerability description, severity score and Common Weakness Enumeration (CWE) [14] identifier) that affects our assessed IT product (viz., Qualcomm SD 820 Firmware). This System-on-Chip (SoC) is commonly used in level 3 and level 4 autonomous vehicles.

With the amount of semantically rich information captured within the generated vulnerability index of the assessed IT component, we can reason and infer various insights in regards to the current vulnerability status of the "Qualcomm SD 820 Firmware" and how many of its vulnerabilities have a damaging impact (if exploited by a malicious actor) to the core of the Cyber-Physical System in operation.

Using this vulnerability index, our NEMESIS architecture can assist in performing various threat modeling, and risk assessment tasks of the for the IT product. This information may be useful towards designing and CPS that are inherently resilient to the modeled threats.

Table I illustrates a sample view of how NEMESIS classifies vulnerabilities (that affect the assessed IT component "Qualcomm SD 820 Firmware") into possible threat types (using STRIDE threat model [15]) that could arise from their exploitation. For instance, "CVE-2018-3594" [16] vulnerability was identified by VULCAN that it affects our assessed IT component, then NEMESIS determines that this vulnerability could lead to "Tampering, Information Disclosure, Repudiation, and Elevation of Privilege" STRIDE threat types (as shown in Table I).

TABLE I. QUALCOMM SD 820 FIRMWARE: THREAT CLASSIFICATION SAMPLE

Vulnerability	S	T	R	I	D	E
CVE-2018-3594	0	1	1	1	0	1
CVE-2017-18140	0	0	1	0	0	0
CVE-2016-10414	0	1	0	0	0	0
CVE-2016-10446	0	1	0	1	0	1
CVE-2016-10434	1	1	1	0	1	1

In Table II we illustrate how NEMESIS ranks all the classified threat types by the average severity of all the found vulnerabilities that can lead to each of the STRIDE threat types. For instance, "Information Disclosure" threat type is the most severe threat that the assessed IT component "Qualcomm SD 820 Firmware" is exposed to.

TABLE II. QUALCOMM SD 820 FIRMWARE: THREAT TYPES RANKING

Threat Type	Severity [0-10]
Tampering	8.19
Denial of Service	5.0
Spoofing	7.5
Information Disclosure	9.0
Repudiation	8.57
Elevation of Privilege	8.78

Security practitioners can use the information for assessing IT products (or cyber component of CPS) to strategize cyber mitigations and resiliency measures to counter any of the perceived threat types that could impact the critical missions of the operational Cyber-Physical System.

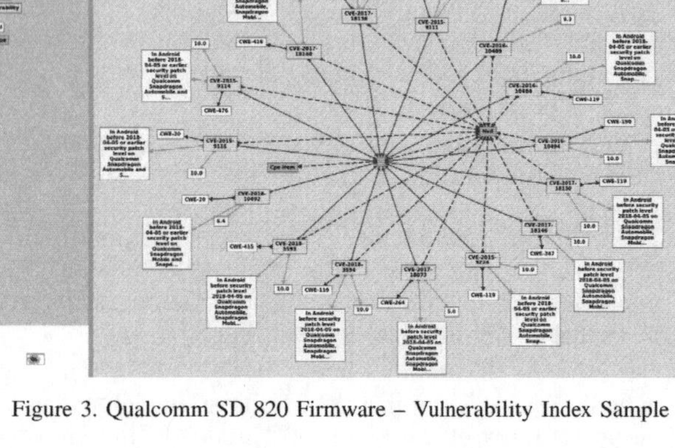

Figure 3. Qualcomm SD 820 Firmware – Vulnerability Index Sample

IV. CPS Ontology design and reasoning process

Cyber systems usually include processors, memory modules, network interfaces and software products. We briefly discussed vulnerability assessment and management for cyber systems by introducing some of our previous work in Section III. We also previously demonstrated the ability to enforce differentiated levels of security for Internet of Things (IoT) devices in [17]. Now, our goal is to understand how these cyber (or IT) vulnerabilities affect physical systems. The challenge is to capture the relationship between cyber and physical components to semantically reason about security and resiliency. The Ontology will be able to provide an insight into potential mitigation techniques, which may involve changes in the design or patching and updating software packages in the cyber domain. The various stages in the reasoning process are listed below.

- Design goals and components of a CPS domain need to be identified in consultation with domain experts.
- The relationships between various components in the domain need to be identified within the context of the design goals identified in the previous step.
- Given all components and their relationships, threat modeling needs to be performed so that only threats relevant to the given CPS are considered.
- The CPS needs to be redesigned if required.
- The redesigned system needs to be validated to ensure it still complies with the design specifications.

We have constructed an Ontology for the trustworthiness concern based on NIST's CPS framework. Figure 4 depicts a preliminary design for the CPS Ontology that is capable of reasoning against a limited set of vulnerabilities that we will discuss in Section V. The Ontology was implemented using OWL web semantic language [18] on Protege Ontology editor [19].

The Ontology identifies components and subcomponents of RLVW system under consideration at conceptual level, assign roles and responsibilities to them and capture dependencies among the components (following NIST CPS Framework [10]). In the realization phase, our framework relates how the conceptual level components will be implemented using cyber systems (processors, memory, network). Since each of these components will be identified using a unique CPE (Common Platform Enumeration), VULCAN system can capture security information about the components from NVD repositories. This information, including vulnerabilities, severity scores, attack vectors, patches are indexed and analyzed, generating comprehensive reports about individual components as well as for the entire cyber system.

NEMESIS [12] uses the VULCAN [11] to collect information in providing a risk score for the cyber components. It uses a Bayesian model that combines vulnerabilities, dependencies among components, severity scores, and threat types exposed by vulnerabilities to compute risks scores and prioritize threat types faced by the system.

The design specifications from Figure 2 were translated into an Ontology. The RLVW concept contains five different knowledge points: physical components and cyber components which are self-explanatory, Abstract, Vehicle and Infrastructure. The infrastructure and vehicle components are mapped

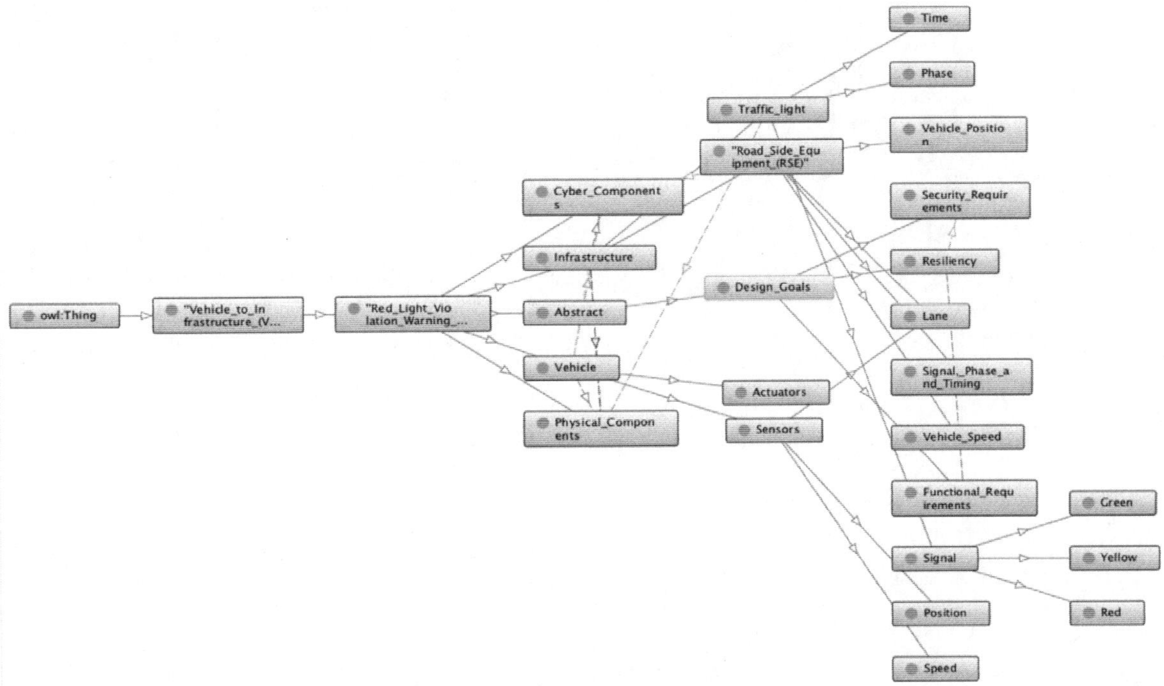

Figure 4. An example of the CPS ontology.

to the cyber and physical concepts. A knowledge point called Abstract captures all the design goals of a CPS domain (The RLVW safety application in this scenario). The two components of interest in this Ontology are the traffic light and RSE. The traffic light interacts with the RSE to display traffic lights and transition between them.

Design goals may be security requirements (from Security Service Level Agreements or SSLAs), Resiliency goals and Functional requirements. Lee et al., [20] describe an Ontology to capture SSLAs, which can be used to understand security agreements of a service provider or to audit compliance to design specifications [20].

V. Case Study

Let us evaluate this Ontology using a few simple examples. We use the STRIDE threat modeling discussed in Section III and the design specifications from Section 2. The configuration of system components is as follows:

- Qualcomm 820a SoC powers a vehicle.
- The DVI is controlled by Android Auto operating system [21].
- RSE is a facility server running Ubuntu 16.04 LTS.
- No identification scheme exists to authenticate entities in the network.
- The data exchanged is not validated (neither by RSE nor the vehicle).
- The traffic light is not designed with any fail-safe modes.
- No personally-identifiable information is collected/stored.

A. An attack on the RSE

Let us consider the RLVW application discussed before. We were able to determine using the CPE identifier for Snapdragon 820a that five significant vulnerabilities could affect the SoC as discussed in section III. One of the most important steps in threat modelling for CPS is to assign a context to a threat/vulnerability i.e, try to understand how a vulnerability affects a physical system. In the first example, let us consider a scenario where an adversary attacks the RSE (as depicted in Figure 5). RSE is no longer trustworthy. Potential attacks are:

- **Spoofing :** The adversary may masquerade as the RSE, sending false data to vehicles or the traffic light. The lights may flash randomly or be turned off. The vehicle may not receive a warning from the RSE even if a potential red light violation is detected. For example, CVE-2018-1111 [22] may be used to create malicious DHCP packets to compromise the server.
- **Tampering :** Data is maliciously modified before being sent to vehicles or the traffic light. The potential impact is similar to that of the Spoofing attack. For example, an adversary may use CVE-2017-1000366 [23] to create a specially crafted environment variable to perform a buffer overflow attack.
- **Repudiation :** Non-repudiation is a state of affairs where a source of specific information denies ever creating/issuing it. In this case, the RSE can deny ever having issued an alert to a vehicle or the traffic light. In this case, the Ontology will help us understand that this attack is not relevant to us because it is easy to

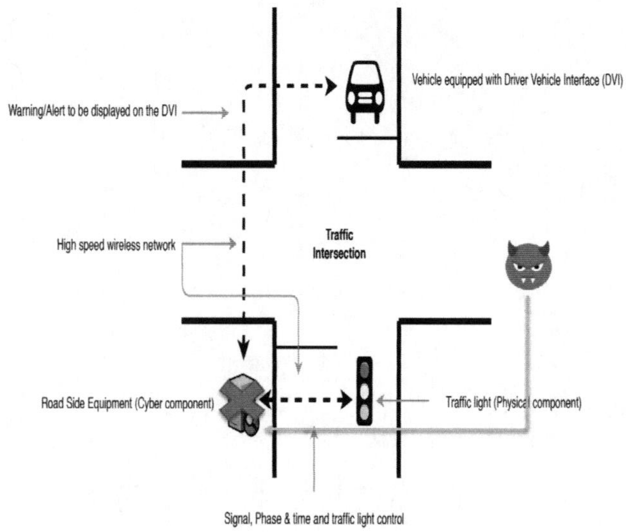

Figure 5. An attack on the RSE.

validate the RSE by using data from the vehicle. This may not be as critical as spoofing or tampering in our system.

- **Information Disclosure :** Since no personally identifiable information is collected, this attack does not substantially impact the physical system. However, if the RSE captures images of the vehicle that violated the red-light, information disclosure may violate privacy goals. If information about the cyber domain is leaked, VULCAN can help mitigate it.
- **Denial of Service :** The adversary may use any of the CVEs previously discussed to render the RSE unresponsive. This means that the vehicles may not receive alerts and the traffic lights are not controlled. The impact may be similar to that of the Spoofing attack.
- **Elevation of Prvilege :** Elevation of privilege or privilege escalation attacks involve gaining escalated access to a resource that is normally protected from a user. This is a cyber-attack so, VULCAN or NEMESIS may be able to suggest mitigation techniques.

B. Mitigation techniques

The Ontology will be able to reason about potential mitigation techniques for a given cyber-vulnerability logically. This also includes changes to the design specification. Let us look at some of them:

- For most of the cyber-attacks like elevation of privilege, updating software packages, applying patches should suffice.
- Cyber system can be designed to protect against spoofing attacks by authenticating network entities using a digital certificate-based identification scheme.
- Physical systems can be designed to protect against spoofing attacks by using a physical unclonable function (PUF) based identification scheme.
- The traffic light can be built to flash yellow lights if no response is received from the RSE for a preset amount of time.
- SPaT data can be transmitted by the RSE so that the vehicles can validate the alerts that were sent.
- Similarly, speed and location information can be sent by the vehicles approaching the intersection. The RSE can validate the data collected by the sensors on the vehicle with the data collected by the RSE. Cross-validation may prove to be a useful design feature.

The Ontology can suggest mitigation techniques. Cost Vs Risk estimates may be used to pick the appropriate mitigation scheme. The insight provided by the Ontology can be used to design resilient physical systems.

C. An attack on the cyber component of a vehicle

We briefly discussed how specific threats that target the cyber component of the RSE might impact the CPS. Similarly, the cyber component of a vehicle (such as the Qualcomm 820a SoC) may be targetted by spoofing, tampering, repudiation, information disclosure, denial of service and elevation of privilege attacks, which may violate the trustworthy concern of the V2I system. However, due to the limitation in space, we are unable to elaborate on this further.

VI. CONCLUSION

In this paper, we have presented an argument for modeling CPS using Ontologies. As systems grow more complex, understanding the relationship between various components becomes harder but, more critical.

We have introduced an Ontology-driven framework that is capable of capturing the relationship between cyber and physical domains. We use the example of a V2I communication model to demonstrate the capability of the Ontology. This Ontology, designed in consultation with domain experts helps identify potential vulnerabilities in the cyber domain that may impact a physical system. Also, it helps in identifying possible mitigation steps (in the cyber or physical domain) that can be used to protect against the threats modeled and also help design resilient physical systems that may provide reduced functionality to meet design specifications (resilient) despite the occurrence of a cyber-attack.

In the future, we intend to develop a more detailed Ontology framework that captures complex relationships between various components. This will also include tools that will be able to translate design specifications from the NIST framework into our Ontology to reason about the trustworthiness of a CPS design.

REFERENCES

[1] Y. Ashibani and Q. H. Mahmoud, "Cyber physical systems security: Analysis, challenges and solutions," Computers and Security, vol. 68, 2017, pp. 81 – 97. [Online]. Available: http://www.sciencedirect.com/science/article/pii/S0167404817300809

[2] Z. DeSmit, A. E. Elhabashy, L. J. Wells, and J. A. Camelio, "An approach to cyber-physical vulnerability assessment for intelligent manufacturing systems," Journal of Manufacturing Systems, vol. 43, 2017, pp. 339 – 351, high Performance Computing and Data Analytics for Cyber Manufacturing. [Online]. Available: http://www.sciencedirect.com/science/article/pii/S027861251730033X

[3] "Why the Ukraine power grid attacks should raise alarm," Mar. 2017, URL:https://www.csoonline.com/article/3177209/security/why-the-ukraine-power-grid-attacks-should-raise-alarm.html/ [accessed: 2018-06-16].

[4] K. Zetter, "A cyber-attack has caused confirmed physical damage for the second time ever," URL:https://www.wired.com/2015/01/german-steel-mill-hack-destruction/ [accessed: 2018-06-13].

[5] K. Zetter, "An unprecedented look at STUXNET, the world's first digital weapon," URL:https://www.wired.com/2014/11/countdown-to-zero-day-stuxnet/ [accessed: 2018-06-16].

[6] "What are Ontologies?" URL:https://ontotext.com/knowledgehub/fundamentals/what-are-ontologies/ [accessed: 2018-06-13].

[7] B. Christie, "Vehicle-to-infrastructure (V2I) safety applications performance requirements, vol. 3, red light violation warning (RLVW)," United States. Dept. of Transportation. ITS Joint Program Office; United States. Federal Highway Administration, techreport, 2015.

[8] B. Christie, "Vehicle-to-Infrastructure (V2I) Safety Applications: Performance Requirements, Vol. 1, Introduction and Common Requirements," United States. Dept. of Transportation. ITS Joint Program Office; United States. Federal Highway Administration, Tech. Rep., 2015.

[9] United States Dept. of Transportation, URL:https://www.its.dot.gov/presentations/pdf/SPaT.pdf [accessed: 2018-06-10].

[10] Cyber-Physical Systems Public Working Group, "Framework for Cyber-Physical SystemsRelease 1.0," National Institute of Standards and Technology, Tech. Rep., 2016.

[11] P. Kamongi, S. Kotikela, K. Kavi, M. Gomathisankaran, and A. Singhal, "Vulcan: Vulnerability assessment framework for cloud computing," in Proceedings of The Seventh International Conference on Software Security and Reliability. SERE (SSIRI) 2013. IEEE, June 2013, pp. 218–226.

[12] P. Kamongi, M. Gomathisankaran, and K. Kavi, "Nemesis: Automated architecture for threat modeling and risk assessment for cloud computing," in The Sixth ASE International Conference on Privacy, Security, Risk and Trust (PASSAT). ASE, December 2014.

[13] National Institute of Standards and Technology, "Common platform enumeration (cpe)," https://nvd.nist.gov/cpe.cfm, June 2018.

[14] MITRE, "Common weakness enumeration (cwe)," http://cwe.mitre.org, June 2018.

[15] "The STRIDE Threat Model," http://msdn.microsoft.com/en-US/library/ee823878(v=cs.20).aspx, June 2018.

[16] National Institute of Standards and Technology, https://nvd.nist.gov/vuln/detail/CVE-2018-3594, June 2018.

[17] R. Y. Venkata and K. Kavi, "CLIPS: Customized Levels of IoT Privacy and Security," in Proceedings of the 12th The Twelfth International Conference on Software Engineering Advances Oct 12–14, 2017, Athens, Greece, pp. 41–47.

[18] "OWL web semantic language," URL:https://www.w3.org/OWL/ [accessed: 2018-06-10].

[19] M. A. Musen and the Protégé team, "The protégé project: A look back and a look forward," AI Matters, vol. 1, no. 4, Jun 2015, pp. 4–12, 27239556[pmid]. [Online]. Available: http://www.ncbi.nlm.nih.gov/pmc/articles/PMC4883684/

[20] C.-Y. Lee, K. Kavi, R. Paul, and M. Gomathisankaran, "Ontology of secure service level agreement," 2015 IEEE 16th International Symposium on High Assurance Systems Engineering, 2015, pp. 166–172.

[21] Google, "The Android Auto Operating System," URL:https://www.android.com/auto/ [accessed: 2018-06-08].

[22] National Institute of Standards and Technology, "CVE-2018-1111," URL:https://nvd.nist.gov/vuln/detail/CVE-2018-1111 [accessed: 2018-05-18].

[23] National Institute of Standards and Technology, "CVE-2017-1000366," URL:https://nvd.nist.gov/vuln/detail/CVE-2017-1000366 [accessed: 2018-05-18].

An Experimental Evaluation of ITL, TDD and BDD

Luis A. Cisneros, Marisa Maximiano, Catarina I. Reis
Computer Science and Communication Research Centre
Polytechnic of Leiria
Leiria, Portugal
email: 2160085@my.ipleiria.pt, {marisa.maximiano, catarina.reis}@ipleiria.pt

José Antonio Quiña Mera
Carrera de Ingeniería de Sistemas Computacionales
Universidad Técnica del Norte
Ibarra, Ecuador
email: aquina@utn.edu.ec

***Abstract*— Agile development embodies a distancing from traditional approaches, allowing an iterative development that easily adapts and proposes solutions to changing requirements of the clients. For this reason, the industry has recently adopted the use of its practices and techniques, e.g., Test-Driven Development (TDD), Behavior-Driven Development (BDD), amongst others. These techniques promise to improve the software quality and the productivity of the programmers; therefore, several experiments, especially regarding TDD, have been carried out within academia and in industry. These show variant results (some of them with positive effects and others not so much). The main goal of this work is to verify the impact made by the TDD and BDD techniques in software development by analyzing their main promises regarding quality and productivity. We aim to conduct the experience in academia, with a group of students from the Systems Engineering Degree of the Universidad Técnica del Norte, Ecuador. The students will receive training and appropriate education to improve knowledge about it, and we aspire to achieve interesting results concerning both quality and productivity. The challenge that it is also desirable, is to reproduce the experiment in industry or other adequate contexts.**

Keywords—Empirical research; ITL; TDD; BDD; Software Engineering; productivity; code quality; Incremental Test-Last; Test-Driven Development; Behavior-Driven Development.

I. Introduction

In software development, quality is probably the most important aspect [1]. The industry in this area is well aware of this because users prefer products that provide a satisfying and productive experience. However, these kind of products are difficult to build. To do this, teams make use of software development methodologies such as: traditional or agile that allow planning and controlling the process of creating a software [2]. Agile methods have been very popular in industry in contrast to traditional methods [1]. They use an iterative approach that responds quickly to the changing needs of the client [2][3]. They improve the quality and also increase the productivity of programmers [4]. A question arises: Do agile practices such as Test-Driven Development (TDD) or Behavior-Driven Development (BDD) help increase product quality and developer productivity? In this context, we intend to run a workshop and a controlled experiment that will answer that question.

The document is structured as follows: Section II introduces software testing and the techniques used in the experiment, Section III provides a summary of the related work, Section IV defines the goals, Section V contains the design of the study. Finally, the expected results and the conclusion and future work are presented in Section VI and VII, respectively.

II. Background

Testing is one of the cornerstones of software development because it ensures the quality of the product [3]. In the traditional software development approach, Test-Last Development (TLD) is usually used. Tests are written at the final phase of the development cycle [4]. This means that the quality of the products is only determined in the final phase and, at that moment, making any change can present severe difficulties. On the contrary, in an agile approach that promotes the early development of tests; changes are welcomed and advancing with functional components and correcting defects is made earlier in the process [5].

A. *Incremental Test-Last*

Incremental software development is modeled around a gradual increase of feature additions to a system. This allows the programmer to take advantage of what was being learned during the development of the earlier ones and provide more user-visible functionality with each addition [6][7].

Incremental Test-Last (ITL) is a natural evolution of the TLD approach and became available upon the introduction of the Revised Waterfall model that enabled the Royce's iterative feedback [8]. Thus, it consists of the development of small portions of the production code, followed immediately by the performance tests of the corresponding unit [9]. The ITL flow is present in Figure 1.

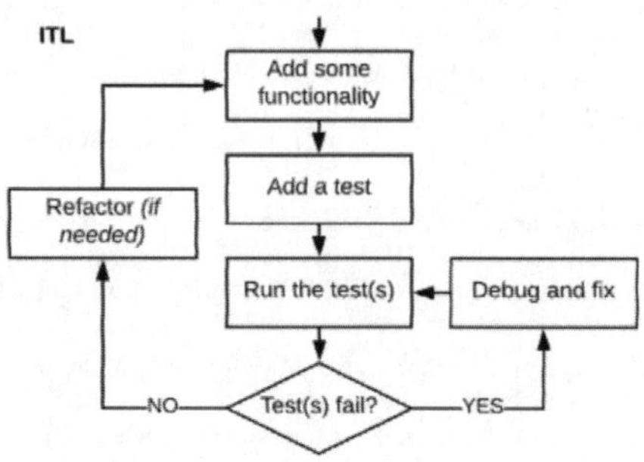

Figure 1. Incremental Test-Last flow.

B. *Test-Driven Development*

TDD, created by Kent Beck (inventor of Extreme Programming [10] and JUnit [11]) refers to a style of programming where three activities are closely intertwined: Coding, Testing (in the form of unit tests) and Design (in the form of refactoring) [12]. Its main idea is to perform initial unit tests for the code that must be implemented [13], and then implement the actual feature.

The TDD process [4][5] is presented in Figure 2, and consists of the following steps: (1) select a user story, (2) write a test that fulfills a small task of the user story and that produces a failed test, (3) write the production code necessary to implement the feature, (4) execute the pre-existing tests again. Where if any test fails, the code is corrected and the test set is re-executed and finally (5) the production code and the tests are re-factored. This method produces some benefits that focus on the promise of increasing the quality of the software product and the productivity of programmers [13][14].

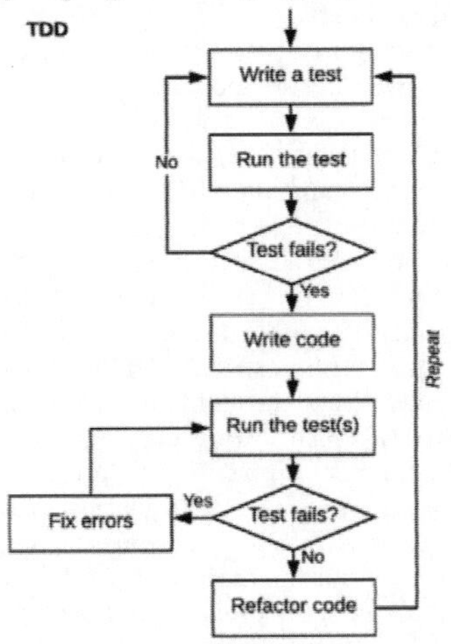

Figure 2. Test-Driven Development flow (*based on* [4]).

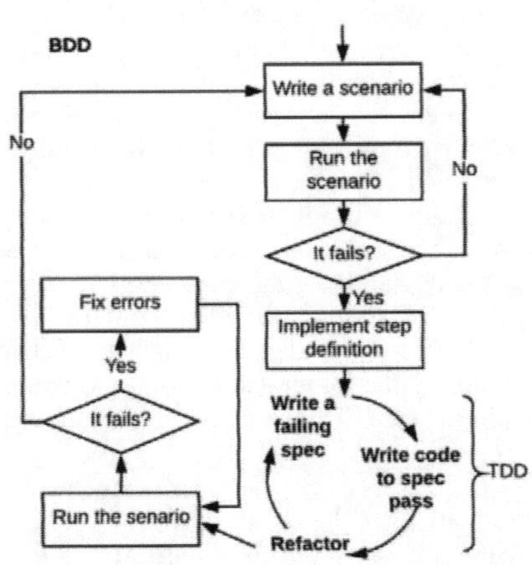

Figure 3. Behavior-Driven Development flow.

C. Behavior-Driven Development

BDD, initially proposed by Dan North [15], is a synthesis and refinement of software engineering practices that help teams generate and deliver higher quality software quickly [16][17]. It has core values that are guided by some agile practices and techniques, including, in particular: Test-Driven Development (TDD) and Domain Driven Design (DDD). Most importantly, BDD provides a common language based on simple structured sentences expressed in something extremely similar to spoken English (Gherkin) [18]. This aspect facilitates communication between project team members and business stakeholders [16]. Gherkin is used to write the acceptance tests as examples and descriptions of scenarios that anyone on the team can read [18].

The BDD process is similar to TDD (see Figure 3) and follows these steps: (1) write a scenario, (2) run the scenario that fails, (3) write the test that corresponds to the specifications of the scenario, (4) write the simplest code to pass the test and the scenario, and lastly, (5) refactor to eliminate duplication.

III. RELATED WORK

Test-Driven Development has been exposed to several scientific experiments developed by researchers in order to validate the advantages offered by its use in software development. O. Dieste et al. [4] studied the produced effect by the technique on the developer's experience through analysis of external quality and productivity. By imparting theoretical and practical knowledge of ITL and TDD to a group of master's students and evaluating the application of techniques in the execution of programming exercises, the study showed that the effectiveness of TDD is lower than ITL. Although the differences are not significant, both productivity and quality improved in half of the cases. They deduced that the technique does not produce immediate benefits and that an intensive training for the subjects is of the utmost importance.

The research directed by Munir et al. [1] was developed in the industry with professional Java developers with previous knowledge of software testing. It aimed to visualize the impact produced by TDD on the quality of internal code, the quality of external code, and productivity, when compared to TLD (Test-Last Development). For this purpose, a programming exercise consisting of 7 user stories was executed. This allowed the participants to put into practice the aforementioned techniques. The results of the analysis by the number of approved test cases: McCabe's Cyclomatic complexity, branch coverage, the number of lines of code per person per hour, and the number of user stories implemented per person per hour. The tests showed slightly significant improvements in favor of TDD, especially in reducing the number of defects. In terms of productivity, the tests suggest that subjects who used TDD achieved an average productivity slightly lower than TLD. This indicates that the adoption of TDD requires compliance with the guidelines of all aspects of software development and adequate training to improve the skill set of the tests.

There is also a recent study designed by Fucci et al. [19], where TDD was compared to ITL through a controlled experiment with professionals within software companies (two in Europe and one in Asia). To achieve a more exact qualification of the effect produced by the techniques within quality and productivity four characteristics were formulated: sequencing, granularity, uniformity, and refactoring effort. The resolution of programming exercises of different levels of difficulty revealed that the improvements found in TDD were associated with granularity and uniformity. The remaining characteristics did not have a relevant influence on the experiment. Thus, the benefits of TDD are due to encouraging stable and precise steps that improve the focus and flow of software development which in turn promise to improve quality and productivity.

Regarding Behavior-Driven Development (BDD), no experiments have been found that evaluate the benefits proposed by the technique, but being based on a set of practices including Test-Driven Development, we hope that it improves or, at least, maintains benefits granted by TDD. In addition, some investigations were found [20][21][22] in which BDD is put into practice in the development of computer solutions while obtaining good results.

IV. STUDY DESIGN

The goal of this empirical experiment is to analyze the impact on software quality and developer productivity produced by applying test-based techniques in software development. The project goal will be achieved through four related steps:

- Step 1: Teach a group of computer systems engineering students about Software Testing, JUnit, Incremental Test-Last, Test-Driven Development, and Behavior-Driven Development.
- Step 2: Provide a workshop about software development and testing techniques with the execution of ***code katas*** (programming exercise).
- Step 3: Provide a challenge to the students so that they can apply the techniques in an autonomous way.
- Step 4: Analyze and evaluate the results obtained by the challenge in order to show the incidence in the quality of the developed software and the productivity with the mentioned techniques.

A. *Research questions*

The experiment is focused on the following research questions with regard to three outcomes: external software quality (fulfillment of stakeholder requirements), internal software quality (the way that the system has been constructed) and developer productivity. External quality is based on functional correctness, and specifically, average percentage correctness [4][19]. Internal code quality deals with the code quality in-terms of code complexity, branch coverage, coupling and cohesion between objects [1]. Developer productivity is based on speed of production, or amount of functionality delivered per effort unit [4][19].

- *RQ1: Does TDD and BDD improve external code quality compared to ITL?*
- *RQ2: Does TDD and BDD improve internal code quality compared to ITL?*
- *RQ3: Does TDD and BDD improve productivity compared to ITL?*
- *RQ4: Does BDD improve external code quality compared to TDD?*
- *RQ5: Does BDD improve internal code quality compared to TDD?*
- *RQ6: Does BDD improve productivity compared to TDD?*

B. *Experimental description*

The experiment will be done with students (approximately 20) from the Systems Engineering Degree of the Universidad Técnica del Norte (Ibarra - Ecuador). It will have an approximate duration of 30 hours and will consist of three phases: knowledge, training, and experimentation.

In the initial phase (**knowledge phase**), information will be given such as: Introduction to agile development, Testing, JUnit, Incremental Test-Last, Test-Driven Development, Behavior-Driven Development, and Cucumber [18]. In addition, at the end of the explanation of each of the techniques, a ***simple calculator*** will be created that allows the calculations of adding and dividing. The application will not have graphical interface so that the students can focus on the understanding of the execution of the technique.

In the **training phase**, jointly done with the students, two code katas will be developed: Rock Paper Scissors (RPS) and Roman Numerals (RM). They will be developed using the techniques chosen for the experiment. RPS is a traditional game involving two players making pre-defined hand gestures while playing against each other, with the winner being decided based on the rules [23]. RM is about the conversion of Arabic numbers into their Roman numeral equivalents, and vice versa [24].

In the third phase (**experimental phase**), students will develop two code katas through the techniques learned: FizzBuzz variant (FB) and String Calculator (SC). FB is a counting and number replacement game, where: any number that is divisible by 3 is replaced with the word 'fizz', any number divisible by 5 is replaced with the word 'buzz', any prime number is replaced with the word 'whiz', any number simultaneously divisible by 3 and 5 is replaced with 'fizz buzz', any prime number divisible by 3 is replaced with 'fizz whiz', and any prime number divisible by 5 is replaced with 'buzz whiz' [21]. SC is about building a *string calculator* with a simple add method [26]. It receives a string with some numbers separated by one or multiple delimiters and returns the sum of all the numbers. An estimation of four hours duration was made to ensure the total resolution of each exercise.

It is important to emphasize that each code *kata* was evaluated with the ***function point metric*** that provides a measure to the difficulty of the exercise. The purpose is to solve exercises of similar difficulty both in the training phase as well as in the practice phase. This metric allows the evaluation of the functionality of a software at any stage of its life cycle [27][28].

C. *Design and threats*

The order of the interventions used in an experiment can affect the behavior of the subjects or elicit a false response due to fatigue, carry-over, resolution order, or outside factors [4][29]. To counteract this, a counterbalanced design could be applied (see Figure 4), which reduces the impact of the order of interventions or other factors adversely influencing the results [29][30]. This process is called "Latin Square".

Our experiment will have three interventions (ITL - A, TDD - B and BDD – C). We will divide the subjects into 6 groups and choose the interventions' order according to the following: ABC, ACB, BAC, BCA, CAB and CBA.

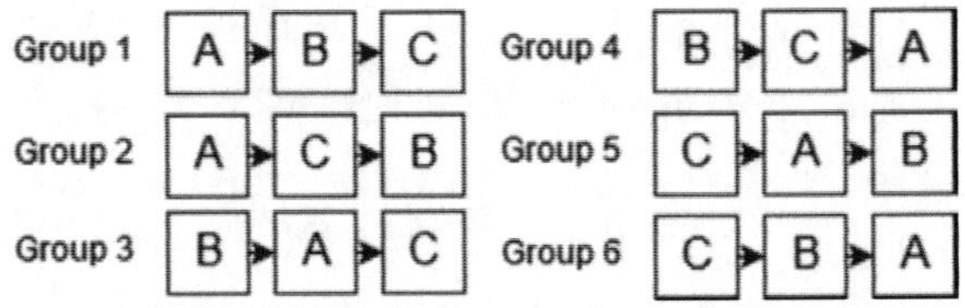

Figure 4. Counterbalanced design for three conditions.

The experimental sessions will be applied contiguously in time, so the main obstacle is fatigue. To counteract this threat, we will provide an adequate time period for the execution of each exercise and grant breaks within the resolution of each technique.

D. Factors and metrics

The experiment will be based upon two factors. The development approach level [4]: ITL, TDD, or BDD, will be used as the main factor. The tasks [4] corresponding to the development of code katas (FB and SC) will be used as the secondary factor. The effectiveness of the development approach will be studied under the perspective of the experiments [1][4][19].

The external quality metric (QLTY) represents the degree of agreement of the system with the functional requirements [4][19]. The formula for calculating QLTY is defined as:

$$QLTY = \frac{\sum_{=1}^{\#TUS} QLTY_i}{\#TUS} \; x \; 100 \qquad (1)$$

where $QLTY_i$ is the quality of the user history *i*th implemented by the subject. $QLTY_i$ is defined as:

$$QLTY_i = \frac{\#ASSERT_i(PASS)}{\#ASSERT_i(ALL)} \qquad (2)$$

In turn, the number of user stories addressed (#TUS) is defined, such as:

$$\#TUS = \sum_{i=0}^{n} \begin{cases} 1 & \#ASSERT_i(PASS) > 0 \\ 0 & otherwise \end{cases} \qquad (3)$$

where *n* is the number of user stories that make up the task. In both cases, it represents the number of passing JUnit assert statements in the set of tests associated with the *i*th user history. Consequently, a user history is considered addressed if it passes at least one of its JUnit assert statements. For example, supposing that a person assesses two user stories (#TUS = 2), this means that there are two user stories for which at least one assert statement passes in the test suite. Let us assume that the acceptance tests of the first analyzed user story contains twelve assertions, out of which six are passing. The acceptance tests of the second user story contain nine assertions, of which three are passing. The quality value of the first assessed user story (QLTY1) is 0.50, while the second user story has a quality value of 0.33 (QLTY2). Therefore, the QLTY measure for the subject is 41.5 percent, i.e., (QLTY = (0.50 + 0.33) / 2 * 100).

The productivity metric (PROD) represents the work done by the subjects with the required quality and within the specified time [19]. Its formula is defined as:

$$PROD = \frac{OUTPUT}{TIME} \qquad (4)$$

OUTPUT symbolizes the percentage of passing JUnit assert statements found in the set of tests for a task.

$$OUTPUT = \frac{\#ASSERT(PASS)}{\#ASSERT(ALL)} \; x \; 100 \qquad (5)$$

TIME (minutes) is an estimate of the amount of work used in the resolution of a task and is based on the time records (milliseconds) collected by the IDE.

$$TIME = \frac{t_{close} - t_{open}}{6000} \qquad (6)$$

For example, a person implements a task with a total of 50 assert statements in a test suite. After running the acceptance test suite against the person's solution, 40 assert statements are passing. Then OUTPUT = (40 / 50) x 100 = 80%. Suppose that the solution was delivered in one and a half hours (i.e., TIME = 90 minutes). The person's PROD is therefore 0.89 (80/90), denoting an assertion passing rate of 0.89 percent per minute.

Regarding the *internal quality* analysis, the metric used in the experiment by Munir et al. [1], McCabe's cyclomatic complexity metric, provides a quantitative measurement of the logical complexity of a software; that is, it indicates how a program can be difficult to test and maintain [1][31]. Furthermore, the Source Code Analyzer PMD will be applied to find common programming flaws like: unused variables, empty catch blocks, unnecessary object creation, and so forth [32].

E. Development Environment Operationalization

The development environment that the participants will use includes: Java 8 using the IDE: IntelliJ IDEA with the 4 additional plugins of Cucumber, Activity Tracker, Metrics Reloaded, and QAPlug. The Cucumber plugin will allow the implementation of the BDD technique in the resolution of the exercises. The Activity Tracker plugin is intended to track and record the activity of the IDE user, such as the time spent on tasks. McCabe's cyclomatic complexity metric will be applied with the use of Metrics Reloaded plugin. In addition, QAPlug plugin implements PMD module to manage code quality.

V. EXPECTED RESULTS

We expect that the descriptive statistics analysis of the information compiled from the code katas implementation by ITL, TDD and BDD responds positively to questions RQ1, RQ2, RQ4 and RQ5. Meaning that the exercises developed through TDD and BDD should present improvement of internal and external quality. A slight decrease of the productivity is expected due to the fact that both TDD and BDD present more steps in its process (RQ3 and RQ6).

VI. CONCLUSION

The experiments that analyze TDD against other techniques mention that the benefits are not very evident and emphasize training as one of the relevant facts for obtaining such results. Therefore, this work focuses on increasing training and performing exercises at the same level of difficulty with the intention of maximizing understanding of the implementation of the techniques used and obtaining better results. This work is now complete after the initial application of the study, held between May and June 2018. We are currently gathering all the information and conducting the statistical analysis that will be of great benefit if the research applied in other environments such as in industry and other countries.

ACKNOWLEDGMENTS

This work is financed by national funds through the FCT - Foundation for Science and Technology, I.P., under project UID / CEC / 04524/2016.

REFERENCES

[1] H. Munir, K. Wnuk, K. Petersen, and M. Moayyed, "An experimental evaluation of test driven development vs. test-last development with industry professionals," *Proc. 18th Int. Conf. Eval. Assess. Softw. Eng. - EASE '14*, pp. 1–10, 2014.

[2] J. Shore and S. Warden, *The Art of Agile Development*. O'Reilly Media, Inc, 2008.

[3] T. D. Hellmann, A. Sharma, J. Ferreira, and F. Maurer, "Agile testing: Past, present, and future - Charting a systematic map of testing in agile software development," *Proc. - 2012 Agil. Conf. Agil. 2012*, pp. 55–63, 2012.

[4] O. Dieste, E. R. Fonseca, G. Raura, and P. Rodríguez, "Efectividad del Test-Driven Development: Un Experimento Replicado," *Rev. Latinoam. Ing. Softw.*, vol. 3, no. 3, p. 141, 2015.

[5] D. Janzen and H. Saiedian, "Test-driven development: Concepts, taxonomy, and future direction," *Computer (Long. Beach. Calif).*, vol. 38, no. 9, pp. 43–50, 2005.

[6] C. Larman and V. R. Basili, "Iterative and incremental developments. a brief history," *Computer (Long. Beach. Calif).*, vol. 36, no. 6, pp. 47–56, 2003.

[7] I. Sommerville, *Software Engineering*. Pearson, 2016.

[8] R. Martin, "Iterative and incremental development (iid)," *C++ Rep.*, vol. 11, no. 2, pp. 26–29, 1999.

[9] D. S. Janzen, "On the Influence of Test-Driven Development on Software Design," pp. 0–7, 2006.

[10] K. Beck and M. Fowler, *Planning Extreme Programming*. Addison-Wesley, 2000.

[11] K. Beck, *JUnit pocket guide*. O'Reilly Media, 2004.

[12] Agile Alliance, "What is Test Driven Development (TDD)?" [Online]. Available: https://www.agilealliance.org/glossary/tdd/. [Accessed: 11-Nov-2017].

[13] R. Martinez, "TDD, una metodología para gobernarlos a todos," 2017. [Online]. Available: https://www.paradigmadigital.com/techbiz/tdd-una-metodologia-gobernarlos-todos/. [Accessed: 11-Nov-2017].

[14] K. Beck, *Test-driven development: by example*. Addison-Wesley, 2003.

[15] D. North, "Introducing BDD | Dan North & Associates," 2006. [Online]. Available: https://dannorth.net/introducing-bdd/. [Accessed: 07-Dec-2017].

[16] J. F. Smart, *BDD In Action: Behavior Driven Development for the Whole Software Lifecycle*. Manning, 2014.

[17] Agile Alliance, "BDD: Learn about Behavior Driven Development." [Online]. Available: https://www.agilealliance.org/glossary/bdd/. [Accessed: 16-Nov-2017].

[18] M. Wynne and A. Hellesoy, *The Cucumber Book: Behaviour-Driven Development for Testers and Developers*, Pragmatic. 2012.

[19] D. Fucci, H. Erdogmus, B. Turhan, M. Oivo, and N. Juristo, "A Dissection of the Test-Driven Development Process: Does It Really Matter to Test-First or to Test-Last?," *IEEE Trans. Softw. Eng.*, vol. 43, no. 7, pp. 597–614, 2017.

[20] M. Rahman and J. Gao, "A reusable automated acceptance testing architecture for microservices in behavior-driven development," *Proc. - 9th IEEE Int. Symp. Serv. Syst. Eng. IEEE SOSE 2015*, vol. 30, pp. 321–325, 2015.

[21] R. A. De Carvalho, F. Luiz, D. Carvalho, R. S. Manhães, and G. L. De Oliveira, "Implementing Behavior Driven Development in an Open Source ERP," pp. 242–249, 2013.

[22] P. L. De Souza, A. F. Do Prado, W. L. De Souza, S. M. Dos Santos Forghieri Pereira, and L. F. Pires, "Combining behaviour-driven development with scrum for software development in the education domain," *ICEIS 2017 - Proc. 19th Int. Conf. Enterp. Inf. Syst.*, vol. 2, no. Iceis, pp. 449–458, 2017.

[23] Agile Katas, "Rock Paper Scissors Kata." [Online]. Available: http://agilekatas.co.uk/katas/RockPaperScissors-Kata. [Accessed: 16-Feb-2018].

[24] Agile Katas, "Roman Numerals Kata." [Online]. Available: http://agilekatas.co.uk/katas/RomanNumerals-Kata. [Accessed: 16-Feb-2018].

[25] M. Whelan, "FizzBuzzWhiz Kata." [Online]. Available: https://github.com/mwhelan/Katas/tree/master/Katas.FizzBuzzWhiz. [Accessed: 16-Feb-2018].

[26] R. Osherove, "TDD Kata 1 - String Calculator." [Online]. Available: http://osherove.com/tdd-kata-1/. [Accessed: 16-Feb-2018].

[27] Ifpug, "Function Point Counting Practices Manual," *Group*, vol. on06/23/. 2010.

[28] F. Sánchez, "Medida del tamaño funcional de aplicaciones software," *Univ. Castilla-La Mancha*, 1999.

[29] N. J. Salkind, *Encyclopedia of Research Design*. SAGE Publications, 2010.

[30] D. J. Saville and G. R. Wood, *Statistical Methods: The Geometric Approach*. Springer New York, 1991.

[31] T. J. McCabe, "A Complexity Measure," *IEEE Trans. Softw. Eng.*, vol. SE-2, no. 4, pp. 308–320, 1976.

[32] PMD Open Source Project, "PMD Source Code Analyzer." [Online]. Available: https://pmd.github.io/. [Accessed: 19-Feb-2018].

Reinforcement Learning for Reliability Optimisation

Prasuna Saka

Advanced Systems Laboratory
DRDO, India
Email: prasunas@asl.drdo.in

Ansuman Banerjee

Indian Statistical Insitute
Kolkata, India
Email: ansuman@isical.ac.in

***Abstract*—Software Reliability Optimization problem is aimed at bridging the reliability gap in an optimal way. In an industrial setting, focussed testing at the component level is the most favored solution exercised to fill the reliability gap. However, with the increased complexity in the software systems coupled with limited testing timing constraints finding an optimal set of test suite to bridge the reliability gap has become an area of intense research. Furthermore, the stochastic nature of the reliability improvement estimates associated with each test suite manifolds the complexity. Here, we propose Reinforcement Learning (RL), as a mechanism to find an optimal solution. We have shown how an interactive learning is used to estimate the true outcome of the selection and the action selection policy so as to maximise the long term reward. The estimation methodology and the selection policy is inspired by Multi-armed bandit solution strategies. Firstly, we employ a sample average estimation technique for deriving the true outcomes. Secondly, a variant of simple greedy algorithm coined as epsilon-greedy algorithm is considered for action selection policy. These two steps are iteratively exercised until the selection criteria converges. The efficacy of the proposed approach is illustrated on a real time case study.**

Keywords–Reliability Optimisation; Reinforcement Learning; Multi-armed bandit.

I. INTRODUCTION

To beat the modern systems software complexity, software designs are built hierarchically - from the conceptual architectural model gradually progressing towards leaf-node components/blocks. In parallel, architectural based software reliability analysis [1][2] has gained prominence in recent years to asses the reliability of the overall system. Intuitively, in an hierarchical system, overall reliability of a system improves by improving the reliability of the underlying components. Often it is found that the existing reliability of the system is less than the intended reliability - we call this difference as the *reliability gap*. Ensuring that the reliability gap is closed is of a major concern for mission critical software and therefore has been the forefront of active research over decades. In general, the reliability of the components can be improved in the following ways:

- By using more *focussed test suites* so that more testing will increase its functional reliability.
- By introducing *redundancy* for weak functional parts.

We may select any (or a combination) of the above mentioned approach. However, improving reliability by focussed testing is the preferred option over providing software redundancy for two notable reasons i) Redundant software adds more to the existing complexity ii) Increased foot print size by incorporating software redundancy leads to undesirable loads on the memory needs of the system.

Focussed testing looks for testing a sub-set of the software components so that the reliability is enhanced to the intended level. As each component testing has different contribution to the reliability improvement figure, their exists *multiple non-dominating solutions* to raise the reliability of the overall software to the desired level. Each of these solutions acts as a representative to the problem. Now, the reliability optimization problem tries to minimize the efforts of testing so that the optimized solution maps to any of the non-dominating solutions.

The remainder of the paper is organised as follows. Section 2 emphasises the problem area using a motivating example. Section 3 presents a brief description of the methodology adopted in seeking the solution. Section 4 describes a real case study, and formulates the numericals of the problem. Section 5 presents experimental results considering several indicative scenarios. Section 6 discusses the related work and Section 7 offers concluding remarks.

II. MOTIVATING EXAMPLE AND PROBLEM FORMULATION

We introduce a small instructive example to disclose the intricacies involved with the problem. For illustration purpose, let us consider a software having 6 basic components swc_1, swc_2,.... swc_6 and each component is provided with a test suite tc_1, tc_2,.... tc_6. As each component has its own contribution to the overall software reliability, reliability improvement figures Ri_i*'s* which can be obtained by testing the component with its associated test suite would be different. Column 2 of Table I represents Ri_i*'s*, and column 3 corresponds to test suite execution times. Assume the current reliability R_{curr} as 0.6 and target reliability R_d be 0.95. Now, our objective is to find an optimal set of test suites such that the reliability gap of 0.35 is closed. In general, one can figure out the solution sets informally by treating it as a combinatorial problem and make different combinations of test suites until the reliability gap is filled or one can attempt on a formal note using heuristic search based algorithms. For this simple case, one can informally derive the solution sets using pen and paper. Multiple solution forms to fill the reliability gap are presented in Table II. Among the various solutions sets, the set represented by S2 is the optimal. Note that these solution sets are not complete and hence there is a possibility of having a better selection set than S2. It is worthy to note that, both pen and paper and heuristic search based methods become intractable with the increase in the test suite collection.

TABLE I. **AN EXAMPLE SHOWING THE RELIABILITY IMPROVEMENT FIGURES Ri$_i$'s and EXECUTION TIMES OF EACH TEST SUITE.**

Test suite	Ri_i	t_i(man hours)
tc_1	0.05	7
tc_2	0.1	5
tc_3	0.15	5.5
tc_4	0.125	6
tc_5	0.195	9
tc_6	0.23	8

TABLE II. **SOLUTION SETS.**

Id	Solution set	t_i(man hours)
S1	$\{tc_6 , tc_5\}$	17
S2	$\{tc_2 , tc_3 , tc_4\}$	16.5
S3	$\{tc_6 , tc_2 , tc_3\}$	18.5
S4	$\{tc_1 , tc_2 , tc_3 , tc_4\}$	23.5

Now, we introduce another element which manifolds the problem scenario - the scenario when the Ri_i*'s* represented are just *estimates* not *actual values*. In this consequence, it is a natural choice to associate a confidence figure for each estimate. These figures represent the certainty (indirectly, the uncertainty factor) element involved with the estimates made. It is to note that, the estimates made would be certain if and only if the testing data is adequate enough to construct a Software Reliability Growth Model (SRGM). However, in case, where test history is not available or limited, estimates are made using subjective guess method. For these estimates to be more effective, one can associate a confidence/certainty factor with each estimate. Now, we try to look for an optimal solution for the same problem illustrated in the previous paragraph with the certainty factors in picture. Table III represents this case, here the numbers in column 3 (P_i) denotes the confidence values. Though, tc_6 has the highest improvement value, as the probability figure associated with it is comparatively much lesser than the confidence figure of tc_5 and also its reliability figure is not much lesser than tc_6 we should favour tc_5 over tc_6. Evidently, with the increase in the number of components, neither pen and paper methods nor heuristics based methods can address this scenario. Also, to the best of our knowledge none of the existing works are fit to handle the software reliability optimisation problem with uncertainty elements in play. The literature review presented in the Section VI strengthens our statement. Now, we proceed ahead with a formal definition of the problem and the solution methodology adopted.

TABLE III. **AN EXAMPLE WITH CONFIDENCE VALUES.**

Test suite	Ri_i	P_i	t_i
tc_1	0.05	0.7	7
tc_2	0.1	0.63	5
tc_3	0.15	0.5	5.5
tc_4	0.125	0.95	6
tc_5	0.195	0.9	8
tc_6	0.23	0.75	8

- Problem Formulation
  Given:
  - A set of software components, swc_1, swc_2 ...... swc_n.
  - A set of test suites, one test suite for each component, tc_1, tc_2,.... tc_n along with their execution times t_1, t_2,.... t_n.
  - Reliability improvement estimates for each test suite, Ri_1, Ri_2,.... Ri_n.
  - Probability/Confidence figure for each estimate, P_1, P_2, ... P_n.
  - The desired reliability of the system as R_d, and current reliability as R_{curr}.

  Assumptions:
  - Test suite is either tested fully or not executed at all (0-1).
  - Time t_n indicates the total time taken to simulate/execute the test suite tc_n and
  - Testing will improve the reliability of components.

  Output:
  Selection of a optimal set of test suites such that the reliability of the system meets the target/desired reliability R_d, having a minimum test execution time.

III. METHODOLOGY OVERVIEW

This section talks in detail about the solution methodology proposed to find an optimal set of test components to be targeted in attaining the desired reliability.

The problem ahead of us can be treated as a class of optimal testing-resource allocation problem concerned with allocating resources among several alternative (competing) options. The options are to be favored keeping the objective function in mind. Here, the objective function involves the cost factor together with reliability, which means that we have multiple objectives in terms of both maximizing system reliability and minimizing testing cost. If there is no uncertainty element involved in the problem domain, we can consider this problem as a multi-objective optimization problem whose solution is trivial: we would always select the test-suites having the maximum outcome, i.e., more reliability improvement in less time. The important point to note here is that, the environment before us now is not a deterministsic environment rather it is a probabilistic environment. It is a well known fact from the history of statistics that, the probabilistic environments are efficiently handled by learning and exploration is a necessary prerequisite of probability learning. The uncertainty about parameters drives learning and it is by exploration and by interactive interaction one can learn the behaviour of the system. Here, we summarise that some learning mechanism is indeed required to address the scenario.

Looking forward for the kind of learning theories that can be considered for, we see that learning under uncertainty can be well handled by *Reinforcement Learning* [3]. RL is a goal directed learning which gathers knowledge about the environment through interaction. Every interaction produces a wealth of information about the consequences of actions, and about what to do in order to achieve goals. The information gain over a number of interactions thus can be used to weed out the uncertainty element involved in and one can come up with a definite average consequence of chosing a particular option.

This is to say until we explore the selections a number of times, it is not trivial to know the true outcomes of each selection. True outcomes of selecting an option can be made by observing the outcome in each trail and refining the expected outcome. It is worthy to note that exploration gives us a opportunity to learn more about the system, but, it may not result in high current rewards. Also, exploring all the time is not a good idea as it cannot give us a quick solution. In order to have a quick solution, it is always better to exploit the current knowledge on the estimates made. Exploitation is the right thing to do to maximize the expected reward on one step, but exploration may produce greater total reward in the long run. Whether we select an action either by exploration or by exploitation, the estimates of the selection are to be refined for every run so that they guide us our future action section policy. In any specific case, whether it is better to explore or exploit depends in a complex way on the precise values of the estimates, uncertainties, and the number of remaining steps. Such problems are paradigms of a fundamental conflict between making decisions that yield high current rewards, versus making decisions that sacrifice current gains with the prospect of better future rewards. However, exploration and exploitation approach will definitely result in a optimal solution.

We now discuss about how exploration and exploitation can be taken up after we introduce some related terminology.

1) *Action list, A* - The set of available choices represent the action list. Here, set of test suites tc_1, tc_2,.... tc_n represent the set of actions available.
2) *Reward, R* - The outcome of selecting a particular action. As our aim is to have more reliability gain in minimum time, we define the reward of selecting an action a as
$$R(a) = \frac{ReliabilityImprovement(Ri_a)}{TestExecutiontime(t_a)}$$
3) *Estimated Reward, $Q_n(a)$* - The estimate of the reward of an action a after n trials.
4) *True Reward, q*(a)* - The true value of selecting an action a.

On a broader view, there are two basic steps needed:

- *Estimation* (the outcome of each action): Whether we explore or exploit, after the selection of every action, we need to refine the outcome of the action. In a simplistic way, action values are estimated/refined using sample-average method. Here, each estimate is an average of the sample of relevant rewards. By the law of large numbers, as the number of iterations increases, estimates converges to real values, i.e., *Qt(a)* converges to *q*(a)*.
- *Action selection policy*: Once the estimates are made, now comes the question of policy to be adopted to choose an action. One natural solution is to select the action having the highest estimated value, expressed as
$$A_t := argmaxQt(a)$$
If we maintain estimates of the action values, then at any time step there is at least one action whose estimated value is greatest. We call these the greedy actions. When we select one of these greedy actions, we say that we are exploiting our current knowledge of the values of the actions. If instead, we select one of the non-greedy actions, then we say we are exploring, because this enables us to improve our estimate of the non-greedy action's value. Greedy action selection always exploits current knowledge to maximize immediate reward; it spends no time at all in sampling apparently inferior actions to see if they might really be better. A simple alternative is to behave greedily most of the time, but every once in a while, say with small probability epsilon (ϵ), instead select randomly from among all the actions with equal probability, independently of the action-value estimates. These methods are coined as ϵ-greedy methods. An advantage of these methods is that, in the limit as the number of steps increases, every action will be sampled an infinite number of times, thus ensuring that all the *Qt(a)* converge to *q*(a)*.

A. Implementation and Performance Aspects

As discussed earlier, rewards are estimated using sample average method. Let R_i denote the reward received after the ith selection of an action a, and let Q_n denote the estimate of its action value after it has been selected *n - 1* times, which we can write simply as

$$Q_n := \frac{R_1 + R_2 + ... + R_{n-1}}{n-1} \quad (1)$$

The above equation can be devised as an incremental formula so that the averages can be updated with minimum computational costs. In other terms, the above equation can be expressed as

$$Q_{n+1} := Q_n + \frac{[R_n - Q_n]}{n} \quad (2)$$

Pseudocode for a complete algorithm using incrementally computed sample averages and ϵ-greedy action selection policy is shown in Algorithm 1. In the Algorithm 1, the function bandit(A) is assumed to take an action and return a corresponding reward.

Algorithm 1 epsilonGreedy

```
Initialise:
for a =1 to k do
    Q(a) ← 0
    N(a) ← 10
end for
while (1) do
    A = argmaxQ(a) with probability 1- ε
                  or
    A = a random action, with probability ε
    R ← bandit(A)
    N(A) ← N(A) + 1
    Q(A) = Q(A) + 1/N(A) (R − Q(A))
end while
```

The algorithm presented has been inspired by the multi-armed bandit solution strategies which is a simplistic form of reinforcement learning. To the best of our knowledge, we say this is the first effort to apply machine learning approach for software reliability optimisation.

IV. DEMONSTRATION USING REAL CASE STUDY

In this section, we present a real case scenario which forms the basis for our motivation to pursue this investigation. As an illustrative example, a relatively simple redundant system is considered, the configuration of which is depicted in Figure 1. The system is a heterogeneous dual redundant system comprising of a main system and a standby system. Each system houses two packages and each package in turn holds 3 sensors. Both Main and Standby systems acquires real time data from these sensors. The dynamics of main system and standby system are heterogeneous in nature. The main system is highly accurate, with less acceptable operational time, whereas the standby system is less accurate with longer operational time.

For the missions, whose working duration is of the order of the performance of main system, it is naturally good to consider the data of the main system so long it is healthy. As the data provided by this system is crucial from mission perspective, the redundancy management is employed at the component (sensor) level. If multiple component failure occurs then system level reconfiguration is considered. Component level redundancy management adds more to the complexity of the software logics coded. Thus, the functional correctness of redundancy management software logics play a significant role in determining the overall reliability of the system. The software architecture of such logics should be failure resilent and robust enough. From the verification perspective, it is of paramount interest to ensure the reliability of these logics. The section below details the software architecture considered for realising the component level redundancy.

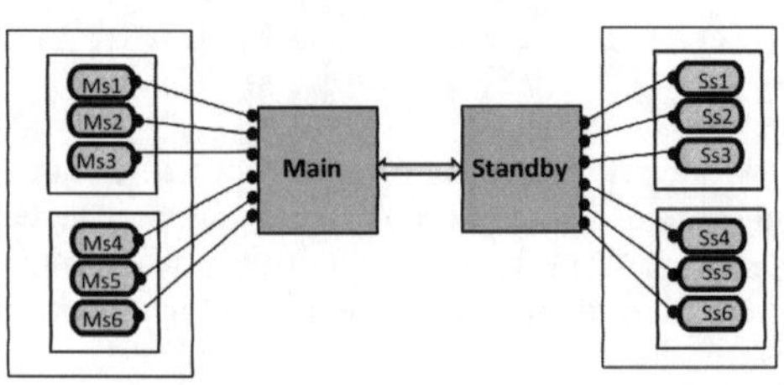

Figure 1. *System Configuration.*

A. Software Architecture

Redundancy management software core has 3 basic modules viz., i) Fault detection module ii) Fault Diagnosis module iii) Reconfiguration module. Fault detection logic recognizes that something unexpected has occurred in the system. To do so, it monitors the behavioral parameters of a component/system to asses the health of it. Once a fault is detected, the next step is to identify the faulty component (failure location), and also the nature of the fault (whether the fault is transient nature or permanent). Finally, a remedial action to be performed based on the decision logics of the system. This phase leads to reconfiguration of the system either at the component level or system level. Successful reconfiguration requires robust and flexible software architecture and the associated reconfiguration schemes.

Software realization for the system is depicted in Figure 2. In total, there are 12 modules labelled as swc_i. Each module is associated with a test suite (tc_i) and its execution time (t_i).

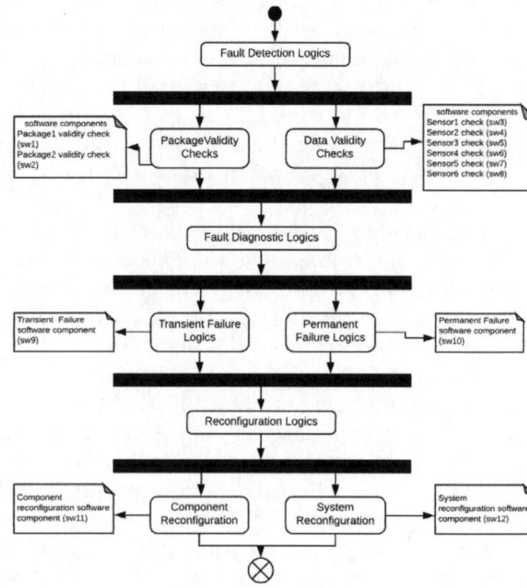

Figure 2. *Software Architecture.*

As stated earlier, each software component has its own contribution to the overall software reliability. The reliability improvement figure *Ri* upon testing different components is different. For the illustrated system, the *Ri* for each component is assigned based on the complexity and the functional criticality of the logic associated with it. In the Table IV, the 2nd row shows the *Ri* that can be obtained by testing a software component swc_i with its test suite tc_i. We see there is a variation in the *Ri's*. For example, software logics identified by swc_2 corresponds to package validity checks of the second package. For the system which is described above, the design elements for package2 are more in number when compared to package1, hence the logics are complex, as a result, the *Ri* is more for swc_2 when compared to swc_1. Similarly, swc_{10} deals with identifying permanent faults. As permanent faults lead to reconfiguration of the system, the decisions are made after observation of the fault for a persistent amount of time. Hence, this logic is obviously the most complex of all the components, hence the *Ri* awarded to it is the highest. 3rd row of the table refers the test suite execution times t_i. As our aim is to find an optimal test suite with minimum execution time, the reward *R* for each test component is

$$R_n = \frac{Ri_n}{t_n}$$

which are placed in 4_{th} row. 5th row corresponds to the uncertainties associated with this reward estimates. The uncertainties are assigned using subjective guess method. When there are more elements of uncertainty in the logics, the probabilities are assigned less. For example, the software logics for package validity checks, which are meant to asses the health of the sensor, depend on operational environmental conditions. The physical quantities like temperature of the chamber, number of operational hours, misalignment factors, calibration state of the package play a role in the sensor behaviour. As per the system design, package2 is highly sensitive and more dependent on the external factors. Hence, it is very difficult to ascertain *Ri* with great confidence, so the probability associated to it is on the lower side. On the other hand, there is no

TABLE IV. **SOFTWARE COMPONENT NUMERICALS.**

Parameter	tc_1	tc_2	tc_3	tc_4	tc_5	tc_6	tc_7	tc_8	tc_9	tc_{10}	tc_{11}	tc_{12}
Reliability Improvement (Ri_i)	9	11.5	6	6	6	8	8	8	7.5	13	10	7
Execution Time *(ti)*	7	8	5	5	5	5	5	5	6	10	9	7
Reward *(R)*	1.285	1.4375	1.2	1.2	1.2	1.6	1.6	1.6	1.25	1.3	1.11	1.0
Probability (P_i)	0.75	0.65	0.65	0.65	0.6	0.6	0.6	0.6	0.9	0.85	0.9	0.9

involvement of external factors on the reconfiguration logics of the system. Only the design criteria as per system needs are to be coded, hence, the uncertainty factor associated to it is less. All components are assigned values following the same analogy.

V. EXPERIMENTAL RESULTS

This section demonstrates the evaluation results of the proposed algorithm to the case study illustrated in the previous section. In essence, two aspects are considered during evaluation. Firstly, the applicability of the bandit algorithm in arriving at an optimal solution is studied. To demonstrate this, 4 case studies each depicting an indicative practical scenario is taken up. Secondly, the aspect of exploration and exploitation tradeoff for the given task at hand is studied. Here, various exploration fractions are considered to arrive at a suitable exploration probability for the illustrated example. Also, on an explorative note, a simple variant of ϵ greedy algorithm termed as ϵ decaying strategy is applied. Here, rather than using a fixed value for ϵ, it is started with a high value initially, and decreased gradually over time. This way, we can favor exploration initially, and then favor exploitation later on. The following subsections elucidates the experimental results on a detailed note.

A. *Application of Bandit Algorithm*

To illustrate the application of bandit algorithm for finding an optimal test suite, four different scenarios/cases considering the different possibilities of having rewards and probability structures are taken. Each scenario results are illustrated using two graphs. The first graph depicts the preferred action choices and the second graph elucidates the reward history. The details of which are stated below:

- *Case1:* This case corresponds to the state where the rewards and probability figures of the case study are kept unchanged. The rewards and confidence figures depicted in Table IV are considered as it is. By intuition we can make some guess on the optimal test suite selection, but it may not be the possible best solution. By running the algorithm designed, we see the order of preference of test suite is as tc_9, tc_{10}, tc_{11}, tc_1, tc_6, tc_{12}, tc_7, tc_2, tc_8, tc_3/tc_4/tc_5. The *Ri's* of tc_6, tc_7, tc_8 are the highest(1.6), but the probabilities associated with them are less. Though the *Ri* of tc_9 is lesser than tc_6, since the associated probability of it is much more than tc_6, tc_9 is given preference. Also, we see the reward of tc_{10} is higher than the reward of tc_9 , but in long run tc_9 is given preference as the certainity factor of it is higher than tc_{10}. Similarly, all other test suites are preferred. The results shown in Figure 3 after running the epsilon greedy algorithm depict the optimal test suite selection for this case.
- *Case2:* This considers the scenario where the estimates made are certain, means there is no element of uncertainty. Thus, all the estimates are assigned a probability of 1 (equal probability distribution). In this case, the test suite having the highest initial estimate should be given preference. For our case, tc_6, tc_7, tc_8 are to be favored first. The graphs illustrated in Figure 4 confirm the expected notion.
- *Case3:* Here, we consider the case where the rewards obtained by selecting each action is equal, but each reward is having its own uncertainty factor. Naturally, the one having the highest probability of occurence should be given preference over the other. For illustration purpose, the initial rewards of all the test suites is set to a value of 1. Here, the test suites tc_9, tc_{11}, tc_{12} with the highest probability are to be favored. The graphs depicted in Figure 5 stand to this opinion.
- *Case4:* This case pertains to the scenario where there is no uncertainty in the estimates made and all components have equal reward. Ideally, in this case all actions are to be chosen with equal importance. The graphs presented in Figure 6 confirm the analogy.

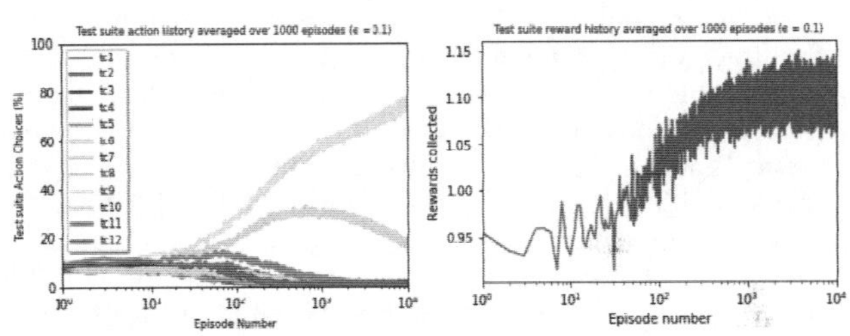

Figure 3. *Case 1 Results.*

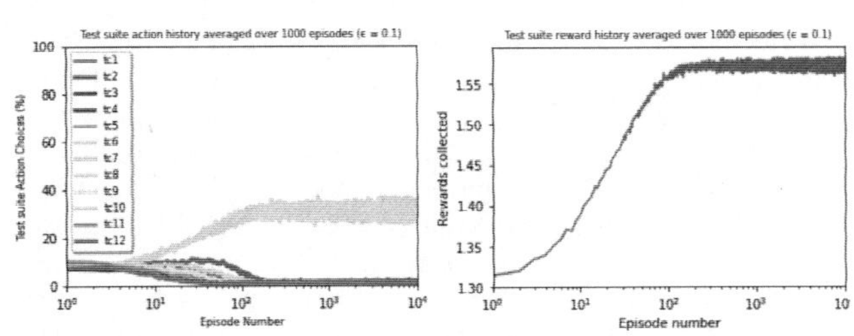

Figure 4. *Case 2 Results.*

The true reward of selecting a particular test suite besides the uncertainty factor in place can be concluded by considering the long term rewards. Table V summarizes the long term rewards R_l of every test suite obtained after running the proposed algorithm for the 4 different scenarios explained in the previous paragraph. For every case, row 1 corresponds to confidence figures, row 2 represents initial reward estimates and row 3 represents the true rewards of each test suite. We

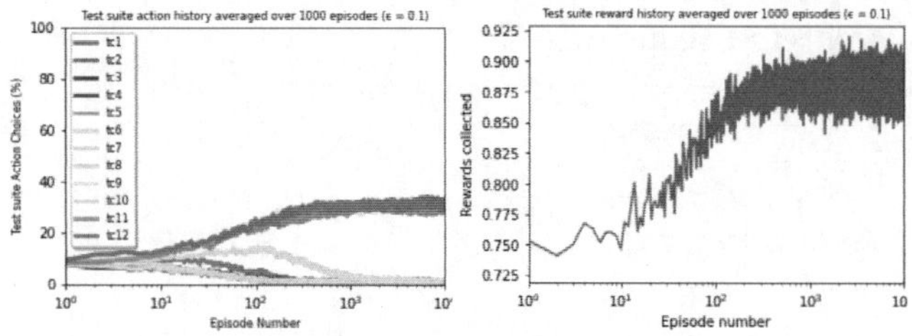

Figure 5. *Case 3 Results.*

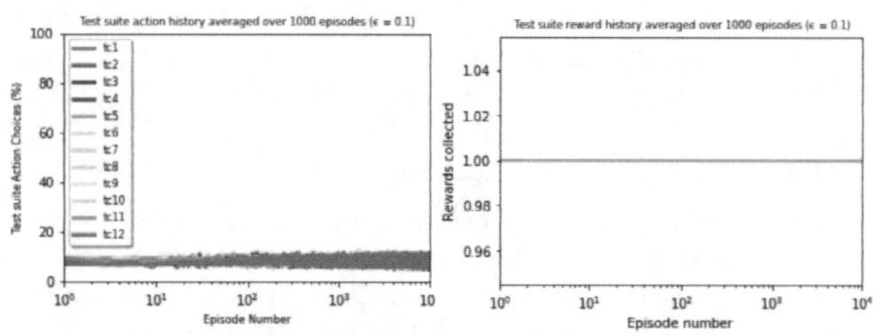

Figure 6. *Case 4 Results.*

see the long term rewards R_l's for each test suite entirely depends on the initial estimates on the probability of occurence of that estimate. The results depicted in Table V are found to be intuitive. Once the true rewards are known for each test suite, choosing an optimal set of test suites to fill the reliability gap is trivial.

B. Exploration-Exploitation Tradeoff

Now we look into the aspect of Exploration and Exploitation trade off by running the algoritm over various exploitation factors. Figure 7 compares a greedy method with three ϵ-greedy methods (ϵ = 0.01, ϵ = 0.1, ϵ = 0.5). All the methods formed their action-value estimates using the sample average technique. The greedy method improved slightly faster than the other methods at the very beginning, but then leveled of at a lower level. It achieved a reward-per-step of only about 1.21, compared with the best possible of about 1.26 on this testbed. The greedy method performed significantly worse in the long run because it often got stuck performing sub-optimal actions.The ϵ-greedy methods eventually performed better because they continued to explore and to improve their chances of recognizing the optimal action. The ϵ = 0.1 method explored more, and usually found the optimal action earlier, but it never selected that action more than 91% of the time. The ϵ = 0.01 method improved more slowly, but eventually would perform better than the ϵ = 0.1 method. As seen from the figures, exploring more often (ϵ = 0.5) is also not good. We say that this exploration-exploitation trade-off varies from problem to problem. For the given case study exploration rate of 0.01 is relatively effective in long run, but this needs more number of iteration to achieve sub-optimal rewards. Hence a choice can be made between exploration rate of 0.1 or 0.01.

One issue with the epsilon-greedy strategy is how to set the value of ϵ, and how we continue exploring suboptimal choices at that rate even after the algorithm identifies the optimal choice. Rather than using a fixed value for ϵ , we can start with a high value that decreases over time. This way, we can favor exploration initially, and then favor exploitation later on. This strategy is known as ϵ decaying strategy. Figure 8 and Figure 9 illustrates this strategy. The initial ϵ is set to 0.1. Figure 8 illustrates the case where the exploration factor is decreased to 0.01 after half the trials are over. We see that there is no performance degradation upon decreasing exploration rate as by half of the trials all the actions rewards might have reached very close to their optimal values, hence little exploration is enough. Figure 9 decreases the exploration factor by a large factor (to 0.001) which is not an advisable scenario for our case study. The initial choice of exploration rate and the decaying factor varies from problem to problem.

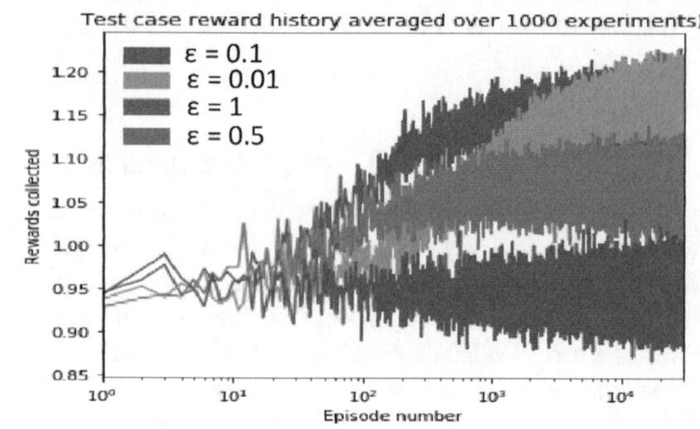

Figure 7. *Exploration-Exploitation tradeoff.*

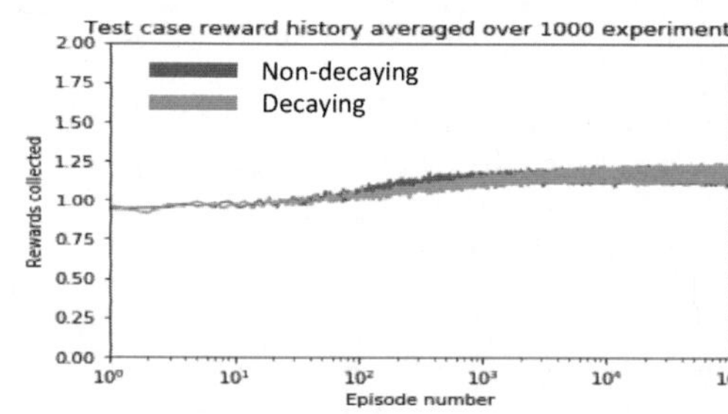

Figure 8. *Epsilon Decreasing Strategy-1.*

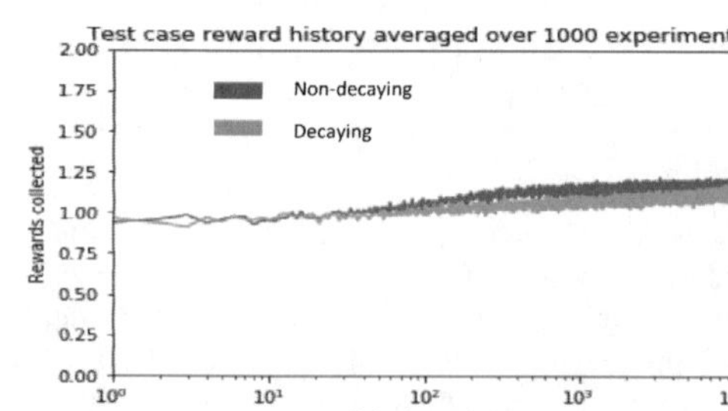

Figure 9. *Epsilon Decreasing Strategy-2.*

VI. RELATED WORK

A lot of work in the past considered the optimal allocation of the reliabilities to minimize a cost function, related to the design or the verification phase costs. Much initial research dealt with hardware systems (e.g., the series-parallel redundancy-allocation problem has been widely studied [4]-[5]); software systems received attention more recently. For a software application, the objective of the optimization will depend on the phase of the software life cycle. During the design phase [6], structural optimisation of the software architecture is paid attention with two leading objectives i) reliability constrained

TABLE V. **OVERALL RESULTS.**

Case No.	Parameter	tc_1	tc_2	tc_3	tc_4	tc_5	tc_6	tc_7	tc_8	tc_9	tc_{10}	tc_{11}	tc_{12}
1	P_i	0.75	0.65	0.65	0.65	0.6	0.6	0.6	0.6	0.9	0.85	0.9	0.9
	Ri_i	1.285	1.437	1.2	1.2	1.2	1.6	1.6	1.6	1.25	1.3	1.11	1.0
	Rl_i	0.96	0.93	0.78	0.78	0.78	0.95	0.95	0.95	1.11	1.09	0.99	0.90
2	P_i	1	1	1	1	1	1	1	1	1	1	1	1
	Ri_i	1.285	1.437	1.2	1.2	1.2	1.6	1.6	1.6	1.25	1.3	1.11	1.0
	Rl_i	1.28	1.43	1.2	1.2	1.2	1.59	1.59	1.59	1.25	1.3	1.11	1.0
3	P_i	0.75	0.65	0.65	0.65	0.6	0.6	0.6	0.6	0.9	0.85	0.9	0.9
	Ri_i	1	1	1	1	1	1	1	1	1	1	1	1
	Rl_i	0.75	0.65	0.65	0.65	0.65	0.6	0.58	0.58	0.88	0.84	0.88	0.88
4	P_i	1	1	1	1	1	1	1	1	1	1	1	1
	Ri_i	1	1	1	1	1	1	1	1	1	1	1	1
	Rl_i	1.0	1.0	1.0	1.0	1.0	0.99	1	1	1	1	0.99	1

cost minimization ii) cost constrained reliability maximization. During the testing phase, the objective of the optimization is to determine the allocation of testing effort so that the desired reliability objective is achieved [7][8]. During the operational phase, optimization is used to explore alternative configurations and to determine an optimal allocation of components to various nodes in a distributed network to achieve the desired performance and reliability.

At the software front, we see much of the research work in the community is biased on design phase optimisation side [9][10]. This work, however, does not consider testing-time of software components and the growth of their reliability. Not many papers considered the problem in the software verification phase, where the issue is either to allocate reliabilities that components need to achieve during their testing or to determine the allocation of testing effort so that the desired reliability objective is reached. Looking at the work in this direction, chronologically, the very initial work by Okumoto and Goel [11] investigated the optimal software release problem by using a software reliability growth model based on NonHomogeneous Poisson Process (NHPP) by considering the cost and software reliability as two different independent criterion. This work was carry forwarded by Shigeru Yamada et al. [12] who consider both cost and reliability criteria.

Also, authors in [7][13] proposed an optimization model with the cost function based on well known reliability growth models. They also include the use of a coverage factor for each component, to take into account the possibility that a failure in a component could be tolerated (but fault tolerance mechanisms are not explicitly taken into account, and the coverage factor is assumed to be known). The authors in [14] also try to allocate optimal testing times to the components in a software system (here, the reliability growth model is limited to the Hypergeometric (S-shaped) Model). Some of the cited papers [7][14][15] also consider the solution for multiple applications, i.e., they aim to satisfy reliability requirements for a set of applications.

In recent times, traditional reliability growth modelling techniques are replaced by machine learning techniques to improve the prediction accuracy of the constructed SRGM. A number of machine learning strategies such as artificial neural networks (ANN), support vector machine (SVM) and genetic programming (GP), are in practice in recent times for reliability modeling. Gene Expression Programming (GEP), a new evolutionary algorithm based on Genetic algorithm (GA) and GP, has been acknowledged as a powerful ML for reliability modelling[16]. We infer from the literature survey that the application of AI in software engineering domain [17] is also concentrated on software relaibility modelling.

Though, SRGM is probably one of the most successful techniques in the literature for software reliability modelling, with more than 100 models existing in one form or another, through hundreds of publications, in practice, however, they encounter major challenges. First of all, software testers seldom follow the operational profile to test the software, so what is observed during software testing may not be directly extensible for operational use. Secondly, when the number of failures collected in a project is limited, it is hard to make statistically meaningful reliability predictions. Thirdly, some of the assumptions of SRGM are not realistic, e.g., the assumptions that the faults are independent of each other, that each fault has the same chance to be detected in one class, and that correction of a fault never introduces new faults. These limitations impediments the use of SRGM based methods. In such cases, subjective knowledge of the system can be taken as an aid in making the reliability estimates. Estimates can be made subject to some criteria like - complexity, functional criticality etc. Since these are just estimates, one can assign confidence factor for the estimates made and can address the optimal selection issue.To the best of our knowledge, no work addresses this scenario and hence motivated us to consider a learning strategy and frame a solution methodology.

VII. CONCLUSIONS

In this paper, we have proposed a learning based paradigm for addressing the software reliability optimisation problem. We have shown how an interactive learning can address the problem of finding an optimal test suite whose rewards are stochastic in nature. In the proposed solution, every interaction is used to learn about the system and in a way the rewards are refined. As a result, over a period of time, the stochastic reward values are converted into true rewards. Once the true rewards are computed, the problem at hand becomes as simple as a multi-objectuive optimisation problem. The learning strategy employed here is inspired by a well known multi-armed bandit solution strategies. The application of the proposed solution strategy to the real case study demonstrates the potential of Reinforcement Learning in addressing the problem stated.

In future, we intend to enhance our existing algorithm by considering various practical scenarios. The random action selection policy considered during exploration phase in ϵ-greedy solution can be improved using Upper-Confidence-Bound strategy. The ϵ greedy action selection forces the non-greedy actions to be tried, but indiscriminately, with no preference for those that are nearly greedy or particularly uncertain. It would be better to select among the non-greedy actions according to their potential for actually being optimal, taking into account both how close their estimates are to being maximal and the uncertainties in those estimates. We find there is a proper mathematical basis to work out this idea. Using this refined startegy, we guess that global optimum can be obtained in a fewer iterations. Furthermore, based on some numerical preference Gradient Bandit Algorithms can be considered to improve further. Furthermore, contextual bandits can be explored for associative search policies. In summary, we see a good potential in the application of RL for optimisation domain.

REFERENCES

[1] M. R. Lyu, "Software reliability engineering: A roadmap," in 2007 Future of Software Engineering, ser. FOSE '07. Washington, DC, USA: IEEE Computer Society, 2007, pp. 153–170. [Online]. Available: http://dx.doi.org/10.1109/FOSE.2007.24

[2] S. S. Gokhale, "Architecture-based software reliability analysis: Overview and limitations," IEEE Transactions on Dependable and Secure Computing, vol. 4, no. 1, Jan 2007, pp. 32–40.

[3] R. S. Sutton and A. G. Barto, Reinforcement Learning: An Introduction. The MIT Press, 2017.

[4] Y. Nakagawa and S. Miyazaki, "Surrogate constraints algorithm for reliability optimization problems with two constraints," IEEE Transactions on Reliability, vol. R-30, no. 2, June 1981, pp. 175–180.

[5] F. A. Tillman, C. L. Hwang, and W. Kuo, "Determining component reliability and redundancy for optimum system reliability," IEEE Transactions on Reliability, vol. R-26, no. 3, Aug 1977, pp. 162–165.

[6] M. E. Helander, M. Zhao, and N. Ohlsson, "Planning models for software reliability and cost," IEEE Transactions on Software Engineering, vol. 24, no. 6, Jun 1998, pp. 420–434.

[7] M. R. Lyu, S. Member, S. Rangarajan, and A. P. A. V. Moorsel, "Optimal allocation of test resources for software reliability growth modeling in software development," IEEE Transactions on Reliability, 2001.

[8] J. Rajgopal and M. Mazumdar, "Modular operational test plans for inferences on software reliability based on a markov model," IEEE Transactions on Software Engineering, vol. 28, no. 4, Apr 2002, pp. 358–363.

[9] F. Zahedi and N. Ashrafi, "Software reliability allocation based on structure, utility, price, and cost," IEEE Trans. Softw. Eng., vol. 17, no. 4, Apr. 1991, pp. 345–356. [Online]. Available: http://dx.doi.org/10.1109/32.90434

[10] O. Berman and N. Ashrafi, "Optimization models for reliability of modular software systems," IEEE Transactions on Software Engineering, vol. 19, no. 11, Nov 1993, pp. 1119–1123.

[11] K. Okumoto and A. L. Goel, "Optimum release time for software systems," in Computer Software and Applications Conference, 1979. Proceedings. COMPSAC 79. The IEEE Computer Society's Third International, 1979, pp. 500–503.

[12] S. Yamada and S. Osaki, "Cost-reliability optimal release policies for software systems," IEEE Transactions on Reliability, vol. R-34, no. 5, Dec 1985, pp. 422–424.

[13] M. R. Lyu, S. Rangarajan, and A. P. A. van Moorsel, "Optimization of reliability allocation and testing schedule for software systems," in Proceedings The Eighth International Symposium on Software Reliability Engineering, Nov 1997, pp. 336–347.

[14] R.-H. Hou, S.-Y. Kuo, and Y.-P. Chang, "Efficient allocation of testing resources for software module testing based on the hyper-geometric distribution software reliability growth model," in Software Reliability Engineering, 1996. Proceedings., Seventh International Symposium on, Oct 1996, pp. 289–298.

[15] N. Wattanapongsakorn and S. P. Levitan, "Reliability optimization models for embedded systems with multiple applications," IEEE Transactions on Reliability, vol. 53, no. 3, Sept 2004, pp. 406–416.

[16] B. Kotaiah and R. A. Khan, "A survey on software reliability assessment by using different machine learning techniques," 2012.

[17] M. Harman, "The role of artificial intelligence in software engineering," in 2012 First International Workshop on Realizing AI Synergies in Software Engineering (RAISE), June 2012, pp. 1–6.

Concurrency Analysis of Build Systems

Vasil Tenev, Bo Zhang, Martin Becker
Fraunhofer Institute for Experimental Software Engineering (IESE)
Kaiserslautern, Germany
Email: {vasil.tenev, bo.zhang, martin.becker}@iese.fraunhofer.de

***Abstract*—In order to derive executable software artefacts, a build system needs to be maintained properly along with the evolution of source code. However, in large software projects the build process often becomes effort-consuming, which is often caused by suboptimal concurrency either in the design of the build system or in the execution of the build process. To cope with these challenges, we present our concurrency analysis with practical experiences in this paper. In particular, we propose a new metric called Degree of Freedom for evaluating the concurrency potential of a build system based on dependencies among build jobs and artefacts. In fact, this metric is not limited to build analysis. It can be used for analyzing the concurrency potential of any executable process in general.**

***Index Terms*—concurrency, build system, control flow**

I. INTRODUCTION

While normal source code (also as known as production source code) implement the behavior of a software, its build system (including build tools and build code such as makefiles) derives the executable software from its production source code. In large industrial software systems, the complexity of the build system is often high (in terms of build jobs and build dependencies), and the build process is time-consuming (over one hour in large systems) even in a distributed environment using high-performance and multi-core computers. This is not acceptable in real continuous integration settings with frequent code revisions and builds per day.

In order to understand the build process and related issues, in our previous work [18] we have depicted the build process via the notion of Build Dependency Structure. Theoretically, the build dependency structure contains two dimensions as illustrated in Figure 1 on page 1. On the one hand, the root build command triggers a flow of build actions that can further run atomic build jobs (e. g., compiling and linking). These build actions and jobs are invoked and executed in a tree structure (vertical in Figure 1 on page 1). On the other hand, the build jobs with different build tools indicate dependencies between input build artefacts and output build artefacts, which further constitute a dependency graph (horizontal in Figure 1 on page 1).

In the build dependency structure, some build jobs need to be executed sequentially due to the dependencies among build jobs and artefacts. However, independent build jobs could be executed in parallel, which helps improving the build efficiency. Therefore, in practice it is important to analyze the build system and make sure that build jobs are executed with optimal concurrency. Although there was some endeavor in build dependency extraction and optimization [6], [12] a comprehensive analysis focusing on build concurrency is still lacking.

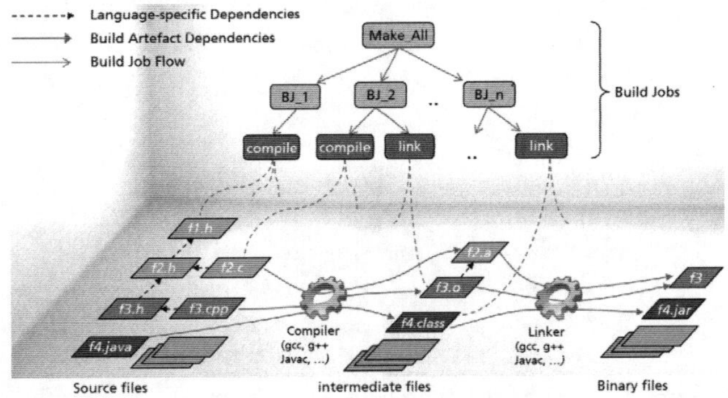

Figure 1: Notion of the Build Dependency Structure

In order to optimize the build concurrency and improve build efficiency, we would like to conduct automated analyses both on the build execution process and also on the build system architecture. At build execution time, we use existing commercial tools for monitoring the build process and analyzing the execution of build jobs in different threads and on different machines. This shows whether build jobs are actually executed in parallel. Moreover, we also conduct static analysis on build dependencies of the build system and measure concurrency potential of the build architecture. This helps identify root causes of concurrency problems in the build process.

In this paper, we provide the following contributions:

- Practices of dynamic and static concurrency analysis in an industrial study.
- An innovative metric called Degree of Freedom for static concurrency analysis.
- Lessons learned during the concurrency analysis and optimization.

This paper is presented in the following structure. Section II presents our practice of dynamic concurrency analysis. Section III introduces our static concurrency analysis approach. While Section Section IV discusses related work, Section V presents conclusions, summarizes lessons learned during our concurrency analysis study, and discusses future work at the end.

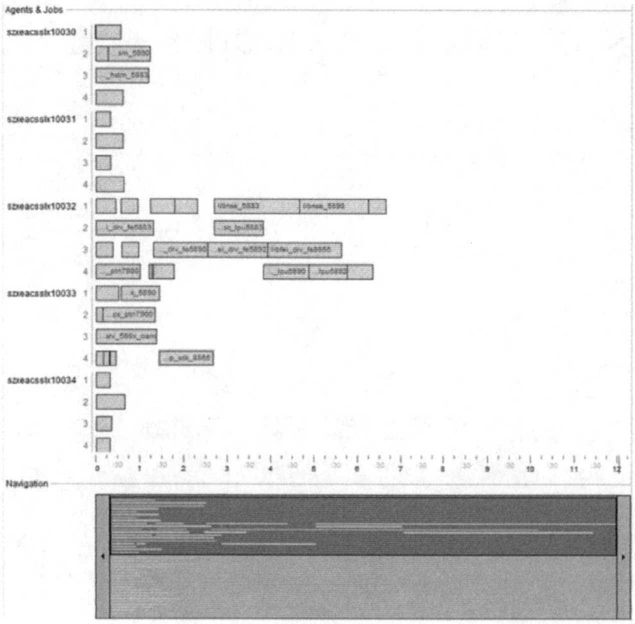

Figure 2: Dynamic Concurrency Analysis by ElectricInsight

II. Dynamic Concurrency Analysis

The dynamic concurrency analysis shows the actual execution of different build jobs in a distributed environment. There exists commercial tools like ElectricInsight [2] for such purpose. Typically, these tools monitor the build process by instrumenting the GNU (GNU is a recursive acronym for "GNU's Not Unix!") make tool or even replacing it with their own make tool. As a result, a build execution graph is generated to visualize concurrent scheduling and execution of build jobs. For instance, in an industrial case study we used ElectricInsight and generated the build execution graph as shown in Figure 2 on page 2. While some build jobs are executed in parallel in different threads (by build agents) and CPU (Central processing unit) cores, other build jobs are executed sequentially in the same thread.

Besides monitoring build execution, ElectricInsight also claims to optimize the scheduling of concurrent build execution (to reduce the overall build duration). However, from our experience the build concurrency is often not optimal. As seen in Figure 2 on page 2, while a few build threads keep executing build jobs sequentially, many other threads finish early and remain idle until the end of the build process. It seems that some build jobs have to be executed sequentially due to build dependencies defined in the build system (e. g., makefiles). In order to investigate the root causes of this suboptimal build concurrency, it is necessary to further analyze build dependencies and identify the actual concurrency potential.

III. Static Concurrency Analysis

While dynamic concurrency analysis shows the actual behavior of build job execution during the build process, static concurrency analysis focuses on the concurrency potential of

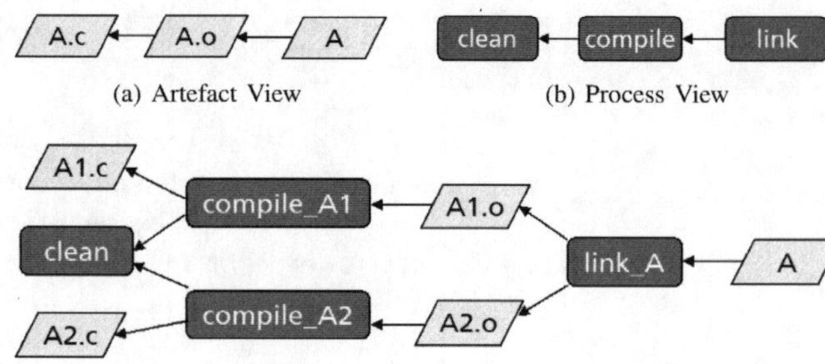

(a) Artefact View (b) Process View

(c) Execution View

Figure 3: Different Views of Build Dependencies.

build jobs and artefacts based on their dependencies. In this section, we assume an arbitrary but fixed environment for the execution of the build process, i. e., number of CPU cores, parallel threads, RAM (Random-access memory) size, etc. Moreover, we assume that the build process has only one connected graph component.

A. Build Dependencies

Various dependencies exist between build jobs and artefacts. We consider three views to analyze the different aspects of the build dependencies structure:

The *Artefact View* contains source code artefacts, intermediate and final artefacts of a build process. In Figure 3a on page 2 an artefact "A.o" depends on artefact "A.c".

On the other hand, the *Process View* shows build jobs and the process dependencies in-between, that represent finish-to-finish relationships. For an example of a clean build see Figure 3b on page 2, where the job "link" can finish, only if job "compile" has finished. The job "link" may however start before, in parallel, or after the job "compile". In any case, "link" can't finish before "compile" is finished.

The *Execution View* describes three kind of dependencies (see Figure 3c on page 2):

- Execution Dependency: Job "compile_A2" executes job "clean";
- Input Dependency: Job "compile_A2" depends on input artefact "A2.c"; and
- Output Dependency: Artefact "A2.o" is result of job "compile_A2".

These views depict all build dependencies in the vertical and horizontal dimensions of the Build Dependencies Structure in [18]. Accounting the different views and the number of possibilities for scheduling build jobs make the basis of the static concurrency analysis.

In any of the views on a well-defined build dependency structure, we deal with an acyclic directed graph. Such structure is equivalent to a partial order over the set of artefacts and build jobs, respectively. This partially ordered set is considered by a build tool (like GNU Make [3], Ninja [5], etc.) to compute a schedule over all build jobs and execute them in the right order. The richer the scheduling possibilities with

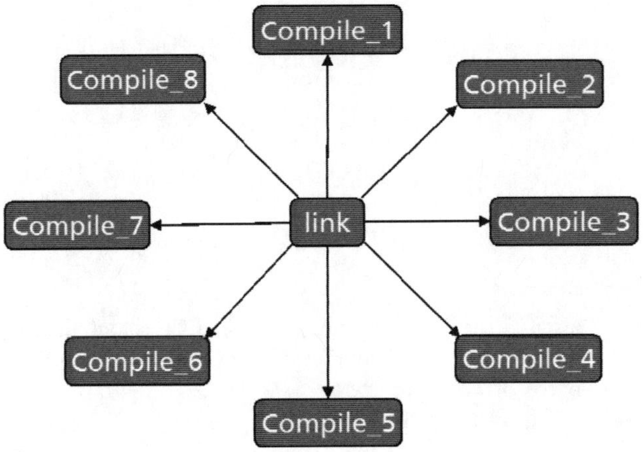

Figure 4: Process view of a best-case example for maximal parallelization

respect to the build dependencies structure, the bigger the optimization space, the greater the degree of freedom for concurrent execution.

B. Degree of Freedom

Here, we propose a new metric called Degree of Freedom that quantifies the parallelization property of a build process, i. e.,the degree to which extent a build process can be parallelized. This stands intuitively in direct correlation with the number of possible scheduling plans.

Examples: (a) Consider a build process where the dependency graph in the process view is a chain (e. g., Figure 3b on page 2). For such a process, there is only one possible plan for scheduling its execution and it is not parallelizable. (b) In comparison, for a star-shaped build process, like in Figure 4 on page 3, there are $8! = 40320$ possible scheduling plans to execute it in one processing thread and 8 of the 9 jobs can be parallelized.

We assume that a build process always has exactly one starting point (i. e., the main build job) and only one final resulting artefact (i. e., the product that is build). Thus, the dependency graph always has exactly one root in every view and therefore a star-shaped build process is the best possible case for maximal parallelization. Using this and the correlation from above, we define a metric that compares a given build process with a same-size, star-shaped build process by the number of possible scheduling plans.

However, the number of scheduling possibilities depends not only on the partial order, but also on the environment, i. e., mostly the number of parallel threads available for the execution. To get an environment independent metric, that is to multiply out the factor depending on the number of threads for parallel computing, we use the number of possible execution sequences for a single thread computation. Therefore, we define the *Degree of Freedom* by

$$\text{Freedom}\,(P) = \log_{S(P^*)} S\,(P)$$

where $S\,(P)$ is the number of possible execution sequences for build process P and $S\,(P^*)$ is the number of possible execution sequences for a star-shaped build process with the same number of build jobs/artefacts as in P. Thus, $S\,(P^*)$ equals$(|P| - 1)!$. Formally, $S\,(P)$ is the number of linear extensions over the partially ordered set (poset) P (see [11]).

Example: Let P be a build process with process view of 9 build jobs, such that P is a sequence. Then the corresponding star-shaped build process P^* is equivalent to this on Figure 4 on page 3. Therefore $\text{Freedom}\,(P) = \log_{S(P^*)} S\,(P) = \log_{8!} 1 = 0$ and $\text{Freedom}\,(P^*) = \log_{S(P^*)} S\,(P^*) = \log_{8!} 8! = 1$.

C. Implementation

At its heart, our metric is based on the number of possible execution sequences for a build process, which is a partial ordered set as discussed in III-A. The number of all sequences with respect to a poset is the number of all linear extensions of the poset [11]. In general, computing $S\,(P)$ is a #P-complete problem for arbitrary posets [8].

Although there are several algorithms that can find one linear extension in linear time [10], it is not clear if there exists even a polynomial time algorithm for computing the number of all linear extensions [16]. However, there are polynomial approximation schemes [9], which can be used to compute the number of all linear extensions by counting. In contrast to these works, we deal with special case of partial ordered sets. From the fact that they correspond to the dependency graph of a build process, we can expect that the posets are 'almost' trees. This means, that they contain a small number of edges that are in contradiction with the tree properties. Thus, we based our approach on the algorithm for computing the number of linear extensions in a tree-shaped poset proposed by Atkinson [7]. He proposes an $\mathcal{O}\left(n^2\right)$ algorithm for trees with n being the number of elements. Since we deal with 'almost' trees, we develop two algorithms for computing a upper and lower bounds for $S\,(P)$.

1) Upper Bound: We apply Atkinson's algorithm in combination with Prim's minimum spanning tree algorithm [15] to approximate a minimum tree-shaped poset that is a superset of P. Firstly, it will take all edges that are conform to the properties of a tree. All remaining edges are evaluated with respect to the minimal number of linear extensions resulting from taking one edge and recursively applying the same procedure until we end up with a tree on which we apply Atkinson's algorithm. This minimal number defines the edge weight. Afterwards, a minimal spanning tree is constructed. The number of linear extensions of that tree gives a upper bound for the number of linear extensions of P, since the set of dependencies (edges) of the tree is a subset of the dependencies of P. This algorithm runs in $\mathcal{O}\left(k^2 n^2\right)$, where k is the number of edges that contradict to the tree properties from graph theory.

2) Lower Bound: For the approximation of the lower bound, we use a simple scheduling strategy that is more restrictive than an optimal strategy for the given poset. We traverse the poset graph bottom-up starting with leaf nodes — elements with no outgoing dependencies — and moving towards a root node — element without ingoing dependencies. Hereby, we detect independent sequences of nodes between branching locations in the graph. This gives us a sequence of layers in the graph. Each layer consists of independent subsequences. The scheduling strategy is to run all subsequences in parallel and synchronizing the build process where a branching takes place. We compute the number of linear extensions l_j for layer j using the multinomial coefficient. More precisely, for every layer j of m independent subsequences, we have

$$l_j = \binom{k_1 + k_2 + \cdots + k_m}{k_1, k_2, \ldots, k_m}$$

with k_i being the number of nodes in i-th subsequence for all $1 \leq i \leq m$. In total, we need the product of all l_j. Computing the lower bound requires only one traversal of the graph without repetitions, as described above, which implies linear time.

Example: In the following, let P be the build dependency graph from Figure 3c on page 2 to illustrate a computation for both lower and upper bounds. We compute the upper bound, as described earlier, based on Prim's minimum spanning tree algorithm. In this example, only two edges contradict to the tree properties from graph theory — these are "clean"←"compile_A1" and "clean"←"compile_A2". Choosing either edge results in equivalent trees with respect to the number of linear extensions due to symmetry. By applying Atkinson's algorithm we get $S(P) < 70$ linear extensions and we get $\mathrm{Freedom}(P) < 0.4$, since $|P| = 9$.

On the other hand, the lower bound is computed very easily. Following the introduced algorithm, we end with three layers (l_1, l_2, l_3). From left to right:

- l_1 consists of 3 independent subsequences each of a single node. These are "A1.c", "clean", and "A2.c" and imply $l_1 = \binom{1+1+1}{1,1,1} = 6$.
- l_2 consists of 2 independent subsequences each of length 2: "compile_A1"←"A1.o" and "compile_A2"←"A2.o". Here we get $l_2 = \binom{2+2}{2,2} = 6$.
- Finally, l_3 consists of one subsequences of 2 nodes "link_A"←"A", that means $l_3 = \binom{2}{2} = 1$.

Since $S(P) > l_1 \cdot l_2 \cdot l_3 = 36$, $\mathrm{Freedom}(P) > 0.337$ holds and in total $\mathrm{Freedom}(P) = 0.3685 \pm 0.0315$.

D. Optimization and Visualization

The Degree of Freedom is a metric for the static concurrency analysis, that measures the parallelization potential of a build process as a whole. While it is an objective measurement, it does not provide direct recommendations for optimization. However, in cases where the build process can be separated in several independent sub-processes (see Figure 5 on page 4), a domain expert would be able to detect high-potential regions by applying our metric.

Here we recommend our »**GAME**-changing« method with:

- The **Goal** to increase concurrency
- by taking **Actions** to restructure dependencies.

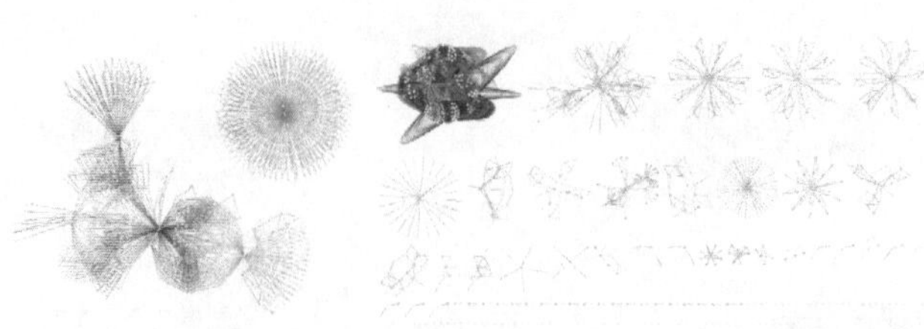

Figure 5: Visualization of Static Concurrency Analysis

- This is achieved by identifying the high potential using **Measurements** to detect large sub-process size with low Degree of Freedom and
- **Executing** the following steps:
  1) relationship analysis in high potential subgraphs by domain experts;
  2) alignment of process and artefact dependency graphs;
  3) reconnection of wrongly routed dependencies; and
  4) removal of unnecessary dependencies.

Additional visualization of the build process can also provide insights and support for further analysis. In Figure 5 on page 4, we provide an example visualization using Cytoscape [1]. Here we see the execution view of a (disconnected) build process, where each edge color represents different execution context, i. e., different execution scripts, different execution variable set, etc. Figure 5 on page 4.

IV. Related Work

There have been approaches and tools for both dynamic and static build analysis. In our previous work [18], we focused on the build process of Android and extracted the build jobs and dependencies by instrumenting the shell of GNU make. Gligoric et al. [12] intercepted file reads and writes in Windows by instrumenting Win32 functions using Detours [13]. In Linux there is the strace tool [14] for capturing such information like file read and write, process invocations, time measurement, etc. Moreover, there are tools for static makefile analysis, such as MAKAO [6], SYMake [17], and Makefile::Parser [4]. However, these tools are for general build extraction and analysis, and they do not support analyzing the concurrency of build execution.

V. Conclusion

This paper presents our approach for concurrency potential analysis we developed to support the maintenance of build system for constantly evolving software in big projects where the build process consumes an important amount of effort. We address these challenges providing our experience on dynamic and static analysis that we gained in our industry case. While conducting the concurrency analysis and optimization in this study, we have the following lessons learned:

1) Conduct dynamic concurrency analysis to monitor the concurrency performance of the actual build process.
2) Conduct static concurrency analysis to evaluate concurrency of the designed build process.

3) In order to optimize concurrency, deficits in the build system (e. g., obsolete/redundant build jobs) should be first fixed.
4) To prioritize concurrency optimization, consider to first focus on larger build subprocesses that have lower Degree of Freedom.

Moreover, we propose a new metric for measuring the concurrency potential of a build process. In fact, this metric is not limited to build analysis. It can be used for analyzing the concurrency potential of any executable process in general. Our implementation also provides a polynomial algorithm for computing lower and upper bounds for the number of linear exertions of a partial order set.

ACKNOWLEDGMENT

Thanks to our colleges from Fraunhofer IESE: Markus Damm for pointing to the right terminology by the problem formulation; and Sören Schneickert for many fruitful discussions and his constructive criticism.

REFERENCES

[1] Cytoscape. http://www.cytoscape.org, August 2018.
[2] ElectricInsight. http://electric-cloud.com/, August 2018.
[3] GNU Make. https://www.gnu.org/software/make, August 2018.
[4] Makefile::Parser. https://github.com/agentzh/makefile-parser-pm, August 2018.
[5] Ninja. https://ninja-build.org, August 2018.
[6] B. Adams, H. Tromp, K. de Schutter, and W. de Meuter. Design recovery and maintenance of build systems. In *Proc. IEEE Int. Conf. Software Maintenance*, pages 114–123, October 2007.
[7] M. D. Atkinson. On computing the number of linear extensions of a tree. *Order*, 7(1):23–25, Mar 1990.
[8] Graham Brightwell and Peter Winkler. Counting linear extensions. *Order*, 8(3):225–242, 1991.
[9] Russ Bubley and Martin Dyer. Faster random generation of linear extensions. *Discrete Mathematics*, 201(1-3):81–88, apr 1999.
[10] Thomas H. Cormen, Charles E. Leiserson, Ronald L. Rivest, and Clifford Stein. *Introduction to Algorithms, Second Edition*, chapter 22.4 Topological sort, pages 549–552. The MIT Press, 2001.
[11] Chaabane Djeraba Dan A. Simovici. *Mathematical Tools for Data Mining*. Springer London, 2008.
[12] Milos Gligoric, Wolfram Schulte, Chandra Prasad, Danny van Velzen, Iman Narasamdya, and Benjamin Livshits. Automated migration of build scripts using dynamic analysis and search-based refactoring. *SIGPLAN Not.*, 49(10):599–616, October 2014.
[13] Galen Hunt and Doug Brubacher. Detours: Binary Interception of Win32 Functions. In *Proceedings of the 3rd USENIX Windows NT Symposium*, pages 135–144, Seattle, Washington, July 1999.
[14] D. V. Levin, R. McGrath, and W. Akkerman. strace. linux syscall tracer. http://sourceforge.net/projects/strace, August 2018.
[15] R. C. Prim. Shortest Connection Networks And Some Generalizations. *Bell System Technical Journal*, 36(6):1389–1401, nov 1957.
[16] Ivan Rival, editor. *Graphs and Order*. Springer Netherlands, 1985.
[17] A. Tamrawi, H. A. Nguyen, H. V. Nguyen, and T. N. Nguyen. Symake: a build code analysis and refactoring tool for makefiles. In *Proc. 27th IEEE/ACM Int. Conf. Automated Software Engineering 2012*, pages 366–369, September 2012.
[18] Bo Zhang, V. Tenev, and M. Becker. Android build dependency analysis. In *Proc. IEEE 24th Int. Conf. Program Comprehension (ICPC)*, pages 1–4, May 2016.

Measuring Success in Agile Software Development Projects: a GQM Approach

Abdullah Aldahmash
Electronics and Computer Science
University of Southampton
Southampton, UK
e-mail: a.aldahmash@soton.ac.uk

Andy Gravell
Electronics and Computer Science
University of Southampton
Southampton, UK
e-mail: amg@ecs.soton.ac.uk

Abstract— **Agile software development has become one of the most commonly used methodologies for developing software. It promises to deliver many benefits, but nevertheless, the implementation of agile practices and techniques require many changes that might be a challenge for organizations attempting to succeed with agile software development projects. Claiming the success of agile software projects is difficult, and there is a need for more measurements with which agile success could be evaluated. This paper develops an instrument with which the success of an agile software development project could be measured. The criteria of the success are driven from the Critical Success Factors (CSFs) of agile development which have been identified prior developing this instrument. The proposed instrument will evaluate the success of agile software development projects in achieving these identified success factors. The instrument was developed following the Goal Question Metric (GQM) approach. This study conducted semi-structured interviews with 13 experts in the field of agile development. The aim of these interviews was to review and confirm the proposed instrument for measuring the success of agile projects. Following comments from the interviews, the instrument was revised. The developed instrument proposes measuring the agile success using 6 goals, 30 questions, and 7 metrics.**

Keywords—Agile; Agile success; GQM; Software metrics; Agile project

I. Introduction

Agile practices and techniques have been adopted by many organizations. These organizations face many challenges during the agile transformation. These challenges are related to a variety of aspects, such as people, culture, and technology. During a previous study [1] we identified the critical success factors of agile software development. Having identified the success factors of agile software development, now we will focus on studying how the success could be measured; claiming the success of agile software development is problematic. Therefore, there should be more metrics and systematic measurements that could evaluate the success of agile software development projects. There is also a need for more measurements with which the adoption of agile practices and techniques could be assessed.

The nature of agile software development requires new metrics that address the agility. One study [2] concluded that not all the software traditional lifecycle metrics are suitable for agile software development. It was suggested that future work should focus on how the use of the traditional software measurement could be adapted to work with agile development or to develop new metrics for agile development. Recent research [3] reviewed a total of 22 software metrics and resulted with only 10 metrics that could be used in agile software development. Therefore, there is a need for more software metrics that could be used to measure the status of agile software development.

This study selected the GQM approach to develop an instrument for measuring the success of agile software development. This selection was based on a suggestion from [4] findings, which revealed that the GQM approach is more relevant to the nature of agile software projects with short-cyclic iterations. GQM will provide measurements with clear purposes and goals and will result in saving the time of developing the measurement which is one of the agile development objectives. In this paper, an instrument is developed using the GQM approach. This instrument aimed to measure the success of agile software development projects.

This paper is organized as follows: Section I is an introduction. Following which, Section II is a background where the literature review is discussed. In Section III, the related work is presented. Section IV discusses the research methodology used in this study is presented. Section V is pertaining to the development of the proposed instrument. Following that, Section VI discusses the review of the instrument. Lastly, Section VII concludes the paper and puts forth the future work.

II. Background

In this section, the relevant literature was reviewed. Section A reviews the literature of the agile software development. Section B discusses the introduction of the GQM approach and how it could be employed.

A. Agile Software Development

In 2001, a group of software engineers established the agile manifesto [5] during which, they introduced four values and twelve principles of agile software development. Since then, agile practices and techniques have evolved. According to Agile Alliance network, agile software development defined as "an umbrella term for a set of methods and practices based on the values and principles expressed in the Agile Manifesto. Solutions evolve through collaboration between self-organizing, cross-functional teams utilizing the appropriate practices for their context" [6].

The main characteristics that the agile development include: communication and collaboration, support innovation/creativity, embrace changes, and the development should be iterative and indivisible [7]. Agile development advocates frequent delivery of working software. This ensures that feedback will be received early and so will be the changes in requirements. Agile development also embraces changes and conflicts during the development rather than rejecting them [8].

The latest State of Agile Survey 2018 [9] revealed that the top three reasons which drive the organizations to adopt agile were to accelerate product delivery, to manage changing requirements, and to increase productivity. According to a survey from Microsoft research, the top three paybacks from agile development are: improve the communication, enhance the delivery, and better respond to the changes. Conversely, the three top difficulties with agile development are: large-scale projects, number of required meetings, and rigorous management culture [10].

B. Goal-Question-Metric Approach

The instrument will be developed by using the GQM approach. GQM was proposed by Basili and Weiss [11] with the aim of introducing a systematic way of defining goals that could easily be refined into questions and linked to metrics. The GQM approach has three levels: conceptual level (Goal), operational level (Question), and quantitative level (Metric).

The goals are usually defined for specific purposes from a certain perspective and for a given object. Therefore, the usage of GQM will help in ensuring that the defined measurements will be defined with the aim of achieving specific goals [12]. The questions are used to describe the approach to achieving the goals and how it is going to be achieved. The metrics are set of data linked to each question aiming to answer it and it could be objective or subjective. Defining goals is beneficial to focus on the important aspects. Writing questions will make the goals more specific and will suggest the relevant metrics [13]. An example of the structure of GQM is illustrated in Figure 1.

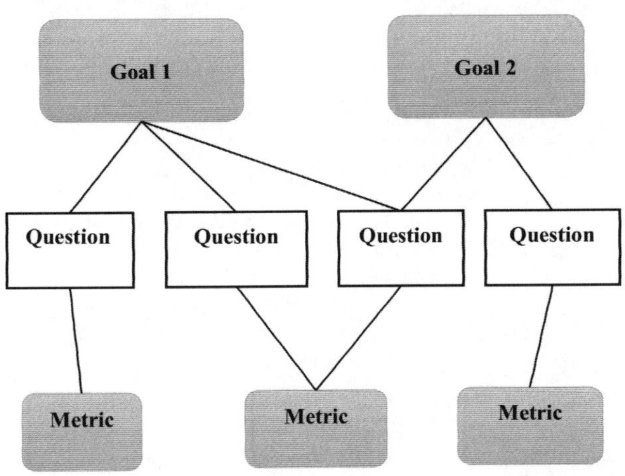

Figure 1. An Example of GQM Structure.

Using GQM approach to develop software measurements is associated with many benefits. Some of these benefits are improving the software product quality, enhancing software processes, and increasing the team cooperation [14]. The GQM-based measurement approach will help in avoiding irrelevant measurements through the regular feedback and by involving the project team to define measurements that are linked to the agreed upon goals [15]. GQM is a systematic approach of representing and combining a set of high-level goals into measurements. The result of implementing GQM is the specification of a set of metrics addressing a particular set of goals and rules for interpreting these results [16]. It is hoped that by implementing the GQM approach it will be possible to define a list of metrics which could measure the success of an agile software development project in an organization.

III. Related Work

A great deal of studies has investigated the status of measurements in agile software development. According to Javdani et. al [17], measurements in agile software development are unlike the measurements in traditional software development. It was suggested that there is a need for more agile measurements especially in the following areas: productivity and velocity, and the changing requirements in agile. Furthermore, Ayed et. al [18] introduced a measurement-based framework for measuring the adoption and customization of agile methods. A set of metrics have been introduced and categorised into three categories: organisation level metrics, product level metrics, and process level metrics. However, the introduced metrics were not introduced in a practical way which the organizations are looking for. Agile measurements need to be confirmed and validated through empirical methodologies in order to gain an acceptance from the agile practitioners. This paper is planning to validate the proposed instrument by conducting experts' interviews. Heidenberg et. al [19] introduced a metrics model following GQM to measure the impact of agile transformation in software development organizations. Their model focused on measuring the business value, lead-time, and efficiency of the agile software development transformation. It was indicated that more measurements are necessary to assess the agile software development status in organizations attempting for agile transformation.

A recent study [20] has also attempted to provide a quantitative measurement of the impact of agile transformation in software development organizations. They proposed a model with quantitative metrics following the GQM approach. The proposed model consists of one goal, four questions, and eight metrics following the structure of the GQM approach. While they introduced quantitative metrics, they indicated that qualitative metrics are needed as well. It was suggested that future work might concentrate on providing qualitative metrics with which the status of agile software development could be evaluated and measured.

Fontana et. al [21] conducted a systematic review on the agile development maturity models and they compared these models aiming to develop a model which could evaluate the adoption of agile practices and techniques in an organisation. They found and reviewed fourteen models which assess the agile maturity, of which six models were introduced in the last four years. Most of these available models are built on a combination between agile principles and Capability Maturity Model Integration (CMMI). Fontana et. al [21] recommended that future works should focus on empirical validation of these measurements which this research already achieved. While our instrument focused on measuring the success of implementing each success factor, these models were designed to measure the maturity of each agile practice independently. Both ways could be used to indicate the success in implementing agile software development projects.

Chita [22] suggested that the activity theory, which is usually used in social science, could be used to assess the factors for successful agile software development implementation, since the agile success is built on organisational, cultural, and social factors. They developed a model following the activity theory for successful agile adoption and they indicated that their on-going research will validate this model by conducting a case study.

Laanti [23] introduced a framework which could assess the agile transformation in large software development organisations. The framework classified the status of the organisations into five categories from beginner organisations to world-class organisations. While the framework assesses the agile adoption in the organisations, it lacks details on how organisations could evaluate their own adoption and how they could improve their agile transformation.

The findings obtained as a result of this paper and of the abovementioned emerging related work focused on understanding how the organizations could succeed in implementing agile practices. Furthermore, how the success in implementing agile practices could be measured and assessed. This shows the needs for more research that could work to validate these measurements and to introduce them to be used by agile software development practitioners.

In this paper, the proposed instrument used a mix of qualitative metrics and quantitative metrics to measure the success of agile software development projects. The proposed instrument will be reviewed by agile experts and it will be validated through conducting practical case studies.

IV. Research Methodology

The proposed instrument was developed using the GQM approach. This study followed a qualitative method which is semi-structured interviews with agile experts. These interviews were necessary to validate the proposed instrument. An invitation of participation was sent to a total of 28 experts. The criterion of selecting the experts which was used is that the expert should have at least 5 years of experience with agile software development. Out of the 28-reached experts, 13 experts were willing to participate in this research. These participants came from various countries, including the USA, Saudi Arabia, the UK, and France. The industries which the interview participants represent include, but are not limited to: Education sector, Finance and Banking sector, and Information Technology & Software sector. The interviewed experts represent different types of organizations which ranges from small organizations with only 15-30 employees to big multi-nation organizations. The participants were shown the instrument, following which they had the chance to ask for clarifications if needed. Then, they were asked about each item and to propose new items to the instrument. The interviews last, on average, approximately from 35 to 60 minutes.

V. Instrument Development

As identified in the literature, more measurements are needed for agile projects. The proposed instrument was developed for the purpose of measuring the success of agile software development projects. The GQM approach was selected to build the instrument considering its effeteness in detecting a systematic way of linking the metrics to the organizational goals and needs.

The first step of following the GQM approach is to identify the goal or the set of goals. The goal of this study was to measure the success of agile projects. Along with 6 sub goals selected as a result of a review of the success factors of agile software development [1], which identified the following factors as critical success factors of agile projects: Communication, Customer Involvement, Team Capability and Training, Top management Support, Organizational Culture, Delivery Strategy, Agile Software Development Practices and Techniques, and Project Management (PM) Process [1].

As suggested by GQM, the eight identified CSFs will be rewritten to be a set of goals. The two success factors of agile practices and techniques, and project management approach merged into one goal. This is because these two factors are about a selection process of available agile techniques and PM approaches; also, this was done to avoid the replication of having two goals about a selection process. Thus, the goal will be to have an appropriate selection of these available agile practices and techniques and PM approaches.

The organization culture is a soft factor which is hard to be measured and it contains many aspects which overlap with other success factors such as communication and top management support factors as per [24]. Thus, in the developed instrument, the organizational culture factor will not be an independent goal. Alternatively, organizational culture success factor will be included in the first, second, third, and fourth goal. The goals of the proposed instrument are listed as follows:

1. Improve the communication throughout the agile project.
2. Increase the customer involvement during the agile project.
3. Improve the training of the agile project team members.
4. Increase the support from top management in the agile project.
5. Enhance the delivery strategy.
6. Appropriate selection of agile techniques, practices, and PM approach.

A. Experts Interviews Design

This research applied semi-structured interviews encompassing open-ended questions and closed-ended questions to review the proposed instrument. The purposes of these interviews were: firstly, to review and confirm the proposed instrument's goals, questions, and metrics, and secondly to suggest any other questions and metrics that need to be considered when measuring the success of an agile software development project. The experts' interview process comprised many steps, which were as follows:

•Emails were sent to experts briefing them on the research and the objectives of the instrument. In the email, the experts were also asked to identify their preferred date and time for the interview.
•Depending on where the experts lived, some interviews were conducted online via Skype and Zoom, which are video calling applications. In contrast, other interviews were conducted on a face-to-face basis.
•Prior to the start of the interviews, all participants were requested to read the participant information sheet, following which they were asked to sign the consent form and return it by email.
•The participants were shown the instrument, and then had the opportunity to ask for further explanation if needed. This lasted approximately 5-10 minutes.
•Following this, the experts were asked about each goal in the instrument, starting with the first goal and ending with the last one. The experts were also asked about each item in the instrument and whether they felt that any additional item(s) needed to be added to the instrument.
•In the last part of the interview, the participants were asked to answer open-ended questions concerning how the instrument could be improved. This allowed the researcher to ensure that, according to the opinions of the interviewed experts, different aspects of agility were addressed in the proposed instrument. This also made it possible to confirm whether or not, according to the experts' interviewee responses, additional items were needed.
•The interviews were recorded and lasted, on average, approximately 35-60 minutes.
•The interviews were voice-recorded and summarised by the researcher using a pen and notebook. However, one participant refused to have his voice recorded, and that interview was hence not recorded.

VI. INSTRUMENT REVIEW

This study applied semi-structured interviews encompassing open-ended questions and closed-ended questions to review the proposed instrument. The aims of these interviews were: firstly, to review and confirm the proposed instrument's goals, questions, and metrics. Secondly, to suggest any other questions and metrics that need to be considered when measuring the success of an agile software development project. Therefore, interviews were conducted with 13 agile experts where the instrument was shown to them in order to review the proposed instrument.

The experts' interviews resulted with many modifications to the proposed instrument. Following the received feedback, the instrument was revised accordingly. These modifications ranged from some language and editing notes to additional questions and metrics to be added. There were number of amendments which were applied to the proposed instrument to address the received feedbacks. It is difficult to list all the discussions with the agile experts about the instrument in this paper. Alternatively, the final version of the instrument is provided. The focus will be shifted now on how the proposed instrument could be validated. The researchers intended to use the instrument in three case studies. The evaluation obtained as a result of these case studies will make it possible to validate the practical usage of the instrument.

The final version of the proposed instrument after the review from the interviewed experts is shown in Tables I, II, and III. The separation of the instrument into three tables is only for presentational purposes.

TABLE I. THE PROPOSED INSTRUMENT (PART 1 OF 3)

Measuring the Success of Agile Software Development Projects	
1st Goal: Improve the communication throughout the agile project	
Q1. Rate your use of the ready communication platforms across the team (e.g. Slack, etc.) or your own developed platform? Q2. Rate the team practice of daily meetings (physical or virtual) where the team sit together to discuss the project progress? Q3. Rate your use of centralized repositories to enable documents and knowledge sharing throughout the project?	• Very Good • Good • Acceptable • Poor • Very Poor
Q4. How often the project team is sharing and communicating development's aspects? Q5. How often the team have access to task boards (or smart boards) to communicate with co-located members and video conferences capabilities to communicate with different-located members? Q6. How often do you communicate informally (face to face communication) during the project when it is possible?	• Always • Often • Sometimes • Seldom • Never
2nd Goal: Increase the customer involvement during the agile project	
Q1. Rate the customers' participation in planning meetings, demos, retrospectives and how they contribute to the success of these events? Q2. Rate the response time (e.g. how fast they are) from the customers to development queries? Q3. Rate the commitment and the support of the customers in the project toward resolving development issues and difficulties?	• Very Good • Good • Acceptable • Poor • Very Poor
Q4. How often do the customers attend the meetings (planning meetings, demos, and retrospectives) when they are requested to do so by the project team? Q5. How often do the customers express their needs to the project team, or suggest improvement for enhancing the project to the team?	• Always • Often • Sometimes • Seldom • Never

TABLE II. THE PROPOSED INSTRUMENT (PART 2 OF 3)

Measuring the Success of Agile Software Development Projects	
3rd Goal: Improve the training of the agile project team members	
Q1. Rate the available training resources in covering all aspects needed by the project team members? Q2. Rate the appropriateness of the contents of the training received by the project team? Q3. Rate the participation (e.g. attending, supporting, and facilitating) of the project team members in the available training programs?	• Very Good • Good • Acceptable • Poor • Very Poor
Q4. How often did the project team members practice self-training (e.g. watching learning videos, attending webinar, etc.)?	• Always • Often • Sometimes • Seldom • Never
4th Goal: Increase the support from top management in the agile project	
Q1. Rate the role of top management support toward the success of the attended planning meetings, demos, and retrospectives during the project? Q2. Rate the role of top management support in facilitating development issues? Q3. Rate the role of top management support in expediting development issues? Q4. Rate the overall support (budget, time, resources, etc.) from top management in the project?	• Very Good • Good • Acceptable • Poor • Very Poor
Q5. How often are the top management involved in planning meetings, demos, and retrospectives when they are requested to be there? Q6. How often do the top management initiate or propose events (meetings, emails, requests, etc.) whenever it is necessarily to do so?	• Always • Often • Sometimes • Seldom • Never

In Tables I, II, and III each question is associated with the corresponding used metric. The developed instrument has been reviewed by 13 agile experts. These experts' interviews allowed the researcher to refine and improve the instrument. It is intended that the proposed instrument will be validated by conducting case studies to use the instrument. Three organizations agreed to use the instrument to measure the success of their agile software development projects. The instrument will be validated by these case studies and the participants' evaluations will make it possible for further improvement of the instrument. By conducting case studies, the researcher will be able to validate the proposed instrument. It is hoped that the evaluation from these case studies will generate further understanding about the concept of success in adopting agile software development practices.

TABLE III. THE PROPOSED INSTRUMENT (PART 3 OF 3)

Measuring the Success of Agile Software Development Projects	
5th Goal: Enhance the delivery strategy	
Q1. How long it takes to deliver a story point?	Story point cycle time
Q2. How much of the sprint's (or iteration) planned story points actually delivered by the end of the current sprint?	Sprint Burndown
Q3. What is the percentage of planned to delivered story points in the current release?	Release Burndown
Q4. What is your schedule efficiency (how fast you are progressing against the rate of progress planned)?	Schedule Performance Index (SPI)
6th Goal: Appropriate selection of agile techniques, practices, and project management PM approach	
Q1. Do the team use an existing agile method "off the shelf" without adjusting it to suit their needs?	Yes/No.
Q2. How often are the current knowledge and capabilities of the team are considered when selecting agile techniques, practices and PM approach? Q3. How often are the needs of the customers and top management considered when selecting agile techniques, practices and PM approach? Q4. How often do the team conduct retrospectives (sprint reviews) to discuss the improvement of the selection of agile techniques, practices and PM approach? Q5. How often do these retrospectives (sprint reviews) lead to a change in agile techniques, practices and PM approach?	• Always • Often • Sometimes • Seldom • Never

The proposed instrument followed a scoring scale with which the success of agile software development projects could be measurement. The scoring is set to be used as an indication of how the participants of the instrument are doing and how they could achieve the defined goals of the proposed instrument, and ultimately achieve success with agile software development projects. With regard to the scoring of the instrument, the final score will range from 0 to 6, whereby 6 is the highest score. The final score is a result of totalling the scores of the six goals, each goal's score ranges from 0 to 1, whereby 1 is the highest score for each goal. The score of each goal is a result of summing of the scores for each question (0 to 1) dividing by the number of questions in that specific goal. This means that each question has the same weight when calculating the goal's score. Eventually, every goal of the six goals has the same weight when calculating the final score of the instrument. The scoring of the instrument will make it easy for the organizations to know their weaknesses and strengths. For instance, if the scoring of the instrument resulted in 0.90 for communication goal and 0.50 for the delivery strategy goal, it will be obvious that the work should be shifted to improve the delivery strategy.

VII. CONCLUSION AND FUTURE WORK

In this paper, an instrument to measure the success of agile software development was proposed. The development of the instrument followed the GQM approach. Semi-structured interviews were conducted with agile software development experts. These experts came from different industries and from different countries. The criterion with which the experts were chosen is that each expert must have at least five years of experience with agile development. The instrument was shown to 13 agile experts. Following this, the instrument was revised and amended based on the feedback received from the experts. The final version of the instrument comprised of 6 goals, 30 questions, and 7 metrics.

With regard to the future work, it is intended that this instrument will be applied in three organizations. These organizations will be used as case studies to apply the instrument. In each case study, the data regarding the agile software development will be gathered and the instrument will be filled. The instrument's score of the agile success will be provided to the organizations. During the case studies, there will be an evaluation of the use of the instrument and how the instrument could be improved. The three organization have been identified and contacted regarding this manner and they approved to host the case studies. By conducting these case studies, the instrument will be validated and further improvement might be added to the instrument.

ACKNOWLEDGMENT

We would like to thank all the 13 experts whom we interviewed during this study for their participation, experience, feedback, and knowledge without which this work could not be completed.

REFERENCES

[1] A. Aldahmash, A. Gravell, and Y. Howard, "A review on the critical success factors of agile software development," In *European Conference on Software Process Improvement EUROSPI2017*, pp. 504-512. Springer, Cham, 2017.

[2] M. Kunz, R. Dumke, and N. Zenker. "Software metrics for agile software development," In *Software Engineering, 2008. ASWEC 2008. 19th Australian Conference on*, pp. 673-678. IEEE, 2008.

[3] K. J. Padmini, H. D. Bandara, and I. Perera, "Use of software metrics in agile software development process," In IEEE Moratuwa Engineering Research Conference (MERCon), pp. 312-317, 2015.

[4] R. Solingen, "Agile GQM: Why Goal/Question/Metric is more Relevant than Ever and Why It Helps Solving the Agility Challenges of Today's Organizations." In *Software Measurement and the International Conference on Software Process and Product Measurement (IWSM-MENSURA), 2014 Joint Conference of the International Workshop on*, pp. 271-271. IEEE, 2014.

[5] Beck, Kent, et al. (2001). Manifesto for agile software development.

[6] Agile 101, Agile Alliance, retrieved: August, 2018, https://www.agilealliance.org/agile101/.

[7] T. Dyba, and T. Dingsoyr. "What do we know about agile software development?," *IEEE software* vol. 26, no. 5, pp. 6-9, 2009.

[8] J. Highsmith and A. Cockburn, "Agile software development: The business of innovation," Computer 34, no. 9, pp. 120-127, 2001.

[9] Agile State Report. (2018). 12th Annual State of Agile Report, State of Agile Report 2018, retrieved: August, 2018, https://explore.versionone.com/state-of-agile/versionone-12th-annual-state-of-agile-report-2.

[10] A. Begel and N. Nagappan, "Usage and perceptions of agile software development in an industrial context: An exploratory study," In *Empirical Software Engineering and Measurement ESEM 2007*, pp. 255-264, 2007.

[11] V. Basili, and V. Weiss, "A methodology for collecting valid software engineering data," *IEEE Transactions on software engineering*, vol. 6. pp. 728-738, 1984.

[12] A. Gray, and S. MacDonell, "GQM++ A Full Life Cycle Framework for the Development and Implementation of Software Metric Programs." In *Proceedings of ACOSM'97 Fourth Austrailian Conference on Software Metrics*, pp. 22-35. 1997.

[13] V. Basili, G. Caldiera, and D. Rombach, "Goal question metric paradigm," *Encyclopedia of software engineering* vol. 1, pp. 528-532, 1994.

[14] A. Birk, R. Solingen, and J. Jarvinen, "Business impact, benefit, and cost of applying GQM in industry: an in-depth, long-term investigation at Schlumberger RPS," In *Software Metrics Symposium 1998*, pp. 93-96, IEEE, 1998.

[15] F. Latum, et al., "Adopting GQM based measurement in an industrial environment," *IEEE software* vol. 15, no. 1, pp. 78-86, 1998.

[16] R. Solingen, and E. Berghout, "Integrating goal-oriented measurement in industrial software engineering: industrial experiences with and additions to the Goal/Question/Metric method (GQM)," In *Software Metrics Symposium 2001*, pp. 246-258. IEEE, 2001.

[17] T. Javdani, H. Zulzalil, A. AbdGhani, A. Sultan, and R.Parizi, "On the current measurement practices in agile software development," *arXiv preprint arXiv*, pp. 1301-5964, 2013.

[18] H. Ayed, N. Habra, and B. Vanderose. "Am-quick: a measurement-based framework for agile methods customisation," In *Software Measurement and the 2013 Eighth International Conference on Software Process and Product Measurement (IWSM-MENSURA)*, pp. 71-80, IEEE, 2013.

[19] J. Heidenberg, M. Weijola, K. Mikkonen, and I. Porres. "A metrics model to measure the impact of an agile transformation in large software development organizations," In *International Conference on Agile Software Development*, pp. 165-179. Springer, 2013.

[20] M. Olszewska, J. Heidenberg, M. Weijola, K. Mikkonen, and I. Porres, "Quantitatively measuring a large-scale agile transformation," *Journal of Systems and Software* vol. 117, pp. 258-273, 2016.

[21] R.M Fontana, R. Albuquerque, R. Luz, A.C Moises, A. Malucelli, and S. Reinehr, "Maturity Models for Agile Software Development: What Are They?," In *European Conference on Software Process Improvement EUROSPI 2018*. Communications in Computer and Information Science, vol. 896. Springer, Cham, pp. 3-14, 2018.

[22] P. Chita, "Agile Software Development – Adoption and Maturity: An Activity Theory Perspective," In Agile Processes in Software Engineering and Extreme Programming. XP 2018.

Lecture Notes in Business Information Processing, vol. 314. Springer, Cham, pp. 160-176, 2018.

[23] M. Laanti, “Agile transformation model for large software development organizations,” In *Proceedings of the XP2017 Scientific Workshops,* ACM, pp.19, 2017.

[24] D. Stankovic, V. Nikolic, M. Djordjevic, and D. Cao, "A survey study of critical success factors in agile software projects in former Yugoslavia IT companies," *Journal of Systems and Software* vol. 86, no.6, pp.1663-1678, 2013.

A Method to Optimize Technical Debt Management in Timed-boxed Processes

Luigi Lavazza, Sandro Morasca and Davide Tosi

Dipartimento di Scienze Teoriche e Applicate
Università degli Studi dell'Insubria
21100 Varese, Italy
Email: luigi.lavazza@uninsubria.it
sandro.morasca@uninsubria.it
davide.tosi@uninsubria.it

***Abstract*—Technical debt is currently receiving great attention from researchers, because it is believed to affect software development to a great extent. However, it is not yet clear how technical debt should be managed. This is specifically true in time-boxed development processes (e.g., in agile processes organized into development sprints of fixed duration), where it is possible to remove technical debt as soon as it is discovered, or wait until the debt reaches a given threshold, or wait until a whole sprint can be dedicated to technical debt removal, etc. We aim at investigating the consequences of different technical debt management options, especially as far as debt removal and program enhancements are concerned. We are interested in the consequences on both the amount of functionality and the quality of the delivered software. We propose a System Dynamics model that supports the simulation of various scenarios in time-boxed software development and maintenance processes. The proposed model is conceived to highlight the consequences of management decisions. Since this is our focus, our model abstracts from a few confounding factors that may be present in software projects, which would basically introduce some noise and blur the effect we want to study. Nonetheless, the model can be easily extended and adapted to represent these other factors adequately. The proposed model shows how productivity and product quality depend on the way technical debt is managed. Our model yields quantitative indications that can support the estimation of the economic consequences of different management strategies. Our study shows that different strategies for managing technical debt in a time-boxed development and maintenance process may yield different results—in terms of both productivity and delivered software quality—depending on a few conditions. Software project managers can use customized System Dynamics models to optimize the development and maintenance processes, by making the proper decisions on when to carry out maintenance dedicated to decreasing the technical debt, and how much effort should be devoted to such activities.**

Keywords–Technical debt; System Dynamics; Technical debt management.

I. Introduction

Both practitioners and researchers are dedicating a growing amount of attention to Technical Debt (TD). In general, TD is connected with a lack of quality in the code. The idea is that, if maintaining a piece of software of "ideal" quality has a given cost, maintaining a piece of software of "less than ideal" quality implies an extra cost.

It is also common knowledge that if no action is performed to improve code quality, a sequence of maintenance interventions will decrease quality, that is, TD increases and the cost of maintenance increases as well. Not managing TD at all could lead to code that is not maintainable.

These considerations pose the problem of managing TD: project managers need to identify the best TD management strategies and methods, and evaluate their effectiveness before putting them in practice.

For this purpose, we propose a System Dynamics model that represents the development of software via a sequence of time-boxed development phases (e.g., Scrum sprints). Like any System Dynamics model, the proposed model can be simulated, thus providing quantitative indications concerning the effectiveness of development in terms of amount and quality of code delivered. The proposed model is used in this paper to illustrate a few development scenarios and the consequences of TD and the adopted TD management practices.

The paper is organized as follows. In Section II, we provide background concerning Technical Debt and System Dynamics. In Section III, we introduce our model of software development and maintenance, characterized by time-boxed incremental phases. In Section IV, the model is used to simulate the behavior of the process when different strategies for allocating effort to repay the technical debt are used. In Section V, we discuss the outcomes of simulations, especially as far as productivity and delivered quality are concerned. Section VI accounts for related work. Finally, in Section VII we draw some conclusions and outline future work.

II. Background

In the last few years, TD has received great attention from researchers. For example, a recent Systematic Mapping Study on TD and TD management (TDM) covering publications from 1992 and 2013 detected 94 primary studies to obtain a comprehensive understanding on the TD concepts and an overview on the current state of research on TDM [1].

An updated Systematic Mapping Study identified elements that are considered by researchers to have an impact on TD in the industrial environment [2]. The authors classified these twelve elements in three main categories: (1) Basic decision making factors, (2) Cost estimation techniques, and (3) Practices and techniques for decision-making. They mapped these elements to the stakeholders' point of view, specifically, for business organizational management, engineering management, and software engineering areas.

Several authors proposed definitions for TD and its interests. Nugroho et al. [3] define TD as *"the cost of repairing quality issues in software systems to achieve an ideal quality level"* and the interests of the debt as *"the extra maintenance cost spent for not achieving the ideal quality level."* Other works try to empirically correlate TD with software size, software quality, customer satisfaction, and other software properties, in the context of enterprise software systems [4].

In a recent Dagstuhl Seminar [5], the following definition of TD was proposed: *"In software-intensive systems, technical debt is a collection of design or implementation constructs that are expedient in the short term, but set up a technical context that can make future changes more costly or impossible. Technical debt presents an actual or contingent liability whose impact is limited to internal system qualities, primarily maintainability and evolvability."*

The Software Quality Assessment based on Lifecycle Expectations (SQALE) method [6] addresses a set of external qualities (like Reliability, Efficiency, Maintainability, etc.). Each of these qualities is associated with a set of requirements concerning internal qualities, each provided with a *"remediation function,"* which represents the cost of changing the code so that the requirement is satisfied. Based on these functions, the cost of TD is computed for each external quality and for all qualities.

The Object Management Group has published a beta version of the specification of a measure of TD principal, defined as *"The cost of remediating must-fix problems in production code"* [7]. The measure can be computed automatically as a weighted sum of the *"violations of good architectural and coding practices,"* detected according to the occurrence of specific code patterns. The weight is computed according to the expected remediation effort required for each violation type.

System Dynamics was developed by Jay Forrester [8] as a modeling methodology that uses feedback control systems principles to represent the dynamic behavior of systems. The elements of System Dynamics models are levels, constants, auxiliary variables and rates. The dynamics of systems is determined by how levels work: given a level L, its value in time is always determined by an equation $L(t + \Delta t) = L(t) + (in(t) - out(t))\Delta t$, where *in(t)* and *out(t)* are rates. Levels and rates can concern anything (e.g., people, rabbits, bricks, lines of code, etc.), depending on the application scope and goal of the model. The value of a rate at time t is defined based on the values of auxiliary variables, other rates and levels at time t. Likewise for auxiliary variables, which are not necessary, but are useful to write readable models.

The elements of a System Dynamics model are interconnected just like in the real world, to form a network, where causes and effects are properly represented. Models can be executed, so that the behavior of the modeled system can be simulated. Via System Dynamics models it is quite easy to perform what-if analyses: you obtain different behaviors by changing the initial state of the system (given by the values of levels), how rates and variable are computed, how they depend on each other, etc.

III. The Proposed Model

As already mentioned, the proposed model describes in an operational way the time-boxed development process, especially in terms of maintenance activities concerning the reduction of Technical Debt. The proposed model aims at evaluating the productivity of development and maintenance activities, and the quality of the released product. Here productivity is defined as the ratio of the amount of product—measured in Function Points (FP) [9][10]—developed in a time period to the amount of effort/resources used.

To focus on the main objectives, we abstract from all those aspects of the model that deal with activities and software products that are not directly connected with TD management. For instance, in a real process, the productivity of individuals tends to increase because of learning effects, the number of developers allocated may change during a project, etc.: we exclude all of these variables because they would introduce noise in our investigation, which focuses on the effects of TD management decisions.

A. Assumptions

The main reason why practitioners and researchers are interested in TD is that maintaining code burdened with a big TD (i.e., low-quality code) costs much more than maintaining code with little TD (i.e., high-quality code). This is because more work is needed to carry out any code-related activity when code is of low quality (e.g., difficult to understand, poorly structured, full of hidden dependencies, etc.).

To account for the relation that links TD to maintenance cost, we need a measure of TD. To this end, we measure TD via a "TD index," an indicator that takes into account the internal qualities of code that concur to determine the amount of TD embedded in the code. Here, we are not interested in defining precisely the TD index, based on the measures of individual internal qualities, because this is not relevant for our purposes. Clearly, accurately modeling individual internal qualities of code would make the model more apt at reproducing the behavior of real development environments. But this is not our purpose: we aim at building a model that shows—at a fairly high level—the effects of decisions concerning TD management in a generic realistic development environment.

We assume that the TD index ranges between 0 (highest quality) and 1 (worst quality). The extreme values represent limiting cases, which may not occur in practice. When the TD index is 1, maintenance is so difficult that one is better off by simply throwing away the code and building a new version from scratch, and productivity is null, i.e., *prod* = 0. When the TD index is 0, maintenance activities attain their optimal productivity $prod_{opt}$. When 1>TD index>0, *prod* steadily increases from 0 to $prod_{opt}$ when the TD index decreases.

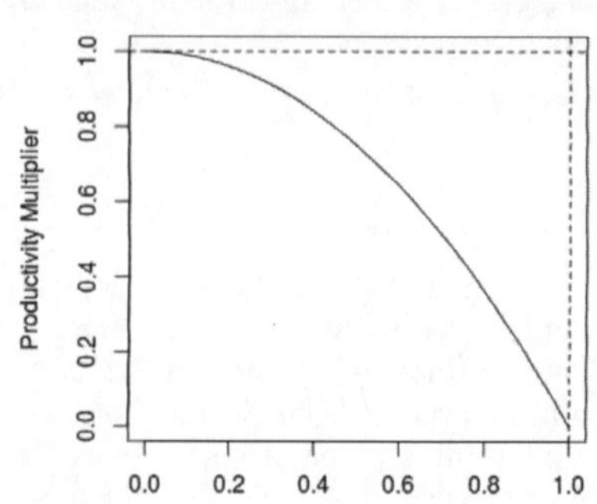

Figure 1. Effect of technical debt on productivity.

The value of productivity for a given value of the TD index *prod(TDindex)* can be expressed as *prodMult(TDindex)* $\times prod_{opt}$. Figure 1 shows a possible behavior of *prodMult(TDindex)*. We use the function illustrated in Figure 1 to build models to exemplify our proposal. Other monotonically decreasing functions that go through points $(0, 1)$ and $(1, 0)$ could be used as well, but that would not change the way we build models in our proposal.

Here, we assume that development is carried out in a time-boxed way. This is coherent with the organization of development in most agile processes. We assume that the development is composed of a sequence of "sprints," each of which has a fixed duration and involves a constant number of developers, hence a sprint "consumes" a fixed number of Person Days (PD). For instance, if sprints last 20 work days and involve 5 developers, then each sprint "costs" 100 PD. If at the end of 5 sprints 416 FP are released, we have achieved a productivity of 416/(5·100)=0.832 FP/PD; if at the end of these sprints 378 FP are released, we have achieved a productivity of 378/500=0.756 FP/PD. Quite clearly, in the former case the management of technical debt was more effective, a higher productivity was achieved, more functionality was released, and bigger returns can be expected.

A consequence of our assumptions is that the amount of effort spent is strictly proportional to development duration, which can be expressed in number of sprints. Given this proportionality between effort and the number of sprints, we can express productivity as the amount of code released after N sprints. Thus, we measure the productivity values above as 416/5=83.2 FP/Sprint (instead of 416/500=0.832 FP/PD) and 378/5=75.6 FP/Sprint (instead of 378/500=0.756 FP/PD).

During each sprint, the developers can carry out two types of activities: 1) increase the functionality of the system, by adding new code, and 2) decrease TD, by refactoring code structure, removing defects and improving the qualities that make development and maintenance easier. Since in each sprint the amount of work is fixed, managers have to decide what fraction of work has to be dedicated to new code development—the remaining fraction being dedicated to TD management. Several different criteria can be used in setting such fraction, as illustrated in Section IV.

We assume that during each sprint a constant fraction of the new code affected by quality problems (hence, increasing the technical debt) is released. This fraction depends on several factors, like the experience and ability of developers, the availability of sophisticated tools, problem complexity, etc. We assume that these factors are constant throughout all the sprints: in this way, we do not generate noise and we can highlight the effects of TDM decisions.

B. The Model

The proposed System Dynamics model involves two level variables: `CodeSize` (measured in FP) and `TDIndex`.

The constants in the model are:
`nominal_maintenance_productivity`, the productivity in FP/Sprint in ideal conditions, i.e., when the TD index is zero. We assume that the nominal productivity is 80 FP/Sprint, corresponding to 0.1 FP/PersonHour, a fairly typical value [11].
`nominal_TDimprovement_productivity`, the amount of code that can be optimized—i.e., whose TD is completely repaid—in a sprint, when the effort is completely devoted to TD improvement. We assume that this value is 40 FP/Sprint. In real developments, this amount is not necessarily constant: a sprint could be sufficient to "clean" 40 FP or relatively good code, but not to "clean" 40 FP of very bad quality code.
`bad_fraction_of_new_code`, the fraction of the new code (released at the end of each sprint) that contributes to increasing TD. We here assume that the value of this constant is 0.2.
`available_effort`: the effort available at each sprint. As already mentioned, we assume it to be a constant. The actual value is not relevant, however, we can take 100 PD as a reference value.

The rate and auxiliary variables of the model are:
`fraction_of_effort_for_quality_maintenance`: the fraction of `available_effort` dedicated to repaying TD. This variable is computed via function `fracEffortForQuality`, which has the TD index as an argument.
`quality_maintenance_effort`: the effort available for improving the quality of code in a sprint.
`maintenance_effort`: the effort available for developing new code in a sprint.
`maintenance_productivity`: the productivity of developing new code in a sprint. It depends on the `nominal_maintenance_productivity`, the `maintenance_effort` and the decrease of productivity due to the TD (computed via function `productivity_considering_TD`).
`TD_dec_rate`: the TD decrease rate.
`TD_inc_rate`: the TD increase rate.

The values of the aforementioned variables are determined by the following equations:

```
available_effort=1
fraction_of_effort_for_quality_maintenance=
 fracEffortForQuality(TDindex)
quality_maintenance_effort=available_effort*
 fraction_of_effort_for_quality_maintenance
maintenance_effort=
 available_effort-quality_maintenance_effort
maintenance_productivity=
 nominal_maintenance_productivity*
 maintenance_productivity_considering_TD(TDindex)
TDimprovement_productivity=
 nominal_TDimprovement_productivity*
   quality_maintenance_effort
TD_inc_rate=bad_fraction_of_new_code*
 maintenance_productivity/CodeSize
TD_dec_rate=TDimprovement_productivity/CodeSize
```

where the following functions are used:
`maintenance_productivity_considering_TD(TDindex)`: the loss of productivity due to TD, as described in Figure 1.
`fracEffortForQuality(TDindex)`: this function describes the strategy used for tackling TD. In Section IV, we use a few different strategies, hence, a few different function definitions.

The levels are computed as follows (where all auxiliary and rate variables are computed at time t):

```
CodeSize(t+Δt)=CodeSize(t)+
    Δt*maintenance_productivity
TDindex(t+Δt)=TDindex(t)+
    Δt*(TD_inc_rate-TD_dec_rate))
```

IV. Simulating the Model

We simulate the model with a few different TD management strategies. The considered case is characterized as follows. Initially, the software system to be maintained has size 80 FP and its TD index is 0.2 (representing the quality gap between the "ideal" quality and the actual initial quality accepted to speed up development and release the product early). The nominal productivity (i.e., new code development productivity in ideal conditions, when no extra effort is due because of TD) is 80 FP/Sprint. The nominal TD repayment productivity (i.e., the amount of functionality for which the TD is completely repaid in a sprint) is 40 FP/Sprint. At the end of every sprint, 20% of the added code is "bad" code.

Our software organization goes through a sequence of 30 maintenance sprints. We assume that there are always enough new requirements to implement to use up the development capacity of sprints. This is a situation that occurs quite often in practice. We also assume that the same amount of effort is allocated to all sprints. In actual developments, this does not always happen. Anyway, simulations that do not depend on variations in the available effort provide better indications of the effects of TD management strategies, since they do not depend on accidental phenomena, like the amount of available workforce.

A. Constant Effort for TD Management

In the first simulation, we assume that the considered software development organization allocates a constant fraction of the effort available in each sprint, to tackle the technical debt. It is reasonable to expect that the achieved results depend on how big the fraction of effort dedicated to TD management is. Hence, we run the simulation a few times, with different fractions of the available effort dedicated to TD management, ranging from zero (i.e., nothing is done to decrease the TD) to 40%. The main results of the simulation are given in Figure 2, which shows, from left to right: the functional size of the software product version released after each sprint; the functional size increment due to each sprint (i.e., the enhancement productivity of each sprint); the evolution of the TD through sprints (i.e., the quality of the software product versions released after each sprint).

We can examine the achieved results starting with the solid black lines, which represent the case in which no effort at all is dedicated to repaying the TD. It is easy to see that the results obtained by this TD management strategy (a no-management strategy, actually) are quite bad. In fact, after 30 sprints we get only 1248 FP: about 500 FP less than the most efficient TD management strategy. Not only: the final product has TD index = 0.84, that is, a very low quality, probably hardly acceptable in practice. The effects of TD on maintenance productivity are apparent: the continuously growing TD makes maintenance less efficient over sprints and, at the end, more than 60% of the initial productivity is lost, due to TD. So, just ignoring the TD is not a good practice. Definitely, we have to allocate some effort to decrease the TD, but how much effort should we dedicate to repaying TD?

By looking at Figure 2, it is easy to see that dedicating 10% of the available effort to repaying TD improves the situation with respect to not managing the TD at all: the final size (1580 FP) is bigger, and the final TD index (0.64) is better, though not really good. When we dedicate 20% of the available effort to repaying TD the results improve further: the final size (1743 FP) is bigger, and the final TD index (0.41) is better, though still not very good.

In summary, by increasing the fraction of effort dedicated to repaying TD from 0 to 20% we improve both the amount of functionality that we are able to release, and the quality of the software product. Hence, it would be natural to hypothesize that, by further increasing the fraction of effort dedicated to repaying TD, we obtain improvements in both the amount and quality of delivered software. Actually, this is not the case: when 30% of the available effort is dedicated to repaying TD, we obtain a fairly good product (the final TD index is 0.13, better than it was initially) but the amount of released functionality is slightly less (1723 FP). When an even bigger fraction (40%) of effort is dedicated to repying TD, we achieve practically ideal quality (the final TD index is 0.007), but substantially less functionality (the final size being 1517 FP).

The explanation of these results is that it is clear that increasing the fraction of effort dedicated to TD improvement improves maintenance productivity by decreasing TD, but at the same time subtracts effort from enhancement maintenance activities. Hence, one should look for a trade-off, to achieve both a reasonably high productivity level and an acceptable quality level (i.e., a sufficiently small TD).

Via a series of simulations, it is possible to find the fraction of effort dedicated to repaying TD that maximizes the released functionality, hence maintenance productivity. In the considered case, allocating 24% of the available effort to TD improvement eventually results in yielding 1758 FP. However, the final TD index is 0.31: not a small debt, and a bigger debt than initially. So, one could easily prefer to go for a bit less functionality but a much better code.

Finally, it should be noticed that in the short term—i.e., in the first 10 sprints or less—not managing TD does not seem to cause relevant negative consequences. For instance, in the considered case, if the goal is to achieve a 500 FP software product, not managing the TD may be a viable choice: you get the product faster than by managing TD. Of course, one should be sure that no further maintenance will be needed, otherwise maintenance cost would be quite high, that is, one has just postponed paying the debt.

B. Variable Effort for TD Management

In the previous section, the fraction of effort dedicated to quality improvement was fixed, i.e., it was constant over the sprints. This is not a good managerial choice, for at least the following two reasons. First, the initial TD could be greater than in the case described in Section IV-A. Hence, it would be a good practice to devote a substantial amount of effort to improve quality at the beginning of development, with the objective of decreasing the TD, and then proceed with easier and more productive maintenance. This corresponds to repaying (all or a substantial part of) the TD in the first sprints: the following sprints will have to pay low or null interests.

Second, the effort dedicated to TD management could be excessive. Consider the evolution of the TD index through sprints illustrated in Figure 2: when the fraction of effort dedicated to quality improvement is 40%, the TD is practically nil after 10 sprints. In the following sprints, the fraction of effort for TD management is partly used to balance the increase

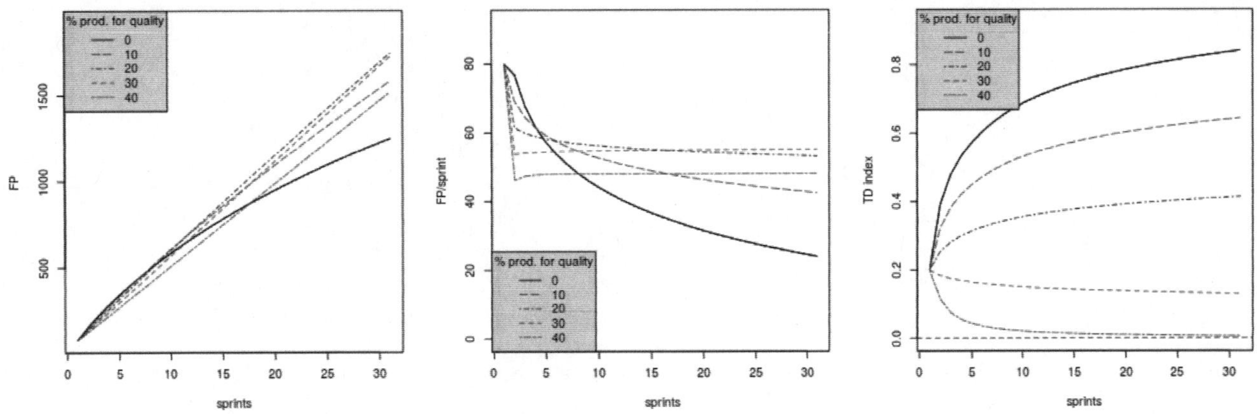

Figure 2. Size of delivered code, Sprint productivity and TD index, depending on a constant fraction of effort allocated to improving the TD.

of debt caused by new code, and part is wasted. This effect is easy to see when you compare the effects of dedicating 30% and 40% of the available effort to TD management. After a few sprints, in both cases the TD index is practically constant (about 0.18 in the former case, about 0.01 in the latter case). Maintenance productivity is also constant in the two cases, but higher in the former case. How is it possible that when 30% of effort is dedicated to TD management, we are using some effort to manage a higher TD, and still we get a higher productivity? Because the effort needed to keep TD close to zero is much less than the allocated 40%: the exceeding part is wasted.

A better strategy for TD management would be to allocate to TD improvement a fraction of effort that is larger when the TD is large and smaller when the TD is little. Of course, there are various ways to decide the fraction of effort to be dedicated to decrease TD. We adopt the function shown in Figure 3, which defines the fraction of effort for TD improvement as $1 - (1 - TDindex)^k$. By changing the value of k we decide how aggressive the approach to debt repayment is: with $k = 1$ the fraction of the effort dedicated to debt repayment is proportional to the debt, with $k > 1$ as soon as TD index raises above zero, a substantial fraction of the effort (the greater k the bigger the fraction) is dedicated to decrease TD.

In this section, the fraction of effort dedicated to TD management is decided at every sprint, as $1-(1-TDindex)^3$: a moderately aggressive policy. When debt increases, we try to decrease it fairly soon, to avoid paying large interests. Figure 4 shows the results of the simulation. The adopted policy provides good results: at the end of the sprints we get 1764 FP, more than in any of the simulations performed in Section IV-A. The final TD index is 0.11: a good result.

It is interesting to note that after a few sprints, the TD index remains constant, and, as a consequence, productivity remains constant as well. The reason is that, at the beginning of each sprint, the effort dedicated to TD management is adequate for repaying the existing TD, but, during the sprint, new TD will be created. This situation is perpetuated over the sprints. To completely repay TD, a policy should allocate enough effort to both repay the existing TD, and to *anticipate* the new TD, by performing maintenance in a way that preserves optimal code structure and quality.

In conclusion, dedicating a large fraction of effort to decrease the TD in the first sprints guarantees optimal results, in terms of both the amount of functionality delivered and the delivered quality.

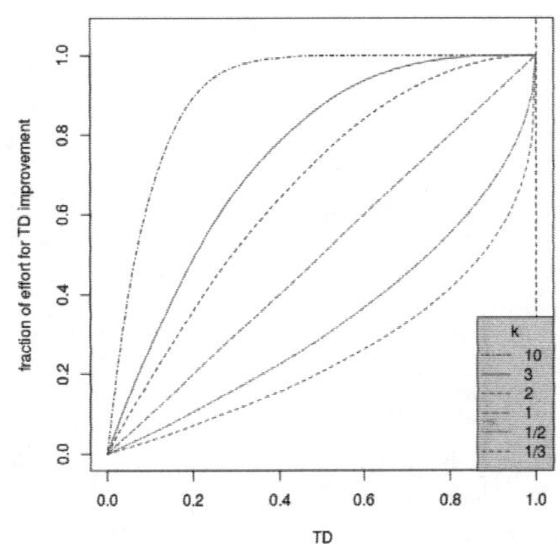

Figure 3. Percentage of effort dedicated to TD improvement, as a function 1-(1-TDindex)^k of TD.

C. Managing TD over a Threshold

In time-boxed development, it is often the case that a sprint is either completely dedicated to enhancement or to decreasing TD (especially via refactoring). So, the policy for allocating effort to TD management is simple: if the TD index is sufficiently high, the next sprint will be completely dedicated to TD repayment; otherwise, the next sprint will be dedicated completely to maintenance. In our case, if a sprint is dedicated completely to TD management, developers will be able to optimize a portion of code 40 FP large. Hence, we can allocate a sprint to TD management when a portion of code of at least 40 FP is affected by TD.

We simulated development with this criterion for allocating effort to TD management and we obtained the results illustrated in Figure 5. It is easy to see that the first sprints are

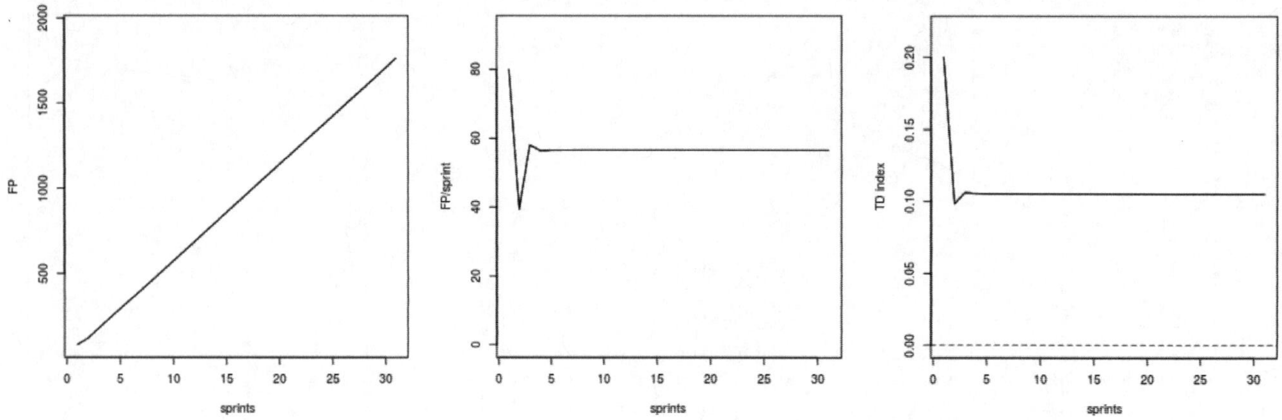

Figure 4. Size of delivered code, Sprint productivity and TD index through sprints, when the fraction of effort for TD improvement is 1-(1-TDindex)^3.

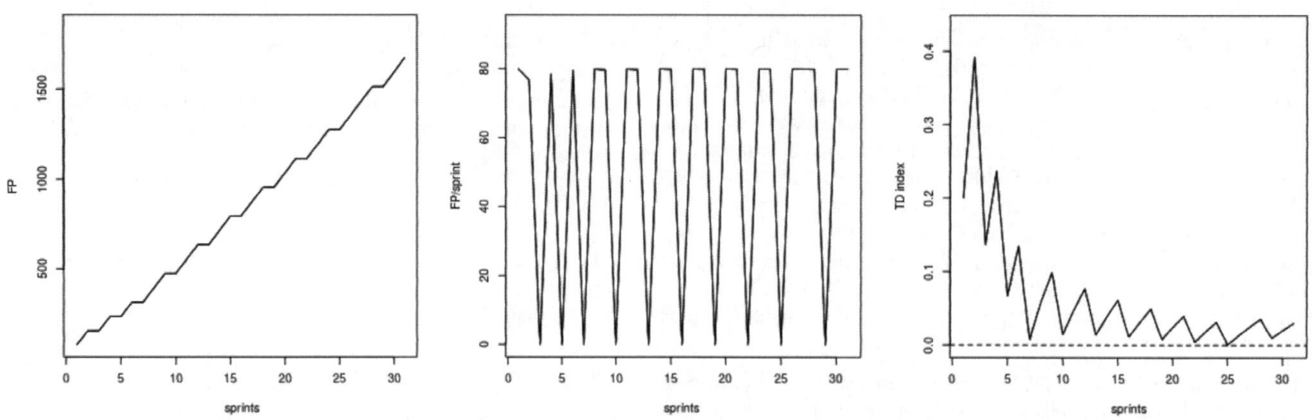

Figure 5. Size of delivered code, Sprint productivity and TD index through sprints, when sprints are dedicated to either TD management or maintenance.

dedicated to TD improvement and enhancement maintenance alternatively. Then, when TD has improved enough, we have a TD improvement sprint every two enhancement sprints. TD progressively decreases until it becomes practically nil (oscillating between 0.01 and 0.03). At the end of sprints, 1674 FP are released, that is, a bit less than with the policy described in Section IV-B. However, the achieved TD index is much better, compared to the 0.11 achieved in Section IV-B.

TABLE I. RESULTS WITH VARIOUS CRITERIA

Criterion	Delivered size	Final TD index
Constant (0%)	1248 FP	0.84
Constant (10%)	1580 FP	0.64
Constant (20%)	1743 FP	0.41
Constant (30%)	1723 FP	0.13
Constant (40%)	1517 FP	0.007
1-(1-TDindex)^3	1764 FP	0.11
1-(1-TDindex)$^{1/3}$	1601 FP	0.51
Threshold	1674 FP	0.01–0.03

V. DISCUSSION

The results obtained with the different criteria for allocating effort to TD improvement are summarized in Table I. Note that in Table I, we have added the results—not given in Section IV-B—obtained when the fraction of effort dedicated to TD improvement is 1-(1-TDindex)$^{1/3}$. In such case, the fraction of effort dedicated to TD improvement decided at the beginning of each sprint, is based on the current TD index, but the approach is not aggressive, on the contrary, a substantial fraction of effort is dedicated to TD improvement only when the TD index is relatively large.

The results given in Table I, along with the more detailed results reported in Section IV, suggest a few observations.

First, allocating a constant amount of effort to TD improvement does not seem a good idea. In fact, if the chosen fraction of effort allocated to TD improvement is too high or loo low, the productivity of enhancement maintenance will be lower than possible. Also, the final quality of the product (as indicated by the TD index) could be quite low. In practice, allocating a constant amount of effort to TD improvement works well only if the right fraction of effort is allocated, but choosing such fraction may not be easy.

On the contrary, computing the amount of effort for TD improvement at the beginning of each sprint, based on the current TD index seems very effective, especially as far as optimizing the productivity of enhancement maintenance is concerned.

One could observe that in some situations it may be hard to separate clearly the effort devoted to enhancements from the effort devoted to TD improvement. This is particularly true when developers perform refactoring activities while they are enhancing the existing code. For this reason, an organization may want to have sprints entirely dedicated to refactoring and other TD improving activities, and sprints entirely dedicated to enhancements. In this case, the evaluations given in Section IV-C show that allocating an entire sprint to TD improvement whenever there is enough TD to absorb one spring effort provides quite good results, in terms of both productivity and quality.

In any case, we have to stress that all the presented strategies for TD management are based on the quantitative evaluation of TD, which results in the TD index. So, devising a way to measure TD appears fundamental to managing TD effectively and efficiently.

VI. Related Work

System Dynamics was first applied in Software Engineering by Abdel-Hamid and Madnick [12], who proposed a model that accounted for human resource management, software development, and planning and control. System Dynamics was then extensively used to model software development and its management. A survey of System Dynamics applied to project management was published by Lyneis and Ford [13], while in [14] De Franca and Travassos propose a set of reporting guidelines for simulation-based studies with dynamic models in the context of SE to highlight the information a study of this type should report.

Cao et al. [15] proposed a System Dynamics simulation model that considers the complex interdependencies among the variety of practices used in Agile development. The model can be used to evaluate—among others—the effect of refactoring on the cost of implementing changes.

Glaiel et al. [16] used System Dynamics to build the Agile Project Dynamics model, which captures each of the Agile main characteristics as a separate component of the model and allows experimentation with combinations of practices and management policies.

Although less comprehensive than the mentioned models, our proposal allows for better undrstanding the consequences of technical debt and the effectiveness of its management strategies.

VII. Conclusions

The term "Technical Debt" indicates several concepts and issues related to software development and maintenance. The latter are complex and multifaceted activities: accordingly, it is not surprising that managing TD is quite difficult [5].

In this paper, we have provided a formal, executable model of time-boxed software development, where the effects of TD are explicitly and quantitatively represented and accounted for. The model is usable to show—via simulation—the effects that TD have on relevant issues such as productivity and quality, depending on how TD is managed, with special reference on how much effort is dedicated to TD repaiment and when—in a sequence of sprints—such effort is allocated.

The model can be used to prove or disprove concepts and hypotheses, to perform what-if analyses, etc. However, our model is not intended to be used in practical software project management as-is, becase, the model illustrated above is too abstract and contains hypotheses that could not match the target development environment. Whoever wants to use the presented model for practical project management should first enhance it; examples of models representing all the main aspects of software development can be found in the papers by Cao et al. [15] and Glaiel et al. [16].

We plan to extend the presented model in several directions: to account for different effects of TD on productivity (i.e., with functions different from the one in Figure 1), to explicitly model defects, to test different debt management policies, etc.

Acknowledgment

This work was partly supported by the "Fondo di ricerca d'Ateneo" funded by the Università degli Studi dell'Insubria.

References

[1] Z. Li, P. Avgeriou, and P. Liang, "A systematic mapping study on technical debt and its management," Journal of Systems and Software, vol. 101, 2015, pp. 193–220.

[2] C. Fernández-Sánchez, J. Garbajosa, A. Yagüe, and J. Perez, "Identification and analysis of the elements required to manage technical debt by means of a systematic mapping study," Journal of Systems and Software, vol. 124, 2017, pp. 22 – 38.

[3] A. Nugroho, J. Visser, and T. Kuipers, "An empirical model of technical debt and interest," in Proceedings of the 2nd Workshop on Managing Technical Debt. ACM, 2011, pp. 1–8.

[4] N. Ramasubbu and C. F. Kemerer, "Managing technical debt in enterprise software packages," IEEE Transactions on Software Engineering, vol. 40, no. 8, Aug. 2014, pp. 758–772.

[5] P. Avgeriou, P. Kruchten, I. Ozkaya, and C. Seaman, "Managing technical debt in software engineering (dagstuhl seminar 16162)," in Dagstuhl Reports, vol. 6, no. 4. Schloss Dagstuhl-Leibniz-Zentrum fuer Informatik, 2016, pp. 110–138.

[6] J. Letouzey, "The SQALE method for evaluating technical debt," in Proceedings of the Third International Workshop on Managing Technical Debt, MTD 2012, Zurich, June 5, 2012, 2012, pp. 31–36.

[7] "Automated technical debt measure – beta," Object Management Group, specification ptc/2017-09-08, September 2017.

[8] J. Forrester, Industrial Dynamics. Cambridge: MIT Press, 1961.

[9] A. J. Albrecht, "Function points as a measure of productivity," in Act as do 53 rd meeting of GUIDE International Corp., Guidance for users of integrated data processing equipment conference, Dallas, 1981.

[10] IFPUG, "Function point counting practices manual, release 4.2," IFPUG, Tech. Rep., 2004.

[11] L. Lavazza, S. Morasca, and D. Tosi, "An empirical study on the factors affecting software development productivity," e-Informatica Software Engineering Journal, vol. 12, no. 1, 2018, pp. 27–49.

[12] T. Abdel-Hamid and S. E. Madnick, Software project dynamics: an integrated approach. Prentice-Hall, Inc., 1991.

[13] J. M. Lyneis and D. N. Ford, "System dynamics applied to project management: a survey, assessment, and directions for future research," System Dynamics Review, vol. 23, no. 2-3, 2007, pp. 157–189.

[14] B. B. França and G. H. Travassos, "Experimentation with dynamic simulation models in software engineering: Planning and reporting guidelines," Empirical Software Engineering, vol. 21, no. 3, June 2016, pp. 1302–1345.

[15] L. Cao, B. Ramesh, and T. Abdel-Hamid, "Modeling dynamics in agile software development," ACM Transactions on Management Information Systems (TMIS), vol. 1, no. 1, 2010, pp. 5:1–5:27.

[16] F. S. Glaiel, A. Moulton, and S. E. Madnick, "Agile project dynamics: A system dynamics investigation of agile software development methods," 2014.

Continuous Improvement and Validation with Customer Touchpoint Model in Software Development

Tanja Sauvola, Markus Kelanti, Jarkko Hyysalo, Pasi Kuvaja and Kari Liukkunen
M3S Research Unit, Faculty of Information Technology and Electrical Engineering,
University of Oulu
PO BOX 4500, FI-90014 University of Oulu, Finland
e-mail: {tanja.sauvola, markus.kelanti, jarkko.hyysalo, pasi.kuvaja, kari.liukkunen}@oulu.fi

***Abstract*—Experimental-driven software development approach has gained momentum as a way to incrementally build and validate customer value. In-depth understanding of customer needs and reasons behind constantly changing requirements are essential for building successful software products. However, identifying, validating and reacting to these changes is often difficult and requires short iteration cycles and feedback from customers. This paper reports a 12-month case study conducted in an agile software team following a practical customer touchpoint (CTP) model for continuous improvement and validation. The objective of the study was to implement CTP into software team practices in order to determine what kind of effect it has on the development of a web application. The contribution of this paper is twofold. First, an in-depth case study is presented that identifies the practices a CTP model should adopt when implemented in the software development process. The CTP model is then extended based on the identified recommendations. Second, the benefits and challenges of the extended CTP in software development are presented. The main benefits relate to learning, decision-making, innovation, co-creation and communication. The model had a positive impact on the software development process, but some challenges, such as stakeholder availability and customer value measurement, were identified.**

Keywords*—*lean UX; service design; customer involvement; software development; continuous improvement.

I. Introduction

Customer value determines the success of a product or a service in the marketplace, and software has become essential to value creation and delivery [1]. Software development teams face high pressure to develop innovative products and services at increasing speeds in a dynamic and continuously changing business environment. To this aim, development teams seek to become more data-driven, which requires using customer feedback and product data to support learning and decision-making during the development process and throughout a product's lifecycle. This presents the challenge in software development to adopt iterative and agile practices for the continuous deployment of new features and enhancements to provide customers with added value [1]-[3]. Customer value and the ability to experiment with business ideas have been considered in Agile methods [4] and the Lean Startup [5] philosophy, both very popular in the software industry. Recently, concepts like continuous experimentation—where software development teams constantly experiment with product value—have been introduced in the literature as well [3][6][7]. The continuous experiment approach involves customers and end-users of the service in the decision-making process, providing feedback to developers by interacting with experimental materials like early prototypes of the features under development.

User experience (UX) has also become an increasingly important determinant of the success or failure of software systems. Approaches such as Design Sprint, introduced by Google Ventures [8], and Lean UX [9] using Lean Startup principles, now appear. These experiment-driven approaches interrelate with business strategy decisions and tend to focus on customer centricity. Forward-thinking companies see the benefits and importance of UX design in their product and service development activities. Even with these methodologies, software teams still encounter challenges when involving customers and integrating customer feedback into short development cycles [2][6].

In this paper, the customer touchpoint (CTP) model introduced by Sauvola et al. [2] is examined as a way for software development teams to become more customer centric and data driven. The study focuses on finding answers to the following research questions:

RQ1: What practices should the CTP model adopt when implemented in the software development process?

RQ2: What are the benefits and challenges of CTP in software development?

To address the research questions, a case study in the software development context has been performed. The CTP model is validated and extended by proposing practices for the continuous validation of customer value in short development cycles to increase customer understanding. The benefits and challenges of the extended CTP model are then identified.

The paper is organized as follows. Section 2 studies the related work. Section 3 presents research approach and describes the case project. Section 4 presents the results and analyses. Section 5 discusses the results. Section 6 concludes the work with a summary and topics for further research.

II. Related Work

A. Value creation through continuous experimentation

In software development, short product development and deployment cycles and shorter feedback loops are enabled by practices such as agile and lean development [4][5], continuous deployment [10] and DevOps [11]. An organisation's ability to deploy new functional and non-functional features continuously enables faster responses to customer needs [10][12]. However, these practices provide only a little guidance on how to constantly validate product assumptions while experiment-driven approaches focus more on value delivery with validated learning.

The literature presents several methods for establishing continuous experimentation with customers. Bosch et al. [13], for example, suggests exposing products to customers in two- to four-week experimentation iterations to solicit feedback. Studies of software engineering also propose ideas for continuous experimentation. Fagerholm et al. [3] suggest their RIGHT model for continuous experimentation, in which the key element is the start-up company's ability to release prototypes with suitable instrumentation. In this model, business strategies form the basis of experiments, and results guide future development activities. Holmström Olsson et al. [6] present the concept of an innovation experiment system (IES) in which software development teams constantly develop hypotheses and test them with customers. The IES approach also recommends that software teams continuously deploy individual features rather than plan larger product releases. This enables short feedback loops and facilitates data-driven decisions, reducing the risk of failing to build customer value by continuously identifying, prioritising and validating product assumptions in all software development phases. Holmström Olsson et al. also coined the hypothesis experiment data-driven development (HYPEX) model, which introduces a set of practices to integrate feature experimentation into the software development process by combining feature experiments and customer feedback. The model aims to improve the correlation between customer needs and research and development efforts [14]. More recently, Holmström Olsson et al. also presented a quantitative/qualitative customer-driven development (QCD) model. This model presents available customer feedback techniques and aims to help companies become more data-driven by combining qualitative feedback with quantitative customer data [15]. Such methods are supported by Kohavi et al. [16], who report that companies use experiments to guide product development and accelerate innovation. Companies adapting the experimentation approach are typically developing internet related product and services, such as Amazon, eBay, Facebook, Google, LinkedIn, Microsoft and Netflix [16]. While experimentations are recognized as beneficial approach to software development, barriers to related resources, organisational culture and data knowledge persist [17].

B. Service design in software development

Service design (SD) is a methodological approach that can be utilized during software development to involve customers and collect feedback. It is a holistic, multidisciplinary approach that aids innovation and improves existing products to make them more useful and desirable to customers [18]. SD provides an outside-in-development approach, where products and services are developed holistically from customers' and end-users' points of view, and applies design thinking and methodologies in product and service development. Recently, some process models and working practices, such as Lean UX [9] and Design Sprint [8], have been introduced under SD and UX design titles with the aim of synthesising design thinking, agile software development and lean start-up philosophies. Lean principles and Lean Startup apply to Lean UX in three ways: 1) removing waste by only creating the design artifact that enables the software development team to move their learning forward; 2) embracing cross-functional collaboration and bringing all relevant stakeholders into the design process; and 3) adopting the experimentation mindset. Lean UX is the evolution of product design, aiming at breaking down the barriers between software development teams, designers and users [9]. Similarly, Google Ventures introduced Design Sprint to integrate product discovery, product validation and delivery activities in a five-day process [8].

Experiments with customers require the ability to elicit customer feedback. For example, visualisation techniques nurture the co-design process and elicit feedback without relying on existing technical infrastructure or up-front development efforts. Different visualisation techniques are used, e.g., in agile development to design a product or a service, support the development process, enhance communication and track the process [19]. The SD approach emphasises the co-design process, whereby stakeholders are involved in concrete, productive design tasks such as workshop sessions. These sessions typically include collaborative prototyping and other means of expressing the information needed in the design and development process [20].

III. Research Approach

The software development process and related activities are presented in this paper through a case study that follows the guidelines set by Runeson and Höst [21]. A qualitative case study method was chosen to gain a practical view on the topic. In principle, the study is an in-depth, single-case study, where the involved participants represent different public and private organisations with fundamentally different roles, such as user, data provider, company representative and ecosystem leader. According to Yin [22], the single-case design is appropriate for testing a specific theory, which in this case is the CTP model. The study is also confirmatory in nature, as it aims to evaluate the robustness of a theory.

A. Case description

Our case study was conducted in the Fenix project (www.fenix.vip), where the software team develops a cloud-based service for real-time business case management for the Allied ICT Finland (AIF) (www.alliedict.fi) In the AIF program, a need was identified as currently information about companies, research institutes, business opportunities and product offerings are scattered into various databases and services. Thus, there is a need to aggregate this information under one digital service-point. Fenix was therefore designed to provide one place for finding and meeting new business opportunities, solution providers, experts, start-ups, business incubators and research institutes. The aim is that the tool would allow users to browse information about potential business partners and opportunities across multiple third-party systems from a single point. For example, the utilization of Business Finland (www.businessfinland.fi) database to follow cases and offers from municipalities and governments as starting cases.

The specific challenge of the Fenix system was to gain the commitment of user stakeholders, namely companies, universities and other organisations, which AIF and Business Finland aimed to support. The idea was that Fenix would promote Finnish industry by increasing overall trade and exports through the improved exposition of business opportunities, expertise and new company and research ecosystem growth. The challenge was that there were no clear requirements to fulfil due to the changing group of stakeholders and the need to develop an efficient mechanism to expose and promote business cases and ecosystem formation. Further more, development funding depended on the success of committing enough stakeholders to create ecosystems in Fenix.

The development team consisted of nine people: a designer/product owner, seven developers and a scrum master in total. During development, one researcher acted as product owner and UX designer and another adopted the role of software architect. Experience levels ranged from novice to expert with several years of industrial experience. The software team followed scrum methodology with iterative two-week development cycles. Customer collaboration was guided by the CTP approach during the design and implementation of the system (see [2] for details).

B. Data collection and analysis

Empirical data was collected between January and December 2017 from observations and field notes, 13 interview recordings and 20 workshops. Semi-structured interviews with open-ended questions [23] were used to collect data from six customer interviews and seven development team interviews. Customer participants were selected to best represent the companies, research institutions and local public actors.

The interviewed customers represented the AIF, Business Finland, trade associations and local companies. The themes discussed in the interviews were customer collaboration practices, agile ways of working and the benefits and challenges involved in the current way of working. The interviews were conducted face-to-face and lasted approximately 60 minutes. All interviews were recorded and transcribed for analysis in QSR NVivo tool (www.qsrinternational.com). The obtained material was analysed in continuous collaboration by three researchers, following the recommendations for thematic analysis in software engineering by Cruzes and Dybå [24]. The interview data was first coded based on the interview topics and then analysed and coded according to emerging themes. The themes were first examined independently, then cross-analysed.

The workshops, besides being an integral part of the development cycles, occurred bi-weekly after every sprint. Workshops lasted approximately one hour and included software product demonstrations and collaborative prototyping sessions. Customers and other stakeholders were invited to see the latest version of the prototype software and to try, test and give feedback. Workshop participant groups consisted of the whole development team and between two and 15 customers. Before these workshops, a new version of the software in question was deployed. During the bi-weekly workshops, the product owner presented the changes and new features introduced in that particular software version and collected feedback and new development ideas. New features ideas were experimented with using UI mock-ups and interactive prototypes during the workshop sessions. The developers summarised the key points of each workshop, and the researchers observed and made notes about stakeholder reactions and documented relevant comments. Following the workshops, the development team analysed the feedback, prioritised next tasks and planned the next iteration.

C. Validity and reliability of the study

The design of the present study was carefully planned to consider validity concerns. We discuss four threats to validity: internal and external validity, construct validity, and reliability [22].

Internal validity regarding cause–effect relations was addressed via multiple sources of evidence, and with iterative research gradually building the final outcome. Evaluation of utility, quality and efficacy was done extensively with the help of industrial experts and real users. Immediate feedback was gathered, and the use of prototypes was observed. Based on the rich feedback and analysis, further development and corrective actions were carried out.

External validity concerning the generalisability of results was addressed by involving several industrial experts to provide their views. In addition, the involvement of several organisations of different types and domains increased the external validity and generalisability of the results. However, further study will be needed to generalise the results fully.

Construct validity was mitigated by several activities. First, an interview guide was developed and piloted. A pilot interview was used to refine and clarify the interview questions. Second, interview candidates were vetted for suitability to the study, and interview themes were introduced with background information.

The reliability of the data and derived results was ensured by applying a peer-reviewed research protocol. Threats to reliability were mitigated, particularly in the analysis phase, by involving all three researchers. The data itself was recorded using Jira (atlassian.com/software/jira) and Confluence tools (atlassian.com/software/confluence), which allowed other researchers and experts to review and correct the data.

Some danger of positive bias exists in the study's results and activities due the way the case study was implemented. The constant communication among researchers, the development team and customer representatives, as well as the inclusion of researchers on the development team, increased the likelihood of producing only positive results. This danger was mitigated by having one researcher to evaluate the plan, results and actions without participating in the development team activities. Further, clear roles and rigorous research methods helped the researchers to maintain an objective perspective throughout the study.

IV. RESULTS AND ANALYSIS

This section presents the extended CTP model (Figure 1.) with identified practices for continuous improvement and customer validation adapted from SD and Lean UX approaches. The practices are defined based on the empirical findings of the data collection and analysis as well as the authors' previous experiences when working with software development teams. The benefits and challenges of applying the extended CTP model in agile software development are then discussed.

A. *Recommended practices for the CTP model*

Continuous improvement of the service unfolds true qualitative and quantitative data collected from customers and products in the field. Various experimentation techniques and combinations can be applied throughout the development process. The role of the CTP model in the present study was to guide the development team to experiment and collaborate with several internal and external stakeholders during the development process and collect feedback.

The purpose of extending the CTP model was to allow the continuous identification, prioritisation and validation of product assumptions in short development cycles with the help of customers, using identified practices presented in touchpoints T_1-T_4 in the model. These practices should be applied as continuous activities to improve service and validate product hypotheses. The findings of this study indicate that to fully utilise the practices, the development team must have an agile and lean mindset, be self-organising and share responsibility. Also, the team must be cross-functional, with one designer onboard. In-depth analysis of the quantitative data requires data analytics and data knowledge expertise, as analysing and utilising data is much more complicated than collecting it.

Discovery: The first customer touchpoint T_1, is used to discover and compile customer needs and translate them into product requirements and product hypotheses, which can be used in experiments. Typically, new ideas and requirements are collected from various sources, including market and competitor intelligence, feedback from customers and product usage data (after the first release of the product has been made).

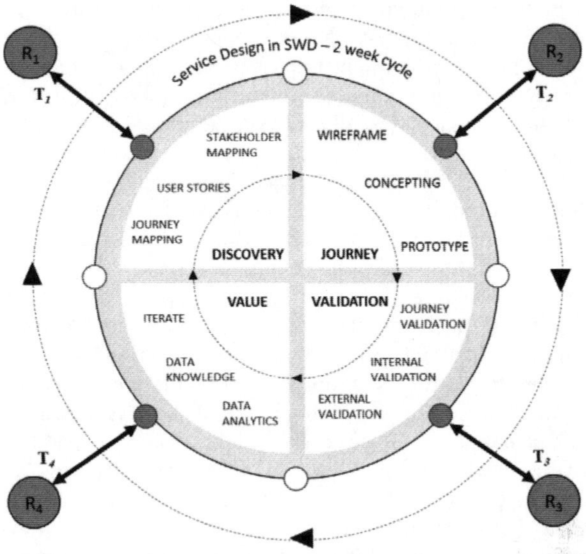

Figure 1. Lean UX practices in extended CTP model. R refers to the main activities: R_1 Collection; R_2 Prioritization; R_3 R&D Verification and R_4 Deployment. T indicate where companies and customers exchange information: T_1 Release learnings or new customer requirements, T_2 Release trade-offs and cost/benefit analysis, T_3 Release features and delivery commitments and T_4 Release configurations and real usage vs. planned usage of the product/feature. R_1–R_4 are also sources for requirements for new product ideas, including market and competitor intelligence, product usage data, customer feedback data collected, etc.

Techniques for collecting qualitative data can vary, from surveys and interviews to observations. Product assumptions are then turned into hypotheses for validation. The practices identified and utilised by the development team in this study included customer journey and stakeholder mapping, user analysis and creation of user stories. Journey mapping [9] provides a structured visualisation of a specific element, be it a single feature or an overview of the entire customer experience. Stakeholder mapping [18] on the other hand governs the overall complex situation and the expectations from various stakeholder groups. Benchmarking through online research and market data collection can also be used as an input to these practices.

Key learning: Balance discovery activities with development efforts by testing only high-risk hypotheses and conducting smaller amounts of research more often.

Journey: The second customer touchpoint T_2, is used to visualise an organisation's service vision and the customer journey. Such visualisation, considered as MVPs in this study, lends insight to improve the understanding of information. In the early phases of product development, many uncertainties related to customer expectations arise. Concept work is required when envisioning the idea for a service, or even at the feature level when designing prototypes and mock-ups. Visualisation techniques like wireframes, UI mock-ups, interactive prototypes and evolutionary prototypes guide development teams to prioritise development tasks continuously through experimentation with product concepts and design artefacts. In terms of prototyping, interactive prototypes are simulations that typically illustrate few predefined scenarios. They look and function like end product but do not handle real data input, processing or output. This technique proposes a quick and cost-effective way to concretise and test new ideas before any development work is done and help software teams to avoid developing unnecessary features. Evolutionary prototypes, build based on lessons learned from the interactive prototypes, however handle real data and form the basis for the actual software evolving after every iteration. Results of the present study indicate that design tasks should be treated as equal to development tasks and executed in the same or parallel cycles during software development. Digital product prototyping tools, such as Invision (invisionapp.com), UXPin (uxpin.com), and Sketch (sketchapp.com) were determined to be useful in this phase because they allowed for more effective collaboration and experimentation with product assumptions.

Key learning: Visualisation techniques create a common understanding by which to resolve communication-related issues. However, adapting these techniques require the role of UX designer in the development team.

Validation: Most of the validation in touchpoint T_3 occurs through testing activities. Testing activities are an opportunity to validate mismatches between customer needs and product offerings. As experienced in our previous research [2], this opportunity is often overlooked. Adopting the journey validation practice, trough different visualisation techniques, helps a development team to identify their needed steps, possible pain points and gaps. Internal validation then covers practices like daily scrum meetings, wikis and other communication channels to provide quick and frequent feedback from executives and team members. During daily scrum meetings in the present study, it was observed that the work that had been visualised on Kanban boards was often the work that got done. This demonstrates the importance of making product discovery and UX design tasks visible in a backlog. In this case, the UX tasks were visualised, executed and tracked in two-week sprint cycles alongside development tasks. External validation was done by exposing experiment materials to customers in two-week cycles to elicit and collect feedback. The experiment materials included interactive prototypes, mock-ups and evolutionary prototypes. Feedback was collected from customer workshops after every cycle, and utilizing usability testing with direct feedback mechanism in the working software integrated into the product development practices. It was concluded that it is important to involve the entire development team in external validation activities like workshops, as doing so helps the team avoid misunderstandings and the incorrect implementation of features.

Key learning: Customer needs and requirements change constantly. Backlog prioritisation should be done with high flexibility in short cycles against validated learnings.

Value: The ability to combine qualitative and quantitative customer feedback data is important, as often they complement each other. For example, by monitoring feature usage, quantitative data can be used to validate qualitative data. Analytic tools and collected product operation and performance data allows development teams to make data-driven decisions to improve the service in customer touchpoint Value T_4 continuously. In the present case, project log files and product usage data such as clicks, page views and number of visits were recorded and analysed. Especially in the field of web development, collecting and analysing product usage data has been eased by general tools such as Google Analytics. Target areas for quantitative data collection can range from system performance and UX improvements to business-level decision-making. In the present study, corrective actions based on quantitative data were done for example by improving the system level performance as well as placement and visibility of UI elements and workflows.

Techniques such as A/B testing can also serve as a potential approach to collect product usage data. In the present case study, A/B testing was not conducted because developing different variations of the same feature required vast resources and a large user base. In addition, a more detailed analysis of the log data would require specific skills and resources, such as adding a data scientist to the team.

Key learning: Quantitative data reveals tacit and complex knowledge of product usage. Detailed analyses of data and systematic, controlled experiments require the active presence of a data scientist.

B. Benefits of the extended CTP model in software development

The use of the extended CTP model with the identified practices as part of the two-week software development cycle was determined to be beneficial from the customer and development team points of view, but some challenges were identified. The benefits (Table I) and challenges (Table II) based on the research data are discussed next.

The most significant observed benefit of using the extended CTP model in software development was that it assisted both business and technical decision-making by promoting a better understanding of information (i.e., tacit knowledge is transformed into tangible knowledge). For the development team, direct interaction with customers enabled them to understand the reasons behind customer requirements and validate which features brought real value. Shared understanding also facilitated faster decision-making, which enabled the team to prioritise tasks 'on the fly' and estimate the validity of tasks in the product backlog.

The findings from this case study demonstrate that at their best, these practices increased customer involvement and nurtured innovation. Involving users in the early phases of development made customers more active and experienced with the product. This increased the motivation of development team and especially users, as they experienced the impact of their involvement during the process.

In terms of decision-making, the present results indicate that visualisation is one of the most important ways to concretise and test new ideas, as information is made visible to both customers and the development team through design artefacts.

TABLE I. IDENTIFIED BENEFITS

Benefit	Description
Learning and decision-making	Accelerate the decision-making process and concretise functions before actual development work.
Innovation and value co-creation	Accelerate co-creation and innovation between development team and users. Receive the first user feedback in the product/service idea phase.
Motivation	Interaction and co-creation between development team and users motivated both the development team and the users.
Communication improvement	Visualisation and prototyping methods improved communication and helped avoid misunderstandings between different stakeholders (e.g., management, development team, customers and end-users).
Transparency	Increase transparency between customers, users and the development team. Reveals grassroots knowledge exploitable in development.
Direct feedback	Presents an opportunity to receive instant and direct feedback from end-users in short cycles.
Integrated UX work	Design activities take place in the same cycle with development activities.
Service vision in communicable form	Developers have a clear, precise schematic by which to see the intended service from the customer perspective and can choose precise specifications.
Prioritisation	Prioritisation 'on the fly' allows the development team to capture changing priorities in short cycles and react flexibly and accurately.
Holistic approach	Holistic approach to software development from customers' and end-users' point of view.

The interviews stressed the need to produce proper visualisations, such as interactive prototypes and UI mock-ups, to concretise the service vision and improve communication to avoid misunderstandings. According to the interviewees, UX work was often perceived as a separate function, one asynchronous with research and development activities. It was also stated in the development team interviews that sometimes UX work was overlooked, as things like code quality, software scalability and security issues were deemed more important. *"Usability and user interface design... perhaps we cannot appreciate these or we consider more important that the software itself works or the code is good quality, the software is scalable and safe and so one, which is of course important... but from my perspective, I see that it is old-fashioned engineering thinking. ...today, in my mind it (usability) is the biggest competitive advantage of software, (senior software developer)."*

Visualisation techniques used in the workshop sessions also bridged the communication gap between those with business mindsets and those more technically oriented. It was important that the whole development team participated in the workshop sessions to get direct and instant feedback from customers. This helped the development team to understand the reasons behind customer needs, the kind of behaviours expected from the service and what created value for customer. During the sessions, the development team was able to identify design improvement ideas for the future and problem areas in the existing design. This had a clear impact on project work such as planning, scheduling and prioritising tasks, as the team was able to capture and react to changing priorities in short cycles. The practices presented in the extended CTP model facilitated better alignment and transparency of different functions, from UX design, business development and product management to short cycles with research and development activities.

By adopting visualisation techniques as suggested in the extended CTP model, the development team was able to obtain their first user feedback after very short iterations (a few days to a few weeks). The model also guided the entire development team to holistic thinking by following a customer centric design and development process throughout the project lifecycle.

C. Challenges of the extended CTP model in software development

Stakeholder availability and commitment represented some challenges for example, if few or no visible functions were delivered in a short iteration cycle, customer and stakeholder commitment to participate in the workshops could suffer. In addition, customers may feel disrupted from their own work by being involved in development activities too often. The development team reported the two-week cycle as optimal, but based on the interviews it could be shortened to one week. For customers, the two-week development cycle with a workshop at the end of each sprint was sometimes seen too often.

New requirements appear all the times and they may disrupt the old ones, often this is related to different user groups and customer roles with conflicting needs. This may also add complexity to defining feature maturity and identifying metrics for measuring customer value.

For a software team to adapt practices presented in the extended CTP model, certain key roles must be filled, which may cause some challenges. The current case study required expertise of back-end and front-end development, database development, server and tool management, a product owner to represent the customer and a UX/UI designer to conduct and facilitate design tasks. While the development team and effort were kept as minimal as possible, it was evident that UX design and different visualisation techniques required significant effort; the person in charge of the design had to discuss and make decisions on the design with different stakeholders who often held conflicting demands and priorities. In order to mitigate this problem, a stakeholder analysis method [25] was used to gain further insight on the conflicting issues and resolve them. The UX work alone was often full-time work for a single person, even in a lightweight web application project. Furthermore, detailed analysis of the log data would require specific skills and resources, such as adding a data scientist to the team and a large user base. In this study, analytic support was integrated to working software and some corrective actions were continuously taken based on quantitative data. However, small user base and lack of resources hindered more detailed analyses. It should be noted that in some industries, laws and regulations or other limitations could prevent quantitative feedback collection.

TABLE II. IDENTIFIED CHALLENGES

Challenge	Description
Stakeholder availability and commitment	Finding suitable time for all stakeholders to participate workshops. Balancing workshop frequency and getting customer commitment to participate and give feedback.
Customer role	Different user groups might have different needs, and those can change according to context.
Measurement of customer value	Identify metrics for how to measure customer value is challenging.
Resources	Successful implementation required having a cross-functional team with an active UX/UI designer and data scientist in the team.
Direct communication	Developers may not always be confident or comfortable with increased and direct customer interaction.
Visualised features might be understood as 'easy to do'	Workload estimation can be challenging from the customer perspective. E.g., features in an interactive prototype and real effort for actual implementation might come as a surprise.
Maturity and definition of done (DOD)	Changing priorities and stakeholders make it hard to analyse the maturity and DOD of features.
Quantitative metrics / analytics	Quantitative metrics and analyses become possible after implementing analytics support, once the software is in use and there is a sufficient stakeholder pool using it. Before that, obtaining quantitative data is nearly impossible.
Physical distances	Technical issues and lack of tools for sharing local demonstrations.

Development team interviews of the present study revealed that some developers were more confident when allowed to focus simply on building the software, preferring to keep their interactions with customers at a minimum or restricted to key individuals.

While a working prototype proved an efficient way to involve stakeholders in the development process, the downside was that customer expectations rose when they saw how 'easy' it was to produce something visible that matched their needs. This led to situations where customers expected that the feature's implementation would be easy as well. The challenge therefore is the increased risk of customers developing unrealistic expectations related to work estimations for the complete functional feature. During the study, this was addressed by maintaining a careful balance between keeping stakeholders satisfied even the workload would be bigger and prioritizing these features over those that are not visible but can be important for system stability, security and other issues that do not show in day-to-day work.

Physical distances reduced the development teams ability to interact with their customers face to face, as well as posed a challenge during the workshops and meetings due to technical issues, such as connection quality and faulty communication equipment. While these technologies enable participation regardless of physical location, communication tools do fail at times, or stakeholders are not used to hold online meetings. Mistakes like using a low volume of voice, moving away from the microphone or demonstrating locally something not visible to those participating remotely can slow down the meeting, make communication difficult and increase the risk of misunderstanding.

V. DISCUSSION

Software development is not an easy or straightforward task. It is even more challenging when requirements are constantly changing and there are many involved customer organisations with different demands. Previous research [2] shows that, delivering value and meeting customer needs in constantly changing markets are key success factors for any business. Multitude of existing methods and approaches for identification, prioritization and validation of customer needs are presented in literature, with more recent being continuous experimentation. From a process perspective, Schermann et al. [26] reports a lack of clear guidelines for conducting experiments. Our extended CTP model fills the gap and presents an approach for continuous improvement and customer validation.

Typically, existing methods and approaches for continuous experimentation (presented in Section II of the paper) are influenced by the 'build-measure-learn' loop and include the phases of planning, collecting customer feedback and analysing of data for learning and decision-making purposes. While some of the approaches focus on the technical implementation and instrumentation for collecting customer feedback data, the extended CTP model offers a more holistic outside-in approach and integrates UX work in the same development cycle. The model can be seen as a framework that guides development team to experiment and collaborate with internal and external stakeholders during the development process. Experimentation does not always require working software as experiments can be conducted with other kinds of experimental artefacts, such as visualizations or mock-ups. Multiple variations of the extended CTP model can be derived based on context and available resources.

The study found two main contributions from the extended CTP model. First, the extended CTP model enhances software development process with practices to improve feedback elicitation, continuous improvement and customer validation through its suggested practises in *1) Discovery, 2) Journey, Validation* and *4) Value* customer touchpoints. Second, the extended CTP model integrates collaborative product discovery with product delivery tasks in short cycles while recognizing the role and importance of UX work. Conducting smaller amounts of research but more often, involving the entire development team and testing the high-risk hypothesis with visualisation techniques are encouraged. In this way, the model offers a new holistic approach to continuous improvement and customer validation.

The research results highlight that teams adopting recommended practices need to have a cross-functional competences, innovative and experimental mindset in which experimentation is seen as a learning opportunity. This is in line with previous continuous experimentation research where organisational culture act as barrier to the incorporation of the practices [17]. In general, adopting these practices benefited both the development team and users and enabled the team to become more customer-driven while focusing on the tasks most relevant to the users. The main benefits relate to learning and decision-making, innovation, value co-creation and communication. We also identified number of challenges that may hinder customer involvement and adapting identified practises, such as stakeholder availability, commitment and measuring customer value. We acknowledge that adapting visualisation practices and quick prototyping requires a cross-functional team with UX design activities and tasks aligned together with the research and development tasks. In addition, experimentation with quantitative data requires a data scientist to be present in the team. Unlike large companies, such as Microsoft [27], this may not always be feasible due to limited resources. We also argue that analysis of quantitative data is not a sole responsibility of a data scientist, as it requires deep customer insight from qualitative data. It this sense, data analysis could fall under product management tasks as the shared responsibility of a product owner, UX designer and data scientist were also business aspects are taken into consideration. This reinforces the fact that there is not one right approach for software teams to become more customer centric. Rather, practices should be tailored to meet specific domain and contexts, distinct business goals and different organisational cultures.

VI. CONCLUSION AND FUTURE WORK

In this paper, we presented a case study aiming to help software teams to continuously validate customer value in short development cycles to increase customer understanding trough practises presented in the extended CTP model. The current findings are based on empirical data gathered from a software development team developing a modern software-as-a-service platform called Fenix. The Fenix system was designed to help companies grow their revenue through digital partnering and ecosystem creation strategies.

This study shows that several methods and practices can be utilised during software development to capture and validate customer needs thus helping development teams to reduce the gap between user expectations and actual implementation. The extended CTP model presents the identified practises through customer touchpoints. By recognising the synergies between continuous customer collaboration, integration of design tasks and involving all the relevant stakeholders, along with the ability to combine qualitative and quantitative feedback, software teams can speed up their delivery process and become more data-driven in their learning and decision-making processes.

Future work on this topic should examine how the extended CTP model works when the web application in question is developed further and the user base is substantial enough to use controlled experiments. This would allow for interesting evaluations of the different practices used in the extended CTP model when used to develop already established software rather than restricting investigations into new software development.

ACKNOWLEDGMENTS

This work was supported by the Six City Strategy (6Aika) and the European Regional Development Fund (ERDF), Business Finland, Allied ICT Finland and its ecosystems.

REFERENCES

[1] A. Nguyen-Duc, X. Wang, and P. Abrahamsson, "What influences the speed of prototyping? An empirical investigation of twenty software startups". In: Software Engineering and Extreme Programming, XP 2017. Lecture Notes in Business Information Processing, vol. 283, pp. 20–36. Springer, Cham, 2017.

[2] T. Sauvola et al., "Towards customer-Centric software development, A multiple-Case study". In: 41st Euromicro Conference on Software Engineering and Advanced Applications (SEAA), 2015, pp. 9–17. IEEE, Funchal, Portugal, 2015.

[3] F. Fagerholm, A. S Guinea, H. Mäenpää, and J. Münch, "The RIGHT model for continuous experimentation". J Syst Software vol. 123, pp. 292–305, 2017.

[4] K. Beck, J. Grenning, and R. C. Martin, Agile Manifesto. http://www.agilemanifesto.org/ [retrieved: August, 2018]

[5] E. Ries, The Lean Startup: How Constant Innovation Creates Radically Successful Businesses. Penguin Group, London, 2011.

[6] H. Holmström Olsson, J. Bosch, and H. Alahyari, "Towards R&D as innovation experiment systems: A framework for moving beyond agile software development". Proceedings of the IASTED, pp. 798–805, 2013.

[7] S. G. Yaman et al., "Transitioning towards continuous experimentation in a large software product and service

development organization: A case study". In: P. Abrahamsson, A. Jedlitschka, A. Nguyen Duc, M. Felderer, S. Amasaki, and T. Mikkonen (eds). Product-focused Software Process Improvement, PROFES 2016. Lecture Notes in Computer Science, vol. 10027, pp. 344–359. Springer, Cham, 2016.

[8] J. Knapp, J. Zeratsky, and B. Kowitz, Sprint: How to Solve Big Problems and Test New Ideas in Just Five Days. Simon and Schuster, New York, 2016.

[9] J. Gothelf and J. Seiden, Lean UX: Designing Great Products with Agile Teams. O'Reilly Media Inc., Sebastopol, 2016.

[10] J. Bosch, "Building products as innovation experiment systems". In: M. A. Cusumano, B. Iyer, N. Venkatraman (eds). Software Business, ICSOB 2012. Lecture Notes in Business Information Processing, vol 114, pp. 27–39. Springer, Berlin, Heidelberg, 2012.

[11] F. Elberzhager, T. Arif, M. Naab, I. Süß, and S. Koban, "From agile development to devops: Going towards faster releases at high quality: Experiences from an industrial context". International Conference on Software Quality, 2017, pp. 33–44. Springer, 2017.

[12] E. Anderson, S. Y. Lim, and N. Joglekar, "Are more frequent releases always better? Dynamics of pivoting, scaling, and the minimum viable product". Proceedings of the 50th Hawaii International Conference on System Sciences, 2017, pp. 5849–5858, 2017.

[13] J. Bosch, H. Holmström Olsson, J. Björk, and J. Ljungblad, "The early stage software startup development model: A framework for operationalizing lean principles in software startups". In: B. Fitzgerald, K. Conboy, K. Power, R. Valerdi, L. Morgan, K.-J Stol, (eds). LESS 2013. LNBIP, vol. 167, pp. 1–15, Springer, Heidelberg, 2013.

[14] H. Holmström Olsson and J. Bosch, "The HYPEX model: From opinions to data-driven software development". In: Bosch J. (ed). Continuous Software Engineering. Springer, Cham, 2014.

[15] H. Holmström Olsson and J. Bosch. "Towards continuous customer validation: A conceptual model for combining qualitative customer feedback with quantitative customer observation". In: J. Fernandes, R. Machado, K. Wnuk (eds). Software Business, ICSOB 2015. Lecture Notes in Business Information Processing, vol. 210, pp 154-166, Springer, Cham, 2015.

[16] R. Kohavi, A. Deng, and B. Frasca. "Online controlled experiments at a large scale". Proceedings of the 19th ACM SIGKDD International Conference on Knowledge Discovery and Data Mining, 2013, pp. 1168–1176, 2013.

[17] E. Lindgren and J. Münch, "Raising the odds of success: The current state of experimentation in product development". Inform Software Tech, vol. 77, pp. 80–91, 2016.

[18] M. Stickdorn and J. Schneider, This is Service Design Thinking (1st ed). 2012.

[19] J. Parades, C. Anslow, and F. Maurer, "Information visualization for agile software development teams". In: Second IEEE Working Conference on Software Visualization (VISSOFT), 2014, pp. 157–166, 2014.

[20] Y. Lee, "Design participation tactics: The challenges and new roles for designers in the co-design process". J Co-design, vol. 4(1), pp. 31–50, 2008.

[21] P. Runeson and M. Höst, "Guidelines for conducting and reporting case study research in software engineering". Empirical Software Engineering, vol. 14(2), pp. 131–164, 2009.

[22] R. K. Yin, Case Study Research: Design and Methods (5th edn). Sage Publications, 2013.

[23] M. D. Myers and M. Newman, "The qualitative interview in IS research: Examining the craft". Inf Organ, vol. 17(1), pp. 2–26, 2007.

[24] D. S. Cruzes and T. Dyba, "Recommended steps for thematic synthesis in software engineering". In: International Symposium on Empirical Software Engineering and Measurement (ESEM), 2011, pp. 275–284, 2011.

[25] M. Kelanti, J. Hyysalo, J. Lehto, S. Saukkonen, P. Kuvaja and M. Oivo "Soft Systems Stakeholder Analysis Methodology". Proceedings of the 10th International Conference on Software Engineering Advances (ICSEA 2015), pp.122–130, Barcelona, Spain, 2015.

[26] G. Schermann, J. Cito, P. Leitner, U.Zdun, and H.C. Gall, "We're doing it right live: A multi-method empirical study on continuous experimentation". Information and Software Technology, 99, pp.41-57, 2018

[27] M. Kim, T. Zimmermann, R.DeLine, and A. Begel. "Data Scientists in Software Teams: State of the Art and Challenges. IEEE Transactions on Software Engineering", 2017, pp. 1–17, http://dx.doi.org/10.1109/TSE.2017.2754374

Measuring and Improving the Quality of Services Provided by Data Centers: a Case Study

Martin Zinner*, Kim Feldhoff*, Michael Kluge*, Matthias Jurenz*, Ulf Markwardt*, Daniel Sprenger*,
Holger Mickler*, Rui Song†, Andreas Tschipang*, Björn Gehlsen*, Wolfgang E. Nagel*
* Center for Information Services and High Performance Computing (ZIH)
Technische Universität Dresden
Dresden, Germany
E-mail: {martin.zinner1, kim.feldhoff, michael.kluge, matthias.jurenz}@tu-dresden.de,
{ulf.markwardt, daniel.sprenger, holger.mickler, andreas.tschipang}@tu-dresden.de,
{bjoern.gehlsen, wolfgang.nagel}@tu-dresden.de
† Technical Information Systems
Technische Universität Dresden
Dresden, Germany
E-mail: rui.song@tu-dresden.de

***Abstract*—As data centers become increasingly complex and deliver services of high importance, it is very important that the quality of the delivered services can be objectively evaluated and can fulfill the expectations of the customers. In this paper, we present a novel, general, and formal methodology to determine and improve the Quality of Services(QoS) delivered by a data center. We use a formal mathematical model and methodology in order to calculate the overall indicator of the service quality and discuss methods of improving the QoS. Since the considerations were conceived and results have been proved in a formal model, the considerations and results also hold in a more general case.**

Keywords–Quality of Services; QoS; Performance data center; Little's Law; Kingman's equation; Flow factor; Operating curve management; Customer satisfaction; Key performance indicators.

I. Introduction

A. Motivation and Short Overview

Nowadays, the services of a data center are indispensable for the good functioning of a company or a research institute. However, due to the advanced digitalization, data centers are becoming more and more complex and difficult to manage. According to a survey of Symantec [1], the main reasons are the raise of the Cloud Computing and the Virtualization. Basically, such complex infrastructures are more error-prone and require more maintenance efforts than simple ones. Thus, it is of crucial importance to measure the Quality of Services (QoS) provided by a data center, in order to detect which components / services are low performers and should be improved. This way, measuring the QoS also avoids service degradations. Services which underperform can be detected and measures can be taken (like relocation of resources) such that these services will perform better again. An optimized usage of the available resources does not only improve the QoS and thus, the image of the service provider, but also helps to save costs.

Furthermore, Butnaru [2] states that "quality has become a strategic element in companies dealing with services because it determines competitiveness at its highest level". Thus, by measuring and improving the QoS provided by companies / research institutes, the service providers can improve their ranking when compared to the competition.

Estimating the QoS of a data center is a complex endeavor. On the one hand, there are objectively measurable indicators like the duration and number of unplanned down times. On the other hand, the customer satisfaction has very important subjective components, which should not be neglected. Thus, if a customer has full confidence in the technical skills, seriousness, and professionalism of the operating staff, then his attitude is permissive and indulgent regarding possible malfunctions. For example, let us consider the scenario that a service has an unplanned downtime. If the operating staff can predict the time when the resumption of the service will occur with satisfying accuracy, the impression of the customer regarding the service provider will be very good. Otherwise, the customer will assume that the service provider does not have his processes under control and a failure of the system will sooner or later occur.

In this paper, we will focus on the perspective from the data center side. We will define and make use of different metrics in order to be able to establish objective criteria which characterize the Quality of Services and the performance of a data center.

B. Main Challenges and Objectives

If a customer is asked about the quality of the services of a data center he or she usually will answer: Yes, quality is good, but it could be better. This answer only describes the subjective perception of the customer. Our aim is to go further. Thus, searching for a positive response to the questions "Is the QoS measurable and if this is the case, how?" is one of the main challenges, we had to accept and take up.

Establishing and choosing meaningful performance indicators form the basis for improving the QoS.

The challenges described above lead us to the following main objectives:

1) Receive responses to the question whether the QoS is quantifiable / metrisable or not, i.e., whether the QoS can be expressed numerically in a reasonable non trivial way, such that this number is independent of the subjective perception of humans.

2) Establish a general approach on the modalities to quantify the QoS such that a single indicator (or only very few) expresses the service quality of the service provider.
3) Find possibilities to improve the QoS and implicitly the performance of the service provider.

C. Outline

The remainder of the paper is structured as follows: Section II gives a short overview of the state of the art and detail some difference of our approach. Section III introduces the proposed strategy for measuring the QoS, first in an informal way, afterwards formalized by introducing a mathematical model. Different metrics are defined and used in order to be able to establish objective criteria which characterize the quality of the services and the performance of a data center. Section IV introduces the formal queuing model, makes the connection to the models used in practice, and discusses modalities to improve the performance of a data center by using the operation curve. In order to be able to balance the performance of the services of different departments of a data center, a formula to calculate the flow factor of the data center out of the flow factor of each department, is established. Section V gives some details of a use case and finally, Section VI concludes this paper and sketches the future work.

II. Related work

An important part of the existing approaches for quality improvement focus merely on the QoS from the user perspective – established through questionnaires (e.g., SERVQUAL and/or SERVPERF [3]) – and on the discrepancies between the user perception and the user expectation of the QoS.

Most approaches concerning the measurement of QoS have tended to avoid the use of pre-defined objective performance indicators and focus instead on the relationship between what consumers expect from a particular service and what they actually get [4]. The conclusion [3] is that customer satisfaction with services or perception of QoS can be viewed as confirmation or disconfirmation of customer expectations of a service offer. The role of emotions in customer-perceived service quality is analyzed [5] by widening the scope of service quality, i.e., by focusing on dimensions beyond cognitive assessment.

We concentrate our study primarily on the service provider perspective by using metrics to characterize the QoS and subsequently establish strategies on how those metrics can be combined together to generate a unique indicator, which characterizes the overall performance of the service provider.

Measuring and ranking service quality has been an issue for study for decades [4], whereby the difficulties lied in the development of the most suitable method of measurement. Approaches to the measurement of QoS are based on the analysis of the relationship between customer expectation of a service and their perceptions of it's the quality. Indices to provide measures of expectation, perceptions, and overall satisfaction from the customer side are set up and compared [4].

In [6], the authors report the insights obtained in an extensive exploratory investigation of quality in four business (retail banking, credit card, security brokerage, and product repair and maintenance) by developing a model of service quality. The most important insight obtained from analyzing the executive responses is the following: "A set of key discrepancies or gaps exists regarding executive perception of service quality and the tasks associated with service delivery to consumers. These gaps can be major hurdles in attempting to deliver a service which consumers would perceive as being of high quality".

Metrics in order to establish the QoS have been used for example by the Systemwalker [7], which supports "Information Technology Infrastructure Library" (ITIL) based IT service management. The focus in [7] is on the service delivery area, such as capacity, availability, and service level management. The composition of metrics is outside the scope of the Systemwalker.

In [8], a framework for the evaluation of QoS for Web Services within the OPTIMACS project is presented, such that Service Level Agreements (SLAs) are established in order to calculate / guarantee the QoS, then the properties are normalized by using statistical functions. The goal is to obtain a final Quality grade, that allows to rank the services. Finally, aggregation is performed using weighted sum of the different quality items.

As a final note, the studies regarding the normalization and composition of metrics considered for QoS for Web Services are straightforward and are based on statistics (min, max, mean value, standard deviation, Z-score) [8], the committed SLA time provides the QoS level. The metrics used to measure the QoS of a data center are so diverse that a case-by-case approach is necessary to determine the normalization and composition strategy. Moreover, statistical values as above are generally not a priori known for unconverted metrics such as "cycle time", etc.

III. Measuring the QoS

We describe the general strategy how to measure the QoS in an informal way in Subsection III-A and formalize this strategy in Subsection III-B.

A. Description of the Strategy

According to ITIL [9] (and similar), the (incomplete) list of processes comprises the following managements:

- "incident management",
- "problem management",
- "information security management",
- "service level management",
- "change management",
- "project management", and
- "release and deployment management".

A list of metrics is specified for each process according to ITIL [9] and / or to the "Key Performance Indicator (KPI) Library"(KPI Library) [10], see [11] regarding developing, implementing and using KPIs. Some of the most important metrics for the ITIL process "incident management" are given in the following:

- "Total number of incidents",
- "Number of repeated incidents, with known resolution methods",
- "Number of incidents escalated which were not resolved in the intended resolution time",
- "Average cycle time associated to the subsequent responses", i.e., including the average cycle time to resolve the incident,
- "Average waiting time from user side associated to the subsequent responses",
- "Average work effort for resolving the incident associated to the subsequent responses",
- "Average time between the occurrence of an incident and its resolution",
- "Total number of incidents resolved within service level agreement (SLA) time divided by the total number of incidents".

In order to establish objective criteria for measuring the QoS, it is not sufficient to consider simply one metric. Indeed, different metrics have to be combined. The following example illustrates this issue.

The metric "Total number of incidents" is a revealing metric regarding the performance of a service provider. Of course, this metric is important for reporting per se, as a non anticipated sharply increasing trend can be the cause for major concerns. Another important metric is "the average cycle time to solve an incident". If the metric "Total number of incidents" is increasing, but in the mean time the "Average cycle time to solve an incident" is decreasing, the balance is restored and the service provider will not face a total collapse of the service.

Hence, composition rules for metrics are needed, such that indicators that characterize the health of the services, can be established. Since we cannot directly compare the different metrics, we transform / normalize the metrics using relative values. By dividing the "Total number of incidents" by an artificially generated "Maximum number of incidents supported", we receive a relative value between 0 and 1. Unfortunately, the value 1 is the worst value you can ever get. In order to circumvent this impediment, we subtract 1 and change the sign. Using the same considerations (by defining the "Minimum average cycle time") analogue relative value for the cycle time can be established. In this case, this new indicator is directed in the sense, that the best cycle time is achieved when this value is equal to 1. This example is just to illustrate the technique. One may argue that an increase of the indicator value "Average waiting time of the incidents during processing" also indicates a congestion.

Thus, in order to combine different metrics, we will normalize them to the range $[0; 1]$ in such a way that the lowest value correspond to the poorest quality, the highest value to the best quality. Once, all the relevant metrics of a process are normalized, we can proceed with the composition such that for each process a single, composed metric is established.

The composed metric should also take values between 0 and 1, such that a greater value implies a better QoS. An example of a straightforward composing strategy is to establish weights for each metric, such that the sum of all weights is equal to 1 and important metrics have bigger weights. Hence, the decisive metrics are much better considered. Of course for practical purposes, we can define groups of incidents having the same importance and accordingly appropriate distribution functions (linear, exponential, etc.). The calculation of the associated weights is then immediate.

Normally, explicitly defining importance grouping and distribution functions is not always necessary. We can set up priority strategies regarding the QoS. As an example, under some circumstances, a fast but not necessarily very detailed answer is more helpful for IT professionals, who can elaborate the details themselves. In other cases, detailed and very accurate answers are necessary, especially for customers with little or no experience. Then, customers could return the ticket of the incident (if the answer is not accurate enough, e.g.) and ask for more information and assistance.

Hence, the development of an appropriate strategy for the quality improvement is essential, in some cases this strategy can be even customer dependent. For example, we can improve the quality:

- by improving only the accuracy of the responses, or
- by reducing only the response times, or
- by minimizing a metric which takes both accuracy and the response time into account.

In accordance with the improvement strategy, the grouping of metrics regarding their performance is more or less straightforward and easy to follow.

In effect, we can establish for each process a unique (abstract) indicator, which characterizes the quality of the process such that a greater value means better quality of the process according to the improvement strategy as above. The absolute value of this indicator has no particular interpretation, only the increment or decrement of this value in time is significant.

Same considerations using the indicators established for the processes lead to a unique indicator of the QoS for the whole service provider, i.e., the data center. By evaluating the time behavior of this indicator and / or the component indicators we can have a good overview which process and / or metrics performed better or worse.

This unique indicator can be deployed for example on daily bases, such that the performance of the service provider can be easily followed and appropriate measures can be taken if performance degradation occurs. Moreover, even if the overall unique indicator has improved in value, there can be some components, whose performance has degraded. By setting up appropriate Graphical User Interfaces (GUIs), and appropriate colors (for example red for degradation and green for improvement) the deviation with respect to the previous day can be visualized.

The only process through which the customers interact with the data center as the service provider is through the "incident management", the performance of the other processes is practically hidden for the regular customer. In order to improve the "incident management" we will analyze the impact of some important processes on the "incident management".

An important direct impact on the "incident management" has the "problem management" in the sense that by a very efficient "problem management" the number of repetitive incidents or the time to solve the repetitive incidents can be dramatically reduced. For this, each incident should be correctly assigned to the appropriate issue, have a correct and exhaustive root analysis, such that the causes of the incident are unambiguously elucidated. It seems a bit of common sense that all the detailed information regarding the incident including good ways of searching, finding, and retrieving the information should be stored in an appropriate knowledge database. Next, the probability of recurring should be estimated and if necessary, appropriate measures should be taken in order to avoid the next occurrence of the same incident.

Proactive methods are very efficient to avoid the occurrence of incidents, e.g., improving "change management", "release and deployment management", etc. By significantly reducing the impact of new releases on the services, the peaks on the QoS can be significantly reduced.

B. *Formalization of the Strategy*

We will formalize the strategy proposed in Subsection III-A by introducing a mathematical model in order to use the advantages of the rigor of a formal approach over the inaccuracy and the incompleteness of natural languages.

Let $\mathcal{A}$ be an arbitrary set. We notate by $2^{\mathcal{A}}$ the power set of $\mathcal{A}$, i.e., the set of all subsets of $\mathcal{A}$, including the empty set and $\mathcal{A}$ itself, and the cardinality of $\mathcal{A}$ by $\mathrm{card}(\mathcal{A})$.

We use a calligraphic font to denote index sets. We denote by $\mathcal{S} := \{S_i \mid i \in \mathcal{S} \text{ and } S_i \text{ is a service}\}$ the finite set of the services. Analogously, we denote by $\mathcal{P} := \{P_i \mid i \in \mathcal{P} \text{ and } P_i \text{ is a process}\}$ the finite set of processes and by $\mathcal{T} := \{[t_1;t_2] \mid t_1 \text{ and } t_2 \text{ are points in time, such that } t_1 \leq t_2\}$ time intervals.

A metric M is a measurement that monitors progress towards achieving the targeted objectives. We denote by $\mathcal{M} := \{M_i \mid i \in \mathcal{M} \text{ and } M_i \text{ is a metric}\}$ the finite set of metrics. Generally speaking, a metric M is defined for an environment containing subsets of $\mathcal{S}$ and $\mathcal{P}$.

For example, let us define the ratio between the "total number of incidents with known resolution method" and the "total number of incidents". Depending on the strategic orientation of the company, different goals can be pursued. On the one hand, having for most of the incidents corrective measures in place can be a targeted objective, one the other hand, avoiding repetitive incidents is crucial for the economic success of companies like fabs running 24x7 continuous manufacturing operations. A mixed strategy (for example 10% known errors) can be also targeted. Hence, the scope of a metric is most of the time business oriented.

In order to be able to compare and compose different metrics in a reasonable way, we introduce the value of a metric such that it is greater or equal 0 and lower or equal 1. A greater value of the metric means a closer value to the targeted business objectives. Formally, the range of values of the *possible* business values, including the targeted ones is $2^{\mathbb{R}}$. Hence, the progress towards achieving the targeted Business Objectives (BO) can be represented as a function.

$$\begin{aligned} BO : \mathcal{M} \times \mathcal{P} \times \mathcal{S} &\rightarrow BusinessObjectives, \\ (M, P, S) &\mapsto BO(M, P, S). \end{aligned}$$

Analogously, the value (V) of a metric is represented as:

$$\begin{aligned} V : \mathcal{M} \times \mathcal{P} \times \mathcal{S} \times \mathcal{T} &\rightarrow [0; 1], \\ (M, P, S, [t_1; t_2]) &\mapsto V(M, P, S, [t_1; t_2]). \end{aligned}$$

A greater value for $V(M, P, S, [t_1; t_2])$ means a closer value to the targeted business objectives for (M, P, S). The definition above highlights the fact that the same metric can have different business objectives and definition (values) depending on the environment (services and/or processes) it is used.

We illustrate the above considerations based on a simple example and consider the "average cycle time" of the incidents. The business demands short cycle times for all departments. In order to be able to compare the cycle times of different departments, we determine the minimal cycle time (i.e., the theoretical cycle time needed if there are no unplanned down times, etc.) and assign the ratio of minimal cycle time to the cycle time as the value of the metric. Hence, the performance of the different departments regarding the same metric (i.e., cycle time) can be easily compared, on the assumption that the respective minimal cycle time has been evaluated correctly.

Our aim is to establish a single indicator for the service performance (i.e., the QoS) of the service provider. In order to evaluate the performance of the different metrics of the same process (for example ITIL process), we set up a methodology to compose the different metrics in a reasonable way, such that the new metric (indicator) outlines the performance of the investigated process.

In order to simplify the notation, we will notate in the following the value of a metric M by $V(M)$, meaning that the metrics involved are defined on the same environment and the same time interval.

Definition III.1 (Composition of metrics) *Let* $\mathfrak{M} := \{M_i | i \in \{i_1, i_2, \ldots, i_k\} \subseteq \mathcal{M}\}$ *a subset of* $\mathcal{M}$. *We define*

$$\begin{aligned} COMP : 2^{\mathcal{M}} &\rightarrow \mathcal{M}, \\ \mathfrak{M} &\mapsto COMP(\mathfrak{M}), \end{aligned}$$

such that there is an aggregation function AGG

$$\begin{aligned} AGG : 2^{\mathcal{M}} &\rightarrow [0; 1], \\ V(COMP(\mathfrak{M})) &\mapsto AGG(V(M_{i_1}), V(M_{i_2}), \ldots, V(M_{i_k})) \end{aligned}$$

and

$$\begin{aligned} & v^1_{i_1} \leq v^2_{i_1}, v^1_{i_1} \leq v^2_{i_1}, \ldots, v^1_{i_k} \leq v^2_{i_k} \\ & \quad \Rightarrow AGG(v^1_{i_1}, v^1_{i_2}, \ldots, v^1_{i_k}) \leq AGG(v^2_{i_1}, v^2_{i_2}, \ldots, v^2_{i_k}) \end{aligned}$$

Except for the case of trivial aggregations, the composition generates a new metric out of known ones.

In order to keep our notation simple and straightforward, we will not make any distinction in the formal representation of the initial metrics and those obtained by consolidation. Hence, $\mathcal{M}$ contains the initial metrics as well as the consolidated ones. Therefore, a consolidated metric can be finally set up for the entire service. We note:

Lemma III.2 (Composition properties) *Let* $\mathfrak{M} := \{M_i | i \in \{i_1, i_2, \ldots, i_k\} \subseteq \mathcal{M}\}$ *a subset of* $\mathcal{M}$ *arbitrarily chosen. Then,* $COMP(\mathfrak{M})$ *is a metric, i.e., fulfills the following properties:*

a) $0 \leq V(COMP(\mathfrak{M})) \leq 1$,

b) *A greater value for* $V(COMP(\mathfrak{M}))$ *means a closer value to the targeted business objectives for this metric.*

Hint *These properties are a direct consequence of Definition III.1.* ∎

Next, we give a small example to illustrate the aggregation strategies. Let $\mathfrak{M} := \{M_{i_1}, M_{i_2}, \ldots, M_{i_k}\}$ be a subset of $\mathcal{M}$. We suppose, that the value of the new characteristic $COMP(\mathfrak{M})$ is a linear combination of the values of the components, i.e.,

$$V(COMP(\mathfrak{M})) := \sum_{i=i_1}^{i_k} \alpha_i \cdot V(M_i)$$

with weights $\alpha_i > 0 \; \forall i \in \{i_1, i_2, \ldots, i_k\}$ and $\sum_{i=i_1}^{i_k} \alpha_i = 1$. If the value of α_i is high, then the metric M_i within $COMP(\mathfrak{M})$ is important. In practice, it suffices to build weight groups $\{G_i | i \in \{i_1, i_2, \ldots, i_l\}\}$ out of $\mathfrak{M}$ such that each $M \in \mathfrak{M}$ belongs to a group G_i and all $M_j \in G_i$ are equally weighted. Furthermore, a weighting function W can be set up, such that all α_i can be explicitly determined, for example set

$$k_i := \frac{\alpha_i}{\alpha_{i+1}} \text{ for all } i \in \{i_1, i_2, \ldots, i_{l-1}\}.$$

The values k_i can be regarded as the "ratio of relevancy" of the corresponding metrics.

IV. Improving the QoS

In the last section, we proposed a strategy how to measure the QoS of a data center. In this section, we will establish metrics controlling the performance of a data center. Thus, we can determine in which cases the service of a data center collapses or the QoS substantially degrades.

A. Queuing Model and Basic Metrics

We model the processing line of a data center by introducing a queuing model and give some basic definitions related to it. In order to keep the presentation accessible and avoid technical complications, we will maintain our model as simple as possible. It is the task of the practitioners to map the real world onto this model according to their needs. We will analyze the entire processing line as well as subsystems of it.

A *queuing system* consists of discrete objects, termed *units* or *items* that arrive at some rate to the system. Within the system, the units may form one or more queues and eventually be processed. After being processed, the units leave the queue.

The finest granularity in our model is *unit, step, time stamp, section* and *classification*. For example, in practice, the unit can be a ticket, the section can be an employee of the service center, a group of employees having the same profile or a specific section of the service center, etc. The classification is the finest attribute which characterizes the unit (like bug, disturbance, project, etc.) and it can be distinguished in the processing phase.

In our model the unit enters the system (service center), is processed according to the specifications and leaves the system. The step is the finest abstraction level of processing which is tracked by the reporting system. When the material unit u enters the system, it is assigned to a classification c. This assignment remains valid till the unit u leaves the system. We will analyze the entire processing line as well as subsystems of it.

We denote by S the set of all steps of the processing line, by U the set of the units that entered the system, and by T the (ordered and discrete) points in time when events may occur in the system. Since we are merely interested in daily calculations, we will set D as the set of all points in time belonging to a specific day D, i.e., $D := \{t \in T |$ t belongs to day D$\}$.

Let $s \in S$ and $u \in U$. We denote by $TrInT_s(u)$ the *track in time* of u, i.e., the point in time when the processing of unit u is started at step s. Analogously, $TrOutT_s(u)$ is the *track out time* of u, i.e., the point in time when the processing of unit u has been finished at the step s.

We assume that for a step s, the function $succ_s(u)$, which identifies the succeeding step of s for the unit u is well defined. Analogously, we assume that the history of the production process is tracked, so the predecessor function $pred_s(u)$ of each step s is well defined. For formal reasons we set $succ_s(u) := s$ for the last step on the route and $pred_s(u) := s$ for the first step on the route.

By *cycle time* (CT), we generally denote the time interval a unit or a group of material units spent in the system / subsystem [12]. We do not make any restrictions on the *time unit* we use, but are merely interested on daily calculations. For formal reasons, – in order to be able to calculate average values – we denote by $24h$ the cardinality of an arbitrary day D. For $t \in T$ we denote by $t \pm 24h$ the point in time t shifted forward or backwards by 24 hours.

We assume that events in the system are repeated on a daily basis, i.e.,

$$\begin{aligned} &\forall u \in U \text{ and } \forall s \in S : TrInT_s(u) = t \\ &\implies \exists v \in U : TrInT_s(v) = t + 24h \text{ and} \\ &\qquad TrOutT_s(v) = TrOutT_s(u) + 24h \end{aligned}$$

and

$$\begin{aligned} &\forall u \in U \text{ and } \forall s \in S : TrInT_s(u) = t \\ &\implies \exists w \in U : TrInT_s(w) = t - 24h \text{ and} \\ &\qquad TrOutT_s(w) = TrOutT_s(u) - 24h. \end{aligned}$$

Under a *stable system* we mean a system according to the conditions above.

In practice, systems pass through a ramp up phase such that the above conditions are eventually reached, i.e., $\exists t_b \in T$ such that the above conditions are satisfied for all $t > t_b$. For our investigations, it is sufficient that the systems reach the stable state after some time (*eventually stable systems*). For reasons of a simple notation, we will use the term *stable system* or *system in a stable state*. However, the statements of this work are also valid for eventually stable systems.

The *raw process time / service time* of unit $u \in U$ related to step $s\ inS$ is the minimum processing time to complete the step s without considering waiting times or down times. We denote the raw process time of unit u related to step s by $RPT_s(u)$.

Let $u \in U$, let $\{s_1, s_2, \ldots, s_n\} \subset S$ be the complete list of steps according to the processing history to process unit u. Let $RPT_{s_i}(u)$ be the raw process times of unit u related to step s_i for all $i = 1, 2, \ldots, n$. Then the raw process time of unit u can be represented as follows:

$$RPT(u) = \sum_{i=1}^{n} RPT_{s_i}(u).$$

The work in progress is defined as the inventory at time $t \in T$ and will be denoted by $WIP(t)$. If the work in process is used in connection with Little's Theorem then it denotes the average inventory for a given period of time. We use the notation $avgWIP$ instead of WIP to denote the average inventory.

We denote by Th the throughput of the material units by. Usually, we consider the daily throughput and refer to it as Th^D for a specific day D.

The cycle time of a unit $u \in U$ spent at a step $s \in S$ in the system can be represented as:

$$CT_s(u) := TrOutT_s(u) - TrOutT_{pred_s(u)}(u).$$

Let $\{u_1, u_2, \ldots, u_n\}$ be the set of units that were processed at step s on a specific day $D \subset T$ i.e., $\forall i \in \{1, 2, \ldots, n\}\ \exists t_i \in D$ such that $TrOutT_s(u_i) = t_i$. Then, the average cycle time $avgCT_s^D$ the units u_i spent in the system at step s on a specific day D can be represented as:

$$avgCT_s^D = \frac{1}{n} \cdot \sum_{i=1}^{n} CT_s(u_i).$$

For $t \in T$, $u \in U$ we define the indicator function 1_s at a process step $s \in S$ as follows:

$$1_s : U \times T \to \{0, 1\},$$
$$(u,t) \mapsto 1_s(u,t) := \begin{cases} 1 & \text{if } t \geq TrOutT_{pred(s)}(u) \text{ and} \\ & t < TrOutT_s(u), \\ 0 & \text{otherwise.} \end{cases}$$

Throughout this work we assume that T is discrete, i.e., units arrive and depart only at specific points in time, since the time is usually measured in seconds or milliseconds.

Lemma IV.1 (Representation of average inventory) *The average inventory $avgWIP_s^D$ for a process step $s \in S$ on a specific day D can be represented as follows:*

$$avgWIP_s^D = \frac{1}{\mathrm{card}(D)} \cdot \sum_{t \in D} \sum_{u \in U} 1_s(u,t) \quad (1)$$
$$= avgCT_s^D \cdot Th_s^D. \quad (2)$$

By interchanging the order of summation, we receive an expression for WIP_s^D, which is much easier to calculate in practice.

Hint *Let $U_{n,D} := \{u_1, u_2, \ldots, u_n\}$ be the set of units that left the step s on a specific day $D \subset T$, i.e., $\forall i \in \{1, 2, \ldots, n\}\ \exists t_i \in D$ such that $TrOutT_s(u_i) = t_i$. Then, in stable systems the following relation holds:*

$$avgWIP_s^D = \frac{1}{\mathrm{card}(D)} \cdot \sum_{t \in D} \sum_{u \in U} 1_s(u,t)$$
$$= \frac{1}{\mathrm{card}(D)} \cdot \sum_{t \in T} \sum_{u \in U_{n,D}} 1_s(u,t).$$

By interchanging the order of summation and considering that for $i \in \{1, 2, \ldots, n\}$ the average cycle time (measured in days) of the material unit u_i at step s is given by:

$$avgCT_s(u_i)$$
$$:= \frac{1}{\mathrm{card}(D)} \cdot \left(TrOutT_s(u_i) - TrOutT_{pred(s)}(u_i)\right)$$
$$= \frac{1}{\mathrm{card}(D)} \cdot \sum_{t \in T} 1_s(u_i, t).$$

Thus, we get:

$$avgWIP_s^D = avgCT_s^D \cdot Th_s^D.$$

Since in stable systems the variables above do not depend on the day chosen for their calculation, Little's Theorem follows. The consideration above do not hold in steady state systems used by Stidham and Sigman (see [13] or [14]). ■

Remark IV.3 (Case: Set of points in time is continuous) *Actually, in theoretical models it is not necessary to consider a discrete set T in order to be able to calculate $avgWIP_s^D$. Let Σ_U be the discrete σ-algebra on U (i.e., the power set 2^U of U). Let μ be the counting measure on Σ_U, i.e., $\mu(\mathcal{U}) := |\mathcal{U}|$ for $\mathcal{U} \in \Sigma_U$. Then, (U, Σ_U, μ) is a measure space. For $T \subset \mathbb{R}_+$ let Σ_T be the σ-algebra of all Lebesgue measurable sets on T and let λ the usual Lebesgue measure on T. Analogously (T, Σ_T, λ) is also a measurable space. Since both spaces are σ-finite, the product measure $\mu \otimes \lambda$ is well defined and for $\mathcal{U} \subset U$ and $\mathcal{T} \subset T$ the equality $\mu \otimes \lambda(\mathcal{U} \times \mathcal{T}) = \mu(\mathcal{U}) \cdot \lambda(\mathcal{T})$ holds. Since 1_s is a simple function (i.e., a finite linear combination of indicator functions of measurable sets) it is $\Sigma_U \times \Sigma_T$ measurable. Then, as expected $\mathrm{card}(D) = \int_D \mathrm{d}\lambda(t) = 24h$ and the theorem of Fubini-Tonelli gives:*

$$avgWIP_s^D = \frac{1}{\mathrm{card}(D)} \cdot \int_D \int_U 1_s(u,t) \mathrm{d}\mu(u) \mathrm{d}\lambda(t)$$
$$= \frac{1}{\mathrm{card}(D)} \cdot \int_{U \times D} 1_s(u,t) \mathrm{d}(\mu \otimes \lambda)(u,t)$$
$$= \frac{1}{\mathrm{card}(D)} \cdot \int_U \int_D 1_s(u,t) \mathrm{d}\lambda(t) \mathrm{d}\mu(u).$$

The last integral is much easier to evaluate.

In stable systems the value $avgWIP_s^D$ does not depend on the specific day D that was considered for the calculation.

B. Expected Inventory

Next, we define one of the relevant metric for bottleneck control and present formulas to calculate them.

$WIP24_{s,c}(t)$ denotes the inventory which is expected in the next 24 hours at a specific step $s \in S$, classification c and $t \in T$. Usually, $WIP24_{s,c}(t)$ at midnight is considered. In this case, we will omit the time constraint and use the notation $WIP24_{s,c}$.

Let us suppose $\{s_1, s_2, \ldots, s_n\}$ is the planned (ordered) list of steps as provided by the route for the classification c. There are of course different strategies to estimate $WIP24_{s_l,c}(t)$ for a specific $l \in \{1, 2, \ldots, n\}$. One alternative supposes that the units moves across the line as planned by the route. Let $refCT_{s_i,c}$ be the target cycle time to process the unit at the step $s_i \in S$, let $WIP_{s_i,c}(t)$ be the inventory at the step s_i for the classification c and time $t \in T$. For l determine $j := min(k : k \leq l)$ such that $\sum_{k \leq i \leq l} refCT_{s_i,c} \leq 24h$. Then the expected inventory can be written as follows:

$$WIP24_{s_l,c}(t) = \sum_{j \leq i \leq l} WIP_{s_i,c}(t).$$

Most of the time, the unit is not processed according to the specifications (route), reworks or alternative processing strategies are necessary. In this case, the formula as above does not hold, and other more complex approaches are necessary.

C. Little's Theorem

In the following, we will introduce Little's Theorem [15] [16]. Little's Theorem which is mostly called *Little's Law* is a mathematical theorem giving a rather simple relation between the average cycle time, the throughput, and the average work in process in the system. It will be used later on for calculating the flow factor and thus, controlling the performance of the data center. The relation of Little's Theorem is valid if some convergence criteria are fulfilled and if the underlying system is in steady state and non-preemptive. The latter means that the properties of the system are unchanging in time, there are no interrupts and later resumes. In many systems, steady state is not achieved until some time has elapsed after the system is started or initiated. In stochastic systems, the probabilities that some events occur in the system are constant. The result is entirely independent of the probability distribution involved and hence it requires no assumption whether the units are processed in the order they arrive or the time distribution they enter or leave the system.

We give now a formal definition for Little's formula. Our explanation is based on [14] slightly modified to use our notations. We consider the queuing system above where – unlimited but countable – units arrive, spend some time in the system, and then leave. Material units enter at most once the system, i.e., units that left do not enter the system again. Let $T := \{t_i | i \in \mathbb{N}\}$ be the countable set of points in time when those events occur. At any point in time $t \in T$ at most a finite number of units enter or leave the system. Let u_n denote the unit which enters the system at the time t_n^e. Upon entering the system, u_n spends CT_n time units in the system (the cycle time of u_n) and then leaves the system at time $t_n^d = t_n + CT_n$. The departure times are not necessary ordered in the same way as the enter times. This means that we do not require that the units leave the system in the same order as they arrived. Let $1_{u_i}^e(t) := 1$ if $t_i \leq t$ and 0 else. We denote by $N^e(t)$ the number of units which entered the system until time t, i.e.,

$$N^e(t) = \sum_{i=1}^{\infty} 1_{u_i}^e(t).$$

Analogously, we denote by $N^l(t)$ the number of units which have left until time t. Let $L(t)$ be the total number of the units in the system by time t. A unit u_n is in the system at time t if and only if $t_n \leq t < t_n + CT_n$. Hence $L(t) = N^e(t) - N^l(t)$. Let be (if the limit exists)

$$Th := \lim_{t \to \infty} \frac{N^e(t)}{t}$$

the arrival rate into the system,

$$avgCT := \lim_{n \to \infty} (\frac{1}{n} \cdot \sum_{j=1}^{n} CT_j)$$

the average cycle time the unit spends in the system,

$$avgWIP := \lim_{t \to \infty} (\frac{1}{t} \cdot \int_0^t L(s) \mathrm{d}s)$$

the average number of units in the system.

Theorem IV.4 (Little's theorem) *If both the arrival rate Th and the average cycle time $avgCT$ exist and are finite, then the above limit in the definition of the average inventory $avgWIP$ exists and it holds:*

$$avgWIP = avgCT \cdot Th. \tag{3}$$

Corollary IV.5 *If both Th and $avgCT$ exist and are finite, then the departure rate exists and equals the arrival rate:*

$$\lim_{t \to \infty} \frac{N^l(t)}{t} = Th.$$

Little used a stochastic framework to define and prove of what is known as Little's Law, the approach we are presenting makes no stochastic assumptions, i.e., the quantities and processes are deterministic. There are other versions of Little's Theorem that allow batch arrivals, see section 6.2 of [14].

D. Calculation of the Flow Factor

Next, we establish a formula for the calculation of the flow factor for the processing line. For this, we restrict to the following queuing model: The *adapted queuing model* is based on the one given in Subsection IV-A with the following modifications:

- Units can enter and leave the system only through a finite number of gates.
- Each gate on the entering side has its correspondence on the exit side.
- The entering and the corresponding exit gate are connected by a lane.
- Once, the person entered the system, he can move forward only on the lane set up by the entering gate.

He cannot switch the lane or leave the system except the exit gates.

- Each lane contains a number of clerks, not defined in detail, such that before each clerk an internal queue is formed and the clerk does not necessarily process the requests instantly.
- The sum of the time the clerks process the requests of a person during his voyage through a given lane (i.e., the raw process time) does not depend on the particular person involved. Hence, the system has a predefined raw process time (RPT^l) for each lane, i.e., the sum of the time the clerks process the requests of a person during his voyage through the lane.

Table I illustrates the queuing model.

Table I. ILLUSTRATION OF A QUEUING SYSTEM WITH 5 LANES $l_1, l_2, \ldots, l_5$ AND 8 PROCESSING STEPS.

l_1	⇒	■	■		■			■	■	⇒
l_2	⇒	■		■	■	■	■		■	⇒
l_3	⇒	■	■				■	■	■	⇒
l_4	⇒	■		■		■			■	⇒
l_5	⇒	■					■		■	⇒

We will denote by L the set of the lanes and by Th^l the throughput at lane $l \in L$.

Definition IV.6 (Flow factor) *Let* $\{u_1, u_2, u_3, \ldots\}$ *be the ordered list of units which enter the system, such that* u_i *enters the system at time* t_i *and* $i < j \Rightarrow t_i \leq t_j$*. The cycle time* CT_i *a unit* $u_i \in U$ *spent in the system can be split into the waiting time (*WT_i*) and raw process time* RPT_i *such that* $CT_i = WT_i + RPT_i$*. If the limit exists, then the (average) flow factor* $avgFF$ *is defined as:*

$$avgFF := \lim_{n\to\infty} \frac{\sum_{i=1}^{n} CT_i}{\sum_{i=1}^{n} RPT_i}. \tag{4}$$

Remark IV.7 *If* $CT := \lim_{n\to\infty}\left(\frac{1}{n} \cdot \sum_{i=1}^{n} CT_i\right)$ *and* $RPT := \lim_{n\to\infty}\left(\frac{1}{n} \cdot \sum_{i=1}^{n} RPT_i\right)$ *exists (and are finite), then the above limit exists and it holds:*

$$avgFF = \frac{CT}{RPT}.$$

Corollary IV.8 (Representation of raw process time) *Let* $N_l^e(t)$ *be the number of units which entered the lane* $l \in L$ *until time* $t \in T$*. Let* $n := N^e(t_n) := \sum_{l\in L} N_l^e(t_n)$*. Then, the average raw process time* RPT *of the whole processing line can be represented as follows:*

$$RPT := \lim_{n\to\infty}\left(\frac{1}{n} \cdot \sum_{i=1}^{n} RPT_i\right) = \sum_{l\in L} \frac{Th^l}{Th} \cdot RPT^l. \tag{5}$$

Hint *We obtain:*

$$\frac{1}{n} \cdot \sum_{i=1}^{n} RPT_i = \frac{1}{n} \cdot \sum_{l\in L} \sum_{i_l=1}^{n} RPT_i^l = \sum_{l\in L} \frac{N_l^e(t_n)}{N^e(t_n)} \cdot RPT^l.$$

Since

$$\lim_{n\to\infty} \frac{N_l^e(t_n)}{t_n} \cdot \frac{t_n}{N^e(t_n)} = \frac{Th^l}{Th} \quad \forall l \in L$$

it follows that

$$RPT := \lim_{n\to\infty}\left(\frac{1}{n} \cdot \sum_{i=1}^{n} RPT_i\right) = \sum_{l\in L} \frac{Th^l}{Th} \cdot RPT^l.$$

■

Corollary IV.10 (Representation of flow factor) *Assumed that the conditions of Little's Theorem are satisfied. Then, the flow factor can be represented as follows:*

$$\frac{1}{avgFF} = \sum_{l\in L} \frac{WIP^l}{WIP} \cdot \frac{1}{FF^l}. \tag{6}$$

Hint *Easy calculations using Little's Theorem for each lane* $l \in L$ *yields to the relationship between the flow factor for the whole system and the flow factors of its components / lanes as given in* (6). ■

We can calculate the average number of units in the system first by considering the whole system and secondly considering the reduced system with one lane. Little's formula is valid in both cases. Since units cannot switch to another lane, it follows that

$$WIP = \sum_{l\in L} WIP^l.$$

Using Little's formula and the definition of the average cycle time it follows that:

$$\lim_{n\to\infty}\left(\frac{1}{n} \cdot \sum_{i=1}^{n} CT_i\right) = CT = \sum_{l\in L} \frac{Th^l}{Th} \cdot CT^l.$$

Hence, as expected:

$$avgFF = \frac{\sum_{l\in L} \frac{Th^l}{Th} \cdot CT^l}{\sum_{l\in L} \frac{Th^l}{Th} \cdot RPT^l} = \frac{CT}{RPT}.$$

Let us suppose that the service center has different departments, such as for "incidents", "problems", "projects", "releases", etc., which operate independently. By abstracting those departments as lanes and calculating for each department the flow factor, the flow factor of the service center can be established as in (6).

Moreover, Equation (6) determines the correlation between the flow factors of each department and the flow factor of the data center. Thus, the flow factor of the data center can be improved within an existing budget, for example by resource reallocation, if the flow factor of some departments will be improved and the flow factor of some other departments will be degraded, see also the discussion regarding the operating curve.

A formula of the type given in (6) was proposed by Hilsenbeck in [17, p. 36]:

$$avgFF = \sum_{l\in L} \frac{Th^l}{Th} \cdot FF^l. \tag{7}$$

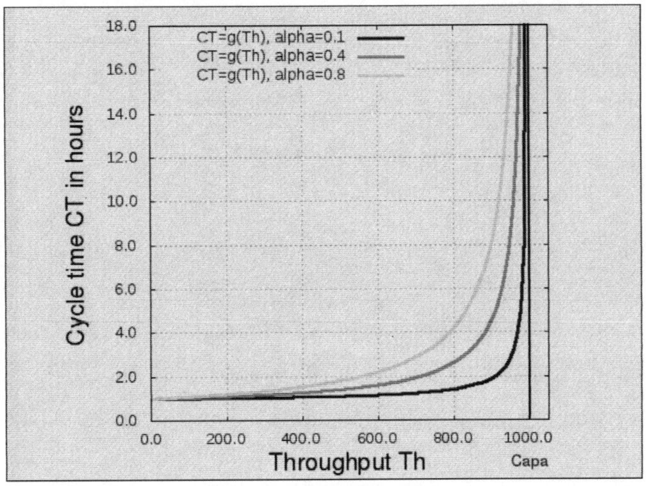

Figure 1. Graph of function g given in (10) (Operating curve). Throughput Th versus cycle time CT for four different values of α.

It seems that the formula (7) is empirical. In particular, no proof of the formula was given.

The flow factor plays an important role in the operating curve management. The operation curve follows from Kingman's equation [18]. One of the representation of the operating curve is based on the following formula (see [19, pp. 55, 58], [17, pp. 41, 44], [20] [21]).

$$avgFF = f(U) := \alpha \cdot \frac{U}{1-U} + 1. \tag{8}$$

U is the *utilization*, i.e., the percentage of the capacity $Capa$ of a tool or production segment (see [22] for a definition and [19, p. 57] for calculation). Introducing $avgFF$ and U in (8), the value for the coefficient α (variability) follows.

The operating curve as a function $avgFF(U)$ can be drawn. However, this relation is rather abstract. Since it holds

$$U = \frac{Th}{Capa}, \tag{9}$$

the flow factor in terms of a function $avgFF = f(U)$ can be easily transformed into a function of the type $CT = g(Th)$ (see [19, p. 40]):

$$CT = g(Th) := \alpha \cdot \frac{Th}{Capa - Th} \cdot RPT + RPT. \tag{10}$$

This relation is more practical as it shows how the throughput directly influences the cycle time. The self-generated graph of the function g is depicted in Figure 1. It is assumed that the average minimal cycle time RPT is 1 hour and that the maximal capacity is $Capa = 1000$. If Th is close to $Capa$, then the graph of g grows asymptotically. Hence, a point at the graph (named *operating point)* has to be chosen, such that a minimal increase of the number of items does not lead to dramatically increased cycle time. The operating curve has been used by Qimonda to improve overall fab performance.

V. Use case: An excerpt

We illustrate the principles of improving the QoS of a data center by means of a simplified example. Let us consider the department which provides the e-mail service of a data center. Firstly, we establish the conditions such that the providing the service is at all possible. Secondly, we set up metrics and compose them in order to be able to track the evolution of QoS.

One of the most sensible indicators whose value has to be estimated is the raw process time RPT which is the (average) minimal cycle time to process an incident. It contains only the effective time to process the incident, for example not including coffee breaks, private telephone calls, etc. Let us suppose that RPT is equal to 1 hour. In real systems (see [19, pp. 46, 48]) the cycle time CT corresponding to a specific throughput, denoted by Th is measured. Let us suppose that by considering the raw process time the maximum capacity $Capa$ is 1000 incidents per month.

Introducing CT and Th in (10), the value 0.4 for the coefficient α (variability) follows. As shown in Figure 1 we can easily follow that a slightly increase of the throughput (after leaving the linear part of the graph) considerably increase the cycle time. In order to avoid the flooding of the departments with tickets, the natural reaction of the employees is to reduce the raw process time and consequently reduce the QoS of the department. Hence, in our example, if the throughput exceeds 800 incidents per month appropriate measures should be taken in order to avoid the collapse of the service. On the contrary, if the throughput is equal to 400 tickets per month (being on the linear part of the graph), a part of the staff can be relocated to assist other services. The relation (6) shows the correlation between the flow factor of the individual departments and the data center and can be used to balance the individual departments.

In order to establish normalized / composite metrics, we consider those presented in Subsection III-A.

We describe below some of the metrics used in incident management, normalized and directed as described in Subsection III-B, i.e., each metric takes values in the closed interval $[0; 1]$ and a greater value for the metric implies a better accomplishment of the business requirements.

$$m_{01} := \frac{1}{\text{“Total No. of incidents”}}$$

$$m_{02} := 1 - \frac{\text{“No. of repeated incidents”}}{\text{“Total No. of incidents”}}$$

$$m_{03} := 1 - \frac{\text{“No. of repeated incidents with known solution”}}{\text{“No. of repeated incidents”}}$$

Unfortunately, the “Maximum No. of incidents” is not a priori known. Hence, generally speaking, it cannot be used in the formula. Furthermore, the business requires that corresponding measures are taken, such that repeated incidents are avoided. Therefore, “No. of repeated incidents” should be kept low. Further metrics, which are considered (SLA refers to Service Level Agreement):

$$m_{04} := \frac{\text{“No. of escalated incidents”}}{\text{Total No. of incidents”}}$$

$$m_{05} := \frac{1}{\text{“Average cycle time to resolve the incident”}}$$

$$m_{06} := \frac{1}{\text{“Average waiting time from user side”}}$$

$$m_{07} := \frac{1}{\text{“Average working time on the incident”}}$$

$$m_{08} := \frac{\text{“Total No. of incidents resolved within SLA time”}}{\text{“Total No. of SLA relevant incidents”}}$$

$$m_{09} := \frac{1}{\text{“First reaction time to repair the incident”}}$$

$$m_{10} := \frac{1}{\text{“No. of responses from service center side”}}$$

Unfortunately, defining metrics fulfilling the conditions as above, is not always straightforward. Let us consider $Incid_{out}$ as the total number of incidents closed and $Incid_{in}$ as the total number of incidents opened in the time frame considered. In order to avoid the flooding of the data center with incidents the metric $k := Incid_{out}/Incid_{in}$ could be tracked. Unfortunately, this metric does not fulfill our requirements, since it can take values outside the interval $[0; 1]$. In order to avoid this impediment, we define $k_{in} := Incid_{in}/$“Total No. of incidents” and $k_{out} := Incid_{out}/$“Total No. of incidents” and set

$$m_{11} := \frac{1 + k_{out} - k_{in}}{2}.$$

Then, m_{11} is normalized and satisfies the above conditions imposed for metrics. Generally speaking, the effective minimal and maximal value of a metric is not known, nor is the distribution a priori known. Thus, for example, a metric m_1 takes values in the interval $[0.5; 0.6]$ and another metric m_2 in the interval $[0.2; 0.7]$ with nearly uniform distribution. Hence, the metric m_2 varies more widely than m_1 and this should be considered – for example using the standard deviation – when setting up the groupings for the composition of the metrics, such that metrics having a low standard deviation should be assigned to more important groups.

Now, let us consider in our use case five composition groups, $G_0, G_1, \ldots, G_4$, such that G_1 is the most relevant group. Let us associate the weight w_i to group G_i and let us consider the weighting according to an exponential function, such that $k_0 := 1$ and $k_i := w_{i-1}/w_i$ for $i > 0$. This yields to the relation: $w_i = w_0/\prod_{l=0}^{l=i} k_l$. In our example $k_1 := e^1$, $k_2 := e^{0.75}$, $k_3 := e^{0.5}$, etc. The values for k_i are illustrated in Figure 2. Let us assign the above metrics to the composition groups, such that index set of the metrics assigned to the group G_l is equal to I_l and let n_l the number of metrics in the group G_l. Then, according to the composition rules: $\sum_{i=0}^{4} n_i \cdot w_i = 1$. Hence, the weight values follow. The value of the composition metric M is:

$$V(M) := \sum_{i=0}^{4} w_i \cdot \sum_{l \in I_i} V(m_l).$$

Examples of services at the ZIH of the Technische Universität Dresden (TU Dresden) are: “E-Mail Service”, “Backup and Archive Service”, “Data Exchange Service”, “Access to High Performance Computing Resources”, etc. [23] We conclude this section by presenting the assistance system for a data center in Figure 4 and by summarizing the composition strategy via the flow diagram given in Figure 3.

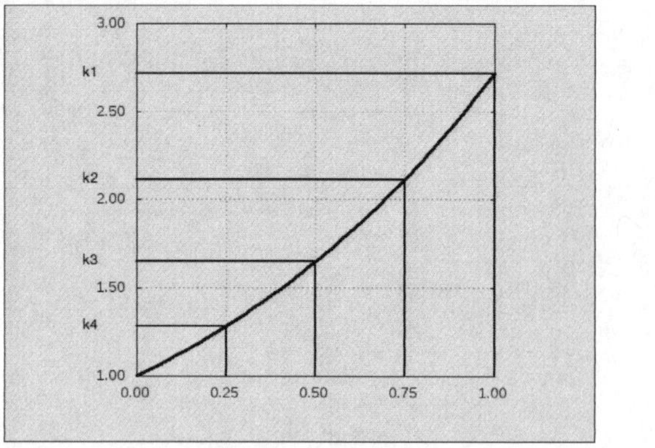

Figure 2. Graphical construction of values k_i such that metrics are weighted according to an exponential function, depicted for $f(x) = e^x$.

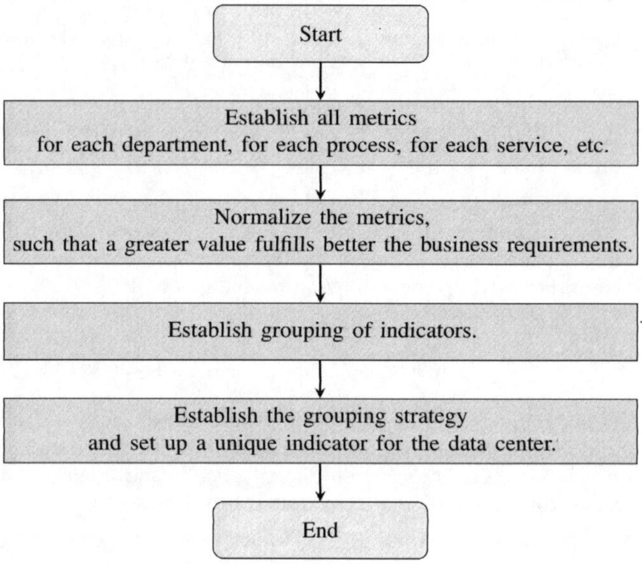

Figure 3. Simplified flow diagram regarding the composition strategy.

VI. CONCLUSION AND FUTURE WORK

We set up a formal, mathematical model and analyzed the QoS and the modalities to enhance it within this model. In that way, the QoS provided by the TU Dresden can be improved, which implicitly leads to a good ranking of the TU Dresden between the universities in Germany and world wide.

The main result of our research is that from a service provider perspective QoS can be characterized in mathematical terms pretty accurately, such that the improvement / degradation of the overall service or part of it can be tracked in IT systems and can be visualized through GUIs. According to Definition of ITU-T Rec. E.800 [24]: QoS is the “Collective effect of service performances which determine the degree of satisfaction of a user of a service”. The long term experience of the first author, working in the semiconductor industry is very similar to the definition above, such that it does not suffice to consider only the service provider perspective, but the user's perception of the QoS should also be considered. Further research is necessary to establish the correlation (or lack of it) between the objectively

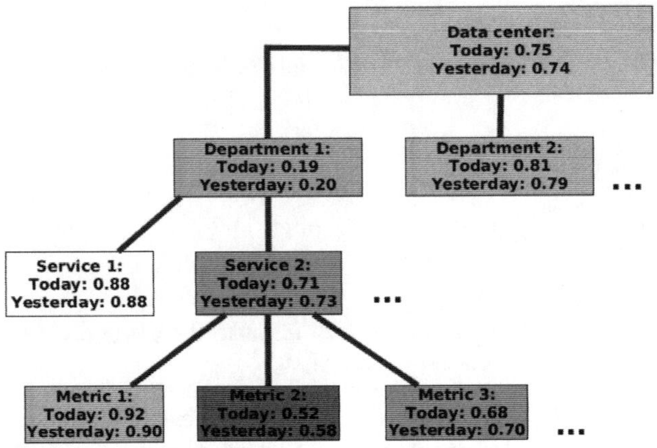

Figure 4. Hierarchical assistance system for a data center consisting of different departments, services, and metrics as levels. Changes will be depicted in green, white or red depending on the indicator's values of today and yesterday.

improved service and the subjective perception of the customer.

The composition strategy of various metrics to form an overall indicator can be a very complex endeavor. If all the metrics improve or degrade, then the overall indicator will improve or degrade accordingly. The question is in which direction will the overall QoS indicator swing if some metrics improve, some other degrade in time. We are not aware of any research in this direction. Similarly, how can the overall QoS be enhanced within the limited budget by improving some components and degrading others by resource reallocation.

The study has been accomplished for the data center of the ZIH, TU Dresden, but it can be used to improve the QoS by any service provider in the event that the real world can be mapped to the formal model used in this approach.

The similitude between a data center and a semiconductor fab regarding performance improvement cannot be denied. It would be then advantageous to identify the major differences, such that the theory developed to improve the performance of a semiconductor fab could be adapted for data centers. This work is a little step in this direction.

ACKNOWLEDGMENT

Part of this paper (including the study regarding Little's Theorem) completes an unfinished study of the first author regarding the performance of semiconductor fabs within the scope of the Cool Silicon Project (2012 - 2014). Part of this work was also supported by the German Federal Ministry for Economic Affairs and Energy (BMWi) by funding the research project "EMuDig 4.0". Furthermore, we acknowledge the assistance and helpful comments of the anonymous referees.

REFERENCES

[1] Symantec Corporation, "State of the data center survey – global results," September 2012, retrieved: September 2018. [Online]. Available: http://www.symantec.com/content/en/us/about/media/pdfs/b-state-of-data-center-survey-global-results-09_2012.en-us.pdf

[2] G. I. Butnaru, "The quality of services in tourism and in the romanian accommodation system," Analele Stiintifice ale Universitatii "Alexandru Ioan Cuza" din Iasi - Stiinte Economice, vol. 56, 2009, pp. 252–269. [Online]. Available: https://EconPapers.repec.org/RePEc:aic:journl:y:2009:v:56:p:252-269

[3] S. Jain and G. Gupta, "Measuring Service Quality: Servqual vs. Servperf Scales," vol. 29, 04 2004, pp. 25–38.

[4] C. Ennew, G. V. Reed, and M. Binks, Importance-Performance Analysis and the Measurement of Service Quality, 03 1993, vol. 27, pp. 59–70.

[5] B. Edvardsson, "Service Quality: Beyond Cognitive Assessment," vol. 15, 04 2005, pp. 127–131.

[6] A. P. Parasuraman, V. Zeithaml, and L. Berry, A Conceptual Model of Service Quality and its Implication for Future Research (SERVQUAL), 01 1985, vol. 49.

[7] K. Ishibashi, Maintaining Quality of Service Based on ITIL-Based IT Service Management, 08 2007, vol. 43, pp. 334–344.

[8] E. L. Hernandez, "Evaluation Framework for Quality of Service in Web Services: implementation in a pervasive environment," Master's thesis, INSA Lyon, France, 2010.

[9] itSMF UK, ITIL Foundation Handbook, 3rd ed. Norwich: The Stationery Office, 2012.

[10] ServiceNow, "Key Performance Indicators (KPI) Examples, Dashboard & Reporting," 2018, retrieved: September 2018. [Online]. Available: http://kpilibrary.com/

[11] D. Parmenter, Key Performance Indicators: Developing, Implementing, and Using Winning KPIs, ser. BusinessPro collection. Wiley, 2015.

[12] L. Turpin, "A note on understanding cycle time," International Journal of Production Economics, vol. 205, 2018, pp. 113 – 117. [Online]. Available: http://www.sciencedirect.com/science/article/pii/S0925527318303748

[13] K. Sigman, "Notes on Little's Law," 2009, retrieved: September 2018. [Online]. Available: http://www.columbia.edu/~ks20/stochastic-I/stochastic-I-LL.pdf

[14] M. El-Taha and S. Stidham Jr, Sample-Path Analysis of Queueing Systems. Kluwer Academic Publishers, 01 1999, vol. 11.

[15] J. D. C. Little, "A Proof for the Queuing Formula $L = \lambda W$," Oper. Res., vol. 9, no. 3, Jun. 1961, pp. 383–387. [Online]. Available: http://dx.doi.org/10.1287/opre.9.3.383

[16] J. Shortle et al., Fundamentals of Queueing Theory, 5th ed., ser. Wiley Series in Probability and Statistics. Wiley, 2018.

[17] K. Hilsenbeck, "Optimierungsmodelle in der Halbleiterproduktionstechnik," Ph.D. dissertation, Technische Universität München, 2005, retrieved: September 2018. [Online]. Available: http://nbn-resolving.de/urn/resolver.pl?urn:nbn:de:bvb:91-diss20050808-1721087898

[18] M. Holweg, J. Davies, and A. D. Meyer, Process Theory: The Principles of Operations Management, ser. BusinessPro collection. Oxford Univ. Press, 2018.

[19] W. Hansch and T. Kubot, "Factory Dynamics Chapter 7," retrieved: September 2018. [Online]. Available: http://fac.ksu.edu.sa/sites/default/files/Factory%20Dynamics.pdf

[20] S. S. Aurand and P. J. Miller, "The operating curve: a method to measure and benchmark manufacturing line productivity," in 1997 IEEE/SEMI Advanced Semiconductor Manufacturing Conference and Workshop ASMC 97 Proceedings, Sep 1997, pp. 391–397.

[21] W. J. Hopp and M. L. Spearman, Factory Physics: Foundations of Manufacturing Management, Burr Ridge, IL, 2nd ed. Irwin/McGraw-Hill, 2001.

[22] D. Baur, W. Nagel, and O. Berger, "Systematics and Key Performance Indicators to Control a GaAs Volume Production," 2012, retrieved: September 2018. [Online]. Available: http://www.csmantech.org/Digests/2001/PDF/12_3_Berger.pdf

[23] TU Dresden, ZIH, "TU Dresden, ZIH, IT services," September 2018, retrieved: September 2018. [Online]. Available: https://tu-dresden.de/zih/dienste

[24] International Telecommunication Union/ITU Telecommunication Sector, "Standard ITU-T E.440: Terms and Definitions Related to Quality of Service and Network Performance Including Dependability – Telephone Network and ISDN Quality of Service, Network Management and Traffic," 1996, retrieved: September 2018. [Online]. Available: https://standards.globalspec.com/std/704295/itu-t-e-440/

The Various Challenges Faced by the Software Startup Industry in Saudi Arabia

Abdullah Saad H., Alqahtani
Imam Abdulrahman Bin Faisal University
Dammam, Saudi Arabia
Email: asalqahtani@iau.edu.sa

Abstract—**With the increasing use of the Internet, Web and mobile technologies at present, software startups, which are newly created software companies with no history, have become an important phenomenon in the software industry. They have a wide impact on the technology market and a significant impact on the global economy. However, even with the increase in the importance of software startups for the economy and communities, little research has investigated the challenges of this phenomenon, especially with new software markets, such as the Saudi Arabia market. This study aimed to investigate the challenges faced by the software startup industry in Saudi Arabia. It presents a mixed-methodology study based on semi-structured interviews and questionnaires. The findings of this study revealed a list of challenges that need to be considered in order to improve the industry for software startups. The lack of transparency and funding can be considered the biggest concern for software startups in Saudi Arabia.**

Keywords-Software startups; startup challenges; small software development; software industry; information startups

I. INTRODUCTION

Software startups are newly created companies with little or no history that aim to grow rapidly in the software industry [16]. Software startups aim at innovation and building software products within a limited time and with few resources [32]. Blank [9] described startups as temporary human organizations with no prior operating history that aim to create new, high-tech products or services. Software startups are considered to be an important phenomenon in the modern economy and society. This phenomenon creates approximately three million new jobs each year in the USA. Information technology companies, such as Facebook, LinkedIn, Instagram and Dropbox, are good examples of how startups can transform into successful businesses, provide tremendous support to their national economies and have a significant impact on the global economy [18]. However, about 60% of startups do not survive the first five years [16]. Early stage software startups face key challenges to success in this industry such as lack of resources and experiences [18]. The competition in the industry drives most of the startups to exit the market within two years form creation [25]. Due to the high failure rates of software startups, communities, organizations and even countries are beginning to investigate this phenomenon. There is a current need for research to support startups with their software engineering practices [25]. This study is aiming to provide deep investigation of the challenges faced by the software startup industry in Saudi Arabia in order to address the current gap of knowledge.

The remainder of this paper is structured as follows: background and previous studies is reported in Section 2. Section 3 addresses the research methodology. Results are reported in Section 4. Then the discussion is presented within Section 5. Finally, the study concludes in Section 6.

II. STATE OF THE ART

Software startups are considered to face several challenges; they may encounter obstacles when attempting to sell their first products, acquire paying customers and establish entrepreneurial teams [32]. Giardino et al. [18] highlighted several challenges for software startups, including lack of resources, lack of experience, dependence on one product, the uncertainty of their conditions, time pressure and lack of sustainability. The nature of software startups, as newly created organizations working in uncertain markets and using cutting-edge technology, make them challenging endeavors [32]. Klonowski et al. [19] investigated software startups in Central and Eastern Europe and placed the challenges into four categories, namely problems with funding, problems with management, the change in corporate culture and acceptance of the business model and financial underperformance. Giardino et al. [16] also reported that the main challenges for many startups are thriving despite technological uncertainty and finding the first paying customers. Giardino et al. [17] reported similar challenges, as well as others such as obtaining initial funding, creating entrepreneurial teams, providing value to customers, starting to make a profit and configuration management. Little relevant research pertaining to software startups exists; Pateronster studied software startups via a systematic map study and reported a few studies in the area of software startups [25]. Unterkalmsteiner et al. [32] stated that research on software startups has increased over the last year, but there is still a need for more investigation in this area.

Alnafjan [2] investigated the applied software practices in Saudi Arabia and reported clear weaknesses in adopting software engineering practices, particularly for small organizations. Alnuem [3], who also investigated the software industry in Saudi Arabia, reported serious issues in the industry, such as culture, communications and understanding the requirements clearly.

The software industry in Saudi Arabia is considered to be in the early stages. A few companies could survive in this industry. The Saudi government has established a new vision called "Vision 2030." One of its goals is to help software startups to develop a successful market in order to support the national economy. The government also aims to support e-government transformation. On the other hand, there is a gap in the current knowledge regarding challenges faced by software startups in Saudi Arabia. There is a lack of empirical updated studies that provide deep investigation of the Saudi software industry. This paper aims to investigate this area in order to provide a better understanding of the challenges software startups face and to help the community to build a better software industry.

III. RESEARCH METHODOLOGY

This paper presents a mixed-methodology study that includes both quantitative and qualitative data. Semi-structured interviews and questionnaires will be used as tools to collect data. The combination of quantitative and qualitative data aims to add more reliability and validity to the study's results. Bryman [12] referred to mixed-methods research as follows: "*This term is widely used nowadays to refer to research that combines methods associated with both quantitative and qualitative research*". Employing the mixed approach matches the study aims and objectives and should allow for a better understanding of the specific challenges of software startups in more detail. The quantitative form will provide the critical numbers and statistics needed to study the challenges, while the qualitative data will be applied as a secondary methodology to provide richer information and an explanation of the study findings. The findings from both approaches will be integrated to form a better understanding of software startup challenges.

A. *Research question*

This study aims to investigate the software industry in Saudi Arabia in order to provide a better understanding of the current barriers that software startups encounter by addressing the following research question:

RQ: What are the main challenges encountered by software startups in the Kingdom of Saudi Arabia (KSA) from the perspective of software development?

B. *Data collection*

1) *The quantitative data*

The quantitative data were collected via a self-completed online survey. About 10 people were invited to pilot the questionnaire, including project managers, software developers and testers, most of whom were experts in software development. The questionnaire was distributed during two main startup events in the KSA (the SAP Startup Focus Forum Saudi Arabia in Riyadh, 2016, and the Small and Medium Enterprise Forum in Jeddah, 2017). It was also distributed online to approximately 120 software companies in the Kingdom. By the end of the data collection phase, 74 completed and eligible responses were received. The questionnaire investigated 19 phrases, which will be treated as possible hypotheses for the challenges faced by software startups in Saudi Arabia.

TABLE I. THE RESEARCH HYPOTHESES: THE EXPECTED OBSTACLES TO SOFTWARE DEVELOPMENT BASED ON PREVIOUS STUDIES

PH1	There is a lack of communication and collaboration during all the development stages. [4][21]
PH2	The development team has estimation difficulties with the development cost, scope, and development schedule. [4] [21]
PH3	There is a lack of communication between the developers and the product owners.[4][21]
PH4	There is lack of team management skills.[16] [19]
PH5	During the development, we face issue with sharing knowledge and information. [13] [18]
PH6	There is a security risk during the development.[2] [3]
PH7	Some development teams have issues with poor infrastructures.[21][25]
PH8	The visibility level of the development progress is low. [13][18][29]
PH9	Customers sometimes do not have a clear idea for their requirement. [1][3]
PH10	There is lack of talent in the software industry in KSA. [13][17][25]
PH11	Provide high quality software is a challenge regarding the development ream's capabilities.[2][13][16]
PH12	There is lack of providing initial funding.[16] [19] [25][29]
PH13	There are barriers to access the market.[16] [17][29]
PH14	Some customers like to work with big software companies. [17][21]
PH15	Government regulations could challenge software companies. [1][3]
PH16	Software projects have issues with building a sufficient business model. [19] [25][29]
PH17	Providing products with competitive prices is a challenge. [13][19]
PH18	There is lack of information and transparency about the software market in Saudi Arabia.[13][17]
PH19	Customers are not aware of how software could add value to their business. [13][17][19][29]

These phrases represent the expected obstacles to software development based on previous studies. A five-point Likert scale was used to explore the questionnaire respondents' degrees of agreement with these challenges. Table I presents the invested hypotheses and their references from the previous studies.

2) *The qualitative data*

The qualitative data were collected via structured interviews. The interviews were face-to-face and were recorded using a voice recorder. In addition, notes of the main ideas and answers were taken during the interviews. The transcribed documents were then compared to the notes from the interviews to ensure the reliability of the data. Following this, a thematic analysis, which is an approach to identify the themes and patterns from the collected qualitative data, was conducted [11][14]. In addition, the data-driven method was selected for the thematic analysis of this study [5]. The interpretation of data has been reviewed by a ccolleague to ensure its accuracy.

IV. RESULTS

This section reports the result of this study. First of all, it states the results of the descriptive analysis. Then, it will address the result of reliability test. Finally, the quantitative results and qualitative results will be reported.

A. *Descriptive analysis*

This section describes the background information about the study participants, including their experience, team size and the location of their development teams.

1) *Development experience*

Table II shows the participants' number of years of experience in software development. Most of the participants had from four to seven years of software development experience, while about 35% had from one to four years of experience. This shows that the study's participants had substantial software development experience.

TABLE II. THE EXPERIENCE OF THE STUDY'S PARTICIPANTS

Answer	Count	Percent
Less than 1	10	13%
1-4	25	35%
4-7	33	44%
More than 7	6	8%
Total	74	100%

2) *Team size*

Table III below indicates the size of the team that developers usually have. Most of the participants (42%) came from teams with five to 15 members; the second highest figure was 15 to 25 team members (37% of the sample), while less than 13% of the sample were from teams that had more than 25 members, and only 8% of the participants came from teams with fewer than five team members. This information is expected due to the nature of startup companies' sizes.

TABLE III. THE TEAM SIZE

Answer	Count	Percent
Less than 5	7	8%
5- 15	30	42%
15-25	27	37%
25-45	3	3 %
45-60	5	7%
Greater than 60	2	3%
Total	74	100%

3) *Outsourced development*

Table IV shows that most of the study's participants had outsourced or offshore teams. About 87% of the sample explained that some of their functions were developed outside of the country. Only 10 participants did not have outsourced teams. This result could relate to the difficulty of the software industry in Saudi Arabia, which leads most companies to outsource some of their development.

TABLE IV. OUTSOURCED DEVELOPMENT

Answer	Count	Percent
Yes	64	87%
No	10	13%
Total	74	100%

B. *Reliability*

According to Bryman and Cramer [12], "*The reliability of measure refers to its consistency.*" Pallant [23] also stated, "*The reliability of a scale indicates how free it is from random error*". With multiple-item scales, such as the Likert scale, variables of internal reliability need to be tested. The aim is to examine whether each scale is measuring a single idea and how each item affects the internal consistency of the scale [12]. Cronbach's alpha coefficient has been applied to test data reliability. This shows the correlation among all the items in the scale. The ideal Cronbach's alpha level is above 0.7 [23]. Table V shows the Cronbach's alpha values for the challenges under investigation. The alpha value was 0.776, which means that the items were internally consistent.

TABLE V. RELIABILITY STATISTICS

Cronbach's Alpha	Cronbach's Alpha Based on Standardized Items	N of Items
0.776	0.784	19

C. *Quantitative results*

TABLE VI. TESTS OF NORMALITY

Phrase	Kolmogorov-Smirnova			Shapiro-Wilk		
	Statistic	df	Sig.	Statistic	df	Sig.
PH1	.358	74	.000	.745	74	.000
PH2	.278	74	.000	.856	74	.000
PH3	.249	74	.000	.828	74	.000
PH4	.250	74	.000	.868	74	.000
PH5	.239	74	.000	.865	74	.000
PH6	.240	74	.000	.890	74	.000
PH7	.279	74	.000	.875	74	.000
PH8	.240	74	.000	.866	74	.000
PH9	.269	74	.000	.861	74	.000
PH10	.269	74	.000	.881	74	.000
PH11	.410	74	.000	.681	74	.000
PH12	.427	74	.000	.652	74	.000
PH13	.369	74	.000	.755	74	.000
PH14	.298	74	.000	.848	74	.000
PH15	.250	74	.000	.853	74	.000
PH16	.255	74	.000	.868	74	.000
PH17	.307	74	.000	.821	74	.000
PH18	.292	74	.000	.805	74	.000
PH19	.336	74	.000	.800	74	.000

Table VI shows the results of the normality test. The results show that the data were not normally distributed, with a significance of less than 0.05 for both the Shapiro-Wilk and the Kolmogorov-Smirnov tests. This means that the data pertaining to those scales will be treated as nonparametric data [23]. The median and mode should be used to describe nonparametric data [10][12]. Table VII shows the mean, median and mode for each phrase. It also shows the results of testing each phrase. The hypothesis will be accepted if the median is above 2.5 and rejected if it is less than 2.5.

TABLE VII. HYPOTHESES RESULTS

Phrase	Mean	Median	Mode	Accepted or Rejected
PH1	3.11	4.00	4	Accepted
PH2	2.35	2.00	2	Rejected
PH3	3.00	3.00	4	Accepted
PH4	2.46	2.00	2	Rejected
PH5	2.43	2.00	3	Rejected
PH6	2.41	2.00	2	Rejected
PH7	2.55	2.00	2	Rejected
PH8	3.01	3.00	4	Accepted
PH9	3.15	3.00	4	Accepted
PH10	3.51	4.00	4	Accepted
PH11	3.89	4.00	4	Accepted
PH12	3.82	4.00	4	Accepted
PH13	3.80	4.00	4	Accepted
PH14	3.73	4.00	4	Accepted
PH15	3.85	4.00	4	Accepted
PH16	3.72	4.00	4	Accepted
PH17	3.95	4.00	4	Accepted
PH18	4.07	4.00	4	Accepted
PH19	3.84	4.00	4	Accepted

Table VII shows that five of the hypotheses "phrases" have been rejected (PH2, PH4, PH5, PH6 and PH7). These challenges were not considered significant based on the median value. The other 14 hypotheses were accepted and are summarized as shown in the table below; they will be discussed in the discussion section. The challenges have been ranked based on their importance according to the degree of agreement on the part of the study's participants and each phrase's mean value, as show in Table VIII.

TABLE VIII. HYPOTHESES RANK

Challenge number	Phrase number	Hypotheses
CH1	PH18	There is lack of information and transparency about the software market in Saudi Arabia
CH2	PH17	Providing products with competitive prices is a challenge.
CH3	PH11	Provide high quality software is a challenge regarding the development ream's capabilities.
CH4	PH15	Government regulations could challenge software companies
CH5	PH19	Customers are not aware of how software could add value to their business
CH6	PH12	There is lack of providing initial funding
CH7	PH13	There are barriers to access the market
CH8	PH14	Some customers like to work with big software companies.
CH9	PH16	Software projects have issues with building a sufficient business model.
CH10	PH10	There is lack of talent in the software industry in KSA.
CH11	PH9	Customers sometimes do not have a clear idea for their requirement.
CH12	PH1	There is a lack of communication and collaboration during all the development stages.
CH13	PH8	The visibility level of the development progress is low.
CH14	PH3	There is a lack of communication between the developers and the product owners.

D. *Qualitative results*

The results of the thematic analysis indicated eight main challenges, as described below:

1) *A1- Lack of funding and financial support:*

Finding sufficient financial support was considered to be one of the main issues for software startups in the KSA. Company A stated, "Providing the needed funding was one of our main concerns, you need to make sure you have enough cash flow." Company B reported that "one of our main challenges was to have enough funds to start our project. We made many meetings with investors and investment companies but, unfortunately, we could not have any financial collaboration with them. In addition, the government's financial support programmes were not sufficient and not available in many cases." Companies C and D both agreed that the funding challenge was one of the main challenges for their projects.

2) *A2- Difficulty of gaining customers' trust and access to the market:*

Company B, which was an online store, reported that "gaining customers' trust was one of the main challenges; first, it is a challenge to have people sell their product using our on-line store and secondly, it is also a challenge to have people buy from our on-line store." Company C stated, "It is a big challenge to access the market; we had our biggest challenge when we tried to sell our product." Company D also reported that signing the first contract was the biggest challenge. Company E mentioned that it had experienced tremendous competition with social media stores and that it was difficult to compete with them in terms of cost.

3) *A3- Making a product that suited the market:*

Company A said that one difficulty was creating a product that did not suit the current market. The company cited the example of having had a product "website" that worked on meta search technologies and failing to sell it to the market because the market was not ready to use this technology to compare hotel prices at the time. Thus, their product was too far ahead of the current market. A few years later, a different company developed and launched an almost identical product and experienced a huge success.

4) *A4- Lack of transparency and market information:*

Company C reported that access to information and data were also major obstacles, citing difficulty when developing a business model due to the lack of transparency in the software market.

5) *A5- Government barriers:*

Company E reported issues with the government's regulations because many steps and complicated processes are required in order to open a software startup.

6) *A6- Access to talent:*

According to Company C, graduates with degrees in software were not qualified to be professionals in the software market, and there was a lack of Saudi talent in the market. Company D's CEO, who is also a professor at one of the larger universities in the Kingdom within the software field, reported a need to create partnerships between colleges and software companies to improve the quality of colleges' graduate student outcomes. Company E reported a lack of expert graduates in the field of software development management and that no courses covering the concepts of "lean" or "agile" were offered in academic programs.

Company B used outsourced teams due to the lack of software developers in Saudi Arabia, which created other barriers in terms of language and cultural differences.

7) A7- Lack of clear ideas about customer requirements:

According to Company C, people do not have sufficient understanding regarding what software could do for their businesses. In addition, customers sometimes did not have a clear idea of their requirements. For example, many customers asked the company to compare their competitors' websites and make better websites for their companies without providing a clear idea of their requirements.

V. DISCUSSION

This section will combine the results of the descriptive analysis (quantitative results) and the results of the thematic analysis (qualitative results). It will provide a general discussion about the challenges in light of previous studies. The challenges will be classified into two main groups. Table IX shows the links between the study's results. It also organizes the challenges into two main groups. The first group contains challenges related to finance and market access, and the second is for software quality challenges.

TABLE IX. STUDY RESULTS

Group	Challenge	Related results
Funding and market access	*Lack of transparency*	CH1, A4
	lack of funding and financial support	CH6, A1
	Government regulations	CH4, A5
	Obstacles of market access	CH2, CH 7,CH8, A2, A3
Software quality and awareness	*Lack of software quality and talent*	CH3, CH9, CH10, A6
	Lacking of clear idea about customer requirement	CH1, CH5, A7
	Lack of communication and visibility	CH12, CH13, CH14

A. *Funding and transparency*

1) Lack of transparency

The quantitative results revealed the lack of information and transparency in the software market in Saudi Arabia (CH1) as one of the main challenges within the market. Startups need information and transparency in order to build their business models and develop strategies. The qualitative data supported this: (A4) "Lack of transparency and market information."

2) Lack of funding and financial support

The first challenge that software startups face is finding funding resources. This barrier was revealed to be one of the main issues according to the quantitative results (CH6), and it was also revealed to be the main concern in the qualitative results. An investigation about the startup industry in Australia reported that around 67% of startups needed financial support to survive until their second year of business, and about 41% of the startups investigated had difficulty with funding [29]. Gilardino et al. [16] reported the challenge of not having initial funding for startups.

3) Government regulations

The government's regulations were reported as a challenge for software startups (CH4 and A5). When establishing a new company, there are many regulations that make the task difficult for startups. Gilardino et al. [16] reported the same issue and agreed that government regulations need to be addressed during software startups' development phases.

4) Obstacles of market access

Accessing the market is the second phase for startups. There are barriers to accessing the market (CH7). Startups will experience challenges in gaining customers' trust (A2). They have no history and not enough experience. Customers usually prefer to work with big software names rather than with small, newly established software companies (CH8). In addition, due to a lack of experience, the software startups could have difficulty providing a product that suits the market (A3). Finally, providing products at competitive prices is a challenge (CH2). Gilardino et al. [16] referred to acquiring the first paying client as one of the main obstacles for software startups. Klonowski et al. [19] mentioned that identifying the available opportunities in the software market was not an easy task due to changes in the clients' requirements and technological uncertainty. Furthermore, the market should be accessed in a time-efficient way [19].

B. *Software quality and awareness*

1) Lack of quality software and talent

Providing high-quality software was a challenge due to the development team's capabilities (CH3). The startups had limited resources, which decreased their development capabilities. They usually had problems with building a sufficient business model (CH9). Furthermore, access to talent was a major challenge due to the lack of talent in the software industry in Saudi Arabia (CH10 and A6). Gilardino et al. [16] identified the general lack of resources as one of the main features of startups. Software startups use external solutions to address the limitations of their resources, such as outsourcing and open-source software [18]. The use of new concepts in software, such as agile methods, is poor, which could reflect on the quality of the software developed [2].

2) Lack of clears idea about customer requirements

Software startups are challenged by the lack of software awareness on the part of their customers (A7). Customers are not aware of how software could add value to their businesses (CH5). They are uncertain about paying for a software service because they are not sure how this service could improve their businesses. Furthermore, customers often lack a clear idea of their requirements.

3) Lack of communication and visibility

The results from the quantitative data showed the lack of communication and collaboration during all stages of development (CH12). The visibility level of the development progress was low (CH13). Moreover, there was a lack of communication between the developers and the product owners (CH14). The quantitative data revealed that about 88% of software projects had outsourced or offshore teams. The distance among teams affects the visibility level of development. The lack of communication could create barriers for customers when attempting to follow the progress of development and could make it difficult for developers to communicate with customers. Therefore, this could decrease the visibility of development [26]. Providing a high-quality communication channel could be expensive and add substantial costs to the project. Sometimes the development teams, particularly those offshore, experienced technical issues such as poor Internet connection or poor infrastructure. As a result, the cost of communication could be increased [35].

VI. CONCLUSION

The software startup industry in Saudi Arabia was investigated in this study. This paper applied a mixed-method approach to collect both quantitative and qualitative data. The lack of transparency and funding can be considered to be the biggest concern. There is a lack of available information about the IT industry, including the size of the market and the existing companies in the market. In addition, the government's regulations limited the startups and created serious difficulties in terms of their business models and plans. The second major difficulty experienced by software startups was access to the market. For a company with no history, gaining customers' trust was considered a major challenge. Customers also lack software awareness and are not aware of how the software can help them to grow their businesses. Furthermore, there is a lack of quality software and talent. Accessing talented people in software development in Saudi Arabia is one of the main issues for the startups. This has an impact on the software's quality and leads many startups to outsource development or to develop software offshore, which is a common practice in software development. However, this could create a lack of communication and decrease the visibility level of development.

In summary, this study reported on the main challenges experienced by software startups in Saudi Arabia, and provided a general investigation into the software industry in order to provide a better understanding of the phenomenon of software startups. This information could be useful for the Saudi government to improve their regulations to support software development industry. The first recommendation of this study is to establish funding channels, either by the government or the private sector. The current regulations need to be updated to attract more investments to the industry. Moreover, it is important to update the current software curricula in universities and computer colleges to provide more qualified developers to the community.

Future work will investigate the relationship between the challenges described and other factors affecting success in the software industry (such as cost, quality and time) in order to identify the factors for success in the Saudi software industry.

REFERENCES

[1] Adebanjo, D., 2010, "Challenges and approaches to customer development in co- located high tech start-ups", Proceedings of the International Conference on Industrial Engineering and Engineering Management (IEEM), pp. 163–167.

[2] Alnafjan, K., 2012, "An empirical investigation into the adoption of Software Engineering Practice in Saudi Arabia", International Journal of Computer Science Issues (IJCSI), vol. 9, no. 3, pp. 328-332.

[3] Alnuem, M. A., Ahmad, A. and Khan, H., 2012, "Requirements Understanding: A Challenge in Global Software Development, Industrial Surveys in Kingdom of Saudi Arabia", IEEE, ,pp. 297-305.

[4] Alqahtani, A.S., Moore, J.D., Harrison, D.K. and Wood, B.M., 2013. The Challenges of Applying Distributed Agile Software Development: A Systematic Review. International Journal of Advances in Engineering & Technology, 5(2), p.23-36.

[5] Asnawi, A., Gravell, A., and Wills, G., 2012, "Emergence of Agile methods: Perceptions from software practitioners in Malaysia" AGILE India, 2012, pp. 30-39.

[6] Bajwa, S. S., Wang, X., Duc, A.N., and Abrahamsson, P., 2017, "Failures to be celebrated: an analysis of major pivots of software startups", Empirical Software Engineering, vol. 22, no. 5, pp. 2373-2408.

[7] Barney, S., Petersen, K., Svahnberg, M., Aurum, A., and Barney, H., 2012, "Software quality trade-offs: a systematic map, Inf. Softw. Technol, pp. 651–662.

[8] Bertram, D., 2007, "Likert scales", Faculty of Mathematics, University of Belgrade.

[9] Blank, S., 2005, "The Four Steps to the Epiphany: Successful Strategies for Startups That Win". Cafepress.com.

[10] Boone, H.N., and Boone, D.A., 2012, "Analyzing Likert Data", Journal of Extension, vol. 50, no. 2, pp. 1-5.

[11] Boyatzis, R., 1998," Transforming qualitative information: Thematic analysis and code development", SAGE publications incorporated.

[12] Bryman, A., and Cramer, D., 2012, "Quantitative data analysis with IBM SPSS 17, 18 and 19: A guide for social scientists", Routledge, Psycholofy Press.

[13] Cbinsight, 2018, The Top 20 Reasons Startups Fail, from: https://www.cbinsights.com/research/startup-failure-reasons-top/

[14] Dawson, C., 2009, "Introduction to research methods: A practical guide for anyone undertaking a research project", Oxford: How To Books Ltd.

[15] Gerald, H.B., Donch, J.C., Fesnak, R., and Stiles, A.R., 2014, "Intellectual Property in Consumer Electronics", Software and Technology Startups, Springer, New York, NY.

[16] Giardino, C., Bajwa, S.S., Wang, X., and Abrahamsson, P., 2015, "Key challenges in early-stage software startups", in Proceedings 16th International XP Conference (XP). Helsinki, Finland: Springer, pp. 52-63.

[17] Giardino, C., Paternoster, N., Unterkalmsteiner, M., Gorschek, T., and Abrahamsson, P., 2016, "Software Development in Startup Companies: The Greenfield Startup Model", IEEE Transactions on Software Engineering, vol. 42, no. 6, pp. 585-604.

[18] Giardino, C., Unterkalmsteiner, M., Paternoster, N., Gorschek, T., and Abrahamsson, P., 2014, "What Do We Know about Software Development in Startups?", IEEE Software, vol. 31, no. 5, pp. 28-32.

[19] Klonowski, D., and Golebiowska-Tataj, D., 2010, "Challenges and opportunities in developing a high-tech business in Central and Eastern Europe", International Journal of Emerging Markets, vol. 5, no. 2, pp. 138-152.

[20] Lee, S., and Yong, H. S., 2010, "Distributed agile: Project management in a global environment", Empirical software engineering, Vol. 15, no. 2, pp. 204-217.

[21] Martinez, M., S., 2016. Good Practices of the Lean Startup Methodology: Benefits, challenges and recommendations, Aato University.

[22] May, B., 2012, "Applying lean startup: an experience report – lean and lean ux by a ux veteran: Lessons learned in creating and launching a complex consumer app", in: Agile Conference (AGILE), pp. 141–147.

[23] Pallant, J., 2013, "The SPSS survival manual: A step by step guide to data analysis using IBM SPSS", Open University Press McGraw-Hill Education, England.

[24] Paspallis, N., et al, 2008, "A pluggable and reconfigurable architecture for a context-aware enabling middleware system", in: Proceedings of the OTM Confederated International Conferences, pp. 553–570.

[25] Paternoster, N., Giardino, C., Unterkalmsteiner, M., Gorschek, T., and Abrahamsson, P., 2014, "Software development in startup companies: A systematic mapping study", Information and Software Technology, vol. 56, no. 10, pp. 1200-1218.

[26] Phalnikar, R., Deshpande, V., and Joshi, S., 2009, "Applying agile principles for distributed software development", Advanced computer control,. ICACC'09. International conference on IEEE, pp. 535-239.

[27] Salamzadeh, A. and Kawamorita Kesim, H., 2015. Startup companies: life cycle and challenges.

[28] Smutny, P., 2012, "Mobile development tools and cross-platform solutions", in: 13th International Carpathian Control Conference (ICCC), pp. 653–656.

[29] Startup Muster, 2015, The most comprehensive data on the Australian startup ecosystem, from:
https://www.startupmuster.com/reports

[30] Sutton, S. M., 2000, "The role of process in a software start-up." IEEE Software 17.4, pp. 33-39.

[31] Terho, H., Suonsyrja, S., Karisalo, A., and Mikkonen, T.O., 2015, "Ways to cross the rubicon: Pivoting in software startups", pp. 555-568.

[32] Unterkalmsteiner, M., et al, 2016, "Software Startups: A Research Agenda," E-Informatica Software Engineering Journal, vol. 10, (1), pp. 89-124.

[33] Unterkalmsteiner, M., et al, 2012, "Evaluation and measurement of software process improvement a systematic literature review", Trans. Softw. Eng. pp. 398–424.

[34] Wulff, M., 2015,"Startup Muster", UTS, pp. 1-18.

[35] Yoo, C., Yang, D., Kim, H., and Heo, E., 2012, "Key value drivers of startup companies in the new media industry – the case of online games in Korea", J. Media Econ. 25, pp. 244–260.

Software Engineering Education: Sharing an Approach, Experiences, Survey and Lessons Learned

José Carlos Metrôlho
R&D Unit in Digital Services, Applications and Content
Polytechnic Institute of Castelo Branco
Castelo Branco, Portugal
metrolho@ipcb.pt

Fernando Reinaldo Ribeiro
R&D Unit in Digital Services, Applications and Content
Polytechnic Institute of Castelo Branco
Castelo Branco, Portugal
fribeiro@ipcb.pt

Abstract—**To provide the best training in software engineering, several approaches and strategies are carried out. Some of them are more theoretical, learned through books and manuals, while others have a practical focus and often done in collaboration with companies. In this paper, we share an approach based on a balanced mix to foster the assimilation of knowledge, the approximation with what is done in software companies and student motivation. A survey was also carried out involving students who had successfully completed the subject in past academic years; some had already graduated, and others are still students. We analyse the results of the survey and share some of the experiences and lessons learned.**

Keywords- agile methodologies; education; software engineering; teaching; teamwork.

I. INTRODUCTION

One of the biggest challenges in teaching software engineering is empowering students with the knowledge and skills they need to be well prepared to face the labour market. This includes providing students with technical skills but also providing them with the non-technical skills associated to the software engineering process. It is also known that the teaching of software engineering cannot be limited to the presentation of concepts and methodologies as a set of abstract concepts. Wherever possible, it should be adequately complemented with the practice of software engineering projects so that the students can assimilate and understand them successfully [1]–[3] Additionally, it is important to consider the growing importance of human factors in the software development process [4] and consequently the role that some of them play in the software engineering process, namely: communication, coordination, collaboration, trust, expert recommendation, program comprehension, knowledge management and culture.

Several approaches and strategies have been proposed and used to improve the teaching and learning of software engineering. They all hold the importance of giving students hands-on experience. However, the way they propose to do so differs greatly.

This paper describes an experience in teaching Software Engineering, of a Computer Engineering program, using a project-based approach. This project-based approach is enriched with the collaboration of two software houses giving the students a real-word experience of software engineering projects development. We also try to understand how the main concepts of the course are assimilated by the students and if they are applied in the professional life of our past students. Finally, we present some lessons learned through our experience and challenges faced.

The remainder of this paper will be as follows: Section 2 presents a brief review of related work; Section 3 we present an overview of our project-based approach for software engineering; Section 4 provides a brief description of the survey that was conducted to achieve feedback from former students; In Section 5 we present the survey results and analysis; Section 6 presents some lessons learned and challenges faced and finally, in Section 7, we present some conclusions and we outline some of the future work.

II. RELATED WORK

To provide the best training in software engineering, several approaches and strategies have been proposed. Some of them are more theoretical, more focused on the study of theory through books and manuals, while others have a more practical focus and often done in collaboration with companies. Nowadays, it seems to be a well-accepted fact that the software engineering training should not be strictly focused on the theoretical study of concepts and methodologies. It is important to provide students with hands-on experience in a software engineering project and provide them with the non-technical skills in a software project. It is important to promote hands-on ability training and the rapprochement between teaching and practice. Additionally, the recent diffusion of agile methodologies in software development brings many difficulties and challenges to software engineering teaching. In this context, several authors refer that current approaches to teaching software engineering are outdated and lack authenticity [5], [6]. However, as referred in [5], it is not clear which should be the best approach and there are different perspectives with different proposed approaches. Some authors (e.g., Clear and Damian [5][7]) suggest that the best approach is to emulate the workplace through distributed software development projects, through cross-university or cross-course courses, others (e.g., [8]–[10] suggest involving students in a project where they have the possibility to experience team working and understanding in the practice of the theoretical concepts dealt with in the course and others (e.g., [11]–[13]) argue for using simulations and games to provide students with a variety of experiences that would not be possible within the constraints of an academic environment. Next, a brief analysis of some works that have been proposed for each one of the perspectives identified before is presented.

The emulation of the workplace through distributed projects or cross-university courses was approached and experienced by some authors. The DOSE [7], a Distributed and Outsourced Software Engineering course, followed an approach to teaching distributed software engineering centred in a distributed software development project. They experienced teaching software engineering using a geographically distributed software project involving various countries with different cultures, native languages and time zones. This approach gives the students the opportunity of facing the challenges of distributed software development and helps them understand typical software engineering issues, such as the importance of software requirements specifications, or the relevance of adequate system design. However, they also identify some time scheduling inconveniences, and difficulties in keeping teams committed to their peers. The Undergraduate Capstone Open Source Projects (UCOSP) program [14] ran for ten terms over six years providing for over 400 Canadian students from more than 30 schools. After this period, the authors identified some lessons they had learned: Students work on real distributed open-source projects as full members of software development teams; They use the same software development processes as regular team members and are provided with explicit mentorship from volunteer mentors from each project; Students integrate and apply the skills they have learned in their courses in a real development setting; Students develop and improve their technical communication skills in a real development setting.

A project-oriented course is followed in several software engineering training programmes. Its purpose is to teach students the theoretical and the practical aspects of developing software systems in a team environment giving students a chance to experience a work scenario that is closer to a real-world experience. A Project-Based learning in software engineering Lab, teaching through an e-Portfolio approach is described in [9]. In this approach, the e-Portfolio allows students to carry out a software project, addressing each phase collaboratively with other students and obtaining appropriate feedback from instructors. The e-Portfolio includes a single problem statement for the development of a complete software project comprising of a set of deliverables. To support the implementation, they chose the Moodle Platform. To assess the students' e-portfolios, various rubrics were implemented by scoring and weighting the sections and categories for every deliverable to be evaluated. Another project-based learning approach for teaching software engineering concepts is described in [10]. Their goal is to teach software engineering concepts using the Scrum framework in real life projects. Usually, projects have a capacity of about 1000 person-hours. To make the projects more relevant real customers were incorporated. They bring in requirements from industry and present their topics during a kick-off meeting. During the project, students work together as self- organized teams (5-7 elements). They chose an appropriate project management and team coordination process and they are only asked to use some core tools that are needed to monitor the projects.

A game-based learning methodology of teaching software engineering is presented in [12]. They suggest a methodology of two-fold use of learning games for teaching software engineers. Students, experienced in programming, develop learning games, and then they use the games that are developed for teaching the next generation of students. Students developing games learn the software development life cycle phases including testing, deployment and maintenance, they contact with customers (teachers of corresponding subjects act as customers) and users (students, learning these subjects). In their approach, they find both advantages and disadvantages. As advantages, they identify the increasing students' motivation and revealing their creativity. The main problems observed include difficulty of organization of team work especially for students of early years and lack of time for coordinating them. Schäfer [13] describes some lessons learned after two teaching periods in using scrum with gamification to learn and train the agile principles. They found that their approach has both advantages and disadvantages. Gamification is motivating and helps to bring participants with different backgrounds together in project teams. The game helps in focusing on the project management part and learning the Scrum methodology. As drawbacks, they refer to the importance of having a real external stakeholder or customer defining a project goal externally in a Scrum learning project.

There are different approaches and strategies that may be followed to provide students with the best training in software engineering. All of them agree that the theoretical study of concepts and methodologies should be complemented with hands-on experiences in a software engineering project. This would allow to provide students with a better understanding of the theoretical concepts and to provide them with the non-technical skills in software projects. However, the way different approaches propose to provide the students with the practical experience is very different. Some of them propose to emulate the workplace through distributed projects, which may involve several entities and thus provide interesting experiences in software engineering. Others suggest a project-oriented course where students can practice requirements analysis, project management, development methodologies and teamwork. Another recommendation is using simulations and games to simulate distinct scenarios in software engineering teaching and training. However, regardless of the approach or strategy, it is necessary to understand whether students have acquired the knowledge and skills they need for the performance of their duties, and whether they apply them in their professional activity in software engineering.

III. Overview of our Project-Based Approach for Software Engineering

In this case a project-based approach was adopted for teaching Software Engineering. It is part of a second year of a computer science course (undergraduate course). This is a discipline that has 5 ECTS and whose semester load is 30 hours for theoretical classes and 45 hours for laboratory classes. The focus of the adopted approach was to combine theory and practice. One teacher is responsible for the course management and theoretical lectures. In these classes, the teacher presents the concepts and methodologies and promotes discussion about them. Students are also provided with an introduction to some software development methodologies namely waterfall, Extreme Programming, SCRUM, Spiral, etc. In the assessment, this theoretical part has a weight of 40% for the final grade; the remaining 60% is from the practical component. Another teacher is responsible for the practical classes. In these classes, students acquire some practice of software engineering through the specification, design, implementation and validation of a software application, as a project for teams of 4-6 students. Scrum is the adopted agile software development methodology. The teacher acts as a product owner. Each team member has a specific function (e.g., Scrum Master, Designer, etc.). Each team develops a different project. However, all the projects are focused on the development of a game from a software engineering perspective. This is important to maintain the students motivated and engaged with the project. The first deliverable is revised to accommodate feedback from the product owner. Trello is used for project management and to track progress on tasks.

A. Additional Realism

One class of the course has been taught by professionals from software house companies. In this class, software development processes like Feature Driven Development (FDD) and Behaviour Driven Development (BDD) were approached and some of their practical aspects are discussed.

Another important initiative to enable students to get in touch with practice in software engineering is a one-day visit to the premises of another software house company. This company (Outsystems) is well-known for the software development platform they hold and that is used by many software companies worldwide. Their platform is a low-code platform for rapid application development. It is especially designed for developing applications in the context of agile projects. During this journey, students were able to have closer contact with some Scrum activities (namely Daily Scrum, Sprint, Sprint Execution) and contact with some SCRUM Roles (Scrum Master, Development Team). Professionals explain to the students what they are doing, and which technologies and tools are used to support their activities. Students also had a brief session about software cost estimation.

These events are very important since they provide students with the contact and interaction with real software engineering projects with real stakeholders. They help to improve the understanding and the assimilation of the concepts learned in the course.

B. Student evaluation

The student evaluation comprises both theoretical and practical evaluation. The theoretical evaluation is a written exam over the course material. The exam consists of 10 questions chosen from the list of 30 questions that were made available to the students at the beginning of the course. This is different from the usual practice on other courses. Most questions are reflexive questions about software engineering subjects. With this approach, the intent is to avoid students wanting to memorise the matters learned along the course period (15 weeks). Also, it is desirable that students learn and acquire knowledge for a long-life period, mainly to be used after graduation on their job integration experience. In section V some gathering data that wants to evaluate results about the achievement to this goal of our approach will be presented.

For the practical evaluation, along the semester, during the 15 working weeks, students´ working teams develop the product on 6 sprints (sprints here are defined as having 2 weeks each). The teacher (i.e. product owner) meets with each team at the end of the sprint to evaluate the work in progress, the achievements and the goals for the next sprint. The team works in class (3h/week) and out of class. Half way through the semester, after sprint 4, and at the end of the semester, after sprint 7, each team has an assessment session were both teachers are present to evaluate different parameters. Some of the parameters are: clear goals, state of the art, requirements (functional and non-functional), software development process (roles, artefacts, timings, hits and misses), team member´s description (roles, skills) task scheduling (monitoring using Trello tool), modelling (user stories), implementation (code), budget (estimated based on the lesson learned during the visit to the company referred to on the previous section of this paper), conclusions (pros and cons) and future work, used literature and citation on the final report, and final presentation and discussion.

One of the achievements that sometimes students realize is learning from mistakes. For instance, if they do not communicate within the team the achieved results are poor, when compared with other more cohesive teams. On the other hand, in collaboration with the "Scrum Master" of the team, a deeper evaluation to eventually gave different grades within the members of the team.

IV. Knowledge Assimilation and Practice

In order to gauge the post-retention cognitive load, a survey of former students was conducted in order to obtain feedback on the importance of the subject to the current professional activity (of those who finished the course and work in the area), and also to know if the knowledge transmitted in the theoretical classes remains. For this last component, the survey included questions that had been already used in the theoretical evaluation of the course. The answers were evaluated with the same evaluation criteria, graded in a scale of 0-20. The questions were selected from the same set of 30 questions referred to in Section III-B. Respondents were informed that the results were for one study and would not be disclosed to third parties. They were asked to respond without recourse to extra help, because what was at issue was whether the concepts and knowledge remained present. The survey was also used to gather insights about the usefulness of the course for the practical life of each graduate. Thus, questions about aspects that may be used in the day to day of their professional activities in the companies where they currently work, were included in the survey.

A. *Survey Description*

The survey was designed to be direct to our objectives and be filled quickly and simply. Some questions were answered in free text (case of questions of theoretical knowledge) and others are multiple choice questions (e.g., used software methodologies). The survey was organized in three parts: Questions about the current professional activity of the respondents; theoretical questions about software engineering; and space for feedback on the importance of topics in their current professional life (for those who had already finished the course).

As examples of questions, we asked if the graduated students are working. If yes, we asked about that actual tasks in their companies (planning, requirements, analysis, design, Code, Quality Control, Tester, Project Management, other), the used methodologies (waterfall, SCRUM, XP, Prototyping, Spiral, FDD, Lean, RUP, other, none). About the theoretical questions we asked about the fundamentals of Software Engineering, Software Quality, Verifications vs Validation, traditional vs Agile, team dimensions and roles, among other questions and feedback.

V. Survey Results and Analysis

This section presents the results gathered in the survey and highlights some of the main findings.

A. *Data Collection/Methodology*

As a universe of respondents, surveys were sent to 97 students. Of these, 56 were undergraduate students (although they had passed in this subject) and 41 graduated.

The survey was done online, using the *LimeSurvey* webtool.

The response rate was of 24.4% of the graduated students and of 21,4% of the undergraduate students.

It is important to note also that some respondents did not answered to all questions.

B. *Results and Analysis*

Figure 1 shows the activities the respondents are involved in in their work. 84% of the respondents are involved in more than one activity. 50% of them are involved in planning, analysis and testing but they are not involved in implementation.

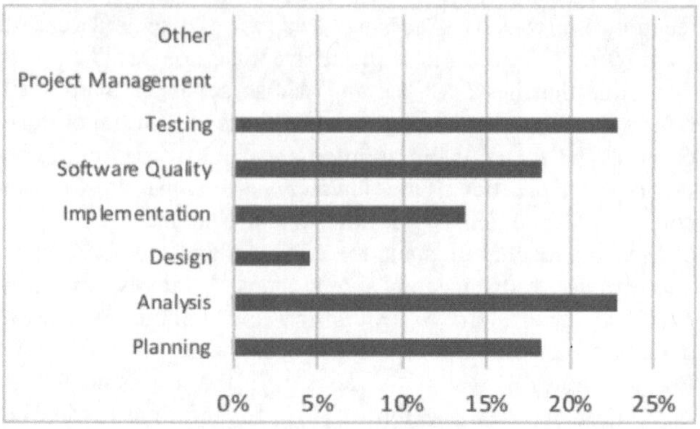

Figure 1. Activities carried out.

Students were also asked to identify the software development methodologies they use in their activities. They were able to identify the methodologies they use considering a list of given methodologies. Results are presented in Figure 2.

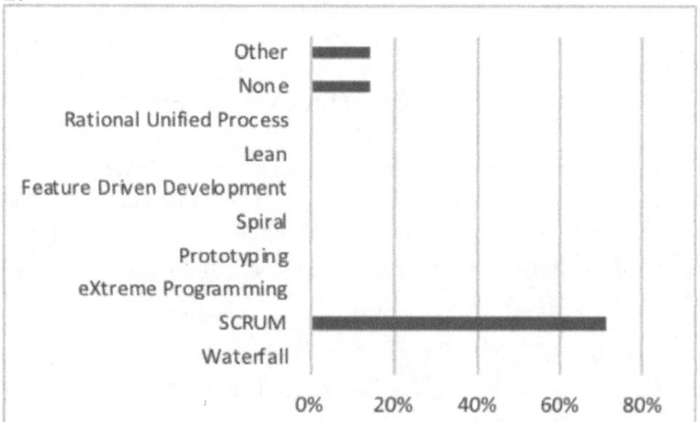

Figure 2. Software development methodologies.

More than 70% of the respondents refer that they use the Scrum methodology. This appears to be in line with the results presented in the "12th annual State of Agile report" [15] that refer that 52% of respondents stated that more than half of the teams in their organizations are using agile practices. And it is also in accordance with the results presented in another survey of more than 2,000 active Scrum and Agile practitioners [16]. This study refers that 94% of agile users use the Scrum approach in their agile practice (78% use Scrum with other approaches).

With respect to the importance of the subjects learned in the course, 87.5 percent, of the 8 graduated students that respond to this question, said that the content learned in the course has been considerably useful for their actual professional activity (see Figure 3).

The second part of the survey was related to theoretical questions about software engineering. This part was evaluated in a 0-20 scale and we compare these results with the results achieved by the same individual during the course. We consider the individual "maintained" if *(grade achieved in the course -1.5 ≤ grade achieved in the survey ≤ (grade achieved in the course +1.5).*

After evaluating the answers to the questions, we conclude that there is a majority (58%) that has maintained or increased the result (41% maintained, 17% increased) (see Figure 4).

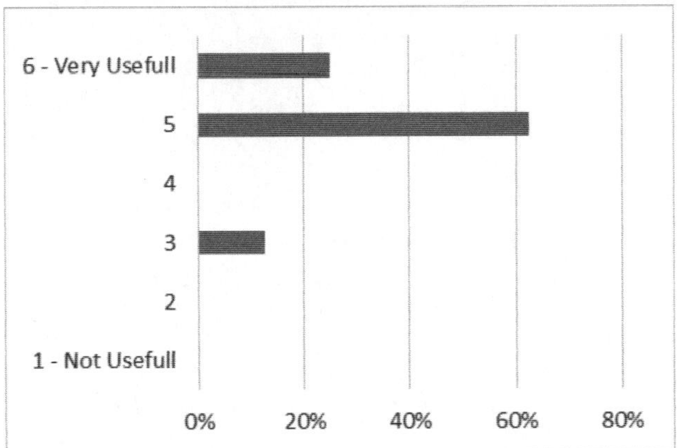

Figure 3. Course content vs profissional activity.

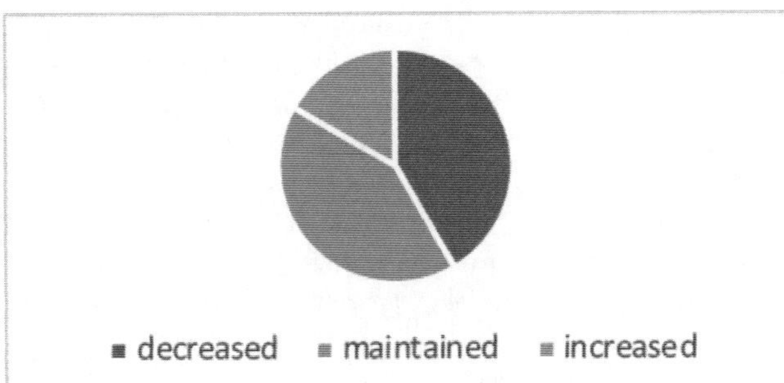

Figure 4. Grades evolution (not graduated respondents).

In the case of students already graduated, the results, presented in Figure 5, are better (less cases (37,5%) of lowering grades). Despite the long period of time after they attend the course, this is probably a consequence of the practical experience they get in the field of software development.

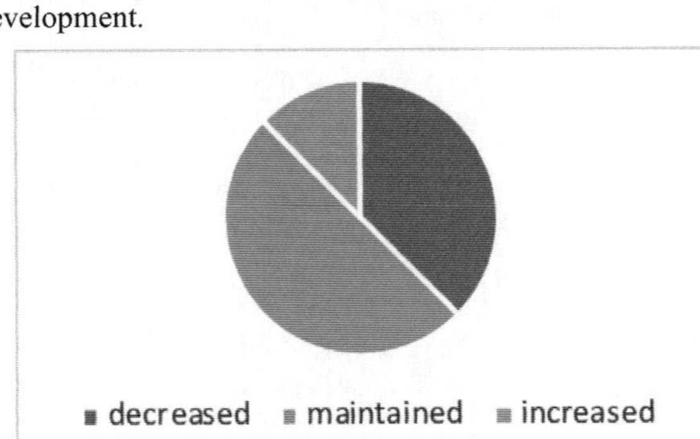

Figure 5. Grades evolution (graduated respondents).

VI. Lessons Learned and Challenges Faced

The contributions of this paper are in the form of the lessons learnt, which may be seen as guidance for others looking to approximate the know-how of students to the methods and techniques used by software companies. In summary, these are:

- Students should learn by doing and, wherever possible, software engineering principles should be assessed in the context of practical work, rather than by regurgitating material taught or extracted from text books.
- Students must have well defined and known goals. The assessment of the theoretical subjects does not need to be a surprise in the exam.
- Opening classes to external stakeholders (by promoting talks or visiting companies) during the last part of the semester helps students to reinforce knowledge (some of which are not in books) and motivate them to the subjects.
- It is very important to get feedback from past students and evaluate if the transmitted concepts and knowledge are still there, and if it was improved by the work experience in the labour market.
- It is important to choose projects that are of interest to the students and that can motivate them and involve them in their development. Projects that are related to games development can be very interesting.

However, during our experience, we faced challenges like:

- Difficulty to maintain all team members equally motivated and engaged in the same way throughout the entire project development period;
- Keeping all students involved in the project. Some students may drop out, leaving the team during the semester, and affecting the workflow and scheduling of the remaining members of the team;
- Allowing students to experience various roles within the team. It is necessary to find a way to rotate the roles of each one within the team, to avoid each student being too focused on just one role. It is important that everyone experiences a diversity, as broad as possible, of different roles;
- Allowing students to experience different methodologies in real environments. More field trips and contact with companies that use different methodologies, must be promoted to foster more diversity of experiences.

VII. Conclusions and Future Work

Our survey was the starting point of a reflexion about the impact of the approach followed in previous years in the course of Software Engineering. Based on the results, we think that allowing students to know the pool of questions in advance, fosters the students on important knowledge in the field and to understand these items, that we want students to maintain over a long period of time.

In future, the pool of questions will be increased to improve the effect of randomisation for the next exams. As for the practical component, based on the results, Scrum is still used as a case study since it is one of the most used processes by companies where our graduated students work. We will work to increase the number of respondents on the survey. Also, in future we will also extend and analyse data from a survey done to the employees of our graduated students and reach more feedback to improve and actualize the contents of this course.

REFERENCES

[1] R. Chatley and T. Field, "Lean Learning: Applying Lean Techniques to Improve Software Engineering Education," in *Proceedings of the 39th International Conference on Software Engineering: Software Engineering and Education Track*, 2017, pp. 117–126.

[2] S. D. Zorzo, L. de Ponte, and D. Lucrédio, "Using scrum to teach software engineering: A case study," in *2013 IEEE Frontiers in Education Conference (FIE)*, 2013, pp. 455–461.

[3] M. Kuhrmann and J. Münch, "Enhancing Software Engineering Education Through Experimentation: An Experience Report." 2018.

[4] C. Amrit, M. Daneva, and D. Damian, "Human factors in software development: On its underlying theories and the value of learning from related disciplines; A Guest Editorial Introduction to the Special Issue," *Inf. Softw. Technol.*, vol. 56, no. 12, pp. 1537–1542, 2014.

[5] S. Beecham, T. Clear, D. Damian, J. Barr, J. Noll, and W. Scacchi, "How Best to Teach Global Software Engineering? Educators Are Divided," *IEEE Softw.*, vol. 34, no. 1, pp. 16–19, 2017.

[6] F. Matthes, C. Neubert, C. Schulz, C. Lescher, J. Contreras, R. Laurini, B. Rumpler, D. Sol, and K. Warendorf, "Teaching Global Software Engineering and International Project Management - Experiences and Lessons Learned from Four Academic Projects," *3rd Int. Conf. Comput. Support. Educ. CSEDU 2011*, p. 12, 2011.

[7] M. Nordio, C. Ghezzi, B. Meyer, E. Di Nitto, G. Tamburrelli, J. Tschannen, N. Aguirre, and V. Kulkarni, "Teaching Software Engineering Using Globally Distributed Projects: The DOSE Course," in *Proceedings of the 2011 Community Building Workshop on Collaborative Teaching of Globally Distributed Software Development*, 2011, pp. 36–40.

[8] D. Dahiya, "Teaching Software Engineering: A Practical Approach," *SIGSOFT Softw. Eng. Notes*, vol. 35, no. 2, pp. 1–5, 2010.

[9] J. A. Macias, "Enhancing Project-Based Learning in Software Engineering Lab Teaching Through an E-Portfolio Approach," *IEEE Trans. Educ.*, vol. 55, no. 4, pp. 502–507, 2012.

[10] A. Heberle, R. Neumann, I. Stengel, and S. Regier, "Teaching agile principles and software engineering concepts through real-life projects," in *2018 IEEE Global Engineering Education Conference (EDUCON)*, 2018, pp. 1723–1728.

[11] M. Yampolsky and W. Scacchi, "Learning Game Design and Software Engineering Through a Game Prototyping Experience: A Case Study," in *Proceedings of the 5th International Workshop on Games and Software Engineering*, 2016, pp. 15–21.

[12] O. Shabalina, N. Sadovnikova, and A. Kravets, "Methodology of teaching software engineering: Game-based learning cycle," *Proc. - 2013 IEEE 3rd East. Eur. Reg. Conf. Eng. Comput. Based Syst. ECBS-EERC 2013*, pp. 113–119, 2013.

[13] U. Schäfer, "Training scrum with gamification: Lessons learned after two teaching periods," in *2017 IEEE Global Engineering Education Conference (EDUCON)*, 2017, pp. 754–761.

[14] R. Holmes, M. Craig, K. Reid, and E. Stroulia, "Lessons Learned Managing Distributed Software Engineering Courses," in *Companion Proceedings of the 36th International Conference on Software Engineering*, 2014, pp. 321–324.

[15] VersionOne Inc, "12th annual State of Agile report," 2018.

[16] Scrum Alliance, "STATE OF SCRUM 2017-2018. Scaling and agile transformation.," 2017.

Multi-Clustering in Fast Collaborative Filtering Recommender Systems

Urszula Kużelewska

Bialystok University of Technology,
15-351 Bialystok, Wiejska 45a, Poland
Email: u.kuzelewska@pb.edu.pl

***Abstract*—Searching the huge amount of information available on the Internet is undoubtedly a challenging task. A lot of new Web sites are created every day, containing not only text, but other types of resources: e.g., songs, movies or images. As a consequence, a simple search result list from search engines becomes insufficient. Recommender systems are the solution supporting users in finding items, which are interesting for them. These items may be information as well as products, in general. The main distinctive feature of recommender systems is taking into account the personal needs and tastes of users. Collaborative filtering approach is based on users' interactions with the electronic system. Its main challenge is generating on-line recommendations in reasonable time when coping with a large data size. Appropriate tools to support recommender systems in increasing time efficiency are clustering algorithms, which find similarities in off-line mode. Commonly, this causes a decrease in prediction accuracy of the final recommendations. This article presents a high time efficiency approach based on multi-clustered data, which avoids negative consequences. The input data is represented by clusters of similar items or users, where one item or user may belong to more than one cluster. When recommendations are generated, the best cluster for the user or item is selected. The best cluster means that the user or item is the most similar to the center of the cluster. As a result, the final accuracy is not decreased.**

***Index Terms*—Recommender systems; Multi-clustering; Collaborative filtering.**

I. Introduction

Recommender Systems (RS) are electronic applications with the aim to generate for a user a limited list of items from a large item set. The list is constructed basing on the active user's and other users' past behaviour. People interact with recommender systems by visiting web sites, listening to music, rating items, doing shopping, reading items' description, selecting links from search results. This behaviour is registered as access log files from Web servers, or values in databases: direct ratings for items, the numbers of song plays, content of shopping basket, etc. After each action users can see different, adapted to them, recommendation lists depending on their tastes [1].

Recommender systems are used for many purposes in various areas. They offer great opportunities for business, government, education, e-commerce, leisure activities and other domains, with successful developments in commercial applications [2]. Recommender systems are often used in e-shops proposing products, which are the most similar to the content of customers' shopping baskets. Some examples include: a shopping assistant on website Qwikshop.com [3] and a mobile personalized recommender system to suggest new products to supermarket shoppers [4]. A practical example is also What2Buy [5] which contains results of a recommender system deployed in an e-store. Multimedia services, such as Netflix [6] or Spotify [7], are places, where recommendations are extremely helpful. A music recommender is described in [8] and a method applied in MoveLens system in [9].

Scalability and performance are key metrics for deploying a recommender system in a real environment [10]. Although they are precise, CF techniques are not time effective, because they calculate items for suggestion by searching similar users or items in the whole archived data. They deal with large amount of dynamic data, however the time of results generation should be reasonable to apply them in real-time applications. A user reading news expects to see the next offer for him/her in seconds, after analysis of millions of archived news.

Clustering algorithms can be used to increase neighbour searching efficiency and thus to decrease the time of recommendations generation. A drawback is that the quality of predictions is usually slightly reduced in comparison to k-Nearest Neighbours (kNN) neighbourhood identification strategy [11] [12]. The reason is due to the way clustering algorithms work. The typical approach is based on one partitioning scheme, which is generated once and then not updated significantly. The neighbourhood of data located on borders of clusters is not modelled precisely (see Figure 1).

To improve the quality of the neighbourhood modelling one can use multiple clustering schemes and select the most appropriate one to the particular data object. As a result, multi-clustering approach eliminates the inconvenience of decreased quality of predictions while keeping a high time effectiveness. Figure 2 presents two different clustering results for the same dataset. For a particular data object, one can select the scheme with this object located closer to the cluster center, thus having more neighbours around.

This paper contains results of experiments on a collaborative filtering recommender system, which is based on similarities among items identified a priori as multi-clusters. The aim of the experiments is to improve quality of recommendation systems (which is typically measured by Root Mean Squared

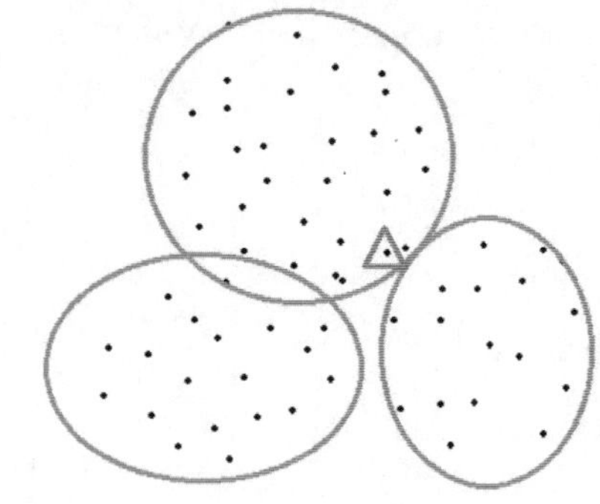

Fig. 1. Inadequate neighbourhood modelling for data located on cluster border in case of conventional k-means clustering

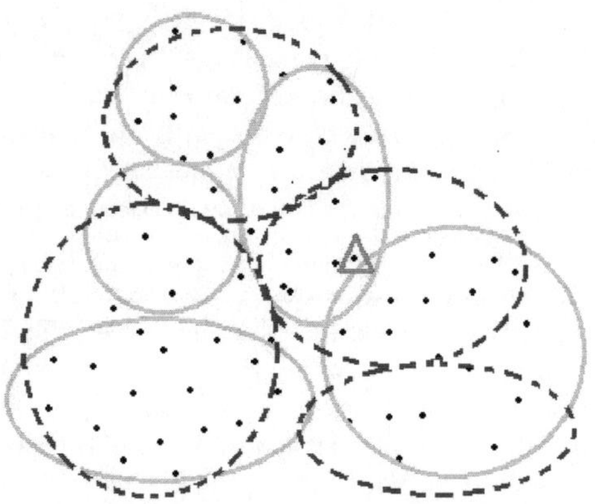

Fig. 2. Various neighbourhood modelling for particular data in case of k-means multi-clustering

Error - RMSE - of estimated vs real ratings) as well as to maintain a short time for recommendations generation (due to a real application - recommender systems in WWW services).

The set of clustering schemes was generated by k-means algorithm with the same values of their input parameters at every time. While searching the most similar items, every cluster is examined, and the one in which the appropriate items are the most similar to the center is selected.

The rest of the paper is organised as follows: Section II describes general aspects in recommendation systems, including problems in this domain and the role of clustering and multi-clustering algorithms. This section contains a description of related work, as well. The following section, Section III describes the proposed approach, whereas Section IV contains the results of the performed experiments. The last section concludes the paper.

II. Determining Neighbourhood in a Collaborative Filtering Domain - Related Work

Collaborative Filtering (CF) techniques search similarities among users or items based on archives of registered users' behaviour. As an example, similar users have mostly the same products in their baskets and similar items are bought by the same customers. Collaborative filtering methods can be classified into model-based and memory-based. The first category builds a model on the ratings, which is then used in the process of generating recommendations. The other category calculates recommendations by searching similar users or items in the whole archived dataset.

Recommender systems face many challenges and problems. The most important one, from the point of view of on-line recommendations, is scalability. Despite dealing with large amounts of dynamic data, recommender systems should generate results reasonably fast to be used in real-time applications. Nowadays, internet users are used to immediate displaying of each website. The most effective recommender systems are hybrid approaches, which combine at least two different methods that are complement to one another. Complementarity means that if one of the methods has a drawback or weakness in a certain area, then the other one has the considered features strong [1]. Clustering algorithms are good tools to analyze the neighborhood before a proper recommendation process, positively influencing its scalability [11].

A. Clustering Methods

Clustering has been and continues to be an important subject of research in the area of recommender systems [12]. The most often used method in memory-based collaborative filtering to identify neighbours is the kNN algorithm, which requires calculating distances between an active user and all the registered ones. In contrast, clustering (in model-based collaborative filtering) reduces computation time, due to the introduction of clusters models.

There are two approaches, which apply clustering in the recommender systems domain, namely: Cluster-based and Cluster-only [13]. In both, the computation efficiency of systems increases as the clustering phase is performed off-line. The first approach is the most common one and focuses only on time efficiency improvement; this is achieved by the application of clustering to find the neighbourhood of active users. Further generation of a recommendation list for the particular active user is performed by memory-based collaborative filtering methods. The process is executed on part of input data and identifies the most similar cluster. The final precision of recommendations can be lower in comparison with memory-based collaborative filtering. The second approach uses clustering as a main module of a recommender system. The partitioning applied on input data builds its model and further calculations are performed only on this model. The final precision of recommendations can be also lower in comparison with memory-based collaborative filtering methods.

B. Multi-Clustering Model of Data

Multi-clustering or alternative clustering is variously defined in literature. This term is usually used to describe the clustering, which is different than a typical partitioning based only on a single scheme. It can be a technique which tries to find different partitioning schemes on the same data, as well as a method that combines the results from clustering items' description with clustering users' demographic data. Bailey [14] provided a thorough survey on alternative clustering methods.

An example of multi-clustering algorithm is COALA (Constrained Orthogonal Average Link Algorithm) [15] that searches for alternative clusterings of better quality and dissimilarity with respect to the given clustering. It starts by treating each object as a single cluster and then iteratively merges a pair of the most similar clusters. The idea bases on $cannot - link$ constraints that guide the generation of a new, dissimilar clustering. Another example is MSC (Multiple Stable Clusterings) [16] that generates stable multiple clusterings. The advantage of this method is that it does not require to specify the number of clusters and provides users a feature subspace to understand each clustering solution.

The advantages of multi-clustering methods can be beneficial to the recommender systems domain. The better quality of the neighbourhood modelling leads to high quality of predictions keeping high time effectiveness provided by clustering methods. Despite of this, there are few publications describing application multi-clustering methods in recommendations.

The method described in [17] combines content-based and collaborative filtering approaches to recommendations. The system uses multi-clustering, however it is interpreted as a single scheme clustering on the following input data: items' description, users' information and item-user ratings matrix. It groups the items and the users based on their content, then uses the result, which is represented by the fuzzy set, to create an item group-rating matrix and a user group-rating matrix. As a clustering algorithm, it uses k-means combined with a fuzzy set theory to represent the level of membership (which is a number from the interval [0,1]) an object has to the cluster. Then, finally, the prediction rating matrix is calculated to represent the whole dataset. In the last step of this process, k-means is used again on the new rating matrix to find a group of similar users. The groups represent the neighbourhood of users in order to reduce a search space for collaborative filtering method.

Another algorithm is presented in [18]. The authors observed that users might have different interests over topics, thus might share similar preferences with different groups of users over different sets of items. The Co-Clustering For Collaborative Filtering (CCCF) method first clusters users and items into several subgroups, where each subgroup includes a set of like-minded users and a set of items in which these users share their interests. The groups are analysed by collaborative filtering methods and the resulting recommendations are aggregated over all the subgroups.

III. The Algorithm Used in the Experiments

The recommendation algorithm proposed in this article is composed of two steps. The first step (off-line) prepares the set of neighbourhoods of the most similar users in the form of a set of many clustering schemes. The method k-means is run several times with the same value of the k parameter. The results are stored as an input for the recommendation process.

In the second step, while calculating items for recommendation for a particular user, the most appropriate neighbourhood is selected for searching for the candidates. The level of adequacy is calculated as a value of similarity between the particular user and a cluster centre. As a similarity value (1) it can be used one of several common measures, e.g based on Euclidean distance, cosine value, Pearson correlation, LogLikehood based, Tanimoto, adopted from mathematical applications [19].

$$\mu_{x_i} = \frac{\sum_{q \in V(x_i)} r(x_{iq})}{|V(x_i)|} \tag{1}$$

An example similarity formula based on Pearson correlation is as follows (2):

$$sim_P(x_i, x_j) = \frac{\sum_{k \in V_{ij}} r_{ik} \cdot r_{jk}}{\sqrt{\sum_{k \in V_{ij}} (r_{ik})^2} \cdot \sqrt{\sum_{k \in V_{ij}} (r_{jk})^2}} \tag{2}$$

where $V_{ij} = V(x_i) \cap V(x_j)$ is a set of ratings present in both user's vectors: i and j, $r_{ik} = r(x_{ik}) - \mu_{x_i}$ and $r_{jk} = r(x_{jk}) - \mu_{x_j}$.

In the recommendation list generation process, a similarity measure is estimated in the same way like it was described above. Then, the candidate clusters are searched by the collaborative filtering item-based technique, but only within the cluster.

The recommendation step of the algorithm is described in Algorithm 1. The input set contains data of n users, who rated a subset of items - $A = \{a_1, \ldots, a_k\}$. The set of possible ratings - V - contains values $v_1, \ldots, v_c$. The input data are clustered ncs times into nc clusters every time giving as a result a set of clustering schemes CS. The algorithm generates a list of recommendations R_{x_a} for the active user.

IV. Experiments

This section contains the results of experiments with multi-clustering recommender system with respect to quality of recommendations and time effectiveness. Quality of recommendations was calculated with the Root Mean Square Error (RMSE) measure in the following way. For every user from the input set, their ratings were divided into training (70%) and testing parts. The values from the testing parts were removed and estimated with the selected recommender system. The difference between the original and the estimated number is taken for calculations. The time effectiveness is measured as the average time of generating recommendations list composed of 5 elements for every of 100 users. The tests were performed on a computer with Windows 7 OS, running on Intel Core i7 3.40 GHz with 8 GB of RAM.

Algorithm 1: A general algorithm of a recommender system based on multi-clustering used in the experiments

Data:
- $U = (X, A, V)$ - matrix of clustered data, where $X = \{x_1, \ldots, x_n\}$ is a set of users, $A = \{a_1, \ldots, a_k\}$ is a set of items and $V = \{v_1, \ldots, v_c\}$ is a set of ratings values,
- $\delta : v \in V$ - a similarity function,
- $nc \in [2, n]$ - a number of clusters,
- $ncs \in [2, \infty]$ - a number of clustering schemes,
- $CS = \{CS_1, \ldots, CS_{ncs}\}$ - a set of clustering schemes,
- $CS_i = \{C_1, \ldots, CS_{nc}\}$ - a set of clusters for a particular clustering scheme,
- $CS_r = \{c_{r,1}, \ldots, c_{r,nc \cdot ncs}\}$ - the set of cluster centres,

Result:
- R_{x_a} - a list of recommended items for an active user x_a,

begin

$\delta_1..\delta_{ncs} \longleftarrow$ calculateSimilarity(x_a, CS_r, δ);
$C \longleftarrow$ findTheBestCluster($\delta_1..\delta_{ncs}, CS$);
$R_{x_a} \longleftarrow$ recommend(x_a, C, δ);

The clustering algorithm as well as the recommendation system were created using Apache Mahout library [20]. The methods were tested with various similarity measures implemented in Apache Mahout: Euclidean based ($Eucl$), cosine coefficient (Cos), Pearson correlation measure (Prs), CityBlock (CBl), Tanimoto (Ta) and loglikehood (LL) similarity.

Recommendations were executed on benchmark LastFM music data [21]. The whole set contains over 16 million ratings: 345 652 users who rated 158 697 songs. The data was split into several smaller sets presented in Table I.

TABLE I. DESCRIPTION OF DATA USED IN THE EXPERIMENTS

Name of dataset	Number of users	Number of items	Number of ratings
100k	2032	22 174	99 998
500k	10 236	49 602	499 992
1M	20 464	66 798	999 981
2M	40 914	86 348	1 999 960
3M	61 367	98 924	2 999 945

First, the data was used as input to the traditional collaborative filtering item-based system. Tables II and III contain results of RMSE values and time (in s) of execution while generating 5 recommendation elements.

The next experiment compared the previous results with the results of the recommender system with modelling of neighbourhood by k-means clusters from a single clustering scheme. Tables IV and V contain results of RMSE values and time (in s) of execution while generating 5 recommendation elements. It can be noticed that in every case of the second experiment RMSE is greater than in the first one, regardless of type of similarity measure. However, the time needed to generate 5 recommendation elements is a few hundred times lower than in the first experiment.

TABLE II. RMSE OF ITEM BASED COLLABORATIVE FILTERING RECOMMENDATIONS

Number of cases in data	*Similarity Measure*					
	LL	*Cos*	*Prs*	*Eucl*	*CBl*	*Ta*
100k	0.58	0.58	0.61	0.48	0.58	0.58
500k	0.58	0.58	0.57	0.51	0.58	0.58
1M	0.58	0.58	0.56	0.52	0.58	0.58
2M	0.58	0.58	0.56	0.52	0.58	0.58
3M	0.58	0.58	0.56	0.53	0.58	0.58

TABLE III. TIME [S] OF ITEM BASED COLLABORATIVE FILTERING RECOMMENDATIONS

Number of in data	*Similarity Measure*					
	LL	*Cos*	*Prs*	*Eucl*	*CBl*	*Ta*
100k	0.090	0.125	0.127	0.121	0.071	0.077
500k	0.71	1.02	1.03	1.03	0.663	0.677
1M	1.774	2.718	2.791	2.800	1.761	1.789
2M	4.587	10.186	10.250	7.954	5.782	5.788
3M	6.516	16.021	16.820	8.020	6.210	6.272

TABLE IV. RMSE OF ITEM BASED COLLABORATIVE FILTERING RECOMMENDATIONS WITH NEIGHBOURHOOD DETERMINED BY K-MEANS

Number of clusters	*Similarity Measure*					
	LL	*Cos*	*Prs*	*Eucl*	*CBl*	*Ta*
20	0.65	0.65	0.64	0.64	0.65	0.66
50	0.67	0.67	0.67	0.66	0.67	0.68
100	0.68	0.67	0.67	0.66	0.68	0.67
400	0.65	0.65	0.64	0.63	0.63	0.65
1000	0.66	0.64	0.65	0.62	0.65	0.66

TABLE V. TIME [S] OF ITEM BASED COLLABORATIVE FILTERING RECOMMENDATIONS WITH NEIGHBOURHOOD DETERMINED BY K-MEANS

Number of clusters	*Similarity Measure*					
	LL	*Cos*	*Prs*	*Eucl*	*CBl*	*Ta*
20	0.017	0.019	0.018	0.019	0.015	0.016
50	0.026	0.027	0.027	0.027	0.024	0.024
100	0.011	0.012	0.011	0.011	0.010	0.010
400	0.036	0.041	0.035	0.040	0.035	0.035
1000	0.010	0.02	0.020	0.020	0.010	0.010

The following experiment was based on 3 clustering schemes generated for 20 and 200 clusters. The dataset used for this experiment contained 100 000 ratings ($100k$). Tables VI and VII contain RMSE and time of recommender system executed separately for every scheme. It is visible that the obtained values differ in all cases of schemes generated for the same number of clusters. Different values of RMSE indicate that, by selecting a suitable clustering scheme, particularly for each active user, it is possible to decrease that value.

The last experiment concerns generating recommendation based on a set of 3 clustering schemes (multi-clustering) generated for 20 and 200 clusters. The dataset used for this experiment is the same - $100k$. Tables VIII and IX contain RMSE and time of recommender system executed for multi-clustering. The time is slightly greater than in the experiments where the neighbourhood was modelled by a single clustering scheme, however the value of RMSE is tremendously lower.

TABLE VI. RMSE OF ITEM BASED COLLABORATIVE FILTERING RECOMMENDATIONS WITH NEIGHBOURHOOD DETERMINED BY K-MEANS PERFORMED FOR SELECTED SCHEMES

Number of clusters	*LL*	*Cos*	*Prs*	*Eucl*	*CBl*	*Ta*
20 (1)	0.637	0.640	-	0.480	0.660	0.660
20 (2)	0.644	0.642	3.36	0.486	0.672	0.672
20 (3)	0.638	0.637	-	0.483	0.663	0.663
200 (1)	0.963	0.954	0.500	0.870	1.004	0.995
200 (2)	0.717	0.716	4.876	0.565	0.753	0.754
200 (3)	0.682	0.682	-	0.545	0.724	0.727

TABLE VII. TIME [S] OF ITEM BASED COLLABORATIVE FILTERING RECOMMENDATIONS WITH NEIGHBOURHOOD DETERMINED BY K-MEANS PERFORMED FOR SELECTED SCHEMES

Number of clusters	*LL*	*Cos*	*Prs*	*Eucl*	*CBl*	*Ta*
20 (1)	0.05	0.051	0.053	0.052	0.050	0.049
20 (2)	0.048	0.049	0.052	0.049	0.057	0.047
20 (3)	0.047	0.049	0.052	0.050	0.048	0.046
200 (1)	0.0002	0.0001	0.0002	0.0002	0.0001	0.0002
200 (2)	0.027	0.025	0.026	0.025	0.025	0.024
200 (3)	0.024	0.049	0.052	0.050	0.048	0.046

The experiments proved that the application multi-clustering in recommender systems and dynamic selection the most suitable clusters is very promising and worthy of further research. Figures 3 and 4 depict the summary of values from our experiments. The charts compare all of the examined methods to determine a neighbourhood: k-Nearest Neighbours (IB), k-means single clustering ($IBSC$), k-means multi-clustering ($IBMC$). The multi-clustering approach, even though it takes additional time for dynamic selection of the most suitable clusters, is very valuable due to its extremely low value of RMSE (green and yellow columns in 3 and 4). In case of greater number of clusters (200) the error is bigger, but the processing time is lower.

TABLE VIII. RMSE OF ITEM BASED COLLABORATIVE FILTERING RECOMMENDATIONS WITH NEIGHBOURHOOD DETERMINED BY MULTI-CLUSTERING K-MEANS

Number of clusters	*LL*	*Cos*	*Prs*	*Eucl*	*CBl*	*Ta*
20	0.15	0.15	-	0.11	0.15	0.15
200	0.18	0.18	-	0.16	0.19	0.19

TABLE IX. TIME [S] OF ITEM BASED COLLABORATIVE FILTERING RECOMMENDATIONS WITH NEIGHBOURHOOD DETERMINED BY MULTI-CLUSTERING K-MEANS

Number of clusters	*LL*	*Cos*	*Prs*	*Eucl*	*CBl*	*Ta*
20	0.0633	0.0707	0.0673	0.0668	0.0717	0.0693
200	0.0316	0.0600	0.0411	0.0323	0.0545	0.0404

V. CONCLUSION

Clustering algorithms support recommender systems in increasing time efficiency and scalability. This benefit usually involves decreased accuracy of prediction while generating recommendations. It results from inaccurate modelling of object neighbourhood in case of data located on borders of clusters. Multi-clustering approach eliminates the inconvenience of decreased quality of predictions while maintaining a high time effectiveness.

This article presented an approach based on multi-clustered data, which prevents the negative consequences, keeping high time efficiency. The neighbourhood is modelled by multiple clustering schemes and the most appropriate one to the particular data object is selected for recommendations. The results confirmed a significant reduction of RMSE without an increase in time.

Future work will concern deeper examination of the multi-clustering technique, as well as testing it in various types of recommender systems and on other benchmark datasets.

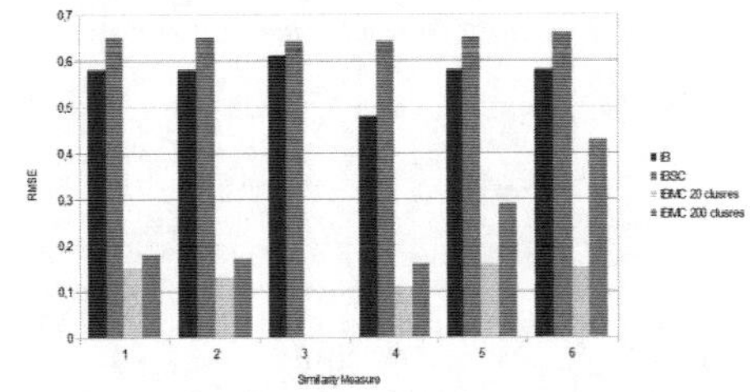

Fig. 3. RMSE of item based collaborative filtering recommendations based on different methods to determine neighbourhood

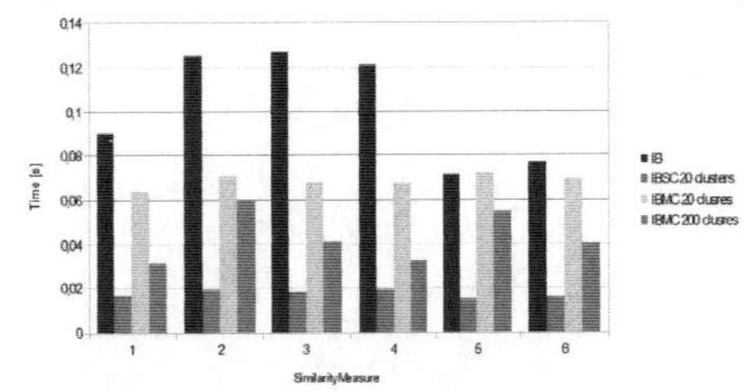

Fig. 4. Time [s] of item based collaborative filtering recommendations based on different methods to determine neighbourhood

ACKNOWLEDGMENT

The present study was supported by a grant S/WI/1/2018 from Bialystok University of Technology and founded from the resources for research by the Ministry of Science and Higher Education of Poland.

REFERENCES

[1] D. Jannach, *Recommender Systems: an Introduction.* Cambridge University Press, 2010.

[2] L. Jie, W. Dianshuang, M. Mingsong, W. Wei, and Z. Guangquan, "Recommender system application developments: A survey," *Decision Support Systems*, vol. 74, pp. 12–32, 2015.

[3] R. Lawrence, G. Almasi, V. Kotlyar, M. Viveros, and S. Duri, "Personalization of supermarket product recommendations," *Data Mining and Knowledge Discovery*, vol. 5, pp. 11–32, 2001.

[4] K. McCarthy, J. Reilly, L. McGinty, and B. Smyth, "Thinking positively-explanatory feedback for conversational recommender systems," in *Proceedings of the European Conference on Case-Based Reasoning (ECCBR-04)*, 2004, pp. 115–124.

[5] U. Kużelewska, *Contextual Modelling Collaborative Recommender System—Real Environment Deployment Results.* Springer, 2016, pp. 119–126.
[6] "Netflix Website," URL: (https://www.netflix.com/) [accessed: 2018-10-02].
[7] "Spotify Website," URL: (https://www.spotify.com/) [accessed: 2018-10-02].
[8] A. Nanopoulos, D. Rafailidis, P. Symeonidis, and Y. Manolopoulos, "Musicbox: personalized music recommendation based on cubic analysis of social tags," *IEEE Transactions on Audio, Speech and Language Processing*, vol. 18, pp. 407–412, 2010.
[9] J. Recio-Garcia, G. Jimenez-Diaz, A. Sanchez-Ruiz, and B. Diaz-Agudo, "Personality aware recommendations to groups," in *Proceedings of the Third ACM Conference on Recommender Systems*, 2009, pp. 325–328.
[10] J. Bobadilla, F. Ortega, A. Hernando, and A. Gutiérrez, "Recommender Systems Survey," *Knowledge-Based Systems*, vol. 46, pp. 109–132, 2013.
[11] B. Sarwar, "Recommender Systems for Large-Scale E-Commerce: Scalable Neighborhood Formation Using Clustering," in *Proceedings of the 5th International Conference on Computer and Information Technology*, 2002.
[12] U. Kużelewska, "Clustering algorithms in hybrid recommender system on MovieLens data," *Studies in logic, grammar and rhetoric*, vol. 37, pp. 125–139, 2014.
[13] J. Rongfei, "A new clustering method for collaborative filtering," in *Proceedings of the International IEEE Conference on Networking and Information Technology*, 2010, pp. 488–492.
[14] J. Bailey, *Alternative clustering analysis: a review.* Chapman and Hall/CRC, 2014, pp. 533–548.
[15] E. Bae and J. Bailey, "COALA: a novel approach for the extraction of an alternate clustering of high quality and high dissimilarity," in *Proceedings of the IEEE international conference on data mining*, 2006, pp. 53–62.
[16] J. Hu, Q. Qian, J. Pei, R. Jin, and S. Zhu, "Finding multiple stable clusterings," *Knowledge and Information Systems*, vol. 51, pp. 991–1021, 2017.
[17] S. Puntheeranurak and H. Tsuji, "A Multi-clustering Hybrid Recommender System," in *Proceedings of the 7th IEEE International Conference on Computer and Information Technology*, 2007, pp. 223–238.
[18] Y. Wu, X. Liu, M. Xie, M. Ester, and Q. Yang, "Cccf: Improving collaborative filtering via scalable user-item co-clustering," in *Proceedings of the Ninth ACM International Conference on Web Search and Data Mining.* ACM, 2016, pp. 73–82.
[19] F. Ricci, L. Rokach, and B. Shapira, "Recommender systems: Introduction and challenges," in *Recommender systems handbook.* Springer, 2015, pp. 1–34.
[20] "Apache Mahout," URL: (http://mahout.apache.org/) [accessed: 2017-07-14].
[21] "A Million Song Dataset," URL: https://labrosa.ee.columbia.edu/millionsong/lastfm/ [accessed: 2017-11-02].

So You Want to Build a Farm: An Approach to Resource and Time Consuming Testing of Mobile Applications

Evgeny Pyshkin and Maxim Mozgovoy
University of Aizu

Tsuruga, Ikki-Machi, Aizu-Wakamatsu, Fukushima, 965-8580, Japan
Email: {pyshe, mozgovoy}@u-aizu.ac.jp

Abstract—**The focus of this research is on improving a process of resource and time-consuming automated software testing. Particularly, we address the problem of testing mobile applications with rich non-native or hand-drawn graphical user interface, as well as resource-consuming dynamic applications, such as mobile games. We introduce an approach to creating a mobile testing farm, which is relatively easy to build with inexpensive components and open source software. This approach can be useful for supporting a product development cycle for a company on lean budget. It is suitable for a wide range of mobile applications with a high variety of human-computer interaction mechanisms.**

Keywords–Non-native GUI; mobile applications; testing framework; human factors.

I. INTRODUCTION

Though there are many existing frameworks supporting software development and testing automation, creating open testing platforms and sharable pragmatic solutions remains one of strategic parts of software quality assurance [1]. For the specific case of mobile testing (including mobile user interface (UI) testing automation), there is a gap between rapid evolution of mobile software and availability of comprehensive automated solutions focusing peculiarities of mobile applications development and testing [2]. One of such particular aspects of mobile software testing is the problem of creating flexible tools that would facilitate running automated tests of large-scale and resource-intensive on mobile applications [3].

One of obvious requirements for automated UI tests is that they should be able to access applications similarly as users do. Particularly, testing graphical UI (GUI) provides a nontrivial case of testing automation for both traditional and mobile applications [4][5]. Existing tools for testing automation (such as Jemmy library [6], Microsoft UI Automation [7], or Android UI Automator [8]) provide features for testing GUI applications in regular cases. They allow accessing programmatically many GUI elements and performing different operations such as pushing a button, scrolling a window, hovering an area, and so on. However, there are specific cases when testing process is time- and resource-consuming. Unlike to traditional applications rewritten to be runnable on mobile devices, applications developed primarily for mobile devices have significant particularities such as connectivity dependency, limitations in available computing resources, battery discharging, specufic GUI based touch screen gestures, rapid evolution and diversity of devices, as well as rapidly evolving new operating systems [9]. Many of these factors are connected and mutually dependent. For example, in mobile games, we might have to run the relatively long-lasting process and collect many screenshots necessary for reproducing the test cases and for making further fine-grain analysis of possible application failures. For arranging such time- and effort-consuming tests, device emulators (being a widely used solution allowing to decrease the testing costs) are often not enough. There are the following reasons:

1) We have to be sure that a program works properly on real devices (it is mentioned above that a wide diversity of mobile devices is one of the significant peculiarities of mobile applications).
2) An emulator could not help in testing applications with intensive CPU and GPU load required for revealing battery drain problems.
3) Test failures might be device-sensitive: a test might successfully pass on one device, while (often unexpectedly) crashing on the another one.
4) Testing on emulators makes difficult to reveal low performance problems.
5) It is hard to model connectivity-sensitive test cases.

In order to decrease testing complexity and save testing time, the developers often use the restricted test suites known as smoke tests, which are useful for some sanity checks: they are aimed at checking whether the whole application works, provides its basic functionality, and operates with user controls properly. Smoke testing is an important element of software deployment process, particularly in case of severe time and cost pressure [10][11].

Simple test scripts can check whether a program works in general, but also they can reveal many potential problems like lack of interaction with a server backend, incorrect processing of user requests, failures in user interactions with UI (probably containing non-standard hand-drawn elements), etc.

In the domain of mobile development including (with respect to the scope of our particular interests) virtualized environments, mobile games, learning environments, etc., arranging smoke tests is far from being a trivial problem. Complex testing scenarios might require the use of specialized smoke testing frameworks. As it has been mentioned above, mobile applications often do not have a platform-native GUI, but a set of hand-drawn elements built without using standard GUI libraries. One relevant project is the recently launched Unity-based mobile game "World of Tennis: Roaring '20s" [12], which is a good example illustrating the complexity of testing gaming applications running primarily on mobile devices [13].

Apart from mobile games, there are more application types that may be built with non-native UI components. For example, map-based travel applications often use GUI elements, which are not ordinary user controls supported by standard testing frameworks, but specially designed components integrated with an electronic map [14]. Hand-drawn GUI is also widely used in educational mobile applications, for example, in language learning applications with non-standard UI elements for representing language grammar structures [15].

The remaining paper is organized as follows. In Section II we describe the application context for our approach and briefly examine recent works in the domain of mobile software testing automation. In Section III we introduce our approach and discuss its current implementation, as well as the lessons learned from using this approach in a mobile development project. In Conclusion we summarize our current contribution and briefly describe the planned future steps.

II. Related Work

The standard approach to mobile application testing is to connect mobile devices to a "test server" running some special software, in order to execute test scripts on a remote machine (as shown in Figure 1).

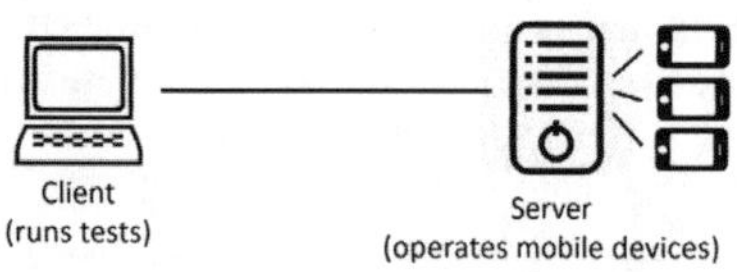

Figure 1. Client-server interaction in a mobile testing environment.

For the server-side software, one can rely on existing solutions, such as Appium [16] and Calabash [17]: a test script is usually a set of instructions containing such activities as waiting, tapping screen location, asserting that an expected UI elements appears on the screen, pressing the button, tapping a certain GUI element within some screen area, etc.

In such test scripts for native GUI applications, user controls can be accessed programmatically: normally, this capability is supported by an operating system. However, in a case of applications that do not rely on the natively rendered GUI components of an underlying operating system and do not use standardized GUI libraries, this approach does not work. Various sources [18][19], including our own works [5][20], suggest to use pattern recognition methods to identify GUI elements on the screen. In a sense, human intelligence (e. g., constructing smoke test scripts) meets the algorithms of machine intelligence (e. g., using image recognition to find GUI elements on the screen).

This technique requires experimenting with the settings of pattern matching and image transformation algorithms (provided, e. g., by OpenCV library), and in general, slows down the testing process. It might be difficult to estimate "typical" duration of a test, since simple smoke tests can reveal the absence of crashes within seconds, while *stress tests*, designed to check the stability of an application in a prolonged time interval, can take hours. Furthermore, ideally every new build should be tested on a variety of mobile devices.

A common way to run automated tests on a selection of real mobile devices is to use cloud mobile farm providers (such as *Amazon Web Services*, or *Bitbar*). Such cloud farms have many advantages: they support many different mobile devices; they can be easily set up; they do not require specific client side equipment. However, there are significant drawbacks as well: most providers still do not support an adequate variety of devices or a selection of devices that can be particularly interesting for the mobile software developers. The testing cost can be quite high for a small team, freelance developer or startup company.

III. Our Approach and Current Implementation

A possible alternative to cloud mobile farms (which are easy to deploy, but expensive and often insufficient) is to build own farms that can be configured to fit exact developers' requirements and specific purposes of the testing process. The expected functionality of such farms includes support for the follwing processes: 1) getting builds from a build machine (such as *TeamCity* [21]); 2) running all tests on all connected devices; 3) generating HTML reports containing the application action logs and screenshots; 4) sending the reports and related data to the subscribed users.

A. Prototype mobile farm

Figure 2 shows the organization of the current prototype we use.

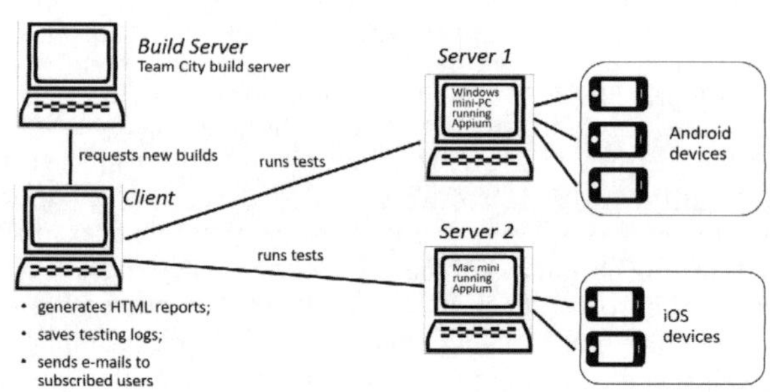

Figure 2. Mobile farm organization: major components.

In our implementation, *Client* testing server is a Windows-based mini-PC, used to run Appium test scripts. There are two servers supporting tests on connected devices: *Server 1* is a Windows-based mini-PC, running Appium server software for Android devices mostly (but Windows devices can also be connected to this server); *Server 2* is a Mac mini computer, running Appium server software for iOS devices mostly. The second server is required, since it is not possible to run iOS tests on the devices connected to non-macOS machines.

Testing devices (where the mobile software under testing is running) are connected with the computers via *Plugable* USB hubs that support simultaneous data transfer and charging with charging rate up to $1.4A$ depending on the device. Figure 3 demonstrates a working mobile farm prototype with three servers, a RAID array based storage and a variety of connected mobile devices under tests.

Though the current implementation is a relatively simple compact solution, it helped us to analyze many difficulties

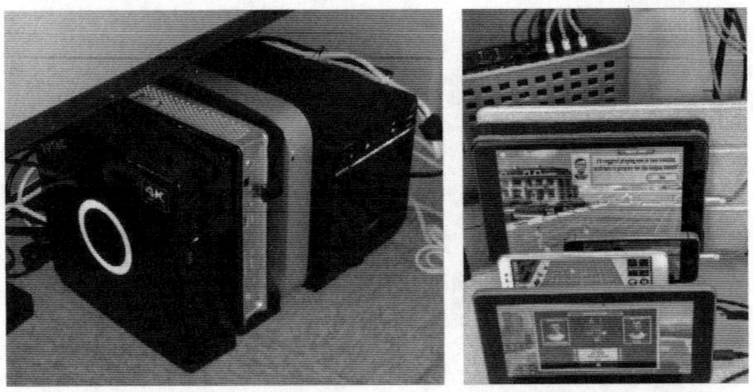

(a) Servers and raid array *(b) Devices under testing*

Figure 3. A prototype mobile farm.

that a quality assurance engineer might face while building a reliable and convenient infrastructure for automated testing of mobile applications on real devices, including (but not limited to) the following problems:

- How to support a representative variety of devices with regards to their operating and eco-systems (e. g., solutions which are perfectly deployed for Android devices might not be working for iOS-based devices).
- How to find appropriate hardware for connecting a reasonable number of devices (with respect to battery draining, difference in charging/connection interfaces, charging rate and time, capabilities to charge and transfer data at the same time, etc.).

B. Case Study: Using Appium and Image Recognition for Testing Non-Native GUI of Mobile Applications

Appium is a test automation framework designed to assist functional testing of compiled native (iOS, Android or Windows) and hybrid applications [22]. By accessing an application from Appium scripts, we can simulate different user interactions. Appium is responsible for the following activities: 1) receiving connections from a client; 2) listening for commands; 3) passing received commands to the application under testing (the application is run on the same machine as Appium or on a USB-connected mobile device); 4) sending responses from the application back to the client.

Thus, Appium just provides a client-server layer that has testing script on the client side and application on the server side. All the work of test scheduling, interaction with TeamCity, storing and retrieving test logs and other things has to be done in our own code, so there is much work for test engineers.

According to the above described process, remote clients connect to Appium servers and run test scripts that send commands for execution. Native application GUI elements can be accessed using a specialized API. However, in order to access non-native or hand-drawn GUI elements, one needs to recognize them on the screen first. From one's first look, identifying objects of interest on the screen (such as non-native GUI controls or game characters) can be reduced to the task of perfect matching of a requested bitmap image inside a screenshot. However, there is a reasonable number of factors making such a naïve approach insufficient for reliable GUI element recognition and thus requiring approximate matching:

- Onscreen objects may be rendered differently (because of GPUs or rendering quality settings.
- Screens vary in dimensions, thus, game scenes might have to be rescaled before rendering. Such a transformation might cause significant distortions.
- Game designers might slightly change the UI elements (fonts, colors, background, etc.).
- Onscreen objects might interfere with complex background or with other objects.
- Many interactions are performed with non-GUI onscreen game objects (such as game characters).

The idea of using OpenCV-supported approximate image matching in Appium is discussed in several tutorials [23][24]. We rely on OpenCV function *matchTemplate()* called with the parameter *TM_CCOEFF_NORMED*. This parameter defines the pattern matching algorithm used by *matchTemplate()*. The pattern matching function allows us to get image similarity coefficients and analyze testing results from the viewpoint of UI elements recognition quality. Unfortunately, *matchTemplate()* function is unable to match scaled patterns. Since a mobile application may run on devices with different screen sizes, we have to scale the screenshots to match the dimensions of the original screen used to record graphical patterns.

Image processing functions (including operations with a large number of screenshots) slows down the testing procedures significantly and makes the whole testing process resource- and time-consuming.

C. Assessment and Lessons Learned

Our current experience to use the suggested approach is based on two prototype farm implementations for testing the large scale software project, which is the above mentioned Unity-based mobile game "World of Tennis: Roaring '20s". Our experiments taught us a number of interesting facts about mobile farms.

Due to very intensive application usage in test runs, mobile devices quickly discharge while testing. Unfortunately, it is not enough to plug a device into a computer or a USB hub to keep the level of battery at an acceptable level: typical USB charging rates are inadequate. Our experiments demonstrated that even powered USB hubs can be insufficient, hence, one might need a hub supporting simultaneous charge and intensive data transfer. However, we realized that even if one uses special powered hubs, there are devices charging very slowly or refusing to charge in such conditions.

Though Appium is a mature project with a significant user base, there are still some unresolved issues that can lead to unreliable test execution. However, we have to admit that there is a visible progress in this project, since many problems (that we faced in the past) have been already fixed.

A device may have its own oddities. While testing, unexpected behavior may be conditioned by a particular version of the operating system or firmware, or even default onscreen keyboard. For example, we tested one device that was randomly crashing until we installed CyanogenMod. Another device reported the lack of available memory space after several dozens of installation-uninstallation cycles of the application under testing. The problem was resolved by installing an alternative Android version.

IV. CONCLUSION

In this contribution, we demonstrated that building a mobile testing farm is not a trivial task. We introduced an approach, which includes a process, a working system, and a set of sample applications using this testing infrastructure. Some primary evaluation results of testing professional software products proves the applicability of the suggested method to the practical cases of mobile software testing.

Particularly, our contribution include a mobile testing infrastructure; a working prototype supporting testing of Windows, Android, and iOS devices; Appium extensions (for handling application distribution across a number of connected devices, load balancing and supporting additional types of UI interaction, which were not included to the Appium implementation we used; and pattern matching-based technique for recognition of non-native GUI elements in test scripts. All above mentioned elements of our solution can be considered as parts of continuous integration process.

We do not argue that creating a farm is always better than renting through the alternatives. However, it is important to note that our approach is not only about implementing smoke tests for a particular case: it should be considered as a stage of a continuous integration pipeline, similar to automated unit testing and automated builds.

We believe that the proposed approach provides a practical solution for real world problems of software analysis and verification automation. Our primary experiments show feasibility of the suggested process for testing automation with the combined use of several technologies including traditional automated unit tests, functional testing frameworks, and image recognition algorithms.

As a future work, we expect to create an open source framework for small-scale mobile farms that would allow users to use facilities of users' own computers and connected devices as a part of the whole testing framework. We expect that such an approach will make smoke testing easier to set up, encourage mobile software developers to extend their testing automation practices, and, therefore, improve mobile software quality. As a result of our efforts, paraphrasing on the the famous Glenn Gould's conceptual composition "So you want to write a fugue" [25], we believe to be able to say: "So you want to build a farm – so go ahead and build a farm".

REFERENCES

[1] D. Amalfitano, A. R. Fasolino, P. Tramontana, and B. Robbins, "Testing android mobile applications: Challenges, strategies, and approaches," in Advances in Computers. Elsevier, 2013, vol. 89, pp. 1–52.

[2] M. Linares-Vásquez, K. Moran, and D. Poshyvanyk, "Continuous, evolutionary and large-scale: A new perspective for automated mobile app testing," in Software Maintenance and Evolution (ICSME), 2017 IEEE International Conference on. IEEE, 2017, pp. 399–410.

[3] T. Ki, A. Simeonov, C. M. Park, K. Dantu, S. Y. Ko, and L. Ziarek, "Fully automated ui testing system for large-scale android apps using multiple devices," in Proceedings of the 15th Annual International Conference on Mobile Systems, Applications, and Services, 2017, p. 185.

[4] K. Moran, M. L. Vsquez, and D. Poshyvanyk, "Automated gui testing of android apps: From research to practice," in 2017 IEEE/ACM 39th International Conference on Software Engineering Companion (ICSE-C), May 2017, pp. 505–506.

[5] M. Mozgovoy and E. Pyshkin, "Unity application testing automation with appium and image recognition," in Tools and Methods of Program Analysis, V. Itsykson, A. Scedrov, and V. Zakharov, Eds. Cham: Springer International Publishing, 2018, pp. 139–150.

[6] "Jemmy library," retrieved: Aug 1, 2018. [Online]. Available: https://jemmy.java.net/

[7] "Ui automation," retrieved: Aug 1, 2018. [Online]. Available: https://docs.microsoft.com/en-us/windows/desktop/WinAuto/entry-uiauto-win32

[8] "Automate user interface tests," retrieved: Aug 1, 2018. [Online]. Available: https://developer.android.com/training/testing/ui-testing/index.html

[9] H. Muccini, A. Di Francesco, and P. Esposito, "Software testing of mobile applications: Challenges and future research directions," in Proceedings of the 7th International Workshop on Automation of Software Test. IEEE Press, 2012, pp. 29–35.

[10] J. Humble and D. Farley, Continuous Delivery: Reliable Software Releases through Build, Test, and Deployment Automation (Adobe Reader). Pearson Education, 2010.

[11] G. Mustafa, A. A. Shah, K. H. Asif, and A. Ali, "A strategy for testing of web based software," Information Technology Journal, vol. 6, no. 1, 2007, pp. 74–81.

[12] "World of tennis: Roaring 20's," retrieved: Aug 1, 2018. [Online]. Available: http://worldoftennis.com/

[13] K. Haller, "Mobile testing," ACM SIGSOFT Software Engineering Notes, vol. 38, no. 6, 2013, pp. 1–8.

[14] E. Pyshkin and M. Pyshkin, "Towards better requirement definition for multimedia travel guiding applications," in Computational Intelligence (SSCI), 2016 IEEE Symposium Series on. IEEE, 2016, pp. 1–7.

[15] M. Purgina, M. Mozgovoy, and V. Klyuev, "Developing a mobile system for natural language grammar acquisition," in Dependable, Autonomic and Secure Computing, 14th Intl Conf on Pervasive Intelligence and Computing, 2nd Intl Conf on Big Data Intelligence and Computing and Cyber Science and Technology Congress (DASC/PiCom/DataCom/CyberSciTech), 2016 IEEE 14th Intl C. IEEE, 2016, pp. 322–325.

[16] "Appium: Automation for apps," retrieved: Aug 1, 2018. [Online]. Available: http://appium.io

[17] "Calabash: Automated acceptance testing for mobile apps," retrieved: Aug 1, 2018. [Online]. Available: http://calaba.sh

[18] T. Yeh, T.-H. Chang, and R. C. Miller, "Sikuli: Using gui screenshots for search and automation," in Proceedings of the 22nd Annual ACM Symposium on User Interface Software and Technology, ser. UIST '09. New York, NY, USA: ACM, 2009, pp. 183–192.

[19] T.-H. Chang, T. Yeh, and R. C. Miller, "Gui testing using computer vision," in Proceedings of the SIGCHI Conference on Human Factors in Computing Systems, ser. CHI '10. New York, NY, USA: ACM, 2010, pp. 1535–1544.

[20] M. Mozgovoy and E. Pyshkin, "Using image recognition for testing hand-drawn graphic user interfaces," in 11th International Conference on Mobile Ubiquitous Computing, Systems, Services and Technologies (UBICOMM 2017), IARIA. IARIA, Nov 2017, pp. 25–28.

[21] M. Mahalingam, Learning Continuous Integration with TeamCity. Packt Publishing Ltd, 2014.

[22] M. Hans, Appium Essentials. PACKT, 2015, retrieved: Aug 1, 2018. [Online]. Available: https://www.packtpub.com/application-development/appium-essentials/

[23] S. Kazmierczak, "Appium with image recognition," February 2016, retrieved: Aug 1, 2018. [Online]. Available: https://medium.com/@SimonKaz/appium-with-image-recognition-17a92abaa23d\#.oez2f6hnh

[24] V.-V. Helppi, "Using opencv and akaze for mobile app and game testing," January 2016, retrieved: Aug 1, 2018. [Online]. Available: http://bitbar.com/using-opencv-and-akaze-for-mobile-app-and-game-testing

[25] G. Gould, So you want to write a fugue? G. Schirmer, 1964.

Considerations for Adapting Real-World Open Source Software Projects within the Classroom

Hyunju Kim
Department of Mathematics and Computer Science
Wheaton College
Wheaton, IL, USA
e-mail: hyunju.kim@wheaton.edu

Abstract—**As Open Source Software (OSS) has become one of the main approaches for developing new software products, efforts to incorporate real-world OSS projects into the computer science classroom have increased. This paper reviews such efforts and discusses the benefits and challenges of adapting OSS projects in software development or engineering courses. It also presents considerations for selecting and using OSS projects for in-classroom software development.**

Keywords-open source software; OSS; software engineering education.

I. INTRODUCTION

Open Source Software (OSS) has been widely used in many areas and has become one of the main approaches for developing new software products. As a result, efforts to adapt OSS and its community structures in computer science education have also increased. Findings from such efforts show that using OSS to teach various aspects of software engineering benefits students by providing opportunities for real-world software development, software reengineering, and team activities, such as project management and group communications. These opportunities are rarely available within the traditional classroom environment; thus, adapting OSS in software engineering education can be an effective supplemental teaching approach to prepare students for their future careers.

Section II of this paper will review previous efforts to use OSS projects in the computer science classroom, along with benefits of using OSS components in software engineering education. Section III will present two different approaches to utilizing real-world OSS projects for software development education, and the corresponding challenges and considerations based on our classroom experience. Section IV concludes our experience and discusses future work that will be necessary for better utilizing real-world OSS projects in the classroom setting.

II. PREVIOUS STUDIES

Several studies have already adapted real-world OSS projects to the computer science classroom environment. A study by Hislop et al. [3] identified the effects of adapting Humanitarian Free and OSS projects in undergraduate software engineering or OSS development courses at diverse educational institutions. Findings from the study indicate that students were motivated by participating in such OSS projects and learned various aspects of collaborative software development. Similarly, a study by Stroulia et al. [8] reported on the Undergraduate Capstone Open-Source Project, which offered a distributed software engineering course to students from multiple universities. The course asked students to work on existing, active OSS projects so that they could learn and participate in real-world team activities for developing software. This distributed environment was helpful for students in learning communication skills, as well as in learning from others and through examples. Another study by Krogstie [4] reported the roles and benefits of a broker between a student development team and an OSS community in a senior project course. While working as the gatekeeper, the broker strengthened the programmer's authority within the team and increased the communication credibility of both parties. As a result, the broker's role became significant for the student team in acquiring the necessary development knowledge from the OSS community.

While most of the previous efforts have introduced OSS projects to the senior level of computer science studies, a couple of them have incorporated OSS projects into second or third year studies [5][6]. Students were asked to contribute to active OSS projects, so they might learn software evolution processes, such as reverse engineering and software maintenance. Students' feedback from those courses was positive and reflected their having learned values of documentation, software development tools, and communication with real-world developers.

It seems obvious that incorporating real-world OSS projects into the classroom provides valuable opportunities for students to learn technical and social aspects of software development, such as:

- Communication skills
- Project management activities
- Distributed software development tools
- Problem analysis and solution development according to given constraints
- Learning from others and by example

However, despite these benefits, one of the challenges is to identify OSS projects that are appropriate for student development. A study by Smith et al. [7] initially considered programming language, code size, team development, and buildability as the criteria when choosing appropriate OSS projects to teach software engineering. Later, the study also considered additional criteria, such as the project's application domain, modular design, recent activity, and documentation quality. Results from this study showed that it was not easy to find appropriate projects of proper size. In addition, buildability problems existed among small, single developer projects; levels of documentation varied; and a project's code organization could mislead its code modularity.

This paper reports findings from adapting two different types of OSS projects into software development courses. We will also discuss the pros and cons of the two adaptation forms so that they can serve as criteria for selecting future OSS student development projects.

III. UTILIZING OSS PROJECTS WITHIN THE CLASSROOM

According to Black Duck's 2015 Future of Open Source Survey [1], over 65% of the companies surveyed took an OSS-first approach in developing or using software for daily business. The 2016 survey revealed that about 65% of the companies contributed to OSS projects to influence OSS markets, and 59% of respondents participated in OSS projects to gain competency [2]. Computer Science education must not only respond to these trends and needs, but also integrate learning opportunities that will prepare students for the contemporary corporate environment. OSS projects provide such opportunities in the following areas:

- Community activities: OSS projects require participants to take on diverse roles, such as end-users, project managers, programmers, and testers. Thus, all levels of computer science students can participate in the community activities, which provide a learning area for students according to their interests and knowledge levels. As members of the community, they can learn from others, including real-world professionals. Students will also learn how to effectively work and communicate with others and how to follow community rules and standards.
- Project management: OSS projects are continuously evolving. Thus, students can witness and participate in ongoing activities for forking and merging projects, release planning, code repository management, risk management, and quality management.
- Software reengineering or reverse engineering: Traditional software engineering courses usually focus more on forward engineering. On the other hand, OSS projects require students to understand existing code, including algorithms, software architectures, data structures, and documentation. The code may include good and bad coding practices, and thus students can learn through examples. This will also be a practical teaching resource for software reengineering.
- Communication and development tools: Although traditional computer science labs provide hands-on exercises with tools, they are usually limited in terms of type and scope. Real-world OSS projects can expose students to diverse and cutting-edge documentation, builds, version controls, and testing tools.

A. *Adapting Two Types of OSS Projects*

Wheaton College is a liberal arts college, and its undergraduate enrollment is about 2,400. In 2017, the computer science program at Wheaton offered a software development course to sophomores and juniors and an OSS development course to juniors and seniors. Both courses were offered to computer science majors and minors. The software development course was required for computer science majors, and the OSS development course was offered as an elective, project course. The sizes of the classes were twelve and three respectively.

Students in each course worked on OSS projects of their choice. Those in the software development course worked on projects that were forked from an existing OSS project, and each of the three students in the OSS development course participated in a different, active OSS project. This paper presents preliminary findings based on the student course evaluations and the instructor's observations. The course evaluations included survey questions about their experiences on OSS projects. Because of the small class sizes, the instructor was also able to closely observe students' project activities and their interactions with the existing projects.

As mentioned, there were two different types of student OSS projects. Students either joined active OSS projects or initiated their own OSS projects by forking existing ones. The former type provides the various learning opportunities outlined above, while benefits of the latter type were identified as follows:

- Students have full control over the projects. They can execute the projects according to their own pace and set their own rules and standards for project activities.
- Students can become involved in various management activities. First-time OSS participants, especially student participants, can hardly contribute to management tasks in a large, active OSS project due to their lack of reputation, knowledge, and experience. However, this type of OSS project allows students to practice the full set of management tasks.
- Students can better exercise reengineering activities. This type of OSS project is relatively small, and thus students can understand the existing code better and more quickly. Consequently, the quality of the outputs from refactoring and documenting the code can be improved.

Despite these benefits, initiating a new OSS project may not provide the full benefits of joining preexisting OSS projects because, in a new project, students' interactions are limited to themselves. Thus, it is necessary to consider the pros and cons of both project adaptation types according to students' needs and constraints.

B. Considerations for Using OSS Projects

As previously discussed, one of the challenges in utilizing OSS projects is identifying appropriate OSS projects for students. Feedback from our two courses shows that the following criteria should be considered when selecting OSS projects:

- Personal interest: Students indicated that a significant factor motivating them the most was their personal interest. Students were interested in particular applications, technologies, systems, subjects, or programming languages. They preferred choosing OSS projects freely rather than choosing ones from a list of pre-selected OSS projects. Maintaining their interest while working on the projects was considered one of the keys to having successful projects.
- Community-related aspects: Project popularity and status (i.e., active or inactive) should be considered. These aspects can be measured by considering the number of developers, weekly downloads, and the organization of project websites.
- Software product-related aspects: Depending on course requirements and students' interests, programming language, lines of code, platform or system, development tools, code modularity, and documentation can be used to screen projects for students.

We found that prompt and helpful responses from the OSS project's existing developers highly encouraged students to become deeply involved in the project's activities. Those students in the OSS development course started to collaborate with the real-world developers, and their contributions to the projects were reviewed by the developers and adapted by the projects. Such collaborative activities encouraged the students to keep working on the projects even after the semester ended. Thus, the criteria to measure community activities should be thoroughly considered. Among the product-related aspects, code modularity and documentation are essential factors for estimating software quality. Yet, it is difficult to automatically measure modularity and documentation levels. Students should be guided to carefully examine these two aspects while investigating potential OSS projects.

Another challenge is the steep learning curve during the early phase of an OSS project. Students need to handle development and/or build tools and set up the specific environment that the development requires. Those tools may be completely new to students, and the project may not provide full instructions for building and configuring the system. Software tools that are frequently involved in the early phase include IDE, version control systems, build tools, automatic testing tools, and bug/issue trackers.

For instructors, assessing students' contributions to the OSS project is a challenging task as well. When real-world projects are brought to the classroom, the traditional methods for evaluating student performance may not work properly. Instructors then need to utilize information and data from the project's version control system and communication tools to evaluate the students' performances. At the same time, the types, scopes, and difficulties of tasks should be considered. Therefore, developing and presenting a rubric for code commits, documentation, and communication activities will be helpful in establishing course expectations.

IV. Conclusion

This paper presents the considerations, benefits, and challenges of adapting real-world OSS projects to software development courses. The use of OSS projects within the classroom can be a good supplement to traditional approaches for teaching software development. Despite the aforementioned challenges, OSS projects provide various opportunities for computer science students to explore and learn new technologies according to their own interests. OSS projects also allow students to take their knowledge from the classroom and apply it to real-world experiences.

Student feedback from our courses shows that participants gained a significant amount of knowledge from different projects and people. Working on an OSS project helped them build a comprehensive understanding of software development, and contributing to real-world projects was highly rewarding for them.

However, to better utilize real-world OSS projects in the classroom, the following future work should be done:

- Criteria must be carefully considered to select appropriate OSS projects according to course requirements and student interests.
- Instructors should formulate guidelines to help students cope with technical difficulties involved in real-world development activities.
- Student performance evaluation criteria and procedures must be specifically developed for non-traditional, real-world, interactive activities.

We will keep utilizing OSS projects as supplementary teaching tools for the software development course as well as other related courses. Student feedback and data form the courses will be used for the future work.

As another approach to better exploit OSS projects within computer science courses, OSS components can be introduced during the early stages of computer science studies. This will encourage students to continuously work on OSS projects according to their interests and knowledge levels, and contributions to the projects will become a great portfolio of their software development activities.

References

[1] Black Duck, *2015 Future of Open Source Survey Results* [Online]. Availave from https://info.blackducksoftware.com/web-future-of-open-source-LP.html, 2018.08.07

[2] Black Duck, *Future of Open Source Survey 2016 Results* [Online]. Available from https://www.brighttalk.com/webcast/13983/199027, 2018.08.07

[3] G. Hislop, et al., "A Multi-institutional Study of Learning via Student Involvement in Humanitarian Free and Open Source Software Projects", Proc. ICER 2015, 2015, pp. 199-206.

[4] B. R. Krogstie, "Power through Brokering: Open Source Community Participation in Software Engineering Student Projects", Proc. ICSE 2008, 2008, pp. 791-800.

[5] R. Marmorstein, "Open Source Contribution as an Effective Software Engineering Class Project", Proc. ITICSE 2011, 2011, pp. 268-272.

[6] R. McCartney, S. Gokhale, and T. Smith, "Evaluating an Early Software Engineering Course with Projects and Tools from Open Source Software", Proc. ICER 2012, 2012, pp. 5-10.

[7] T. Smith, R. McCartney, S. Gokhale, and L. Kaczmarczyk, "Selecting Open Source Software Projects to Teach Software Engineering", Proc. SIGCSE 2014, 2014, pp. 397-402.

[8] E. Stroulia, K. Bauer, M. Craig, K. Reid, and G. Wilson, "Teaching Distributed Software Engineering with UCOSP: The Undergraduate Capstone Open-Source Project", Proc. CTGDSD 2011, 2011, pp. 20-25.

Sentiment-aware Analysis of Mobile Apps User Reviews Regarding Particular Updates

Xiaozhou Li, Zheying Zhang, Kostas Stefanidis

Faculty of Natural Sciences, University of Tampere
Tampere, Finland
Email: xiaozhou.li@uta.fi, zheying.zhang@uta.fi, kostas.stefanidis@uta.fi

***Abstract*—The contemporary online mobile application (app) market enables users to review the apps they use. These reviews are important assets reflecting the users needs and complaints regarding the particular apps, covering multiple aspects of the mobile apps quality. By investigating the content of such reviews, the app developers can acquire useful information guiding the future maintenance and evolution work. Furthermore, together with the updates of an app, the users reviews deliver particular complaints and praises regarding the particular updates. Despite that previous studies on opinion mining in mobile app reviews have provided various approaches in eliciting such critical information, limited studies focus on eliciting the user opinions regarding a particular mobile app update, or the impact the update imposes. Hence, this study proposes a systematic analysis method to elicit user opinions regarding a particular mobile app update by detecting the similar topics before and after this update, and validates this method via an experiment on an existing mobile app.**

Keywords–Mobile app; review; sentiment analysis; topic modeling; topic similarity

I. Introduction

The increasing number of smart phone users has led to a continuous increase in the number of mobile apps and their overall usage. Users browse and download apps via different digital distribution platforms (e.g., Apple app store, and Google Play). These platforms also provide an important channel enabling the users to provide feedback to the app. The ratings and comments given by the users at a particular time reflect their opinions regarding the overall app and the specific version of that app. While the app developers, continuously or sporadically, update their apps, the retrieved user reviews reflect not only their overall opinion changes throughout the evolution time but also their specific complaints and praises regarding the specific app version [1]. Such specific complaints, regarding various aspects [2], shall enable the developers to be aware of the issues and tackle them accordingly.

Existing studies have proposed different approaches to identifying change requests from user reviews for mobile app maintenance. With various opinion mining techniques, such as Natural Language Processing (NLP), Sentiment Analysis (SA) and supervised learning, many studies have been conducted regarding the classification of reviews towards different issue perspectives [3] [4]. Other perspectives, such as user preferences, app evaluation, user satisfaction, relation between download and rating, feature extraction, review prioritization and so on, have also been widely studied [5]–[9]. However, limited studies focus on the use of such methods in opinion mining on particular updates of a mobile app and the impact on the app's updates in the following releases, despite the importance of such information. It is unclear how users' attitude towards a particular issue changes when new updates are released and how the reviews have impacts on app's maintenance and evolution.

In this paper, we investigate the correlation between users' positive and negative reviews before and after an app's release. We consider two dimensions: time and sentiment. Specifically, we divide user reviews based on major updates, and distinguish them between those precede and follow the particular updates. Each group of reviews are further divided into positive and negative ones using sentiment analysis. We devise an approach to measuring the similarity of each group of reviews. The measurement reveals the similarity and changes between different groups of reviews and helps to gain insight into how to detect users' opinion changes regarding a particular update. Furthermore, detecting the users' update-specific opinions shall also help the developers be aware of the users opinion on a particular release and guides them proactively to address the most important issues early.

The remainder of this paper is organized as follows. Section II introduces the method with details. Section III presents a case study using this method. Section IV introduces the related works when Section V concludes the paper.

II. Method Description

In this section, we introduce our method with the main goal to detect the correlation between the content of app reviews before and after the app updates done by the app company through the app maintenance lifecycle. Such correlation shall show the degree in which the users comments are reflected in the sequence of updates and such updates are accepted by the users. The factors that influence and reflect such correlation include the main topics of the reviews between each two updates, the sentiment of those reviews, and the topics similarities before and after each update. Next, we illustrate how to detect the correlation via investigating these factors. Accordingly, Subsection A introduces the overall procedure of the method and brings forth the hypotheses it aims to verify. Subsection B and C introduce respectively how to analyze the sentiment and topics of user reviews. Subsection D introduces how to calculate the similarity between topics, when Subsection E presents how to identify the matching similar topics between review sets.

A. Preliminaries

Let R be a collection of user reviews for a particular mobile app A, covering a particular time period. Therein, each review r_i R is associated with a particular time point, at which the review r_i is published. Let also U be the set of updates released by the app developers within the time period with each update u_i is released at a particular time point as well. Therefore, we consider each review r_i, which is published after the release time of update u_i and before that of the next update u_{i+1}, as a review regarding the update u_i. Hence, for the n updates $\{u_i|i \in N, k \leq i < k+n\}$ where $k \geq 1$ and $n > 0$ for the app A within a time period, the review set R can be divided into $n+1$ subset where each $R_i \subseteq R$ is the set of reviews commenting on the according u_i. R_0 is the review set correlated with the last update before u_1 or the first version of A if u_1 is the first update of A. For each review $r_j \in R_i$, a sentiment score shall be calculated and assigned to r_j, whose the sentiment is either $positive$ or $negative$. In this way, by identifying the sentiment of each individual review in R_i, we can divide R_i positive review set R_i^+ and negative review set R_i^+, where $R_i^+ \cup R_i^- = R_i$ and $R_i^+ \cap R_i^- = \emptyset$ with an acceptable accuracy.

We further investigate the main topics for each of the positive and negative review sentence sets. We assign T_i^+ and T_i^- as the topic set for the positive and negative reviews. Therefore, we investigate the merits and issues of a particular update u_i by comparing the similarities and changes between T_{i-1}^+, T_{i-1}^-, T_i^+, and T_i^-. Specifically, the following hypotheses shall be verified.

- H1. The topic similarities between T_{i-1}^+ and T_i^+ reflect the merits regarding the app A in general.
- H2. The topic similarities between T_{i-1}^+ and T_i^- reflect the uncomfortable changes in the update u_i.
- H3. The topic similarities between T_{i-1}^- and T_i^+ reflect the improvement in the update u_i.
- H4. The topic similarities between T_{i-1}^- and T_i^- reflect the remaining issues regarding the app A.

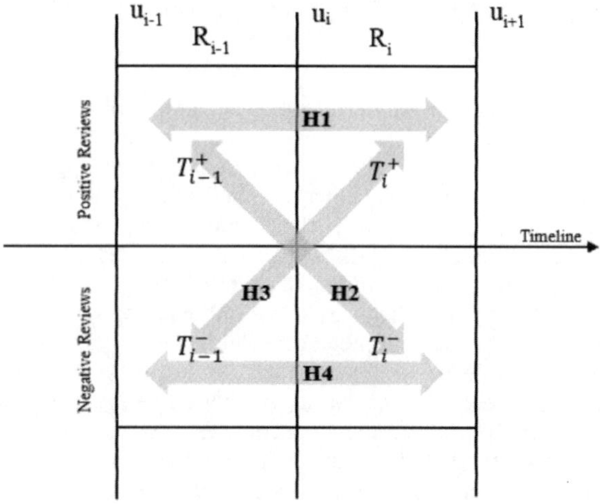

Figure 1. Relationship between hypotheses and updates.

Thus, the results obtained from these hypotheses for updating u_i provide the following information: 1) the merits and issues for the app A in general, 2) the merit and issues specific to the update u_i, and 3) the improvements and drawbacks of u_i compared with u_{i-1}. The merits and issues for app A and those for each $u_i \in U$ shall be recorded as the evolution status of app A throughout period T, which can be used as the reference to guide planning the following updates. Figure 1 visually depicts the focus of our hypotheses for updating u_i.

B. Sentiment Classification

The aim of sentiment classification in this method is to classify each review set R_i into two subsets, i.e., R_i^+ and R_i^-. Herein, R_i^+ denotes the set of positive reviews from R_i, and R_i^- denotes the set of negative reviews. Therefore, each r_j in R_i shall be determined whether it is positive or negative.

To do so, we assign a sentiment score to each review by exploiting a robust tool for sentiment strength detection on social web data [10]. As each r_j can be seen as a list of words W_j, we first select a lexicon that will determine the sentiment score of each word w_z in W_j. The lexicon for sentiment analysis is a list of words used in English language, each of which is assigned with a sentiment value in terms of its sentiment valence (intensity) and polarity (positive/negative). To determine the sentiment of words, we assign a rational value within a range to a word. For example, if the word "okay" has a positive valence value of 0.9, the word "good" must have a higher positive value, e.g., 1.9, and the word "great" has even higher value, e.g., 3.1. Furthermore, the lexicon set shall include social media terms, such as Western-style emoticons (e.g., :-)), sentiment-related acronyms and initialisms (e.g., LOL, WTF), and commonly used slang with sentiment value (e.g., nah, meh).

Algorithm 1 Sentiment Classification

```
procedure SENTIMENT ANALYSIS
lexicons ← selected sentiment lexicon
R_i ← review set
W_j ← word set of r_j(r_j ∈ R_i)
For each r_j in R_i
    For each w_z in W_j
        s_z ← polarity and valence analysis(w_z, lexicons)
        list ← list.append(s_z)
    S_j ← grammatical and syntactical heuristics
      (r_j, list, heuristics)
    if S_j > 0 then
        R_i^+.append(r_j).
    if S_j = 0 then
        R_i^0.append(r_j).
    if S_j < 0 then
        R_i^-.append(r_j).
trainMatrix ← train(R_i^+[: 8000], R_i^-[: 8000])
R_i^{0+}, R_i^{0-} ← naive bayes classifier(R_i^0, trainMatrix)
R_i^+.extend(R_i^{0+})
R_i^-.extend(R)i^{0-})
return R_i^+, R_i^-
```

Figure 2. Algorithm for Sentiment Classification

With the well-established lexicon, and a selected set of proper grammatical and syntactical heuristics, we shall then be able to determine the overall sentiment score of a review. Namely, the sentiment score of a review r_j is equal to S_j, where $S_j \in (-1, 1)$. The grammatical and syntactical heuristics are seen as the cues to change the sentiment of word sets. Therein, punctuation, capitalization, degree modifier, and contrastive conjunctions are all taken into account. For example, the sentiment of "The book is EXTREMELY AWESOME!!!" is stronger than "The book is extremely awesome", which is stronger than "The book is very good.". With both the lexicon value for each word of the review, and the calculation based on the grammatical and syntactical heuristics, we can then assign unique sentiment values to each review. That is, each review r_j is classified into positive, neutral or negative, as following:

$$r_j \text{ is } \begin{cases} \text{positive, if } 0 < S_j < 1, \\ \text{neutral, if } S_j = 0, \\ \text{negative, if } -1 < S_j < 0. \end{cases}$$

Overall, each review set R_i is divided into R_i^+, R_i^0, and R_i^-, denoting the positive, neutral and negative review sets. To further investigate the information in R_i^0, after experimentally observing that typically includes a big number of reviews, we classify it into positive and negative using the Naive Bayes Classifier with the training data from R_i^+ and R_i^-. This way, R_i^0 is classified into R_i^{0+} and R_i^{0-}, which in turn, are added to R_i^+ and R_i^-, respectively. The reason to perform supervised classification after sentiment analysis instead of directly applying classification is twofold. Firstly, manually creating training data is time-consuming and less accurate than using existing sentiment analysis methods. Secondly, training the sentiment classified reviews will provide domain specific and reliable results. The process is described in Figure 2.

C. Topic Analysis

After dividing the review sets R_i and R_{i-1}, i.e., the review sets related to update u_i, into R_i^+, R_i^-, R_{i-1}^+ and R_{i-1}^- based on the sentiment classification method, we elicit the main topics from each of the classified review sets by exploiting the Latent Dirichlet Allocation (LDA) method [11]. First, we consider each review sentence r_j in a particular set of reviews as a list of words W_j, where the sequence of the words is not recorded. The number of topics in this review set is set as t. Presumably, there is a distribution for the probability of a particular word appears in a particular topic, when there is also one for that of a particular review in a topic. We build the set of $Review-Topic$, where each word of each review is assigned with a topic out of the t topics. As preparation, we define $Review-topic-numbers$, $Topic-words-numbers$, and $Topic-numbers$ denoting the number of occurrence of each topic in each review, the number of occurrence of each word in each topic, and the number of words in each topic, respectively. For example, $Review-topic-numbers(r_j, k)$ denotes the number of occurrences of topic k in review r_j. Then, we randomly assign each word w_z of each review r_j with a topic t_k. Accordingly, the $Review-topic-numbers$, $Topic-words-numbers$, and $Topic-numbers$ will be updated as the referencing weight of the distribution the words for each topic. Then iteratively, for each word, we assign a new topic based on such weight of distribution and adjust the weight with the $Review-topic-numbers$, $Topic-words-numbers$, and $Topic-numbers$ for the next iteration. After a given number of iteration, t topics will be determined by the $Topic-words-numbers$, which is the number of occurrences of the words in each topic. Each t_k is then denoted by the most common keywords used in this topic. Then, the set of topics T are returned as result. For the review sets R_i^+, R_i^-, R_{i-1}^+ and R_{i-1}^-, we will have the topics sets T_i^+, T_i^-, T_{i-1}^+ and T_{i-1}^- accordingly.

D. Calculating Topics Similarities

Based on the topic sets T_i^+, T_i^-, T_{i-1}^+ and T_{i-1}^- elicited from the review sets R_i^+, R_i^-, R_{i-1}^+ and R_{i-1}^-, we further analyze the similarities between the individual topics between each pair of the topic sets. As the result from the previous topic analysis, each topic set T encompasses k topics, each of which is represented by the list of the most possible appearing keywords. Thus, each topic set T with k topics each of which is represented by w keywords, can be denoted as:

$$T = \begin{bmatrix} kw_{1,1} & kw_{1,2} & \dots & kw_{1,w} \\ \dots & \dots & \dots & \dots \\ kw_{k,1} & kw_{k,2} & \dots & kw_{k,w} \end{bmatrix}$$

with each $t_i \in T$ can be denoted as $[kw_{i,1}, kw_{i,2}, ...kw_{i,k}]$. To compare the similarity between two topic sets, each consisting of t topics, we compare all pairs of topics. Due to the fact that each topic is represented as a set of keywords, the similarity of two topics shall be denoted by the common keywords of these topics. Hence, an easy way for calculating the similarity between any two topics t_i and t_j is by using the Jaccard similarity. This similarity function reflects the percentage of the common keywords of the two sets in the whole keywords set of the two: $J(t_i, t_j) = \frac{|t_i \cap t_j|}{|t_i \cup t_j|}$.

However, by using the Jaccard Similarity, we consider two given topics are similar only when they contain a particular number of common keywords, regardless of the probability of them. The meaning of each topic $t_i \in T$, denoted as $[kw_{i,1}, kw_{i,2}, ...kw_{i,k}]$, shall be more likely reflected by the high-probability keywords of t_i. Furthermore, the subset of only low-probability keywords may reflect different meanings. For example, a topic is denoted as {'update': 0.143, 'problem': 0.096, 'fix': 0.064, 'install': 0.03, 'uninstall': 0.029, 'open': 0.027, 'stop': 0.025, 'plea': 0.025, 'get': 0.022, 'reinstall': 0.019, 'bug': 0.019, 'start': 0.019, 'need': 0.014, 'application': 0.014, 'issue': 0.011, 'battery': 0.011, 'help': 0.01, 'face': 0.009, 'frustrate': 0.009, 'day': 0.008}. From the high-probability keywords of this topic, we can summarize that the topic is regarding the problems of updating, which requires being fixed. However, the low-probability keywords hardly reflect the topic, e.g., a keyword subset, {'reinstall', 'bug', 'start', 'need', 'application', 'issue', 'battery'}, reflects a very different issue regarding bugs and batteries.

Hence, when comparing the similarity of two given topics, the probability of the common keywords shall be taken into account. Considering that Jaccard coefficient is the normalized inner product [12], we herein adopt the similarity measure method incorporating also the inner product, the Kumar-Hassebrook (KH) similarity [13]. Provided between topic t_i and t_j, the c common keywords are denoted as $[kw_{ij,1}, kw_{ij,2}, ...kw_{ij,c}]$, with the according probability list in t_i and t_j is $[p_{i,1}, p_{i,2}, ...p_{i,c}]$ and $[p_{j,1}, p_{j,2}, ...p_{j,c}]$. The similarity of the two given topics are calculated as follows.

$$KH(t_i, t_j) = \frac{\sum_{x=1}^{c} p_{i,x} \cdot p_{j,x}}{\sum_{x=1}^{k} p_{i,x}^2 + \sum_{x=1}^{k} p_{j,x}^2 - \sum_{x=1}^{c} p_{i,x} \cdot p_{j,x}}$$

The probability for each keyword of any topic belongs to (0,1). Hence, for this formula, when t_i and t_j contain more common keywords, the numerator increases monotonically, and the denominator decreases monotonically. Therefore, $KH(t_i, t_j)$ increases when t_i and t_j have more keywords in common. In addition, when the probability of the common keywords increases, $\sum_{x=1}^{c} p_{i,x} \cdot p_{j,x}$ increases. Because the denominator is greater than the numerator, and both are greater than 0, $KH(t_i, t_j)$ increases when the probabilities of the common keywords of t_i and t_j increase.

In this way, for two given topics t_i and t_j, when each keyword of these two topics is assigned the average value of the probability value set, then $KH(t_i, t_j) = J(t_i, t_j)$. Considering the monotonical increasing of the KH Similarity formula, it means that for t_i and t_j, when $KH(t_i, t_j) < J(t_i, t_j)$, the common keywords of these two topics hardly reflect the meaning of them. For example, two topics, denoted as the following set of keywords with the according probability of each keywords, are listed in Table I.

TABLE I. EXAMPLE TOPICS WITH KEYWORDS AND PROBABILITY

Topic 1	{'problem': 0.145, 'fix': 0.081, 'download': 0.051, 'please': 0.032, 'use': 0.025, 'reason': 0.021, 'service': 0.02, 'user': 0.015, 'issue': 0.015, 'data': 0.014}
Topic 2	{'version': 0.197, 'please': 0.121, 'go': 0.069, 'use': 0.043, 'option': 0.036, 'one': 0.028, 'lot': 0.027, 'revert': 0.021, 'way': 0.018, 'download': 0.018}

The Jaccard Similarity of these two topic is 0.176 when the KH Similarity is 0.064. We can observe that the common keywords, {'download', 'please', 'use'}, are of low probability in Topic 1 and keywords {'please', 'use'} in Topic 2, while neither topic is reflected by the common keywords. Topic 1 can be seen regarding the requests of fixing problems/bugs when Topic 2 is more related to keyword 'version' instead of 'download'. Thus, these two given topics cannot be considered as similar despite the high Jaccard Similarity.

E. Identifying Matching Topics

After computing similarities between pairs of review topics with KH similarity, we shall identify which are the matching topics when cross-comparing the topics of the topics sets T_i^+, T_i^-, T_{i-1}^+ and T_{i-1}^-. Hence, to identify the matching topics between two review topic sets T_a and T_b, the aim is to identify all the topic pairs (t_{ai}, t_{bj}), $t_{ai} \in T_a$ and $t_{bj} \in T_b$, that have the high similarity. Starting from the pair of topics with highest similarity values,

We firstly use the Jaccard Similarity value of two particular topics as the threshold for their KH similarity. According to the formula of KH similarity given previous, we set the probability of each keyword in each topic equal to the average. Then

$$KH(t_{ai}, t_{bj}) = \frac{\sum_{x=1}^{c} p^2}{\sum_{x=1}^{k} p^2 + \sum_{x=1}^{k} p^2 - \sum_{x=1}^{c} p^2}$$

$$= \frac{c}{k+k-c} = J(t_{ai}, t_{bj})$$

Therefore, we select the topic pairs, whose KH similarity value greater than their Jaccard similarity value, as similar topics. Furthermore, from the topic pairs with the highest KH similarity value, we select the top n pairs of topics to investigate the changes and similarities of users opinion regarding the app.

Algorithm 2 Matching Topics Identification

procedure MATCHING TOPICS IDENTIFICATION
$k \leftarrow$ number of topics
$n \leftarrow$ number of selected similar topics
Ta $\leftarrow \{t_{a1}, t_{a2}, ..., t_{ai}, ..., t_{ak}\}$
Tb $\leftarrow \{t_{b1}, t_{b2}, ..., t_{bj}, ..., t_{bk}\}$
$KHs_{ij} \leftarrow KHSimilarity(t_{ai}, t_{bj})$
$Js_{ij} \leftarrow JaccardSimilarity(t_{ai}, t_{bj})$
For $i, j \in \{1, 2, ..., k\}$
  if $KHs_{ij} \geq Js_{ij}$ **then**
    $S \leftarrow s_{ij}$
If $len(S) > n$
  For each (t_{ax}, t_{by}) in S[:n]:
  Result.append(Summarize(t_{ax}, t_{by}))
Else:
  For each (t_{ax}, t_{by}) in S:
  Result.append(Summarize(t_{ax}, t_{by}))
Return Result

Figure 3. Algorithm for Matching Topic Identification

The aim of the algorithm (shown in Figure 3) is to select the similar topic pairs with the highest similarity value. When a particular topic pair is selected, the other pairs, which either of these two selected topics is also pairing with and have also high similarity, will be considered as references to interpret the users opinions. Each particular topic generated by the LDA model contains a number of perspectives that can be interpreted by the keywords. Thus, it is possible that one particular topic have the similar similarity value to multiple topics, when they are similar regarding different perspectives which represented by their different common keywords.

TABLE II. EXAMPLE TOPICS WITH KEYWORDS AND PROBABILITY

Topic 1	{'time': 0.12, 'friend': 0.091, 'talk': 0.081, 'way': 0.069, 'see': 0.048, 'people': 0.045, 'communication': 0.038, 'want': 0.03, 'face': 0.023, 'world': 0.02 }
Topic 2	{'friend': 0.111, 'bring': 0.07, 'connect': 0.068, 'talk': 0.06, 'keep': 0.059, 'family': 0.054, 'application': 0.037, 'way': 0.021, 'touch': 0.017, 'contact': 0.016 }
Topic 3	{'see': 0.077, 'use': 0.056, 'people': 0.046, 'want': 0.044, 'contact': 0.034, 'thing': 0.031, 'year': 0.027, 'find': 0.023, 'know': 0.023, 'number': 0.019 }

For example, in Table II Topic 1 has the same Jaccard similarity value to both Topic 2 and 3. The two pairs of common keywords are {'friend', 'talk', 'way'} and {'people', 'see', 'want'}. Their KH similarity values are different but both high (0.276 and 0.137). From Topic 1, we could summarize that it is regarding using the app enabling people to communicate with friends any time they want and can see their faces as well. Despite it is considered similar to both Topic 2 and 3, Topic 2 focuses on the perspective of enabling communication between families and friends, when Topic 3 focus more on the perspective of contacting people with phone numbers and seeing them. Thus, by identifying both similar topic pairs, we shall have more thorough understanding of the users' opinions regarding the app.

III. CASE STUDY

A. Preprocessing

Before starting the experiment with the proposed method, preprocessing on the raw review data is required. The whole preprocessing work can be divided into three individual steps as follows.

Filtering non-English reviews. The raw review data may contain a number of review items that are not written in English, which needs to be filtered out. Also, similar to social media text, user reviews usually contain many commonly used slurs that are not regular English vocabularies. Our goal is to not filter out these words, as they likely contain sentiment related information, without which shall influence our experiment results. Overall, we screen out the non-English review sentences using Langdetect [14], a convenient language detecting package for Python language. Compared with PyEnchant [15], another language detecting package, Langdetect enables determining the language of text on sentence level. It shall remain the review data containing such English slurs.

Focusing on sentence-level granularity. Due to the fact that each user review can contain more than one sentence, a multi-sentence review can contain multiple meanings, one for each sentence. Thus, we divide each review from a review set R_i into individual sentences. Hereafter, we use r_j to denote a review sentence in R_i. We use the sentence tokenizer feature from the NLTK [16] python package, with a further checking on the legitimacy of the sentences.

Filtering stop-words and lemmatization. In addition, the collected English review sentences are also transformed into lower cases, screened with stop-words, and lemmatized before topic modeling. In order to obtain more meaningful topic modeling results, we add the words that connect to only general information but have significant appearing rate in the reviews to the list of stop words. For example, the name of the app and the word app are of neither help towards topic modeling nor towards sentiment analysis. In addition, considering the fact that the sentiment of each review item is identified, we eliminate all adjectives from the obtained tokens and select only nouns and verbs as tokens via the pos_tag function of NLTK.

Sentiment Classification with VADER. To perform sentiment analysis on the collected app reviews, we select the Valence Aware Dictionary for sEntiment Reasoning (VADER) approach [10]. Compared with other sentiment analysis tools, VADER has a number of advantages regarding this study. Firstly, the classification accuracy of VADER on sentiment towards positive, negative and neutral classes is even higher than individual human raters in social media domain. In addition, its overall classification accuracies on product reviews from Amazon, movie reviews, and editorials from NYTimes also outperform other sentiment analysis approaches, such as SenticNet [17], SentiWordNet [18], Affective Norms for English Words [19], and Word-Sense Disambiguation [20], and run closely with the accuracy of individual human. On the other hand, VADER approach is integrated in the NLTK package, which can be easily imported and performed using Python.

B. Dataset

Our study relies on real data. In particular, we focus on reviews submitted for 1-year period of Skype on the Android platform. We collected 153,128 user reviews submitted from 1.9.2016 to 31.8.2017. The reviews are tokenized into 234,064 individual sentences. After filtering the non-English review sentences, the number is reduced to 174,559.

We investigate the merits and issues concerning the major update of Skype released on Android platform on 1.6.2017 (u_i = version-1.6.2017). Within this period from 1.9.2016 to 31.8.2017, 76 updates were released. On average, the app has been updated nearly every five days. By observing the content of each update from the given information of Google Play, we find that some consecutive updates contain exact same content based on their descriptions. Therefore, we consider the first update of a set of updates which contain same descriptions as a major update, when the rest of the update set as minor update. Amongst the major updates of Skype during this period, the update u_i provide significant changes in UI design and user experiences. By classifying all selected review sentences into positive and negative using sentiment analysis and supervised classification with Naive Bayes Classifier, the number of review sentences in each segment is listed in Table III. Accordingly, the review sets R^+_{i-1}, R^-_{i-1}, R^+_i, and R^-_i, for this study, consists of 65580, 29970, 36703, and 42306 reviews.

TABLE III. POSITIVE AND NEGATIVE REVIEWS AROUND A PARTICULAR APP UPDATE

	Positive reviews	Negative reviews	Total
Before 1.6.2017	65,580	29,970	95,550
After 1.6.2017	36,703	42,306	79,009
Total	102,283	72,276	174,559

Overall, the total number of positive reviews around the particular update is bigger than the number of negative reviews. Meanwhile, the monthly review number increased sharply after this particular major update. Opposite to the situation before the update, we observe that after the update more negative reviews are given by the users than the positive ones, meaning that many users are not satisfied with this particular update or the app overall.

TABLE IV. NUMBER OF REVIEWS PER TOPIC

$t^+_{(i-1)1}$	$t^+_{(i-1)2}$	$t^+_{(i-1)3}$	$t^+_{(i-1)4}$	$t^+_{(i-1)5}$
13627	3104	3168	6283	4725
$t^-_{(i-1)1}$	$t^-_{(i-1)2}$	$t^-_{(i-1)3}$	$t^-_{(i-1)4}$	$t^-_{(i-1)5}$
8692	6016	4122	6105	9738
t^+_{i1}	t^+_{i2}	t^+_{i3}	t^+_{i4}	t^+_{i5}
3519	2892	4204	1895	3433
t^-_{i1}	t^-_{i2}	t^-_{i3}	t^-_{i4}	t^-_{i5}
2409	2700	2794	2408	3716
$t^+_{(i-1)6}$	$t^+_{(i-1)7}$	$t^+_{(i-1)8}$	$t^+_{(i-1)9}$	$t^+_{(i-1)10}$
7768	2796	3134	3186	3391
$t^-_{(i-1)6}$	$t^-_{(i-1)7}$	$t^-_{(i-1)8}$	$t^-_{(i-1)9}$	$t^-_{(i-1)10}$
4810	3399	3244	2798	2177
t^+_{i6}	t^+_{i7}	t^+_{i8}	t^+_{i9}	t^+_{i10}
4818	4132	4463	3237	4635
t^-_{i6}	t^-_{i7}	t^-_{i8}	t^-_{i9}	t^-_{i10}
3139	3893	3229	6252	4508

After sentiment analysis and classification, we perform the LDA topic analysis to identify the topics of the review set R^+_{i-1}, R^-_{i-1}, R^+_i, and R^-_i, in order to investigate the users opinions concerning the update and further verify the previously proposed hypothesis. To train the LDA topic models, we need to set the number of topics k. Based on an experimentally study regarding the quality of the topics produced for different k values, and select $k = 10$.

Overall, for the collected 174,559 review sentences on Skype, we perform an LDA topic analysis on the review set R^+_{i-1}, R^-_{i-1}, R^+_i, and R^-_i. For each of the 4 sets of review data, we use the Gensim topic modeling toolbox to train the 10-topic LDA models. For the 4 LDA models, each individual topic is represented by 20 keywords. Then, we assign each review sentence in the LDA models to the topic to which it has the highest probability to belong. The numbers of reviews for each topic of the 4 data sets appear in Table IV (t^+_{in} represents the nth topic of R^+_i). In general, reviews are divided into topics smoothly and, in most cases, each topic consists of around 4000 review sentences.

C. *Topics Similarity Analysis*

With the 40 identified topics, each of which is represented by 20 keywords, we compare the similarity between each topic from the 20 topics before the update and each one from the 20 topics after the update, which provides 400 topics pairs. The Jaccard similarity values for those 400 pairs range from 0 to 0.429 (i.e., 0 - 12 common keywords between two topics). Meanwhile, the KH similarity values range from 0 to 0.676. Therein, we identify the potential similar topics from the highest KH similarity value and eliminate the results where the KH similarity value is lower than the according Jaccard similarity value. In this way, we guarantee the common keywords of each identified topic pairs contain the overall probability value greater than average. We select the seven topic pairs with the highest KH similarity values for each comparison set. For each topic pair, we analyze the similarity of the two topics by observing their common keywords. Furthermore, from the unique keywords of each topic from one particular topic pair, we could also see the topic changes. The seven topic pairs with the highest KH similarity value are depicted in Table V.

TABLE V. PAIRS OF SIMILAR TOPICS

T^+_{i-1} - T^+_i	$(t^+_{(i-1)8}, t^+_{i5})$ $(t^+_{(i-1)6}, t^+_{i6})$ $(t^+_{(i-1)7}, t^+_{i9})$ $(t^+_{(i-1)6}, t^+_{i1})$ $(t^+_{(i-1)6}, t^+_{i5})$ $(t^+_{(i-1)1}, t^+_{i7})$ $(t^+_{(i-1)8}, t^+_{i3})$
T^+_{i-1} - T^-_i	$(t^+_{(i-1)6}, t^-_{i10})$ $(t^+_{(i-1)6}, t^-_{i5})$ $(t^+_{(i-1)8}, t^-_{i7})$ $(t^+_{(i-1)5}, t^-_{i6})$ $(t^+_{(i-1)7}, t^-_{i8})$ $(t^+_{(i-1)8}, t^+_{i10})$ $(t^+_{(i-1)2}, t^+_{i3})$
T^-_{i-1} - T^+_i	$(t^-_{(i-1)3}, t^+_{i6})$ $(t^-_{(i-1)7}, t^+_{i3})$ $(t^-_{(i-1)5}, t^+_{i1})$ $(t^-_{(i-1)3}, t^+_{i5})$ $(t^-_{(i-1)10}, t^+_{i8})$ $(t^+_{(i-1)1}, t^+_{i4})$ $(t^+_{(i-1)6}, t^+_{i9})$
T^-_{i-1} - T^-_i	$(t^-_{(i-1)3}, t^-_{i10})$ $(t^-_{(i-1)10}, t^-_{i3})$ $(t^-_{(i-1)6}, t^-_{i8})$ $(t^-_{(i-1)7}, t^-_{i9})$ $(t^+_{(i-1)7}, t^+_{i6})$ $(t^+_{(i-1)8}, t^+_{i6})$ $(t^-_{(i-1)8}, t^-_{i9})$

By further analyzing the common keywords in the obtained similar topic pairs, we verify the hypothesis H1 - H4 as follows.

H1. The topic similarities between T^+_{i-1} and T^+_i reflect the merits regarding the app A in general. The common keywords of the seven topics pairs with the highest KH similarity value appear in Table VI. For example, the common keywords of topics $(t^+_{(i-1)8}, t^+_{i5})$ reflects the acknowledgement from the users before and after the update. Because, the common keywords 'work' and 'call' indicate that the core function of the app works properly. The common keywords of topics $(t^+_{(i-1)6}, t^+_{i6})$ reflect the users acknowledge also the benefits brought by the app, e.g., enabling people to chat in groups, with video or by calling, so that people can see and hear from their friends. On the other hand, topic pair $(t^+_{(i-1)7}, t^+_{i9})$ contains the common keywords that reflect the users needs in adding features and fixing bugs. Considering the overall positive sentiment of the review sets, it is also possible the users reflect their satisfaction towards the work done by the developers regarding such matters. Topic pair $(t^+_{(i-1)6}, t^+_{i5})$ reflects the users satisfied with the video and audio quality of the app. As topic t^+_{i5} is also similar to $t^+_{(i-1)8}$, both topic pairs reflect similar information. Topic pair $(t^+_{(i-1)1}, t^+_{i7})$ reflects the contribution of the app to the society in a bigger picture, regarding the communication between friends and family and helping people keep in touch. Topic pair $(t^+_{(i-1)6}, t^+_{i1})$ contain few common keywords; however, as $t^+_{(i-1)6}$ is also similar to topic t^+_{i6} and t^+_{i5}, all these topic pairs reflect similar information.

TABLE VI. COMMON KEYOWRDS IN POSITIVE-POSITIVE REVIEWS

Topic Pairs	Common Keywords
$(t^+_{(i-1)8}, t^+_{i5})$	['call', 'phone', 'sound', 'work']
$(t^+_{(i-1)6}, t^+_{i6})$	['call', 'chat', 'friend', 'group', 'hear', 'make', 'people', 'person', 'phone', 'see', 'video']
$(t^+_{(i-1)7}, t^+_{i9})$	['add', 'bug', 'everything', 'fix', 'hope', 'issue', 'make', 'need', 'please']
$(t^+_{(i-1)6}, t^+_{i1})$	['people', 'use', 'year']
$(t^+_{(i-1)6}, t^+_{i5})$	['call', 'make', 'phone', 'quality', 'video', 'voice']
$(t^+_{(i-1)1}, t^+_{i7})$	['application', 'communicate', 'connect', 'family', 'friend', 'get', 'help', 'touch', 'way']
$(t^+_{(i-1)8}, t^+_{i3})$	['connection', 'internet', 'keep', 'nothing', 'work']

H2. The topic similarities between T^+_{i-1} and T^-_i reflect the uncomfortable changes in the update u_i. The common keywords of the selected similar topic pairs are shown in Table VII. The common keywords of topics $(t^+_{(i-1)6}, t^-_{i10})$ reflects negative user reviews regarding the apps core feature exist, despite the positive feedback before this update. According to t^-_{i10}, the aspects which users complain about include calling in general, the user interface, video and sound quality, and connections. Meanwhile, t^-_{i10} is also considered similar to $t^+_{(i-1)8}$. Topic $t^+_{(i-1)8}$ indicates that before the update many users like the internet connection of this app with wifi on computer and tablet. Topic pair $(t^+_{(i-1)5}, t^-_{i6})$ reflects that issues concerning the user accounts, including logging in, signing up, passwords emerge after the update, where the users complain quite often. Furthermore, the topic pair $(t^+_{(i-1)7}, t^-_{i8})$ indicates that many users complain about the developers fixing problems negatively, despite many others reflect the issue with positive sentiment (see topic pair $(t^+_{(i-1)7}, t^+_{i9})$).

TABLE VII. COMMON KEYOWRDS IN POSITIVE-NEGATIVE REVIEWS

Topic Pairs	Common Keywords
$(t^+_{(i-1)6}, t^-_{i10})$	['call', 'connect', 'hear', 'make', 'person', 'phone', 'quality', 'video', 'voice']
$(t^+_{(i-1)6}, t^-_{i5})$	['make', 'use', 'year']
$(t^+_{(i-1)8}, t^-_{i7})$	['need', 'work']
$(t^+_{(i-1)5}, t^-_{i6})$	['account', 'go', 'keep', 'let', 'log', 'password', 'sign', 'try', 'win']
$(t^+_{(i-1)7}, t^-_{i8})$	['fix', 'please', 'problem', 'thing']
$(t^+_{(i-1)8}, t^-_{i10})$	['call', 'connection', 'drop', 'phone', 'sound', 'work']
$(t^+_{(i-1)2}, t^-_{i3})$	['conversation', 'get', 'take', 'time', 'type']

H3. The topic similarities between T^-_{i-1} and T^+_i reflect the improvement in the update u_i. The common keywords of the selected similar topic pairs are shown in Table VIII. The common keywords of topics $(t^-_{(i-1)3}, t^+_{i6})$ reflect that before the update, many users have complaint regarding using the app for phone calls in general. After the update, a number of positive reviews towards this matter appear. Considering the topic pair $(t^-_{(i-1)3}, t^+_{i5})$, users also switch the attitude regarding the video and sound quality to positive after the update. Topic pair $(t^-_{(i-1)7}, t^+_{i3})$ reflects the general positive acknowledgement of the update. Topic pair $(t^-_{(i-1)10}, t^+_{i8})$ reflects the users attitude towards the message notification feature has changed into positive. $(t^-_{(i-1)1}, t^+_{i4})$ reflects the general positive feedback regarding the new version while $(t^-_{(i-1)6}, t^+_{i9})$ reflects the positive feedback on having some bugs fixed in this version.

TABLE VIII. COMMON KEYOWRDS IN NEGATIVE-POSITIVE REVIEWS

Topic Pairs	Common Keywords
$(t^-_{(i-1)3}, t^+_{i6})$	['call', 'get', 'hear', 'make', 'people', 'person', 'phone', 'see', 'talk', 'time', 'video']
$(t^-_{(i-1)7}, t^+_{i3})$	['get', 'update', 'win', 'work']
$(t^-_{(i-1)5}, t^+_{i1})$	['get', 'try', 'use', 'year']
$(t^-_{(i-1)3}, t^+_{i5})$	['call', 'make', 'phone', 'quality', 'sound', 'time', 'video', 'voice']
$(t^-_{(i-1)10}, t^+_{i8})$	['message', 'notification', 'open', 'see', 'send', 'show', 'take']
$(t^-_{(i-1)1}, t^+_{i4})$	['version']
$(t^-_{(i-1)6}, t^+_{i9})$	['bug', 'fix', 'get', 'lot', 'please']

H4. The topic similarities between T^-_{i-1} and T^-_i reflect the remaining issues regarding the app A. The common keywords of the selected similar topic pairs are shown in Table IX. For example, the common keywords of topics $(t^-_{(i-1)3}, t^-_{i10})$ reflects the users complaint regarding the general quality of the app remains after the update, specifically concerning connections, calling, audio and video quality, etc. On the other hand, topic pair $(t^-_{(i-1)10}, t^-_{i3})$ reflects the problem with sending and receiving messages with notifications still exist. Furthermore, crashing is also a persisting issue that many users complained about based on topic pair $(t^-_{(i-1)6}, t^-_{i8})$. Topic pair $(t^-_{(i-1)7}, t^-_{i9})$, despite having only one common keyword, reflects the users general negativity towards the update. Topic pair $(t^-_{(i-1)7}, t^-_{i6})$ and $(t^-_{(i-1)8}, t^-_{i6})$ reflect the issues regarding logging in and signing up with Microsoft account. Topic pair $(t^-_{(i-1)8}, t^-_{i9})$ reflects the issues regarding user contact list when specially t^-_{i9} reflects the users' complaints regarding contact list syncing and status.

TABLE IX. COMMON KEYOWRDS IN NEGATIVE-NEGATIVE REVIEWS.

Topic Pairs	Common Keywords
$(t^-_{(i-1)3}, t^-_{i10})$	['call', 'connect', 'drop', 'hear', 'make', 'person', 'phone', 'quality', 'sound', 'time', 'video', 'voice']
$(t^-_{(i-1)10}, t^-_{i3})$	['get', 'message', 'notification', 'open', 'see', 'send', 'show', 'take', 'time']
$(t^-_{(i-1)6}, t^-_{i8})$	['crash', 'fix', 'give', 'keep', 'please', 'problem', 'star', 'think', 'time']
$(t^-_{(i-1)7}, t^-_{i9})$	['update']
$(t^-_{(i-1)7}, t^-_{i6})$	['let', 'login', 'microsoft', 'time', 'try', 'turn', 'update', 'win']
$(t^-_{(i-1)8}, t^-_{i6})$	['account', 'keep', 'make', 'sign']
$(t^-_{(i-1)8}, t^-_{i9})$	['add', 'contact', 'list', 'sync']

Conclusively, we could summarize the users' opinion before and after the particular update (version 1.6.2017) as follows:

The merits in general:

1) $(t^+_{(i-1)8}, t^+_{i5})$: calling feature works.
2) $(t^+_{(i-1)6}, t^+_{i6})$, $(t^+_{(i-1)1}, t^+_{i7})$: people can chat in group with video and calls, connecting with family and friends.
3) $(t^+_{(i-1)7}, t^+_{i9})$: added features and bugs fixed.
4) $(t^+_{(i-1)6}, t^+_{i5})$: the video and sound quality.

The uncomfortable changes:

1) $(t^+_{(i-1)6}, t^-_{i10})$: user interface, connection, and calling quality in general.
2) $(t^+_{(i-1)5}, t^-_{i6})$: the user accounts, including logging in, signing up, passwords.
3) $(t^+_{(i-1)7}, t^-_{i8})$: bugs fixes.

The improvement:

1) $(t^-_{(i-1)7}, t^+_{i3})$: update in general.
2) $(t^-_{(i-1)10}, t^+_{i8})$: message notification.
3) $(t^-_{(i-1)3}, t^+_{i6})$, $((t^-_{(i-1)3}, t^+_{i5})$: calling in general, video and sound quality.

The remaining issues:

1) $(t^-_{(i-1)3}, t^-_{i10})$: update in general.
2) $(t^-_{(i-1)10}, t^-_{i3})$: sending and receiving messages with notifications.
3) $(t^-_{(i-1)6}, t^-_{i8})$: crashing.
4) $(t^-_{(i-1)7}, t^-_{i9})$: the new version
5) $(t^-_{(i-1)7}, t^-_{i6})$, $(t^-_{(i-1)8}, t^-_{i6})$: login and signup with Microsoft accounts.
6) $(t^-_{(i-1)8}, t^-_{i9})$: contact list syncing and status update.

Interestingly, these points are verified by the short notes of Skype developers regarding their updates [21]. Specifically, the above topics can be associated with the following original developers claims: (a) General performance and reliability improvements (Version 2017.08.15, Version 2017.08.29: phone calls, video calls and messaging quality), (b) Improved sign in - sign back into your account more easily (Version 2017.08.15: "log in" features, user account related functions), (c) New controls added to help users manage vibration and LED notification alerts. (Version 2017.07.05: notification), (d) Improvements to PSTN call stability (Version 2017.07.05: connection), (e) Messaging improvements Add content to chats via the + button and enjoy more room for your messages. (Version 2017.08.02: messaging), (f) The ability to add or remove contacts from your profile (Version 2017.08.01), (g) Activity indicators - see who's currently active in your Chats list (Version 2017.08.02: contacts and statuses). Hence, due to the correlation between the previously mentioned issues detected using our method and the content of the following up updates, we can verify the existence of those issues. However, whether the reason of the according update is the user reviews is unknown. On the other hand, we can also detect the disagreement amongst users' opinions. For example, a number of users think the calling quality deteriorated after the update while many others think it was improved $((t^+_{(i-1)6}, t^-_{i10})$ and $(t^-_{(i-1)3}, t^+_{i6}))$. A number of users also think the update improves the app when other users think it is just as bad as the previous $((t^-_{(i-1)7}, t^+_{i3})$ and $(t^-_{(i-1)3}, t^-_{i10}))$. We can obtain more details regarding users' different opinions by further investigating the keywords-related review texts.

IV. Related Work

The spontaneous feedback from the users, i.e., the user reviews, helps effectively the evolution of the target system, where a key to enable such feedback is to ease the users effort in composing and uploading it [22]. For the contemporary mobile apps, the app distribution platforms, e.g., Apple AppStore, and Google Play, enable such spontaneous reviews of the users and facilitate the developers in terms of maintaining and evolving mobile apps [23]. Such feedback and reviews contain helpful information for developers in terms of identifying missing features and improving software quality [24]. From those review information, user requirements can be elicited continuously and, in a crowd-based fashion [25] [26].

The reviews of the mobile app users reflect a variety of topics, which majorly cover the perspectives of bug reports, feature requests, user experiences, solution proposal, information seeking and giving, and general ratings [2]–[4].

For such purpose, NLP, SA, and supervised learning are the common techniques used to classify user reviews [3] [4]. According to recent studies, the combination of NLP and SA techniques has high accuracy in detecting useful sentences [4]. These techniques are also used in many other studies in terms of review opinion mining [7] [9] [24].

Many studies have contributed to the user opinion mining of mobile apps. Fu et al. [5] proposes WisCom, which can detect why the users like or dislike a particular app based on the users reviews throughout time and provide insights regarding the users concerns and preferences in the app market. Similar studies regarding mining information from app stores data focus on different perspectives of the issues, e.g., the correlations between ratings and download rank [6], ratings and API use [27], review classification and useful sentences detection [4]. On the other hand, Chen et al. [7] provides the AR-miner framework, which facilitates the informative reviews extraction, review grouping based on topics, review prioritization and informative reviews presentation with visualization. Guzman and Maalej [8] proposes an approach focusing on feature extraction and sentiment analysis, which facilitates the evaluation of individual app features. Similarly, Iacob and Harrison [9] focuses also on the feature requests extraction but via means of linguistic rules and LDA topic modeling. Many studies also provide methods of using automatic classification method to study mobile app user reviews [28] [29] [30]

Compared to the previous mentioned approaches in user review opinion mining, our method aims towards the similar topic detection and analysis concerning not only the app in general but also the particular major updates. Furthermore, we focus on the topic similarity of data segments, classified by sentiment analysis and supervised learning, which is different from the methods mentioned above. It enables the developers to acquire information regarding each individual update and will provide insights on the future updates.

V. Conclusion

In this study, we propose a method for analyzing the correlation of mobile apps user reviews before and after a particular app updates in order to detect how users' opinions change with the update released. After classifying the reviews before and after a particular update by positive and negative sentiment, we extract the topics of each segment. By comparing the similarities of these extracted topics, we identify both the positive and negative issues reflected by these reviews regarding the particular update and the app in general. Overall, this study is an exploratory investigation on using user review opinion mining techniques in detecting update-specific issues. The future studies shall extend the use of this method to the whole maintenance lifecycle of mobile apps to investigate the broader correlation between users feedback and the apps' update trends. Releasing strategies improvement based on this method will also be studied. Other factors, e.g., the different app categories, different platforms, and different mining and analysis techniques will also be taken into account.

References

[1] X. Li, Z. Zhang, and J. Nummenmaa, "Models for mobile application maintenance based on update history," in Evaluation of Novel Approaches to Software Engineering (ENASE), 2014 International Conference on. IEEE, 2014, pp. 1–6.

[2] H. Khalid, E. Shihab, M. Nagappan, and A. E. Hassan, "What do mobile app users complain about?" IEEE Software, vol. 32, no. 3, 2015, pp. 70–77.

[3] W. Maalej and H. Nabil, "Bug report, feature request, or simply praise? on automatically classifying app reviews," in 2015 IEEE 23rd international requirements engineering conference (RE). IEEE, 2015, pp. 116–125.

[4] S. Panichella, A. Di Sorbo, E. Guzman, C. A. Visaggio, G. Canfora, and H. C. Gall, "How can i improve my app? classifying user reviews for software maintenance and evolution," in Software maintenance and evolution (ICSME), 2015 IEEE international conference on. IEEE, 2015, pp. 281–290.

[5] B. Fu, J. Lin, L. Li, C. Faloutsos, J. Hong, and N. Sadeh, "Why people hate your app: Making sense of user feedback in a mobile app store," in Proceedings of the 19th ACM SIGKDD international conference on Knowledge discovery and data mining. ACM, 2013, pp. 1276–1284.

[6] M. Harman, Y. Jia, and Y. Zhang, "App store mining and analysis: Msr for app stores," in Proceedings of the 9th IEEE Working Conference on Mining Software Repositories. IEEE Press, 2012, pp. 108–111.

[7] N. Chen, J. Lin, S. C. Hoi, X. Xiao, and B. Zhang, "Ar-miner: mining informative reviews for developers from mobile app marketplace," in Proceedings of the 36th International Conference on Software Engineering. ACM, 2014, pp. 767–778.

[8] E. Guzman and W. Maalej, "How do users like this feature? a fine grained sentiment analysis of app reviews," in Requirements Engineering Conference (RE), 2014 IEEE 22nd International. IEEE, 2014, pp. 153–162.

[9] C. Iacob and R. Harrison, "Retrieving and analyzing mobile apps feature requests from online reviews," in Proceedings of the 10th Working Conference on Mining Software Repositories. IEEE Press, 2013, pp. 41–44.

[10] C. H. E. Gilbert, "Vader: A parsimonious rule-based model for sentiment analysis of social media text," in ICWSM, 2014.

[11] D. M. Blei, A. Y. Ng, and M. I. Jordan, "Latent dirichlet allocation," Journal of Machine Learning Research, vol. 3, 2003, pp. 993–1022.

[12] T. T. Tanimoto, "Ibm internal report," Nov, vol. 17, 1957, p. 1957.

[13] B. V. Kumar and L. Hassebrook, "Performance measures for correlation filters," Applied optics, vol. 29, no. 20, 1990, pp. 2997–3006.

[14] Langdetect, https://pypi.python.org/pypi/langdetect, last accessed on 06/20/18.

[15] Pyenchant, https://pypi.python.org/pypi/pyenchant, last accessed on 06/20/18.

[16] NLTK, http://www.nltk.org, last accessed on 06/20/18.

[17] E. Cambria, R. Speer, C. Havasi, and A. Hussain, "Senticnet: A publicly available semantic resource for opinion mining." in AAAI fall symposium: commonsense knowledge, vol. 10, no. 0, 2010.

[18] S. Baccianella, A. Esuli, and F. Sebastiani, "Sentiwordnet 3.0: an enhanced lexical resource for sentiment analysis and opinion mining." in Lrec, vol. 10, no. 2010, 2010, pp. 2200–2204.

[19] M. M. Bradley and P. J. Lang, "Affective norms for english words (anew): Instruction manual and affective ratings," Citeseer, Tech. Rep., 1999.

[20] M. Stevenson and Y. Wilks, "Word sense disambiguation," The Oxford Handbook of Comp. Linguistics, 2003, pp. 249–265.

[21] "Skype on Google Play," URL: https://play.google.com/store/apps/details?id=com.skype.raider, last accessed on 06/20/18.

[22] K. Schneider, "Focusing spontaneous feedback to support system evolution," in RE, pp. 165–174.

[23] D. Pagano and W. Maalej, "User feedback in the appstore: An empirical study," in Requirements Engineering Conference (RE), 2013 21st IEEE International. IEEE, 2013, pp. 125–134.

[24] L. V. Galvis Carreño and K. Winbladh, "Analysis of user comments: an approach for software requirements evolution," in Proceedings of the 2013 International Conference on Software Engineering. IEEE Press, 2013, pp. 582–591.

[25] N. Seyff, F. Graf, and N. Maiden, "Using mobile re tools to give end-users their own voice," in Requirements Engineering Conference (RE), 2010 18th IEEE International. IEEE, 2010, pp. 37–46.

[26] E. C. Groen, J. Doerr, and S. Adam, "Towards crowd-based requirements engineering a research preview," in International Working Conference on Requirements Engineering: Foundation for Software Quality. Springer, 2015, pp. 247–253.

[27] G. Bavota, M. Linares-Vasquez, C. E. Bernal-Cardenas, M. Di Penta, R. Oliveto, and D. Poshyvanyk, "The impact of api change-and fault-proneness on the user ratings of android apps," IEEE Trans. on Soft. Engin., vol. 41, no. 4, 2015, pp. 384–407.

[28] S. McIlroy, N. Ali, H. Khalid, and A. E. Hassan, "Analyzing and automatically labelling the types of user issues that are raised in mobile app reviews," Empirical Software Engineering, vol. 21, no. 3, 2016, pp. 1067–1106.

[29] W. Maalej, Z. Kurtanović, H. Nabil, and C. Stanik, "On the automatic classification of app reviews," Requirements Engineering, vol. 21, no. 3, 2016, pp. 311–331.

[30] Z. Sun, Z. Ji, P. Zhang, C. Chen, X. Qian, X. Du, and Q. Wan, "Automatic labeling of mobile apps by the type of psychological needs they satisfy," Telematics and Informatics, vol. 34, no. 5, 2017, pp. 767–778.

Database Model Visualization in Virtual Reality: A WebVR and Benediktine Space Approach

Roy Oberhauser
Computer Science Dept.
Aalen University
Aalen, Germany
e-mail: roy.oberhauser@hs-aalen.de

***Abstract* - As the data era and the Internet of Everything unfolds, databases are becoming ubiquitous and an integral part of software while alternative database types such as NoSQL grow in popularity. Thus, software engineers, not just database specialists, are more likely to encounter and need to deal with these databases. While Virtual Reality (VR) technology has increased in popularity, its integration in software development tooling has been limited. One application area for WebVR technology includes database-model visualization, permitting web-based cross-platform and remote VR access. This paper describes Virtual Reality Immersion in Data Models (VRiDaM), a generic database-model approach for visualizing, navigating, and conveying database-model information interactively in a web browser using WebVR technology utilizing Benediktine space visualization for heterogeneous (relational and NoSQL) database models. A prototype shows its viability and an empirical study looked at usability, effectiveness, and efficiency.**

Keywords - virtual reality; database visualization; database tools; visual development environments; database modeling; software engineering; WebVR; Benediktine space.

I. INTRODUCTION

Data has become the most coveted "raw material" of both our time and the foreseeable future, in some respects analogous to a gold rush. Cisco estimates there will be 27bn networked devices by 2021 [1]. The ongoing digitalization involving Industry 4.0 and the Internet of Everything will imply a large increase in databases to be able to store and retrieve this data, in particular embedded databases. IDC estimates the current annual data creation rate at 16.1ZB (Zettabytes), and by 2025 163ZB, with embedded data by then constituting nearly 20% of all data created [2]. As data explodes, software engineers are increasingly faced with the daunting task of structuring and analyzing such databases across various DataBase Management System (DBMS) types, including relational and NoSQL types such as document (semi-structured), key-value, wide column (extensible record), in memory, and graph [3].

Thus, software engineers are increasingly faced with developing and maintaining software that integrates some form of data repository, data store, or database. While the original developers may have a clear (and correct to a certain degree) mental model of their actual data model, the maintenance situation is exacerbated by proliferation of relational (mostly SQL) and NoSQL database types and the relatively high turnover rates common in the software industry, resulting in developers unfamiliar with the data models attempting to quickly comprehend the database structures involved with these software applications.

Humans tend to be visually-oriented and can detect and remember visual patterns well. Information visualization has the potential to support human understanding and insight while dealing with resource constraints on the human as well as computer side. Common ways for visually conveying database structures include 2D entity-relationship (E-R) modeling and diagrams [4], but these are typically applied to relational databases (RDB) and NoSQL databases may or may not have a tool that includes visual support. As to DBMS tools, often a database product has a preferred product-specific tool offering web-based or standard 2D graphical user interfaces (GUIs), while certain tools support multiple database products of one specific type (e.g., MySQL workbench for SQL databases).

Contemporaneously, VR has made inroads in its accessibility as hardware prices have dropped and capabilities have improved. The VR market is rapidly expanding, with VR revenue reaching $2.7bn in 2016, a 10-fold increase to $25bn by 2021 [5]. However, software engineers mostly do not have access to integrated VR capabilities in their development tools. Broad VR usage is relatively new and this market segment small compared to the general VR market.

This application paper contributes Virtual Reality Immersion in Data Models (VRiDaM, pronounced like freedom), a generalized approach to heterogeneous (relational and non-relational) database-model visualization in VR , using WebVR in a web browser and a Benediktine-space [6]-[9] visualization paradigm. Thus, database models from different data store types can be visualized and navigated (locally or remotely) in VR via a cross-platform web browser and a VR headset and controller. We describe its principles and features for visualizing, navigating, and conveying database information interactively to support exploratory, analytical, and descriptive cognitive processes [10]. A prototype implementation demonstrates its viability and its usability is evaluated in an empirical study.

The paper is organized as follows: the following section discusses related work; Section 3 presents our solution approach. In Section 4, our implementation is described. An evaluation is described in Section 5, followed by a conclusion.

II. Related Work

We are unaware of directly related work regarding database visualization using VR. VR Juggler [11] provides VR support for developing VR applications, but not for database modeling and visualization. As to VR approaches for software structure visualization, ExplorViz [12] is a WebVR application that supports VR exploration of 3D software cities using Oculus Rift together with Microsoft Kinect for gesture recognition. As to non-VR visualization, [13] provides an overview and survey of 3D software visualization tools across various software engineering areas. Software Galaxies [14] gives a web-based visualization of dependencies among popular package managers and supports flying, with each star representing a package clustered by dependencies. CodeCity [15] is a 3D software visualization approach based on a city metaphor and implemented in SmallTalk on the Moose reengineering framework. X3D-UML [16] provides 3D support with UML grouping classes in planes. In contrast, VRiDaM focuses on visualizing database structures and leverages WebVR capabilities without requiring gestures.

Database management (DBM) tools are typically DB type-specific and require some installation. Each professional RDB product usually offers its own tool, but since most RDBs support the Structured Query Language (SQL), certain RDB tools can access other RDBs using RDB-specific drivers. For example, MySQL Workbench works across multiple databases and supports reverse-engineering of 2D E-R diagrams. Schemaball [17] provides a 2D circular composite schema diagram for SQL databases. As to 3D RDB tools, DIVA (Database Immersive Visual Analysis) uses stacked rings with rectangular tables attached to them (forming a cylinder), with the tables with the most foreign keys sorted to the top of the stack. Alternatively, stacked square layers of tables can be displayed and 2D E-R diagrams shown. Actual data values are not visualized. For NoSQL databases, each database type differs and the associated DBM tools. One example of a popular wide-column database (WDB) is Apache Cassandra, for which DataStax Studio is a Java-based DBM tool with a web GUI (Graphical User Interface). As to document-oriented databases (DDBs), MongoDB is a popular example and MongoDB Compass, Robomongo, and Studio 3T being example DBM tools. For graph databases (GDB), Neo4j is popular and graph DBM tools include Neo4j admin, Structr, Gephi, Graffeine, etc. In contrast, the VRiDaM approach is more generalized to work across heterogeneous DB types, thus permitting users to only ramp up on one tool, it is cross-platform and provides an immersive web-based VR experience. Furthermore, in contrast to the 3D DIVA or 2D Schemaball, our approach avoids the visual connection 'yarnballs' as the number of connections and tables scale.

Work on big data visualization techniques in conjunction with VR is discussed by Olshannikova et al. in [18]. Herman, Melançon, and Marshall [19] survey work on graph visualization and navigation for information visualization. In contrast, our focus is displaying the database-model structure, not on displaying and analyzing large amounts of data per se, and we apply Benediktine spatial placement in conjunction with a dynamic self-organizing force-directed graph [20].

III. Solution

Visualization, especially VR with its wide viewing angles, can leverage peripheral vision for information, whereby visual data is both consciously and unconsciously seen and processed. If leveraged well, visualization can be cognitively easier in providing insights than an equivalent textual analysis would require. Traditional text-centric tabular formats or boxes in E-R diagrams do not explicitly take advantage of such visual capabilities. Also, if the contents of each database table were visualized as a rectangular 2D object, as it scales both in number of tables and the size of various tables, lucidity issues occur that nullify the advantage of VR visualization.

To provide some background context for our solution, we describe several perspectives that were considered. Information can be grouped and large amounts of information provided in a relatively small amount of graphical space. Yet humans are limited in their sensory perception and focus, and thus visualization considerations include: determining the proper balance for what to place into visual focus in which context, what to place into the periphery, what to hide or show, and to what extent and at what point should what be visualized. To develop actionable insights from visualization, the knowledge crystallization cognitive process involves acquiring information, making sense of it, creating something new, and acting on it [21]. Regarding visual perception, gestalt psychology [22] is based on the four principles of emergence, reification, multistable perception, and invariance. Formulated gestalt grouping laws regarding visual perception include proximity, similarity, closure, symmetry, common fate, continuity, good gestalt, past experience, common region, and element connectedness. For visual representation, we considered Don Norman's design principles, in particular affordance, consistency, and mapping [23]. Other concepts considered were [9] information space, cognitive space, spatialization, ordination, and pre-attentive processing, which refers to the accumulation of information from the environment subconsciously [24]. Visualization techniques explicitly analyzed with regard to their appropriateness for displaying data models in VR included books, cone trees, fisheye views, information cubes, perspective walls, spheres, surface plots/cityscapes/3D bar graphs, viewpoints, workspace/information space/3D rooms, worlds in worlds, and Benediktine space [19][21].

A. *Benediktine Space*

Benediktine space transforms or maps an information object's attributes to extrinsic (e.g., Cartesian coordinates, time) and intrinsic (e.g., size, shape, color) information spatial dimensions. To keep objects from overlapping, mapping principles include exclusion, maximal exclusion, scale, and transit [6][7][8][9].

B. *WebVR*

WebVR is a Mozilla JavaScript API that enables web browsers to access VR hardware. A-Frame is an open source framework for displaying VR content within HTML. It is based on an entity component system architecture in which each object in a scene is an entity (a container) consisting of components that provide desired functionality or behavior for that entity. A-Frame uses the three.js library to provide 3D graphics display in the browser and simplify WebGL programming. Systems are data containers. In contrast to game or PC station VR solutions, the use of VR within web browsers is relatively new, thus in deciding on the visualization techniques to use we considered the limitations and available capabilities and performance offered with WebVR for standard hardware (such as notebooks) that developers might use. Visualization considerations included selecting what and how many objects are displayed at any given time. Furthermore, in contrast to games, there is no real upper limit on the number of simultaneous entities a database or database model may have, which may overtax the computing and rendering capabilities and have negative impacts on the frame rates in VR, making the experience unsatisfactory and possibly resulting in VR sickness.

To characterize WebVR performance, we experimented with the implementation, some measurements of which are shown in Table 1. They are averaged across 10 measurements for 10 tables with 50 columns each on a notebook with Intel Core i5-3320M 2.6Ghz, 8GB RAM, Win7 x64, Intel HD Graphics 4000, Chrome 60.0.3112.113 and A-Frame 0.6.1.

TABLE I. AVERAGE A-FRAME PERFORMANCE (FRAMES PER SECOND)

Variants	Loading (fps)	Running (fps)
spheres, no edges	25	61
spheres, with edges	21	53
labeled spheres, no edges	11	19
circles, no edges	25	57
spheres, no edges (10x nodes)	3	12

Based on our experience and measurements with the A-Frame implementation, the following performance findings were made and affected our solution: 1) the number of rendered objects has a major impact on performance, 2) edges have a negative effect on performance, 3) text labels have a severe impact, 4) circles and spheres are equivalent.

For Finding 1, that implies that only the minimum number of objects should be displayed. Thus, rows (data values) will only be shown for selected column, not for all columns. Due to Finding 2, objects will be displayed without edges and connectors between objects will be avoided (force-graph). Due to Finding 3, text will be limited and the data value only shown when a circle (tuple) is selected.

C. *VRiDaM Solution*

Our VRiDaM solution architecture is based on the information visualization reference model by Card et al. [25] (see Figure 1) and involves transforming the raw data and its metadata to internal structures (the first two being purely data forms), and then mapping these to visual element structures, and transforming these to the views seen be the user (the last two being visual forms). To adjust the views, the user provides interaction input affecting one of the aforementioned transformation steps.

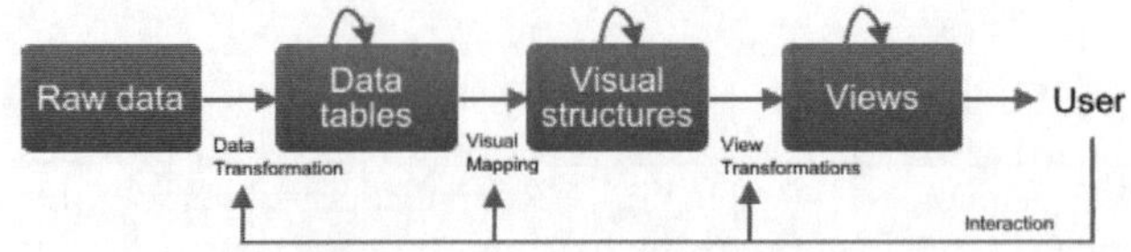

Figure 1. VRiDaM architecture.

The VRiDaM solution principles (P:) are as follows:

Support heterogeneous database-model types. Our VR approach works across different databases products and database types (SQL and NoSQL), thus familiarity with a single VR app could be leveraged across the various database types. Alternatively, currently developing unique VR app tools for each database and/or database type would be exorbitant relative to the number of software engineers that have VR capabilities and have database-model interests, and inefficient from a learning/training perspective.

Leverage spatial visualization in VR using a Benediktine spatial object placement approach. Our approach leverages the additional dimensional visualization and navigational capabilities VR provides (within current limitations of WebVR). Specifically, we utilize a Benediktine space visualization technique [6] with visual object spatial placement based on extrinsic spatial dimensions, whereas other entity properties are represented by intrinsic dimensions (form, size, color, etc.). The principle of exclusion ensures no two objects occupy the same spatial location, and the principle of maximal exclusion ensures that different data items are separated as much as possible [7].

Leverage dynamic self-organizing force-directed graph visualization to indicate the strength of relationship between objects via proximity. For visualizing relations, dynamic self-organizing force-directed graph placement [20] can be used in place of connectors to indicate via proximity more strongly related entities from those that are less- or unrelated. This is combined with visual highlighting of related objects when selecting an object. In this way we intend to avoid the "ball of yarn" issue with visual connectors as database models scale.

Cross-platform web-centric VR access. Our approach utilizes a browser-based implementation based on WebVR to enable cross-platform access to VR content assuming the user has a VR headset. Software engineers often work across different operating systems (Windows, Linux, etc.), and this permits them to utilize the app from any platform with appropriate WebVR browser support.

IV. IMPLEMENTATION

The WebVR-based prototype uses A-Frame and D3.js, which produces dynamic, interactive data visualizations in web browsers. For a self-organizing force-directed graph, our implementation uses the d3-force-3d physics engine from D3. Firefox and Chrome were used as web browsers. For database connectivity, the Spring Framework 4.3.1 was used and tested with PostgreSQL, MSSQL, MongoDB, Cassandra, and Neo4j. Content for the force-directed graph component was transformed to JSON format. The Northwind Trading sample database consisting of 13 tables and 6635 records was used, primarily, . Figure 2 shows the class diagram regarding database integration.

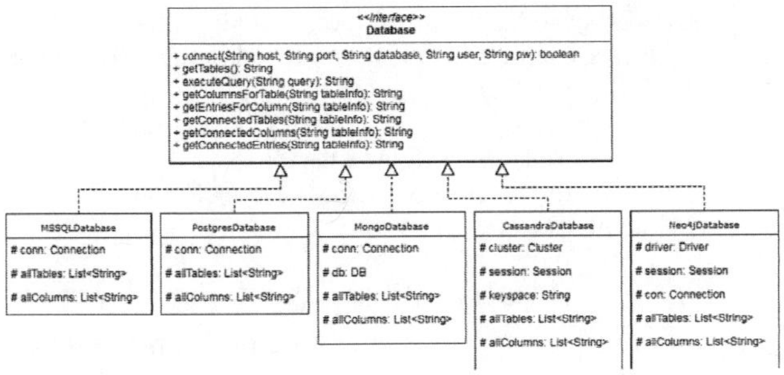

Figure 2. Class diagram of database integration.

The following visual object forms were selected:

Cubes are used to represent database tables (collections for document stores, or labels for graphs), analogous to cube furniture that can be used as a table (Figure 3).

Cylinders are used to represent database columns (set of similarly typed data, known as keys for document stores or graphs), analogous to columns in a building (Figure 4).

Planes are used for projecting the database data records (rows, tuples, or entries - the actual data values) since these can be very large in both columns and records and would thus occupy a large amount of VR space Figure 5). A plane supports maximum readability and permits VR navigation around it.

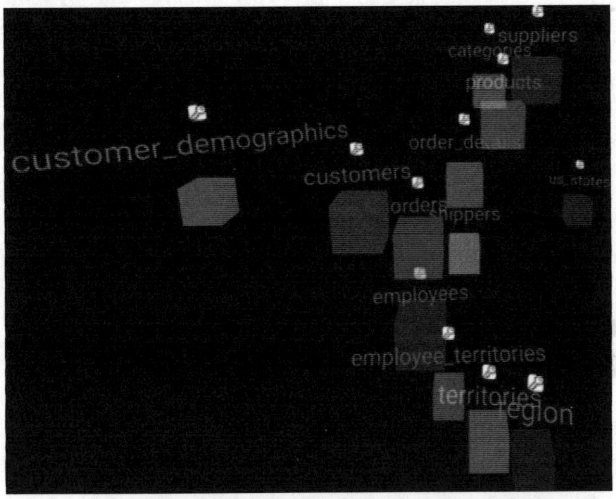

Figure 3. VRiDaM showing Northwind tables in Benediktine space.

Figure 4. Columns visible orbiting selected table (identical color).

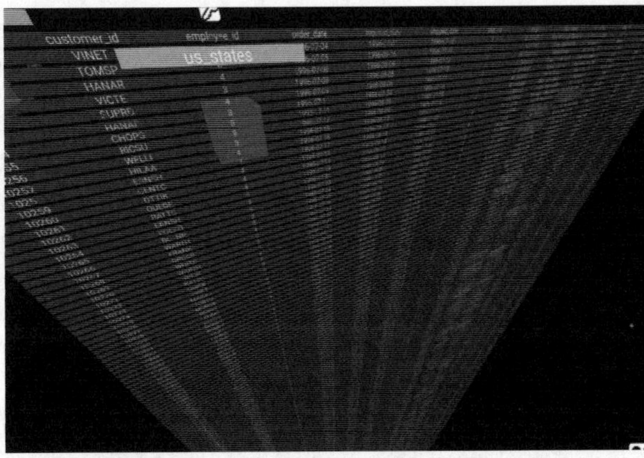

Figure 5. Table records projected onto a plane.

As to navigation and interaction, users can move objects as desired using standard VR controllers (we used an HTC Vive) or can use a mouse and keyboard. As seen in Figure 6, besides using spatial proximity to indicate closer associations, if a user selects an object, that object and all its directly referenced objects are highlighted. A key image is provided as an affordance and, if selected, a popup shows the primary and foreign keys names. If desired, lines can optionally be used to emphasize relations as shown in Figure 7.

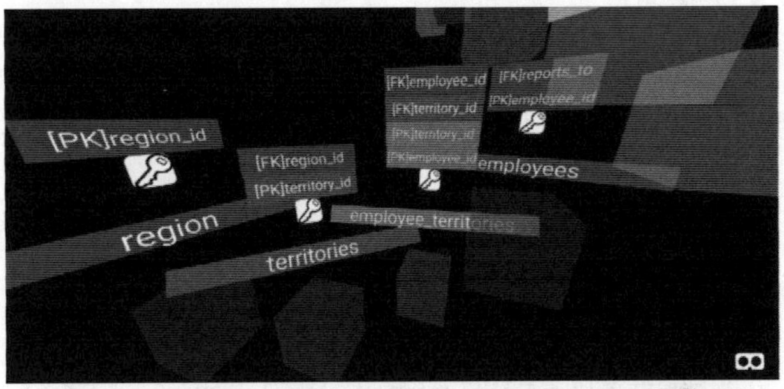

Figure 6. Primary and foreign keys for table shown as popups.

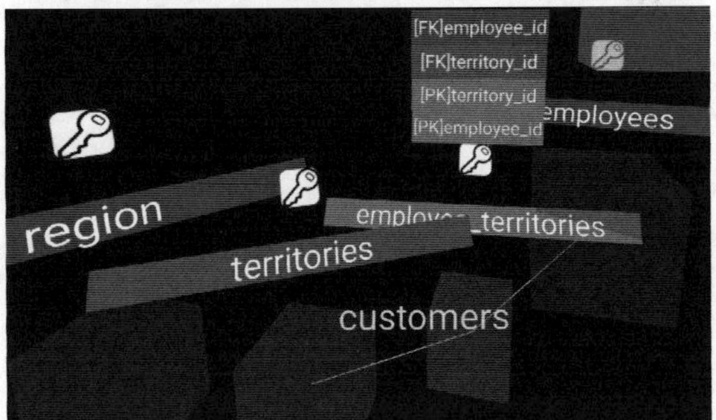

Figure 7. Example optional relation visualization using lines.

The configuration menu is overlaid and can be used to connect to a database and query (e.g., SQL, Cypher, etc.) by typing on the keyboard and executed via enter. In order to quickly find a table, they are listed on the menu for selection and navigation to the visual object.

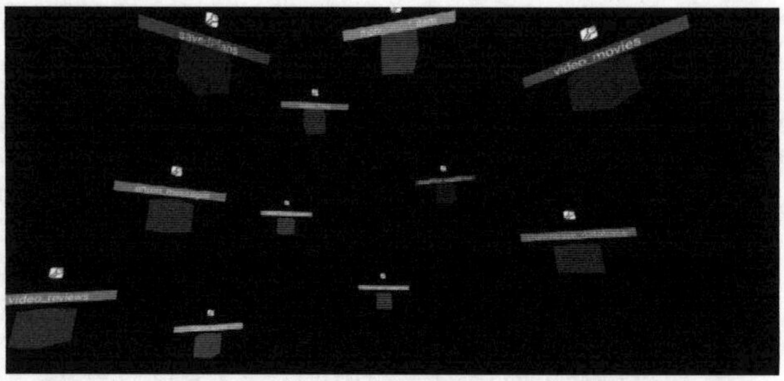

Figure 8. VRiDaM of MongoDB with dbkoda example data [26], showing spatial orientation and not intended to be readable.

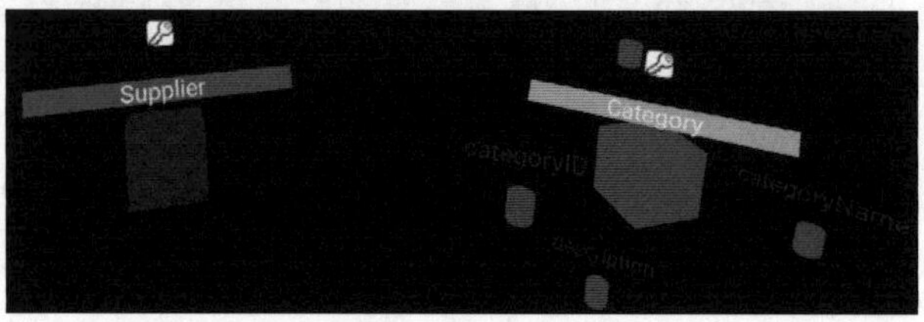

Figure 9. VRiDaM of Neo4j with Northwind example data.

Figure 8 shows the VRiDaM visualization for MongoDB with dbkoda example data [26] (a Northwind port was no longer available), while Figure 9 shows Neo4j with Northwind example data.

V. Evaluation

To evaluate VRiDaM, we compared its usage with a typical 2D database tool, DbVisualizer 10.0.13 (Free), shown in Figure 10 with the Northwind database loaded to provide an impression of the model's complexity, not meant to be readable. A convenience sample of eleven computer science students was selected. One experienced VR sickness symptoms and thus only the remaining ten were included in the results. All indicated they had some familiarity with SQL and they lacked NoSQL experience, so we chose to compare VRiDaM with an SQL tool. Three had not experienced VR before. The subjects were randomly selected to start in either VR mode (6) or the common tool (4). PostgreSQL Version 10 with the Northwind sample database (Figure 11Figure 10.) was used. Java 8 update 151, Apache Tomcat v8.0, AFRAME 0.8.2, Firefox 61, and SteamVR Version 2018-05-24 (1527117754).

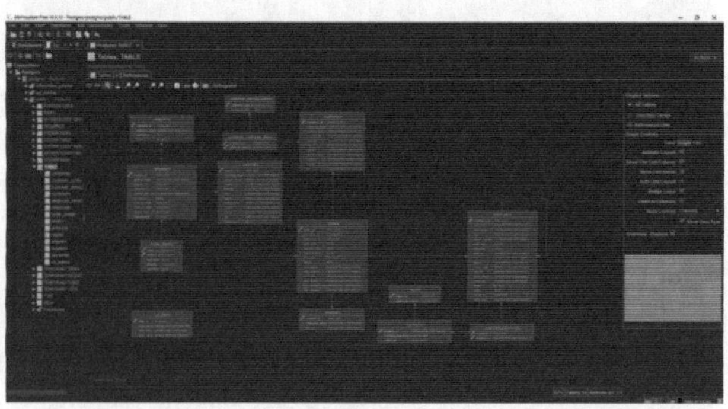

Figure 10. Northwind Traders data model in DbVisualizer.

These database tasks were given verbally and equivalent but not the exact same five questions asked in the other mode:

1) Which tables have a relation to table X?
2) To which table(s) does the table X have a relation?
3) What columns does table X have?
4) What are the foreign or primary keys of table X?
5) What are the keys in table X?

TABLE II. VRiDaM vs. DbVisualizer Tasks (averaged)

	VRiDaM	DbVisualizer
Task duration (mm:ss)	4:48	1:46
Cumulative answers given (total/incorrect/missing)	130/6/4	140/1/6
Task correctness	92%	95%

The tasks results are shown in Table II. VRiDaM task duration was 2.7 times longer, and this can be expected since VR requires navigation time through space that 2D tools do not incur. The number of correct answers across the five tasks were 13 in VR and 14 in DbVisualizer, with ten subjects resulting in 130 or 140 cumulatively correct answers respectively. These longer VR task durations may be acceptable for certain user scenarios, and gives insight into what liabilities can be expected. A correctness difference of 3% across ten subjects is not necessarily significant and shows that the users were able to immerse themselves within minutes into a Benediktine space paradigm and perform tasks effectively. The task correctness differences could be attributed to personality, human alertness, distraction, or other factors beyond the paradigms or VR influence, as only 4 subjects in VR and only 3 subjects in non-VR were responsible for all errors, the rest had no mistakes.

Subjective impressions are shown in Figure 11 for VRiDaM intuitiveness and suitability of the controller interface and visualization as well as overall enjoyment. We note no significant difference between the interaction and the visualization intuitiveness or suitability. Only one preferred VRiDaM. This may indicate that more training and experience would be needed for them to feel more comfortable with a VR tool than with a 2D tool. Various debriefing comments indicated that the Benediktine spatial arrangement was either liked or not an issue for the subjects. When debriefed about what they liked about VRiDaM, comments included that it was a better database-model visualization, that tables were real objects instead of text boxes, how tables where displayed in space, and the highlighting effect.

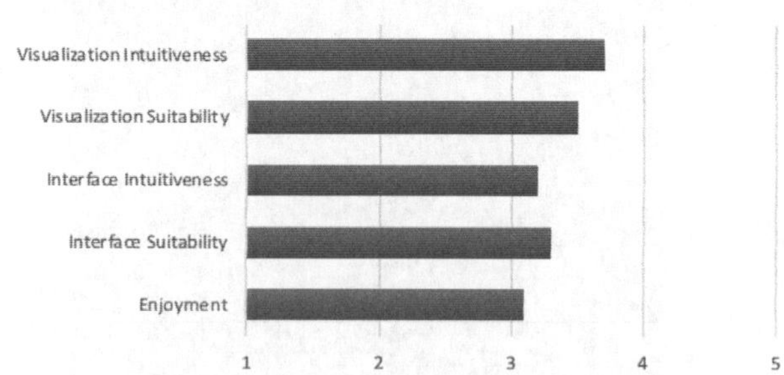

Figure 11. Average responses for VRiDaM (scale of 1 to 5 with 5 best).

The evaluation shows some of the challenges in utilizing VR for database-model visualization and interaction. VR object interaction is not standardized nor do users have familiarity and experience with it as they do with 2D mouse-based user interfaces. While VR enables new immersive paradigms and metaphors, these are not necessarily immediately intuitive. VR movement (moving the camera perspective) is more time consuming than scrolling or zooming a 2D perspective. For simpler tasks, VR tends to require more interaction time to accomplish the same task and thus entails efficiency costs. A 3D space permits objects to hide other objects, and for opaque objects requires movement to determine that no other objects are hidden. Given that the subjects were already familiar with E-R diagrams and SQL tools, yet had no prior training with VRiDaM and Benediktine space, we are satisfied with the ratings on suitability and intuitiveness. Based on comments about what subjects liked about VRiDaM we see it as a positive indicator and intend to investigate this approach further.

VI. CONCLUSION

This paper contributes VRiDaM, an immersive WebVR heterogeneous database visualization approach, applying Benediktine space visualization and force-directed graphs to (relational and non-relational) database models. It thus avoids the connection "yarn-balls" other techniques have in visualizing connections by leveraging spatial locality. A prototype was used to verify its viability and an empirical study evaluated its usability.

The empirical evaluation showed VRiDaM to be less efficient for equivalent analysis tasks while correctness was slightly worse. Intuitiveness, suitability, and enjoyment were given a better than neutral rating on average. One case of VR sickness occurred and we hope to address it in future work.

One ongoing challenge for a generic tool approach is the plethora of non-standardized interfaces to NoSQL and other databases. However, by providing driver plugins we believe that the adaptation overhead is small in relation to the advantages of a VR visualization that VRiDaM brings. Future work includes a more comprehensive empirical study and will investigate various optimizations to improve usability, performance, and scalability.

ACKNOWLEDGMENT

The author thanks Christoph Bauer and Camil Pogolski for assistance with the design, implementation, and evaluation.

REFERENCES

[1] Cisco. The Zettabyte Era: Trends and Analysis. (Jun 7, 2017). Whitepaper. Available from https://www.cisco.com/c/en/us/solutions/collateral/service-provider/visual-networking-index-vni/vni-hyperconnectivity-wp.html 2018.07.24

[2] D. Reinsel, J. Gantz, and J. Rydning, "Data Age 2025: The Evolution of Data to Life-Critical," IDC Whitepaper (April, 2017).

[3] R. Cattell, "Scalable SQL and NoSQL data stores," Acm Sigmod Record 39, no. 4, pp. 2-27, 2011.

[4] P. Chen, "Entity-Relationship Modeling: Historical Events, Future Trends, and Lessons Learned," In Software pioneers. Springer-Verlag, pp. 296-310, 2002.

[5] T. Merel, "The reality of VR/AR growth," Jan 11, 2017. Available from http://techcrunch.com/2017/01/11/the-reality-of-vrar-growth/ 2018.07.24

[6] M. Benedikt, "Cyberspace: some proposals," In Cyberspace, Michael Benedikt (Ed.). MIT Press, Cambridge, MA, pp. 119-224, 1991.

[7] P. Young, "Three Dimensional Information Visualisation," Technical Report, University of Durham, 1991.

[8] U. Fayyad, A. Wierse, and G. Grinstein (Eds.), Information Visualization in Data Mining and Knowledge Discovery. Morgan Kaufmann, 2002. ISBN: 1558606890.

[9] S. Fabrikant and B. Buttenfield, "Formalizing Semantic Spaces for Information Access," Annals of the Association of American Geographers, 91(2), pp. 263-280, 2001.

[10] D. Butler, J. Almond, R. Bergeron, K. Brodlie, and R. Haber, "Visualization reference models," In Proc. Visualization '93 Conf., IEEE CS Press, pp. 337-342, 1993.

[11] A. Bierbaum et al, "VR Juggler: A virtual platform for virtual reality application development," In Proc. IEEE Virtual Reality. IEEE, pp. 89-96, 2001.

[12] F. Fittkau, A. Krause, and W. Hasselbring. "Exploring software cities in virtual reality," In Proc. IEEE 3rd Working Conf. on Software Visualization (VISSOFT). IEEE, pp. 130-134, 2015.

[13] A. Teyseyre and M. Campo, "An overview of 3D software visualization," In IEEE Trans. on Visualization and Computer Graphics. IEEE, 15(1), pp. 87-105, 2009.

[14] A. Kashcha, "Software Galaxies," Available from http://github.com/anvaka/pm/ 2018.07.24

[15] J. Rilling and S. Mudur, "On the use of metaballs to visually map source code structures and analysis results onto 3d space," In Proc. 9th Work. Conf. on Reverse Engineering. IEEE, pp. 299-308, 2002.

[16] P. McIntosh, "X3D-UML: user-centered design, implementation and evaluation of 3D UML using X3D," Ph.D. dissertation, RMIT University, 2009.

[17] M. Krzywinski, "Schemaball: A New Spin on Database Visualization," In Dr. Dobb's: The World of Software Development,, 2004.

[18] E. Olshannikova, A. Ometov, Y. Koucheryavy, and T. Olsson, "Visualizing Big Data with augmented and virtual reality: challenges and research agenda," J. of Big Data, 2(22), 2015.

[19] I. Herman, G. Melancon, and M. Scott Marshall, "Graph visualization and navigation in information visualization: A survey," In IEEE Transactions on visualization and computer graphics, 6(1), pp. 24-43, 2000.

[20] G. Di Battista, P. Eades, R. Tamassia, and I. Tollis, Graph drawing: algorithms for the visualization of graphs. Prentice Hall PTR, 1998.

[21] S. Card, "Information Visualization," In: Human Computer Interaction Handbook: Fundamentals, Evolving Technologies, and Emerging Applications (Ed: Jacko, J.), Third Edition. CRC Press, pp. 544-545, 2012.

[22] S. Palmer, Vision Science. MIT Press, Cambridge (USA) 1999, ISBN 978-0262161831.

[23] D. Norman, The Design of Everyday Things: Revised and Expanded Edition. Hachette UK, 2013.

[24] A. Van der Heijden, "Perception for selection, selection for action, and action for perception," Visual Cognition, 3(4), pp. 357-361, 1996.

[25] S. Card, J. Mackinlay, and B. Schneiderman (editors), Readings in Information Visualization: Using Vision to Think. Morgan Kaufman, 1999.

[26] [Online] Available from https://github.com/SouthbankSoftware/dbkoda-data 2018.08.12

Redefining KPIs with Information Flow Visualisation – Practitioners' View

Jarkko Hyysalo, Markus Kelanti and Jouni Markkula
M3S Research Unit, Faculty of Information Technology and Electrical Engineering,
University of Oulu
Oulu, Finland
e-mail: {jarkko.hyysalo, markus.kelanti, jouni.markkula}@oulu.fi

***Abstract*—We investigate Key Performance Indicators (KPIs) in a large and multi-national telecommunication company and discover needs and requirements for understanding, analysing and using KPIs from practitioner's perspective. Utilising an action research approach, we identified the existing challenges with KPIs in a large-scale software-intensive systems development in a global setting. Our study revealed several issues with organisations KPIs, e.g., measuring the wrong things or not basing the measurements on reliable data. Based on the identified issues, a visualisation and modelling approach was introduced to reform the KPI representation and formulation to improve understanding and communicating KPIs, as well as their use in decision-making. We suggest that KPI information flow visualisation with appropriate tool support allows redefining usable, valid and reliable KPIs. The problem is addressed with a simple solution that is easily adopted and taken into use at all levels of an organisation.**

Keywords—key performance indicators; KPIs; modelling; visualisation.

I. INTRODUCTION

Managing the development of software systems requires careful attention. Companies operate in turbulent environment with fierce competition and tight time-to-market requirements [1], where knowledge of the performance of the development process, in addition to understanding the system and its development is necessary [2]. Companies use Key Performance Indicators (KPIs) to provide this vital information. KPIs are used to measure, for example, the quality of the product, the features developed, the resources spent in the development and the value delivered to customers. KPIs provide a way to evaluate and improve the product and the process.

There is evident value in defining KPIs for the company. However, it is challenging to formulate KPIs so that they provide useful, valid and reliable information, and many organisations struggle to measure their projects, products and units [3]. Thus, our research question: "How to easily formulate KPIs so that they effectively and reliably measure the product development process performance?"

In this paper, we report an action research study, conducted within a large telecommunications company. The study revealed critical practical challenges in defining and using KPIs in organisation. For solving the challenges, the visualisation of the KPI information flow was found to be essential to provide a better understanding of the process. An approach and supporting tools were developed for the modelling and visualisation of the KPI information flow. Supporting the developers' understanding about the KPI formulation process resulted in KPIs that provide more real value for the organisation, and thus improve the KPI process. Visualisation and supporting tools provided means also to understand and communicate KPIs.

The rest of the paper is organised as follows. Section 2 discusses the related works, Section 3 presents the research approach, Section 4 presents the action research intervention and its results, Section 5 discusses the findings of the empirical work, and Section 6 concludes this work.

II. RELATED WORK

KPIs provide many kinds of information about the development, thus, it is important to select KPIs according to organisation's strategy and objectives [4][5]. Deep understanding of the software development process is needed—providing the understanding of the "why", "what" and "how", defining also the motivations and rationales for activities and flows [6]. Different stakeholders have different views of and needs for the process [6]: Process performers often focus on the "hows", process managers on the "whats", and process engineers on the "whys". Thus, different views are necessary, and KPIs address different needs. Our focus is on how KPIs are used and defined, as well as understanding KPIs and recognising stakeholders' views.

A. Formulating KPIs

Production of good KPI values starts from the reliable source data, but in practice it is hard to collect consistent and comparable data. Further challenge is to decide upon the importance of individual performance measures for decision-makers and prioritisation is a challenge as well. There are approaches that guide KPI work and measure organisational performance; some of them are shortly introduced next.

del-Rey-Chamorro et al. [4] presents a framework for creating KPIs for knowledge management solutions, with eight steps to create KPIs from the strategic level business plan all the way to operational level measurable KPIs utilising templates for KPI formulation and how to bridge the strategic level and operational level. The aim is to evaluate the effectiveness of knowledge management solutions.

Analytical Hierarchy Process (AHP) constructs a pairwise comparison between different KPIs and their hierarchies to evaluate and prioritise them based on SMART (Specific, Measurable, Attainable, Realistic, Time-sensitive) goal setting [5]. The focus is the prioritisation of KPIs to find the most relevant KPIs for the organisation [5]. However, it does not consider how KPIs should be formulated.

Balanced Scorecard [7] measures the organisational performance and aims at transforming the vision and strategy into concrete objectives, aligning departments and units towards common goals, etc. Yet, the following shortcomings are identified: Inaccurate and subjective measures, communication is not participative (only top-down), and inappropriate benchmarks are used for evaluation [8].

ISO standards provide guidelines as well. ISO 9001:2015 specifies requirements for a quality management system. It does not specifically mention "KPIs" but requires metrics to measure the system to ensure: a) the ability to consistently provide products and services that meet customer and applicable statutory and regulatory requirements, and b) aims to enhance customer satisfaction through the effective application of the system, including processes for improvement of the system and the assurance of conformity to the customer and applicable statutory and regulatory requirements [9]. ISO quality management principles [10][11] aims for customer focus, leadership, the involvement of people, process approach, system approach to management, continual improvement, factual approach to decision making, and mutually beneficial supplier relationship.

However, several challenges are identified in current ways for defining KPIs and ensuring that they are based on valid data [12]-[15]: Selecting and defining KPIs is not easy. KPIs are often defined in siloed terms instead of considering the whole organisation, e.g., they only focus on financial aspects and may lack the other aspects like manufacturing. Accurate calculations are hard to create and they easily measure something else than the intended objective. It is difficult to have metrics reflecting strategic drivers and be in line with the organisation's visions and goals. KPIs must also be aligned through the whole organisation and every level of work, from visions and goals to actual implementation. Local optimisation should be avoided, and short-term and long-term goals should be balanced. There are nuances and unforeseeable variables that affect the measures. Finally, KPIs must be put in practice in order to see how they impact the performance and behaviour, and they should be adjusted accordingly. Hence, continuous refining is necessary.

To address the identified issues, improvements are necessary. Properly selected and measured KPIs help decision-making, but getting the measures right requires considerable effort [16]-[18]: Even though the measures are classified into different categories, they are often correlated due to the inherent internal relations of different processes in the supply chain. Complex dependencies, changing goals and tight deadlines make organisations prone to making rushed decisions. Thus, it is important to have a simple way to identify and analyse the KPI data flows and relationships in order to avoid flawed decisions. Due to the complicated relationships, dependencies and conflicts, modelling the relationships is proposed and quick feedback loops are suggested. Furthermore, the goals and KPIs should be adjusted when they are no longer realistic.

In a nutshell, KPIs should be based on data that is available and measurable, and KPIs should provide relevant information. Effective performance measurement system "should provide timely, accurate feedback on the efficiency and effectiveness of operations" [19]. Measurements are also necessary for process improvement purposes—if it can't be measured it can't be improved [20].

B. KPI Visualisation

It is important to understand how to present the measurements and act accordingly. Visualisation helps ensuring that the actions are taken and transparency is achieved [21]. Benefits of KPI visualisation are many: Visualisation is an important factor in thought and communication [22]; Information visualisation and graphical representation help in complex cognitive tasks [23]; Information visualisation supports comprehension and data analysis [24], especially for non-technical users [12]; Visualisation enables smarter decisions and improved productivity [12]; Groups supported by visualisation achieve better productivity, the better quality of outcome and greater knowledge gains than groups without such support [24].

Often KPIs and different measures are correlated and create a complex network of interdependencies [18], thus, understanding the results and the process of formulating KPIs is challenging. Visualisation enables the analysis of activities, the flows (i.e., inputs and outputs), dependencies, and the contexts [25]. It can also be used to visualise the components where KPIs are built from, decomposing the higher level KPIs into lower-level components in order to trace the sources of problems [26]. Visualising the process can be done in several ways with different levels of formalism and detail (cf. [27][28]). Finding the correct level depends on the purpose.

There are examples to KPI visualisation, like del-Río-Ortega et al. [29], who propose an XML-based way for a graphical or a template-based textual notation for business processes. To help selecting the visualisation approach, Staron et al. [30] provide a model based on seven dimensions: type of reporting, data acquisition method, type of stakeholders, method of delivery, frequency of updates, aim of the information, and length of data processing flow. However, formal visualisation and modelling approaches can be cumbersome and "too heavy", e.g., for persons who are not familiar with process modelling concepts [25]. Thus, their benefits are lost. Instead, a simpler approach is proposed. Presenting detailed processes as higher-level entities makes the visualisations more comprehensible, and multiple views or representations for managing the complexity is suggested [25]. Rationale and justification for processes and activities must also be presented as those express why the work is needed. Rationale and reason tell what is meant to be accomplished and why [31][32].

III. RESEARCH APPROACH

The case company was chosen as it could provide data related to the research question. The case organisation is one of the largest data networking and telecommunication technology providers in the world in its field. The organisation is distributed across the globe, operating in over 100 countries, with over 50000 employees globally. The case organisation uses both traditional and agile development methods, depending on the product and development teams. The role of KPIs in the company is to evaluate the performance and ability to meet the organisational goals of every product line. A number of factors make KPI design and calculation complex, like: a) vast number of product lines operating under different organisational units, b) different processes used by development teams, c) different data formats for work items, d) knowledge and data are distributed over several systems, e) several persons are required to handle knowledge and data, and f) copying of data from one format to another and one system to another.

To monitor their product development process, the case company utilised metrics that measure the process on different levels. Data was collected and analysed from various stakeholders to synthesise KPIs and analyse those with the aim to get an accurate picture on product development. The data was provided and calculated by multiple units, a part of the work was done manually and partly assisted by tools. The company was interested to minimise manual data collection and work and improve the tools, as well as the accuracy of the KPI process. In order to reach these goals, the company needed a method for collecting and structuring information to describe the current KPI process from multiple perspectives. It was seen that an action research intervention is needed to analyse the problem and provide improvements. A typical action research cycle is shown in Figure 1. The research started with a pre-study to familiarise the topic and understand the state of the practice.

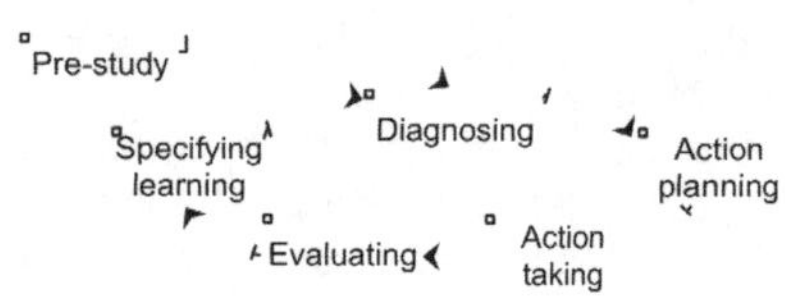

Figure 1. Research process [33].

Experts and managers from different levels of the organisation were interviewed. Eight production lines were involved with at least one production line manager from each attended the modelling session. In each modelling session, the product line manager was assisted with engineer working in the production line who could provide technical details when needed. The persons attending the modelling session were senior engineers or managers, each at least ten years of working in the company. Hence, the results represent the experiences in the case organisation.

In each iteration, the results of the previous iteration were presented first, i.e., the visualisation of the KPI process. In the diagnosing phase, the learnings were diagnosed to commence the action planning. This was done in co-operation with the company. Based on the diagnosis, actions were defined and then carried out. Actions were conducted by implementing a construct and applying it in its intended settings, thus, providing empirical evidence of its use. The action taking phase lasted over two months to ensure the agreed actions were implemented. Then, the results were evaluated and discussed in a workshop. Based on the evaluation and workshop, the learning was specified.

The action research cycle was repeated four times during the study consisting of a total of 30 modelling sessions with 20 stakeholders and 5 analysis workshops. In the modelling session, each participant's viewpoint to the process was modelled and visualised by the researchers, who asked the developers and experts to present the process from their own perspective. The participants were asked to think out loud so that the researchers could understand what they were thinking of. Questions were also asked to elaborate things when necessary. These sessions were also recorded for later use. Researchers made notes and observed the use of the construct. After each evaluation phase, experiences were discussed in a meeting. Gathered feedback, observed challenges and identified issues in the construct were documented. The researchers and the case company representatives also held regular meetings to review the results and decide on further actions. These actions provided rich data for analysis and for specifying learning.

Soft Systems Methodology (SSM) was selected as a basis for our modelling approach. SSM, a problem structuring method popularised by Checkland [34], was applied in the study for structuring KPIs and the KPI process. SSM was chosen because it is an efficient way to understand and address the complex situations, especially when there is no clear problem definition, and it is also useful for information visualisation, to show flows, bottlenecks, inconsistencies and contradictions. It also supports information discovery and decision-making, and it frees cognitive resources that can be used for, e.g., solving development problems [22][35]. Figure 2 presents the basic elements of our approach.

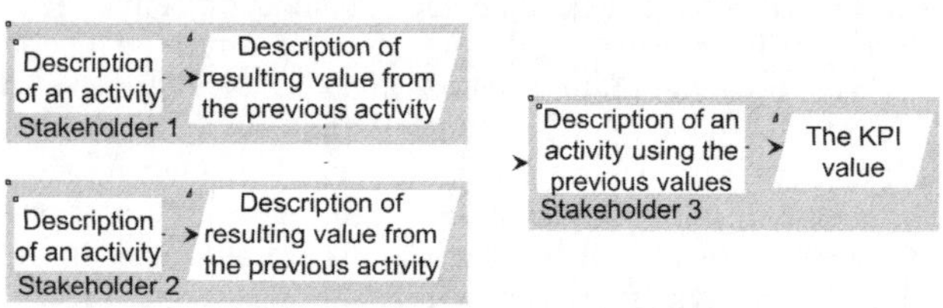

Figure 2. Basic structure of a KPI.

In this approach, practitioners simply model the values and activities from their perspective, regardless of whether the activity or data matches the documented KPI descriptions. It gives the building blocks utilising existing UML notations. Enabling users to construct representations from their perspective and viewpoint is important, as it helps them to come up with solutions to problem issues, and enables them to know what to do next [4].

IV. RESEARCH EXECUTION

The action research intervention consisted of pre-study and four action research cycles. In the pre-study, existing company documentation defining their KPI structure, visualisation and implementation was analysed. The provided information described the intent of each KPI and how those should be formulated. In addition, the company provided a list of persons and organisational units that were involved in the KPI process, including also description how they provided or processed KPI information in the process. In addition, related research was also analysed.

A. *First Action Research Cycle*

DIAGNOSING: The pre-study revealed that the system was more complex than the company documentation indicated. The process included hundreds of stakeholders and multiple variations of the data items. Based on the pre-study, it became necessary to study the overall information flow and stakeholder involvement to determine how the actual system providing the KPIs was structured.

ACTION PLANNING AND TAKING: The plan was to start the KPI system modelling with the pre-study information to formulate a proper soft system model based on SSM. UML flowchart approach and SSM [34] were used to create a KPI soft system model.

EVALUATION AND LEARNING: At the end of the first cycle, the resulting model was evaluated in a workshop with the company representatives. The participants agreed that the model allowed examining KPIs in more detail, which showed that the company documentation did not represent the real KPI behaviour or process. The lack of information about how the data is obtained, undocumented sources, how data is created and how data is used in the decision-making demonstrated that KPIs did not present accurate information or what KPIs were intended to present. Moreover, a simple collapse/expand feature was requested from the tool hiding the complexity or bringing out the details when needed. Participants agreed that this kind of feature would improve visualisation and understanding. Finally, a decision was made to include the stakeholders of KPI modelling in the next research cycle to provide the information missing from the model.

B. *Second Action Research Cycle*

DIAGNOSING: At the previous cycle, the soft system model of the KPI process showed that there was missing information and dead ends not documented in the official documentation. This indicated that there are information only known by involved stakeholders and they should be contacted to provide the missing information.

ACTION PLANNING AND TAKING: The plan was to involve the stakeholders to add the missing information to the model. The stakeholders who would know how data items were created or what information was used to create them were invited to a modelling session, where the information provided by the stakeholder was added to the soft system model created in the previous research cycle. Each modelling session continued updating the same KPI soft system model created in the first cycle. After the sessions, a workshop was organised to evaluate, correct and analyse the KPI soft system model.

EVALUATION AND LEARNING: The new version of the soft system model was discussed with company representatives in a workshop. Based on the analysis of the soft system model, workshop participants thought that the visualisation was complex. They suggested that using stakeholder viewpoints allowed adjusting abstraction levels to manage the complexity. With viewpoints, they were able to examine selected parts of the process and keep the visualisation comprehensible. The feedback for the soft system model indicated that it allowed stakeholders to understand how KPIs were constructed and the model offered enough information to interpret KPIs correctly. According to the participants and the analysis in the workshop, both the UML visualisation and SSM principles created a KPI model that was easy to interpret, translated concepts from one domain to another in a meaningful way and allowed the evaluation of KPIs. Finally, the participants considered it necessary to adjust the way the model was created to support simpler notation and logic to allow users with varying experience to contribute. They thought that the current approach was labour intensive and required deep knowledge of modelling and SSM methodology, which was seen as hindrance as it required an expert to help.

C. *Third Action Research Cycle*

DIAGNOSING: The ability to understand how KPIs actually work was very important for the company personnel as the KPIs did not work as intended and they did not provide the correct information. The modelling of the KPI process needed to continue to provide a better big picture. However, the process needed to be simplified, allowing anyone to understand it and input his or her own viewpoints without the help of the researcher or an expert.

ACTION PLANNING AND TAKING: The existing KPI soft system model was transformed to a digital format utilising Microsoft's Visio tool, allowing anyone to access the model at any time. In addition, the participating stakeholders, developers and managers were taught the modelling method so that they could add their own viewpoints. Teaching the approach also allowed the researchers to develop it further and make it easier to understand and learn. In addition, modelling sessions were continued with those stakeholders who preferred to work with the researchers instead of doing the modelling alone.

EVALUATION AND LEARNING: At the end of the cycle, a workshop was held to discuss the results with all company stakeholders involved in the cycle. Based on the discussion and analysis of the new version of the KPI soft system model, it was quickly noticed that the selected visualisation approach was approved and the process representation it provided was very informative and usable. The KPI soft system model provided a shared understanding about the process and work activities regardless of the expertise or work position. It was easy to discuss the specifics of the process with the representation as a reference point, where each participant could pinpoint the activity or information flow they were interested in.

Further, the findings from second research cycle were re-examined, as more data was available from different teams and product lines. The model started to show its efficiency, as it confirmed that the data that the organisation bases its KPI measurements is not sufficient and that lead to situation where KPIs were not indicating the measurements that they were intended to do. For example, two different organisational units could get different figures based on their source information or interpretation during the data handling. Another concrete example was that the calculation of delivered backlog items didn't take into account the size of the items or items finalised by collaborators, thus, resulting in skewed efficiency measures. Finally, simplifying the modelling process was seen as a way to speed up the modelling process and to help others to understand the modelling process and the modelling language [cf. 36]. This also allowed persons with no prior knowledge on UML to understand process and contribute.

D. *Fourth Action Research Cycle*

DIAGNOSING: Diagnosis of the previous action research cycle called for an analysis of KPIs and presentation on how they can be re-constructed as meaningful KPIs that accurately reflect the development process. Furthermore, additional focus was needed on KPI visualisation due the growing amount of information in a single model. A proper system visualisation was required from different stakeholder perspectives in order to effectively communicate the KPIs to different levels of management, developers and support staff.

ACTION PLANNING AND ACTION TAKING: Based on the diagnosis, this action research cycle was focused on analysing which KPIs the company would benefit on utilising, and use that information to propose how the previously modified KPIs should be constructed. In order to do so, in addition to the existing model, a new KPI soft system model was created to represent the meaningful and accurate KPIs perceived by company management. In addition, special attention was given to the viewpoints to make the visualisation easier to read. The analysis and modelling were done in separate sessions with management stakeholders, similarly to previous research cycles. After a selection of 8 KPIs was fully remodelled, they were compared to the original KPI soft system model to show the current implementation and how the KPIs should be changed to match the desired situation.

EVALUATION AND LEARNING: After the action planning and taking, a workshop was held with all participants. Based on the workshop discussions, it was clear that the stakeholders preferred this approach as it provided the following benefits: 1) It allowed stakeholders to see the current situation and what should be made to the existing KPI system to have meaningful KPIs. 2) The model showed the disparities between stakeholder viewpoints that weren't visible before and the visualisation enabled effective communication on disparities. 3) The resulting model allowed practitioners to re-evaluate their current process and data in order to determine the best course of action. 4) The model was easy to comprehend and it provided reliable results that were accurately reflecting the state of the process.

The fourth action research cycle was the final iteration, as the results were satisfying for both researchers and case organisation. The resulting model worked as the description of KPIs and allowed to construct, analyse and describe KPIs with a single model. The participants also agreed that the measures could now be relied upon, and the KPIs showed effectively what they were supposed to show.

V. Discussion

Our action research intervention revealed several issues with the organisations KPIs and KPI formulation process. The company's process provided KPIs that did not fulfil their intended purpose. There was a clear need to understand the process better—to know more about the reasons KPIs were used for and from what source data the analyses were done from. This called for modelling the KPI information flows from stakeholders' perspectives that contribute to or calculate any KPI data. The focus was to provide visualised and accurate KPIs. Table 1 summarises our findings.

TABLE I. SUMMARY OF THE MAIN FINDINGS

Finding	Implication
Describing KPI as an information flow allowed stakeholders to comprehend the actual meaning of KPI versus what was described in the official documentation.	- Modelling, visualisation and constant analyses are necessary to find out the relevant KPIs and to keep the KPI process up to date. - Modelling and visualisation enables to see where the data originates and how it is manipulated. - Modelling and visualisation enables simplification. - Modelling and visualisation enables the evaluation of the validity of the data and whether KPIs perform as intended.
Visualising the KPI information flow eased communication between stakeholders with different backgrounds.	- Visualising the workflow improves the coordination and understanding of others work. - Modelling and visualisation enables more accurate analyses, reveals bottlenecks and problem areas, and finally makes possible process improvement activities. - Visualisation improves understanding and communication.
Showing different stakeholder viewpoints as a part of the information flow allowed comprehension of KPI, data items and complexity of the implementation in different parts of the organisation.	- Viewpoints can be used to adjust the abstraction levels and to manage the complexity. - Hiding and expanding parts simplifies the presentation. - Viewpoints allows for focusing on the matter at hand. - Modelling tools should provide viewpoints functionality.
Allowing stakeholders to see their viewpoints and modify them motivated stakeholders to participate and extend the model further.	- Understanding the process for KPIs is paramount for motivation. - Modelling KPIs reveals information on how the data is obtained and created, and how it is used in the decision-making. - Showing the viewpoints help understanding and agreeing upon the perspectives (e.g., quality vs. efficiency).
With the proposed approach the KPI information flow model became both the actual description and formulation of a KPI.	- Stakeholders should be involved in the modelling. - Accurate and reliable source data is required for meaningful KPIs. - Measurements and comparisons over the product lines can be achieved.

Utilizing common UML-tools (e.g., Visio) and the modelling method presented in [36] as our tools we could provide the visualisations. With the help of the visualisations, the case organisation personnel understood better KPIs and how they were formulated, and they noticed serious flaws. KPIs were neither reliable nor commensurable between different units or product lines, e.g., there was inconsistency with measurements, as management focused on effectiveness and engineers focused on quality. In sum, visualisation made the organisation rethink their KPIs and how they are formulated.

Visualisation revealed that the source data was different than originally understood by those who formulate KPIs, providing different results than what originally was intended, and hence decisions were made based on flawed KPIs.

Furthermore, KPIs were not immediately available, instead data was gathered once a month and KPIs were then calculated, KPI data was different between product lines/units, and KPI process had unnecessary workload and loops. One of the key findings was that the changes to the existing process did only change the local processes and work; it did not guarantee that KPIs were changed elsewhere. It was realised that in order to properly formulate KPIs, the whole KPI process and its information flows should be analysed, not just the data sources. Based on our study, we propose that KPI visualisation as a flow is necessary for recognising who is contributing and what data is used in that contribution. It also helps to see if KPIs provided by different teams are commensurable.

The study showed that KPIs were found problematic, as they are often taken for granted and the way that KPIs are implemented is not visible for stakeholders. It is seldom considered where KPIs come from and what they are representing. It is necessary to think carefully what calculations are useful and whether those calculations reveal the issues they are meant to.

Figure 3 below presents a KPI example that shows the average development hours of two different products. In this example, two teams work for product A and input their working hours directly to Jira for each feature. For product B, the product owner estimates the working hours spent on each feature based on team members compiled a list of features. The example presents a visualised KPI that informs what is the source data used to calculate the KPI and how it is formed. With proper tool support, the data and activity elements can be made to represent real data. Essentially, the visualisation allows stakeholders to identify and ask the questions that matter in regards to validity, representation and usage of a KPI. With a systematic analysis, we found the issues with KPIs and KPI formulation process. Modelling and visualisation enabled the stakeholders to understand the KPI process better and it made the stakeholders think about the relevant data and information concerning KPIs.

With our approach, a soft system model could be built systematically. The model showed where the data originated and how it was manipulated throughout the process. Thus, validating the usefulness of our approach to modelling of KPI information flows. We believe that our approach would be fit for other cases also, however that still requires further validation. Due to improved understanding, modelling and visualisation was found useful as a process improvement tool: It allowed the identification of problems in the process, and unnecessary activities could be identified and the process could be streamlined accordingly. Coordination of activities was also improved.

Our modelling and visualisation approach addresses several needs and is generic enough to be used in various situations and purposes. Our approach is suitable for visualising and analysing the activities and information flows, and showing the dependencies. Moreover, it was easily adopted and personnel committed to use it. Presenting the KPI process as a graphical model provided better understanding for developers and experts, and it also improved communication and helped to analyse the work. It motivated the personnel and they came up with new ideas to further improve their work, work practices and processes. Visualisation was also found to be useful in pinpointing the bottlenecks and problem areas.

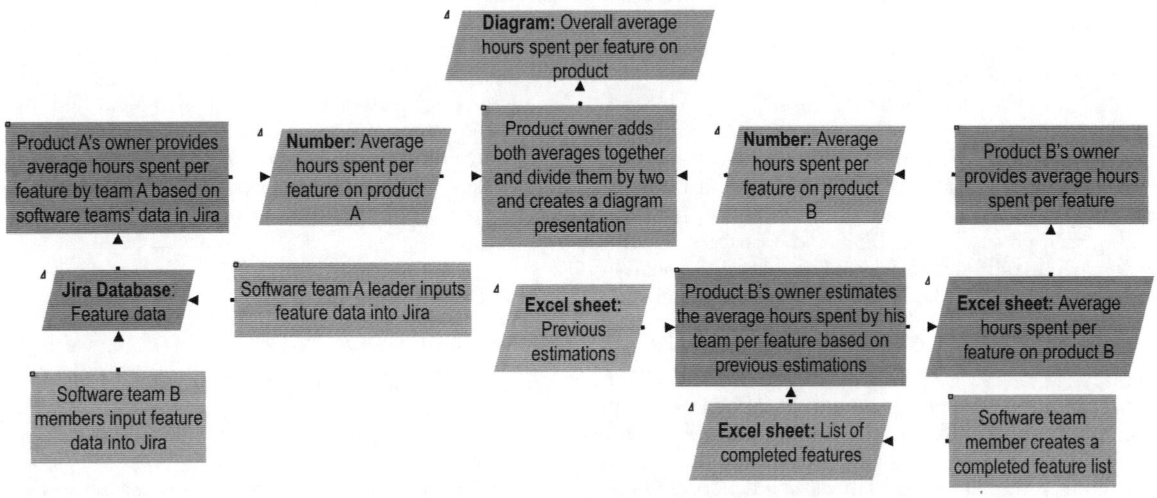

Figure 3. Example KPI formulation for a system.

Being able to construct representations also improve the readability of visualisations [37]. Our approach complements, e.g., the dashboard selection model by Staron et al. [30] and ways to elicit information by Staron et al. [38], which is more based on a set of questions, and it can also be used as a simple visualisation mechanism on top of other established approaches, such as Balanced Scorecards by Kaplan and Norton [7]. The findings are also in line with Staron [3], stressing the importance of completeness, reliability and early warning signs.

A. *Validity of the Study*

The reliability of the data and results was ensured via rigorous research protocol with peer reviews by researchers and company representatives. The action research cycles were documented throughout the research. The modelling sessions were recorded and transcribed by the researchers.

The way the action research was implemented introduces a danger of positive bias within researchers and company participants—due to the constant communication and interventions; the company participants could be positively biased, producing only positive results. However, having many different viewpoints presented in the workshops and modelling sessions addressed this issue. Also, agreement over clear roles and rigorous research methods helped participants remain neutral observers.

This study was conducted within a large ICT organization that utilizes product line based development, hence limiting the generalizability of the results. In order to make wider conclusions more domains, smaller companies and different production models should be studied.

VI. Conclusion and Future Work

This paper presents an action research study with the aim to understand organization's KPI process and to formulate a meaningful set of KPIs. Several issues in the case organisation were identified during the study, with the most significant being that the original KPIs didn't measure what they were intended to measure. KPIs were not giving the right information; they were not well defined and were not based on complete and reliable information. When the information was not correct, it caused harm as the decision-making was relying on false data.

Modelling and visualisation was used to understand, analyse and to model the KPI process. Using simple visualisation mechanisms to model and represent the KPI process helped in understanding the purposes and needs of measurements, as well as the source data and its handling during the KPI process. Modelling and visualisation also clearly revealed the different stakeholders that participated in the KPI process, and further improved understanding and communication between the stakeholders; especially non-technical persons' understanding was improved considerably.

The improved KPI process and well-defined KPIs, in turn, lead to more effective decision-making, as the measurements were more accurate, reliable and descriptive. Also, different units and product lines could be compared when the measurements were commensurable.

Study showed that the KPI information flow should be carefully analysed and KPIs should be based on real needs and real measurable values. To address our research question, KPIs should be formulated in a way that provides real results. For this purpose, the proposed modelling and visualisation approach is a very useful tool. It allows for redefining usable, valid and reliable KPIs so that KPIs and the whole KPI process, with all the interdependencies, can be well understood and analysed. It is also important that the whole product development process is analysed, not just the data sources for KPIs. Analysing the process provides an understanding how KPIs are build from the original data, what the measurements really indicate and how they can be used to understand and improve the development process. Constant follow up and process refining is also an integral part of the process, which helps to keep the KPI process always up to date.

Our approach solves many issues related to KPIs and it is useful especially when there are several teams working on their tasks and the overall picture may be hard to see. Our approach concretises abstract work and defines the relationships of activities associated to it. It provides graphical presentations that are accessible and easy to use for understanding, analysing, communicating and improving processes. The resulting model can be used for presenting the actors, activities and information flows, and describing their logical order and dependencies. Graphical models and modelling helps in understanding the complex problems by enabling breaking those down to understandable entities.

This work benefits both research and industry. Research benefits from new knowledge and the experiences from the industry to expand the knowledge base. Industry practitioners can adopt a simple modelling and visualisation approach to improve their KPI process. We propose simple modelling and visualisation as a recommended practice in formulating KPIs, especially in sociotechnical systems, where persons are in interaction with technology. The solution is simple on purpose. The problems are common in industry and, e.g., in the case organisation the heavy weight solutions have not been useful – they have not been well embraced. However, simple and intuitive solutions are more easily taken into use also at the lower levels of an organisation.

Topics for further studies were also identified, including confirming the results in other domains to improve the generalizability. Furthermore, the question about how to help organisations to act upon KPIs and implement the changes still remains.

References

[1] P. Helo, "Managing Agility and Productivity in the Electronics Industry," Industrial Management & Data Systems 104(7), pp. 567–577, 2004.

[2] J. Froehlich and P. Dourish, "Unifying artifacts and activities in a visual tool for distributed software development teams," Proceedings of the 26th International Conference on Software Engineering, pp. 387–396. IEEE Computer Society Press, Los Alamitos, CA, 2004.

[3] M. Staron, "Critical role of measures in decision processes: Managerial and technical measures in the context of large

software development organizations," Information and Software Technology, 54(8), pp. 887–899, 2012.
[4] F. M. del-Rey-Chamorro, R. Roy, B. van Wegen, and A. Steele, "A framework to create key performance indicators for knowledge management solutions," Journal of Knowledge management 7(2), pp. 46–62, 2003.
[5] A. Shahin and M. A. Mahbod, "Prioritization of key performance indicators: An integration of analytical hierarchy process and goal setting," International Journal of Productivity and Performance Management 56(3), pp. 226–240, 2007.
[6] E. S. Yu and J. Mylopoulos, "Understanding "why" in software process modelling, analysis, and design," Proceedings of the 16th International Conference on Software Engineering, pp. 159–168. IEEE Computer Society Press, Los Alamitos, CA, 1994.
[7] R. Kaplan and D. Norton, "The Balanced Scorecard-Measures that Drive Performance," Harvard Business Review, 70(1), pp. 71–79, 1992.
[8] M. A. Malina and F. H. Selto, "Communicating and controlling strategy: an empirical study of the effectiveness of the balanced scorecard," Journal of management accounting research 13(1), pp. 47–90, 2001.
[9] ISO 9001:2015 Quality Management Systems–Requirements. Available from: https://www.iso.org/standard/62085.html 2018.08.01
[10] ISO 9000:2015 Quality Management Systems–Fundamentals and Vocabulary. Available from: https://www.iso.org/standard/45481.html 2018.08.01
[11] ISO 9004:2018 Quality management–Quality of an organization–Guidance to achieve sustained success. Available from: https://www.iso.org/standard/70397.html 2018.08.01
[12] D. Stodder, "Data visualization and discovery for better business decisions," TDWI Best Practices Report. The Data Warehouse Institute, Renton, WA, 2013.
[13] K. Bauer, "KPIs - The metrics that drive performance management," DM Review 14(9), 63, 2004.
[14] M. Resinas et al., "KPIshare: A Collaborative Space for BPM Practitioners for Full Definitions and Discussions on Process KPIs," In BPM (Demos), pp. 61–65, 2014.
[15] W. W. Eckerson, "Creating Effective KPIs," Information Management 16(6), p. 15, 2006.
[16] A. del-Río-Ortega et al., "Enriching decision making with data-based thresholds of process-related KPIs," International Conference on Advanced Information Systems Engineering, pp. 193–209. Springer, Cham, 2017.
[17] J. Cai, X. Liu, Z. Xiao, and J. Liu, "Improving supply chain performance management: A systematic approach to analyzing iterative KPI accomplishment," Decision Support Systems 46(2), pp. 512–521, 2009.
[18] E. R. Randall, B. J. Condry, M. Trompet, and S. K. Campus, "International bus system benchmarking: Performance measurement development, challenges, and lessons learned," 86th Annual Meeting of the Transportation Research Board, Washington, D.C, pp. 1–12, 2007.
[19] R. S. Kaplan, "New systems for measurement and control," The Engineering Economist 36(3), pp. 201–218, 1991.
[20] H. J. Harrington, "Improving business processes," The TQM Magazine 3(1), pp. 39–44, 1991.
[21] W. W. Eckerson, "Performance dashboards: measuring, monitoring, and managing your business," John Wiley & Sons, Hoboken, New Jersey 2010.
[22] J. B. Ellis, S. Wahid, C. Danis, and W. A. Kellogg, "Task and social visualization in software development: evaluation of a prototype," Proceedings of the SIGCHI conference on Human Factors in Computing Systems, pp. 577–586. ACM New York, NY, 2007.
[23] S. K. Card, J. D. Mackinlay, and B. Shneiderman, "Readings in information visualization: Using vision to think," Morgan Kaufman, San Francisco, CA, 1999.
[24] S. Bresciani and M. J. Eppler, "The Benefits of Synchronous Collaborative Information Visualization: Evidence from an Experimental Evaluation," IEEE Transactions on Visualization and Computer Graphics 15(6), pp. 1073–1080, 2009.
[25] L. Scott, L. Carvalho, R. Jeffery, and J. D'Ambra, "An evaluation of the spearmint approach to software process modelling," European Workshop on Software Process Technology, pp. 77–89. Springer, Berlin, 2001.
[26] W. W. Eckerson, "Performance management strategies," Business Intelligence Journal 14(1), pp. 24–27, 2009.
[27] R. S. Aguilar-Saven, "Business process modelling: Review and framework," International Journal of Production Economics 90(2), pp. 129–149, 2004.
[28] K. Schneider, K. Stapel, and E. Knauss, "Beyond documents: visualizing informal communication," Proceedings of the third International Workshop on Requirements Engineering Visualization, pp. 31–40. IEEE, 2008.
[29] A. del-Río-Ortega, C. Cabanillas, M. Resinas, and A. Ruiz-Cortés, "PPINOT tool suite: a performance management solution for process-oriented organisations," International Conference on Service-Oriented Computing, pp. 675–678. Springer, Berlin, Heidelberg, 2013.
[30] M .Staron, K. Niesel, and W. Meding, "Selecting the Right Visualization of Indicators and Measures–Dashboard Selection Model," International Workshop on Software Measurement, pp. 130–143. Springer International Publishing, Switzerland, 2015.
[31] M. Kelanti, J. Hyysalo, P. Kuvaja, M. Oivo, and A. Välimäki, "A Case Study of Requirements Management: Toward Transparency in Requirements Management Tools," Proceedings of the Eighth International Conference on Software Engineering Advances, pp. 597–604. Curran Associates, Inc., Red Hook, NY, 2013.
[32] J. Hyysalo, M. Kelanti, J. Lehto, P Kuvaja, and M. Oivo, "Software development as a decision-oriented process," Proceedings of the International Conference of Software Business, pp. 132–147. Springer, Cham, 2014.
[33] G. Susman and R. Evered, "An Assessment of the Scientific Merits of Action Research," Administrative Science Quarterly 23(4), pp. 582–603, 1978.
[34] P. B. Checkland, "Systems Thinking, Systems Practice," John Wiley & Sons Ltd, Chichester, 1981.
[35] Y. Rogers, H. Brignull, and M. Scaife, "Designing Dynamic Interactive Visualisations to Support Collaboration and Cognition," Sixth International Conference on Information Visualisation, pp. 39–48. IEEE, London, 2002.
[36] M. Kelanti et al., "Soft System Stakeholder Analysis Methodology," Proceedings of the Tenth International Conference on Software Engineering Advances, pp. 122–130. Associates, Inc., Red Hook, NY, 2015.
[37] A. Dix and G. Ellis, "Starting simple - adding value to static visualisation through simple interaction," Proceedings of the working conference on Advanced visual interfaces, pp. 124–134. ACM New York, NY, 1998.
[38] M. Staron, W. Meding, G. Karlsson, and C. Nilsson, "Developing measurement systems: an industrial case study," Journal of Software Maintenance and Evolution: Research and Practice, 23(2), pp. 89–107, 2011.

Tracing and Reversing the Run of Software Systems Implemented by Petri Nets

Radek Kočí and Vladimír Janoušek

Brno University of Technology, Faculty of Information Technology,
IT4Innovations Centre of Excellence
Bozetechova 2, 612 66 Brno, Czech Republic
{koci,janousek}@fit.vutbr.cz

Abstract—**Application run tracing and application interactive debugging are integral part of the software systems development process. In many cases, the possibility to execute reverse steps of the system run would make debugging easier and quicker due to examination of the system state before it got into the wrong or disabled state. Currently, techniques of reversing the system run are not widespread, but there are experimental implementations. Nevertheless, these solutions increase overhead of the application run due to the logging of the information needed to restore previous states. Moreover, many of them increase overhead in a significant way. This article focuses on the possibility of reversing the run of systems whose behavior is described by Petri nets. The work follows the methodology of designing and validating system requirements using functional models that combine formal notation with objects of production environment and can be used as a full-fledged application. Due to the nature of Petri Nets formalisms, it is possible to define reverse operations to reduce the overhead of application run.**

Keywords–Object Oriented Petri Nets; debugging; tracing; reverse debugging; requirements validation.

I. Introduction

This work builds on the concepts of formal approach to design and develop system requirements and, consequently, their implementation using Petri Nets [1]. It is part of the *Simulation Driven Development* (SDD) approach [2] combining basic models of the most used modeling language Unified Modeling Language (UML) [3][4] and the formalism of Object-Oriented Petri Nets (OOPN) [5]. This approach is based on ideas of model-driven development dealing with gaps between different development stages and focuses on the usage of conceptual models during the development process of simulation models—these techniques are called *model continuity* [6]. Model continuity concept works with simulation models during design stages, while the approach based on Petri Nets focuses on *live models* that can be used in the deployed system.

When testing models or implementations, developers often use the interactive debugging technique, which allows to go through the system run and investigate its state step by step. The logging technique and subsequent analysis of the running system is less often used. These techniques are linked to the limits of their use, notably the inability to make reverse steps. In this case, it is difficult to determine the system states before stopping (e.g., at breakpoints). However, the introduction of reverse interactive debugging leads to increased overhead especially for running an application where it is necessary to collect the information needed to reconstruct the previous states. There are several approaches that differ in their possibilities and overhead. A very important factor is, in addition to higher demands on the runtime of application, that there is a higher demand for memory that keeps the collected information. Another issue is the overhead of reverse debugging, which is not as important as the run overhead.

There are three basic approaches to solving this problem. The first one records the system run and then performs all the steps from the beginning to the desired point (*record-replay* approach). The second approach records all the information needed to return to the previous step (*trace-based* approach). The third approach records only selected checkpoints so they are reliably replicated (*reconstruction-based* approach). Reverse debugging is done by reconstructing the appropriate checkpoint state and then making forward steps. The approach presented in this paper is based on the trace-based reverse debugging. Due to the nature of used OOPN formalism, which has a formal base working with unambiguously defined events, there is no problem to define and perform reverse operations associated to each event.

The paper is organized as follows. Section II introduces related work. Section III summarizes basic definitions of OOPN formalism needed to define tracing concepts. Section IV discuss the possibilities of OOPN models simulation tracing and introduces the simple demonstrating model. Section V focuses on recording states and event during the simulation and Section VI describes reverse events and operation when reverse debugging performed. The summary and future work is described in Section VII.

II. Related Work

The solution based on recording simulation run and replaying it from the beginning to the breakpoint may be time consuming and, for a long run of the application, unsuitable due to time lags when debugging. As examples we can mention Instant Replay debugger [7] or Microsoft Visual Studio 2010 IntelliTrace [8].

The trace-based solution logs all steps, so it is possible to determine the current state and the sequence of steps that led to this state. In many cases, the simulators record everything and, therefore, it is possible to go back to one of the previous steps. The scope of that solution is limited by what and how can be traced, especially using multi-processors is very difficult to work. As examples we can mention Green Hills Time Machine [9], Omniscient Debugger [10] fo Java Virtual Machine, or gnu reverse debugger gdb 7.0 [11]. The last mentioned, gdb debugger, is very slow, but is the only open-source solution. There are tools based on Petri nets that allow reverse debugging, e.g., the TIme petri Net Analyzer TINA [12]. Nevertheless, these tools focus on a specific variant of Petri nets that are not not usable for the application environment. Besides, there are also tools suitable for these purposes, e.g., Renew [13], that are similar to the SDD approach but do not allow reverse debugging.

Some solutions allow to go back in the operation stack, change the current state and proceed from this step. An example may be the Smalltalk language [14]. Even in this case, however, we do not have the state of the system associated with the appropriate step, but only the current state whose image we see in the context of methods that were called.

III. Basic definition of OOPN formalism

In this section we will introduce the basic definition of Object-oriented Petri Nets (OOPN) formalism necessary for the presented purpose.

A. System of classes and objects

For the purposes of this work, we define the Object Oriented Petri Nets (OOPN) as a system of classes and objects that consists of the individual elements [15].

Definition 1: System OOPN is $\Pi = (\Sigma, \Gamma, c_0, o_0)$, where Σ is a system of classes, Γ is a system of objects, c_0 is an initial class and o_0 is an identifier of the initial object instantiated from the class c_0.

Definition 2: System of classes Σ consists of sets of elements constituting classes and is defined as $\Sigma = (C_\Sigma, MSG, N_O, N_M, SP, NP, P, T, CONST, VAR)$, where C_Σ is a set of classes, MSG is a set of messages, N_O is a set of object nets, N_M is a set of method nets, SP is a set of synchronous ports, NP is a set of negative predicates, P is a set of places, T is a set of transitions, CONST is a set of constants and VAR is a set of variables. Messages MSG correspond to method nets, synchronous ports, and negative predicates.

Definition 3: System of objects Γ is a structure containing sets of elements constituting the model runs (the model run corresponds to the simulation, so that we will use the notation of simulation). $\Gamma = (O_\Gamma, N_\Gamma, M_N, M_T)$, where O_Γ is a set of object identifiers, N_Γ is a set of method nets identifiers, $M_N \subset (O_\Gamma \cup N_\Gamma) \times P \times U^M$ is place markings and $M_T \subset (O_\Gamma \cup N_\Gamma) \times T \times \mathcal{P}(BIND)$ is transition markings.

Definition 4: The OOPN system universe U is defined $U = \{(cnst, cls, oid) \mid cnst \in CONST \wedge cls \in C_\Sigma \wedge oid \in O_\Gamma\}$. The system universe represents a set of all possible values that may be part of markings or variables.

We can use the following notation to simplify writing. For constants, we write down their values directly, e.g., 10, $'a'$. For classes, we write down their names directly without quotes or apostrophes. To identify an object, we will write its identifier with a @ character.

Definition 5: The set of all variable bindings BIND used in OOPN is defined $BIND = \{b \mid b : VAR \longrightarrow U\}$.

Definition 6: We define operators for instantiating classes $\amalg_C$ and method nets $\amalg_N$ that create the appropriate instances and assign them identifiers from sets O_Γ, resp. N_Γ. When creating a new instance of the class $c \in C_\Sigma$, we will write $\amalg_C(c) = o$ or $\amalg_C(c, o)$, where $o \in O_\Gamma$. Similarly, for the method net instance $m \in N_M$, we will write $\amalg_N(o, m) = n$ or $\amalg_N(o, m, n)$, where $o \in O_\Gamma$ is an object where the method net instance $n \in N_\Gamma$ is created.

Individual class elements are identified by their fully qualified names consisting of sub-element names separated by a dot. The class is identified by its name, e.g., C. The method is identified by class and method names, e.g., C.M, the method place C.M.P, and so on. In the case of object net, the elements will be written directly without method identification, e.g., C.P. Similarly, we will introduce the identification of Γ object system elements. Objects and nets instances are uniquely identified by their identifiers, net elements (transitions and places) by their names. For instance, the transition $t \in T$ of the method net $m_i \in N_\Gamma$ can be identified by following notations: $m_i.t$ or (m_i, t). The object net describes the autonomous activities of the object, its instance is always created with the instantiation of the class, and is just one. For this reason, the notation $o \in O_\Gamma$ can identify the class instance as well as its object net. Method nets describe the object's response to the sent message. In case the message is received, the instance $n \in N_\Gamma$ of the respective net N_M is created and its simulation starts.

B. Place

The place is represented by a named multi-set. The multi-set A^M is a generalization of the set A such that it can contain multiple occurrences of elements. Thus, the multi-set can be defined as a function $A^M : A \rightarrow \mathbb{N}$, which assigns to each element $a \in A$ the number of occurrences in the multi-set. The number of occurrences will be denoted by the term *frequency*. We will denote $|A|$ the cardinality of the set A, i.e., the number of elements in the set A. We will denote $|A^M|$ the cardinality of multi-set A^M, i.e., the sum of frequencies of all elements in the set A. For an individual element x of the place $p \in P$, we will write $x \in p$ a for its frequency m‘x.

Definition 7: The place marking corresponds to its content and is defined as a multi-set $M_P = \{(m, o) \mid m \in \mathbb{N}^+ \wedge o \in U\}$, where m is frequency of the member o in the multi-set. Members of multi-set will be written in the form m‘o, marking of the place $p \in P$ will be written in the form $M_P(p) = \{m_1‘o_1, m_2‘o_2, \ldots\}$.

C. Arc Expression

Arc expression matches the usual approach used in Petri nets. Each arc expression has a form of m‘o, where $m \in \mathbb{N}^+ \cup VAR$ and $o \in U \cup VAR$. The expression element m represents the frequency of o in the multi-set and can be denoted by a numeric value or a variable. If the variable is used at the position m, the frequency of the member o in multi-set is assigned to that variable. The element o represents the object stored in multi-set and can be defined by the element of the universe U or the variable. If a variable is used at the position o, an object from multi-set, whose frequency corresponds to specified m, is bound to that variable. If both parts of an expression are defined by variables, any object and its frequency are bound to these variables. If the content of multi-set does not match the given expression, the bounding process fails.

D. Set of Classes

The formalism of OOPN works, in addition to the OOPN objects (O_Γ and the corresponding set of classes C_Σ), with objects that are not a direct part of the formalism. Principle of their usage is based on Smalltalk, which is also used as the inscription language of the formalism of OOPN. These objects are especially *basic constant objects* (sometimes also called *primitive objects*) such as numbers, symbols, characters, and strings. The corresponding classes will be denoted Number, Symbol, $\mathrm{Character}$ and String and their set, in sum, $\mathrm{C}_\mathcal{C}$. Objects of these classes are part of the set of constants CONST. In addition to these basic objects, OOPN formalism can work with other objects and classes. In particular, it covers collections, graphical user interface objects, user-defined classes, etc. We will call the set of these classes as *domain classes* and denote with the symbol $\mathrm{C}_\mathcal{D}$, $\mathrm{C}_\mathcal{C} \subset \mathrm{C}_\mathcal{D}$. A set of object identifiers created from classes $\mathrm{C}_\mathcal{D}$ is denoted $\mathrm{O}_\mathcal{D}$.

Definition 8: Let $\mathrm{C}_\Pi = \mathrm{C}_\Sigma \cup \mathrm{C}_\mathcal{D}$ be a set of all classes that can be used by the formalism of OOPN. Let $\mathrm{O}_\Pi = \mathrm{O}_\Gamma \cup \mathrm{O}_\mathcal{D}$ be a set of all object identifiers that can be instantiated (created) from classes C_Π.

Definition 9: Extended Universe U_Π of OOPN is defined $\mathrm{U}_\Pi = \{(\mathrm{cnst}, \mathrm{cls}, \mathrm{oid}) \mid \mathrm{cnst} \in \mathrm{CONST} \wedge \mathrm{cls} \in \mathrm{C}_\Pi \wedge \mathrm{oid} \in \mathrm{O}_\Pi\}$.

IV. Simulation Tracing

In this section, we briefly outline the sample model and discuss the possibilities of tracing the run of software system described by the formalism of OOPN. We will call that run *simulation*.

A. Sample Model

The basic concept will be outlined using a simple example. Figure 1 shows classes of that example. Figure 1a) depicts the initial class $\mathrm{A1}$ with its object net and Figure 1b) depicts the class $\mathrm{A2}$ having the only method $\mathrm{calc:}$ with one parameter x.

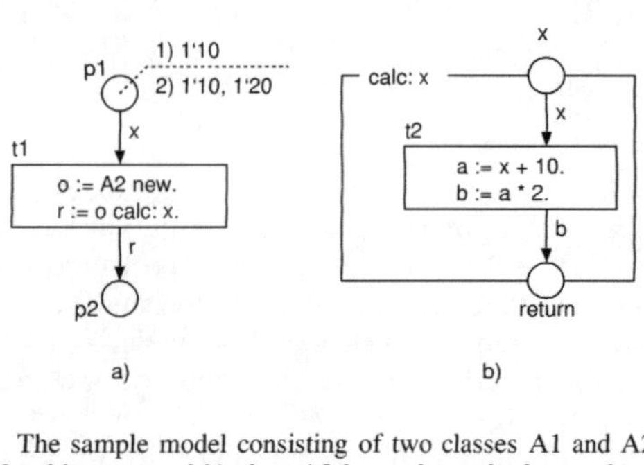

Figure 1. The sample model consisting of two classes A1 and A2; a) class A1 has only object net and b) class A2 has only method net calc:.

At the simulation start, an instance o_0 from the initial class $\mathrm{A1}$ is created, $\Pi_\mathrm{C}(\mathrm{A1}, \mathrm{o}_0)$. The object net o_0 creates an instance of the class $\mathrm{A2}$, $\Pi_\mathrm{C}(\mathrm{A2}, \mathrm{o}_1)$, and calls its method net $\mathrm{calc:}$ from the transition $\mathrm{o}_0.\mathrm{t1}$, $\Pi_\mathrm{N}(\mathrm{o}_1, \mathrm{calc:}, \mathrm{n}_1)$. The method net n_1 executes the transition $\mathrm{n}_1.\mathrm{t2}$. This example works with two variants of initial marking of the object net A1; 1) $\mathrm{M}_\mathrm{P}(\mathrm{p1}) = \{1`10\}$ and 2) $\mathrm{M}_\mathrm{P}(\mathrm{p1}) = \{1`10, 1`20\}$.

B. Tracing Tree

The simulation progress can be recorded as a tree, where nodes represent the relevant unit of simulation run and edges represent a sequence of units execution including the bindings. The relevant unit is understand as the least set of events that the tracer records. Tree root represents the input point of the calculation. If a parallel calculation occurs during the execution of the relevant unit, this unit has more successors in its tree view. The current state of the calculation is then represented by all tree leaves. In Figure 2, we can see such a tree for the model from Figure 1 for the variant of initial marking $\mathrm{M}_\mathrm{P}(\mathrm{p1}) = \{1`10, 1`20\}$. In this example, the relevant unit is one executed command. Edges are recorded with a full-line arrow. Nodes capture on which network and transition the command has been performed.

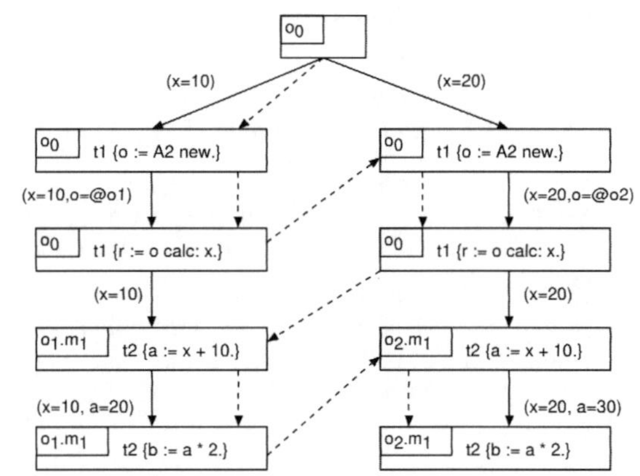

Figure 2. Scenario model of one simulation run.

The tree constructed by that way represents threads that may appear while running the simulation. It does not, however, capture the succession of steps that are important for making backward steps. The sequence of steps can be different and depends on the specific conditions of the simulation run. One such variant is captured in Figure 2 with the dashed line arrows.

C. Event

The simulation run is driven by events. Each executed (fired) event changes the system state, and, therefore, represents one step of model simulation. The set of states S of the system has a character of the net instances marking, which includes marking of places and transitions. One step from the state $\mathrm{s} \in \mathrm{S}$ to the state $\mathrm{s}' \in \mathrm{S}$ is written in the form $\mathrm{s}\ [\mathrm{ev}\rangle\ \mathrm{s}'$, where ev is an executed event .

Definition 10: Event is $\mathrm{ev} = (\mathrm{e}, \mathrm{id}, \mathrm{t}, \mathrm{b})$, where e is a type of event, $\mathrm{id} \in \mathrm{N}_\Gamma \cup \mathrm{O}_\Gamma$ is the identifier of net instance the event executes in, $t \in T$ is the transition to be executed (fired), and $b \in \mathcal{P}(BIND)$ is variables binding the event is to be executed for.

Event types can be as follows: A represents an atomic event, the entire transition is done in one step; F represents sending a message, i.e., creating an instance of a new method net and waiting for its completion; J represents completion of the method net called at F event.

D. Event flow subgraph

The object net can describe multiple scenarios, either interconnected or totally disjoint. The structure of each net is defined by a graph of the Petri net, so we can define the scenarios as subgraphs of such nets.

Definition 11: Let $\mathcal{S}(O_\Gamma \cup N_\Gamma)$ be a set of all valid subgraphs of object nets O_Γ and method nets N_Γ. Individual scenarios will be denoted $\delta_c(n) = (ev_0, ev_1, \dots)$, where $n \in O_\Gamma \wedge c \in \mathbb{N}$.

Now, we return to the step (i.e., event) sequence entry shown in Figure 2 and write the presented scenario in the form of net subgraph, $\delta = ([A, o_0, t1, (x = 10)\rangle, [F, o_0, t1, (x = 10, o = @o_1)\rangle, [A, o_0, t1, (x = 20)\rangle, [F, o_0, t1, (x = 20, o = @o_2)\rangle, [A, o_1.m_1, t2, (x = 10)\rangle, [A, o_1.m_1, t2, (x = 10, a = 20)\rangle, [A, o_2.m_1, t2, (x = 20)\rangle, [A, o_2.m_1, t2, (x = 20, a = 30)\rangle)$.

E. Composite Command

If the transition contains a sequence of messages, either step-by-step or composite ones, this transition can be understood, from the OOPN theory point of view, as a sequence of simple transitions, each of which contains just one simple command. An example of such equivalence is shown in Figure 3.

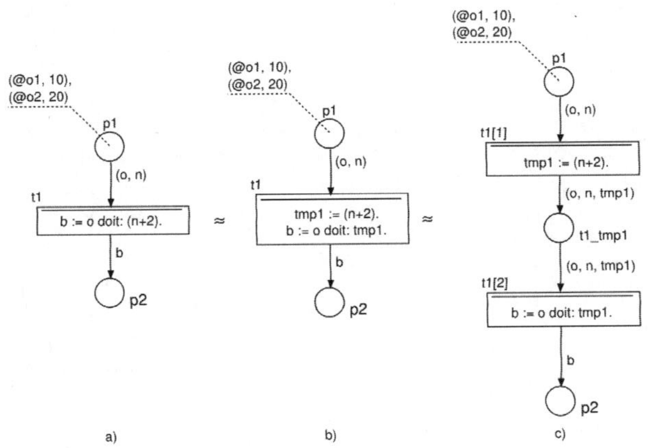

Figure 3. Composite command of the transition.

This model has four variants of execution. In the following example, only one is listed, the others are a combination of different interleaving of two concurrently running transitions t1. The notation of a transition using index, e.g., t1[1], refers to the corresponding command of the composite transition.

$$\begin{aligned}\delta_1(o_0) = ([&A, o_0, t1[1], \{o = @o1, n = 10\}\rangle,\\ [&F, o_0, t1[2], \{o = @o1, n = 10, tmp1 = 12\}\rangle,\\ [&J, o_0, t1[2], \{(o = @o1, n = 10, tmp1 = 12\}\rangle,\\ [&A, o_0, t1[1], \{(o = @o2, n = 20\}\rangle,\\ [&F, o_0, t1[2], \{o = @o2, n = 20, tmp1 = 22\}\rangle,\\ [&J, o_0, t1[2], \{o = @o2, n = 20, tmp1 = 22\}\rangle)\end{aligned}$$

V. Recording the Simulation

This section focuses on recording states during simulation. We will describe each of the monitored events and how the state changes are recorded. To record the entire state would be very time consuming and memory intensive, and from the means offered by OOPN formalism point of view also unnecessary. For the purpose of stepping, it is sufficient to save partial state changes. This avoids storing the whole simulation image after every step.

A. State Changes Processing

A partial state change may involve inserting or selecting an element from a place, assigning the result to a variable, creating or destroying an object, creating or completing a method net instance (associated with calling and terminating this method), and creating or completing a transition instance.

1) Changing Place State: Changing the place state is the easiest operation corresponding to removing elements when transition fires, or adding elements when transition is complete. Within one step, more elements can be inserted or removed into or out of more places. The change will be recorded in the following notation. Operation $add(p, m, o)$ for adding element to the place and operation $del(p, m, o)$ for removing element from the place, where $p \in P$ is the place and $m \in \mathbb{N}^+$ is the frequency of element $o \in U$.

2) Firing and Completing Composite Transition: Although the composite command in the transition is always interpreted by individual commands, it is necessary to maintain a relationship to the original entire transition. Additionally, the transition can be run multiple times for different bindings, so it is necessary to uniquely identify the specific transition instance. Therefore, we will introduce a special event type B, which represents the transition firing for a given binding, and at the same time assigns a unique identifier to the fired transition. Similarly, we will introduce a special C event type to completing the fired transition.

Definition 12: For the purpose of writing state changes, we will extend the definition of the system of objects Γ to the set of transition instance identifiers T_Γ, i.e., transitions fired with a specific binding, $\Gamma = (O_\Gamma, N_\Gamma, T_\Gamma, M_N, M_T)$.

3) Changing Variable State: Changing the state of the variable when executing the transition is denoted by operation $swap(t_i, v, o_{new}, o_{old})$, where $t_i \in T_\Gamma$ is a transition, $v \in VAR$ is the transition variable, $o_{new} \in U$ is a universe object assigned to the variable v and $o_{old} \in U$ is the original object assigned to the variable v before this event occurs.

4) Creating Object: Creating an object (a class instance) corresponds to the creation of an object net and its initialization. In terms of state recording, it is important to keep information about identification of newly created object Π_C and changes of the object net's places, i.e., adding objects into places during the net initialization process.

5) Creating Method Net Instances: Creating a method net instance corresponds to a method invoking by sending a message. As with the object, it is necessary to keep information about identification of newly created instance Π_N and inserting objects (values) into the net's parameter places.

6) Completing Method Net Instances: After the method net instance is completed, two possible options can be applied to record changes. First, the current state of entire net is recorded, i.e., marking of all places and all fired transitions (instances). Second, no state is recorded. The first option is more demanding for time and memory space during simulation, but it is not necessary to reconstruct the net's state so that it matches the state before its completion. The second option is more efficient during simulation, but it is more demanding to reconstruct the net's state during backward stepping. At this point we will focus on the option without state recording. We will introduce a special operation $\Delta_N(m_i)$, which indicates the completion and cancellation of the net instance m_i.

B. Example of Tracing Simulation

We demonstrate the concept of simulation tracking on the model shown in Figure 1 for variant 1, i.e., with the initial marking $M_P(p1) = \{1`10\}$. For the reasons given in Section V-A2, we will modify the event definition as follows:

Definition 13: Event is $ev = (e, id, t, t_i, b)$, where e is a kind of event, $id \in N_\Gamma \cup O_\Gamma$ is the identifier of the net instance the event executes in, $t \in T$ is the transition to be executed (fired), and $b \in \mathcal{P}(BIND)$ is variables binding for which this event is executed, and $t_i \in T_\Gamma$ is the identifier of fired transition.

The sequence of fired transitions does not necessarily correspond to the tracing tree, which also takes into account the simulation branching. Sequence of fired transitions captures a specific sequence of events, which is always unambiguously given. Figure 4 captures the sequence of events (scenario) completed with state change operations. This is about tracing a simulation with storing relevant information for backward stepping. We can see individual state changes in the *State* column. For the purpose of this text, we will simplify writing events so that we do not specify the binding b.

Event	*State*
	$\Pi_C(A1, o_1)$
	$add(o_1.p1, 1, (10, \varepsilon, \varepsilon))$
$[B, o_1, t1, t1_1\rangle$	$del(o_1.p1, 1, (10, \varepsilon, \varepsilon))$
	$swap(t1_1, x, (10, \varepsilon, \varepsilon), \varepsilon)$
$[A, o_1, t1[1], t1_1\rangle$	$\Pi_C(A2, o_2)$
	$swap(t1_1, o, (\varepsilon, \varepsilon, o_2), \varepsilon)$
$[F, o_1, t1[2], t1_1\rangle$	$\Pi_N(o_2, A2.calc:, m_1)$
	$add(o_2.m_1.x, 1, (10, \varepsilon, \varepsilon))$
$[B, o_2.m_1, t2, t2_1\rangle$	$del(o_2.m_1.x, 1, (10, \varepsilon, \varepsilon))$
	$swap(t2_1, x, (10, \varepsilon, \varepsilon), \varepsilon)$
$[A, o_2.m_1, t2[1], t2_1\rangle$	$swap(t2_1, a, (20, \varepsilon, \varepsilon), \varepsilon)$
$[A, o_2.m_1, t2[2], t2_1\rangle$	$swap(t2_1, b, (40, \varepsilon, \varepsilon), \varepsilon)$
$[C, o_2.m_1, t2, t2_1\rangle$	$add(o_2.m_1.return, 1, (40, \varepsilon, \varepsilon))$
$[J, o_1, t1[2], t1_1\rangle$	$\Delta_N(m_1)$
	$swap(t1_1, r, (40, \varepsilon, \varepsilon), \varepsilon)$
$[C, o_1, t1_1\rangle$	$add(o_1.p2, 1, (40, \varepsilon, \varepsilon))$

Figure 4. Scenario record.

VI. REVERSE DEBUGGING

In this section, we describe steps that are performed when stepping backwards.

A. State Changes Reverse Processing

There is a sequence of reverse operations for each state change that allows to return to the previous step. We explain the operations associated with each recorded event. Some of the operations will be demonstrated on discussed example, first steps of reverse debugging are shown in Figure 5.

1) C-Event Type: The event C represents completing the transition instance t_i. In a step back, our goal is to reconstruct this instance. It is necessary perform the reverse operations that are associated with this event. Since these operations refer to the insertion of elements into the output places, the reverse operations are therefore the removal of these elements. The next step is to reconstruct the state of transition instance t_i. We find the first entry regarding the instance t_i, i.e., $[B, t, t_i\rangle$, create this instance and perform all the swap operations. In our example, this would be a sequence of events $[B, t1, t1_1\rangle$, $[A, t1[1], t1_1\rangle$, $[F, t1[2], t1_1\rangle$ and $[J, t1[2], t1_1\rangle$. Event B ensures creation of the appropriate instance with the $t1_1$ identifier. The associated sequence of swap operators is as follows: $swap(t1_1, x, (10, \varepsilon, \varepsilon), \varepsilon)$, $swap(t1_1, o, (\varepsilon, \varepsilon, o_2), \varepsilon)$ and $swap(t1_1, r, (40, \varepsilon, \varepsilon), \varepsilon)$. This way we filled all the variables with appropriate values, and we are in a state where the transition instance $t1_1$ was completed. If the object, resp. its identifier, that has been destroyed (e.g., because it was removed by a garbage collector) is assigned to the variable, it is not essential at this point. The object will be reconstructed at the first access to it (state handling, work with method net, etc.).

2) J-Event Type: The event J represents completing the call of method. The reverse swap operation is executed, i.e., the value is removed from the variable and replaced with the original (previous) value. The next step is to perform a reverse operation $\overline{\Delta}_N(m_i)$ to destroying the method net $\Delta_N(m_i)$, i.e., creating net instance m_i and reconstructing its last state. Using operation $\overline{\Delta}_N(m_i)$, we get a sequence of operations over the net m_i starting with $\Pi_N(o_i, class.method\_name, m_i)$ operation. From this sequence, we will perform add and del operations on the net instance m_i. In our example, it would be a sequence of operations $add(o_2.m_1.x, 1, (10, \varepsilon, \varepsilon))$, $del(o_2.m_1.x, 1, (10, \varepsilon, \varepsilon))$ and $add(o_2.m_1, return, 1, (40, \varepsilon, \varepsilon))$. As a result, we made method net in the state, where the place return contains the object representing number 40.

Step	*State*
$[\mathrm{C}, \mathrm{o}_1, \mathrm{t1}_1\rangle$	$\mathrm{del}(\mathrm{o}_1.\mathrm{p2}, 1, (40, \varepsilon, \varepsilon))$
$[\mathrm{J}, \mathrm{o}_1, \mathrm{t1}[2], \mathrm{t1}_1\rangle$	$\mathrm{swap}(\mathrm{t1}_1, \mathrm{r}, \varepsilon, (40, \varepsilon, \varepsilon))$
	$\bar{\Delta}_\mathrm{N}(\mathrm{m}_1) \Rightarrow$
	$\quad \amalg_\mathrm{N}(\mathrm{o}_2, \mathrm{A2.calc:}, \mathrm{m}_1)$
	$\quad \mathrm{add}(\mathrm{o}_2.\mathrm{m}_1.\mathrm{x}, 1, (10, \varepsilon, \varepsilon))$
	$\quad \mathrm{del}(\mathrm{o}_2.\mathrm{m}_1.\mathrm{x}, 1, (10, \varepsilon, \varepsilon))$
	$\quad \mathrm{add}(\mathrm{o}_2.\mathrm{m}_1.\mathrm{return}, 1, (40, \varepsilon, \varepsilon))$
$[\mathrm{C}, \mathrm{o}_2.\mathrm{m}_1, \mathrm{t2}, \mathrm{t2}_1\rangle$	$\mathrm{del}(\mathrm{o}_2.\mathrm{m}_1.\mathrm{return}, 1, (40, \varepsilon, \varepsilon))$
	$\mathrm{swap}(\mathrm{t2}_1, \mathrm{x}, (10, \varepsilon, \varepsilon), \varepsilon)$
	$\mathrm{swap}(\mathrm{t2}_1, \mathrm{a}, (20, \varepsilon, \varepsilon), \varepsilon)$
	$\mathrm{swap}(\mathrm{t2}_1, \mathrm{b}, (40, \varepsilon, \varepsilon), \varepsilon)$
$[\mathrm{A}, \mathrm{o}_2.\mathrm{m}_1, \mathrm{t2}[2], \mathrm{t2}_1\rangle$	$\mathrm{swap}(\mathrm{t2}_1, \mathrm{b}, \varepsilon, (40, \varepsilon, \varepsilon))$

Figure 5. Reverse scenario.

It may happen that there are still instances of transitions that are not terminated at the method net completion. These instances must also be reconstructed. From the sequence of operations $\bar{\Delta}_\mathrm{N}(\mathrm{m}_\mathrm{i})$, we find such sequences that correspond to unfinished transitions starting with $[\mathrm{B}, \mathrm{t}, \mathrm{t}_\mathrm{i}\rangle$ event, but having no event $[\mathrm{C}, \mathrm{t}_\mathrm{i}\rangle$. For each such sequence we perform actions similarly to the backward step of $[\mathrm{C}, \mathrm{t}_\mathrm{i}\rangle$ event.

3) F-Event Type: The event F represents the method invoking on the object. In the reverse step, the appropriate instance of method net specified in $\amalg_\mathrm{N}$ operator is destroyed.

4) A-Event Type: The event A represents the atomic execution of the operation. The reverse swap operation is executed, i.e., the value is removed from the variable and replaced with the original (previous) value. If the atomic operation is a creation of a class instance $\amalg_\mathrm{C}$, this instance is destroyed.

5) B-Event Type: The event B represents the start of transition execution (creation of a transition instance). In the reverse step, the transition instance t_i is destroyed and the add reverse operation is performed. There is no need to swap variables, as the entire fired transition is canceled.

B. Object Reconstruction

At the time of access to the object, e.g., due to the reconstruction of the method net, it may happen that the object no longer exists. The reason may be the loss of all references to this object and its removal by the garbage collector. At this point, it is necessary to create the object and reconstruct its last state. Because the object was destroyed, it means that there were no existing method nets. It is necessary to reconstruct the state of the object net, which is done in the same way as the method net reconstruction. The sequence of corresponding operations on the object net o_i is obtained by using $\bar{\Delta}_\mathrm{O}(\mathrm{o}_\mathrm{i})$ operation, which is similar to $\bar{\Delta}_\mathrm{N}(\mathrm{o}_\mathrm{i})$ operation, but the obtained sequence starts with $\amalg_\mathrm{C}(\mathrm{class}, \mathrm{o}_\mathrm{i})$ operation and the class instance is created instead of method net instance.

VII. Conclusion

The paper dealt with the concept of tracing and reversing run of software system modeled by Petri Nets, especially the formalism of Object Oriented Petri nets. Presented concept is fully functional, but has not yet taken into account all the possibilities of use. We were only concerned with pure Petri Nets objects and passed the domain objects, e.g., collections, objects of user classes etc. We have also abstracted the possibility of having objects that have running method nets, even though they were collected by garbage collector. The reason is an existence od cyclic dependencies but unavailable from the initial object. The last constraint is to omit the method from the external (domain) object. At present, we have an experimental partial implementation of the tool supporting reverse debugging. We will complete the implementation in the future and focus on the above-mentioned limitations.

Acknowledgment

This work has been supported by the internal BUT project FIT-S-17-4014 and The Ministry of Education, Youth and Sports of the Czech Republic from the National Programme of Sustainability (NPU II); project IT4Innovations excellence in science - LQ1602.

References

[1] R. Kočí and V. Janoušek, "Specification of Requirements Using Unified Modeling Language and Petri Nets," International Journal on Advances in Software, vol. 10, no. 12, 2017, pp. 121–131.

[2] R. Kočí and V. Janoušek, "Modeling and Simulation-Based Design Using Object-Oriented Petri Nets: A Case Study," in Proceeding of the International Workshop on Petri Nets and Software Engineering 2012, vol. 851. CEUR, 2012, pp. 253–266.

[3] J. Rumbaugh, I. Jacobson, and G. Booch, The Unified Modeling Language Reference Manual. Addison-Wesley, 1999.

[4] C. Raistrick, P. Francis, J. Wright, C. Carter, and I. Wilkie, Model Driven Architecture with Executable UML. Cambridge University Press, 2004.

[5] M. Češka, V. Janoušek, and T. Vojnar, "Modelling, Prototyping, and Verifying Concurrent and Distributed Applications Using Object-Oriented Petri Nets," Kybernetes: The International Journal of Systems and Cybernetics, vol. 2002, no. 9, 2002.

[6] D. Cetinkaya, A. V. Dai, and M. D. Seck, "Model continuity in discrete event simulation: A framework for model-driven development of simulation models," ACM Transactions on Modeling and Computer Simulation, vol. 25, no. 3, 2015.

[7] T. LeBlanc and J. Mellor-Crummey, "Debugging Parallel Programs with Instant Replay," IEEE Transactions on Computers, vol. 36, no. 4, 1987, pp. 471–482.

[8] I. Huff, "IntelliTrace in Visual Studion 2010 Ultimate," MSDN Blogs, http://blogs.msdn.com/b/ianhu/archive/2009/05/13/historical-debugging-in-visual-studio-team-system-2010.aspx, 2009.

[9] M. Lindahl, "The Device Software Engineers Best Friend," in IEEE Computer, 2006.

[10] B. Lewis and M. Ducasse, "Using Events to Debug Java Programs Backwards in Time," in Proc. of the ACM SIGPLAN 2003 Conference on Object-oriented programming, systems, languages, and applications (OOPSLA), 2003, pp. 96–97.

[11] The GNU Project Debugger, "GDB and Reverse Debugging," GNU pages, https://www.gnu.org/software/gdb/news/reversible.html, 2009.

[12] F. V. B. Berthomieu, F. Peres, "Model-checking Bounded Prioriterized Time Petri Nets," in Proceedings of ATVA, 2007.

[13] O. Kummer, F. Wienberg, and et al., "Renew User Guide," http://www.informatik.uni-hamburg.de/TGI/renew/renew.pdf, January 2016.

[14] A. GoldBerk and D. Robson, Smalltalk 80: The Language. Addison-Wesley, 1989.

[15] R. Kočí and V. Janoušek, "The Object Oriented Petri Net Component Model," in The Tenth International Conference on Software Engineering Advances. Xpert Publishing Services, 2015, pp. 309–315.

ADA Language for Software Engineering

Diana ElRabih
Research & Development Department
Monty Holding Company
Beirut, Lebanon
E-mail: diana.elrabih@montyholding.com

***Abstract*— Software engineering is significantly more complex than just programming and as a result, then different tools are needed since software reliability cannot be compromised. ADA was designed as a coherent programming language for complex software systems, unlike other languages which grew by gradual addition of features. ADA is a modern programming language designed for large, long-lived applications and embedded systems in particular where reliability and efficiency are essential. Also ADA can be used as a communication language for some aspects of the needs and for some aspects of the design. In this paper, we present the concepts of ADA, as well as the strengths of ADA for software engineering.**

Keywords-ADA, software engineering, embedded systems, real time systems

I. Introduction

Software engineering is significantly more complex than just programming, and it should not be surprising that different tools are needed. The structure of the software market for personal computers has caused reliability to be consciously neglected. Software packages are compared by lists of features as performance (46 seconds is better than 47 seconds), and occasionally price. Vendors feel pressured to bring new versions to market, regardless of the reliability of the product. They can always promise to fix the bug in the next version. But word-processors, presentation graphics and interactive games are not the only type of software being developed. Computers are now controlling the most complex systems in the world: airplanes, spacecraft, communications networks, international banks, stock markets, military systems and medical equipment. The social and economic environment in which these systems are developed is totally different from that of packaged software. Each project pushes back the limits of engineering experience, so delays and cost overruns are usually inevitable. A company's reputation for engineering expertise and sound management is more important in winning a contract than a list of features. Consistent, up-to-date, technical competence is expected, not the one-time genius of a startup. Above all, system reliability cannot be compromised. The result of a bug is not just a demoted reporter or the loss of a sales commission. A bug in a medical system can mean loss of life. The crash of a communications system can disrupt an entire economy. The failure of a spacecraft can cost hundreds of millions of dollars. In fact, all these have occurred because of software faults. Software engineering is the term used to denote the set of techniques for developing large software projects. It includes for example, managerial techniques, such as cost estimation, documentation standards, configuration management and quality assurance procedures. It also includes notations and methodologies for analysis, design and testing of the software itself. There are many of us who believe that programming languages play an essential role in software engineering. In the end, a software system is successful if the 'code' of the program executes reliably and performs according to the system requirements.

The best managed project with a superb design is a failure if the delivered 'code' is no good. Thus, managerial techniques and design methodologies must be supplemented by the use of a programming language that supports reliable programming. The alternative to language support for reliability is 'bureaucracy'. The project manager must write conventions for interfaces and specifications of data representations, and each convention must be manually checked in code inspections. The result is that all the misunderstandings, to say nothing of cases where conventions were ignored by clever programmers, are discovered at best when the software components are integrated, and at worst after the software is delivered. Why cannot these conventions be formalized in the programming language and checked by the compiler? It is strange that software engineers, who make their living from automating systems in other disciplines, are often resistant to formalizing and automating the programming process itself.

ADA is a modern programming language designed for large, long-lived applications and embedded systems in particular where reliability and efficiency are essential. In fact, ADA is a design language as much as a programming language. It is designed to be read by ADA programmers and programmers not knowing ADA. Then from the point of view of the software engineers, in addition to being a programming language, ADA can be used as a communication language for some aspects of the needs and for some aspects of the design with its embodiment of modern software engineering principles. In this paper, we present the concepts of ADA, as well as the strengths of ADA for software engineering. ADA has rigid requirements for making entities such as subprograms and variables visible globally. This leads to a separation of ADA code into specifications or "specs" and bodies.

In section 2 we describe what ADA is, section 3 presents how ADA can be used for software engineering. In section 4 we talk about the development of ADA, while in section 5 we show the concepts of ADA. In section 6 we present the strengths of ADA. Section 7 concludes the paper.

II. What is ADA

The ADA language was designed to present a general language, unifying, standardized and supporting the precepts of software engineering. ADA is beginning to prove itself of reliability, robustness but has youthful defects. From 1990 to 1995 the revision of the standard leads to ADA95 , which corrects small defects, fills a big lack by making the language completely object (ADA is the first object language normalized). ADA95 adds its lot of novelties still unpublished 10 years later. Today ADA does not seem to have the place he deserves especially in first learnings of computer science where we must mix the programming itself with the good practice of programming. Since a long time ADA can largely replace Pascal the excellent teaching language. Paradoxically, ADA is more readily taught in high-level training because, again, it makes it possible to teach clearly, this time qualified and more arduous concepts. ADA is well used (even unavoidable) in avionics and embedded computing (rocket Ariane for example), as well as for traffic control (air, rail) where reliability is crucial. It is also appreciated when the code to develop is consequent (so very difficult to maintain). But the fact remains that currently few small or medium-sized companies admit to using ADA. Modest, productivity gains with ADA are proven and very significant.

Computer teachers eager to develop a quality code will be able to use ADA which is the culmination of procedural languages. A free, open and portable compiler (GNAT) allows (especially for academics) to run it and to adopt the language for a formation (or a culture) of computing.

Advantages of ADA by comparing to others: ADA appears more cost-effective compared to other similar languages [5]. ADA, unlike other languages which grew by gradual addition of features, was designed as a coherent programming language for complex software systems. In many instances in other similar languages to ADA such as C language, rules require a non-trivial amount of code development and verification, while the ADA solution is trivial [5]. For instance, achieving object initialization in similar languages requires the use of carefully implemented constructors, while specifying default initialization for ADA records is relatively trivial [5]. Another example is multi-threading with several rules for the use of locks, and condition variables. For ADA, the built-in facilities for direct task communication with protected objects for communication through shared buffers, includes implicit control of locks, and condition variables [5].

III. ADA for Software Engineering

The ADA language is complex because it is intended for developing complex systems, and its advantages are only apparent if engineers are designing and developing such a system. Then, and only then, they will have to face numerous dilemmas, and they will be grateful for the ADA constructs that help them resolve them. Next, we ask questions on ADA and we respond on these questions: How can I decompose the system? I can decompose the system into packages that can be flexibly structured using containment, hierarchical or client-server architectures. How can I specify interfaces? I can specify interfaces in a package specification that is separate from its implementation. How can I describe data? I can describe data with ADA's rich type system. How can I ensure independence of components of my system? I can ensure independence of components of my system by using private types to define abstract data types. How can data types relate to one another? Data types can relate to one another either by composition in records or by inheritance through type extension. How can I reuse software components from other projects? I can reuse software components by instantiating generic packages. How can I synchronize dozens of concurrent processes? I can synchronize dozens of concurrent processes synchronously or asynchronously. How can I get at the raw machine when I need to? I can get at the raw machine by using representation specifications. How can I make the most efficient use of my expensive testing facility? I can make the most efficient use of my experience testing facility by testing as much of the software as possible on a host machine using a validated compiler that accepts exactly the same standard language as the target machine.

Programming in ADA is not, of course, a substitute for the classical elements of software engineering. ADA is simply a better tool. The software engineers design their software by drawing diagrams of the package structure, and then each package becomes a unit of work. The effects caused by incompetent engineers, or by personnel turnover, can be localized. Many, if not most, careless mistakes are caught by type checking during compilation, not after the system is delivered. Code inspections can focus on the logical structure of the program, because the consistency of the conventions and interfaces is automatically checked by the compiler. Software integration is effortless, leaving them more time to concentrate on system integration. Though ADA was originally intended for critical military systems, it is now the language of choice for any critical system.

IV. Development of ADA

The ADA language was developed at the request of the US Department of Defense which was concerned by the proliferation of programming languages for mission-critical systems. Military systems were programmed in languages not commonly used in science, business and education, and dialects of these languages proliferated. Each project had to acquire and maintain a development environment and to train software engineers to support these systems through decades of deployment. Choosing a standard language would significantly simplify and reduce the cost of these logistical tasks. A survey of existing languages showed that none would be suitable, so it was decided to develop a new language based on an existing language, such as Pascal. There were several unique aspects of the development of ADA: The ADA language was developed to satisfy a formal set of requirements. This ensured that from the very beginning the

ADA language included the necessary features for its intended applications. The language proposal was published for scientific review before it was fully implemented and used in applications. Many mistakes in the design were corrected before they became entrenched by widespread use. The standard was finalized early in the history of the language, and facilities were established to validate compilers against the standard. Adherence to the standard is especially important for training, software reuse and host/target development and testing.

V. CONCEPTS OF ADA

This part is a quick overview of some of the strong points of the ADA language that allow engineers to discipline the development process and thus satisfy the precepts of software engineering.

A. Typing

ADA proposes few predefined types (so-called standard or primitive). Types: character, string, Boolean, integer numeric and actual numeric (comma floating). Their implementation is not specified by the standard and therefore it is recommended to define one's own, even the most basic, types in particular the numerals (integers, real floating and even real fixed) pledge of a safer programming (especially portability). ADA offers unparalleled power for the declaration of new types (and not necessarily numerical). This declaration inserts into the code a knowledge of the domain that usually stays in the comments, or in documents, or ... nowhere. This statement is portable and, in addition, the overflows are checked in the code generated. ADA is strongly typed which implicitly forbids mixtures.

B. Encapsulation

This property remains relevant with classes and objects. It is a question of rendering specific statement, closely intertwined the data of a software component and associated operations. Today, we are talking about member data and methods. In ADA, this software envelope is realized with the packages (package). But unlike Java (which takes this concept 20 years later). It is, in ADA, of a very concrete entity since declared in a clean file. This property is the pledge of a great federation of concepts where nothing is scattered. The package remained with ADA95 the basic structure of the language as it is a Robust and elegant code factorization technique.

C. Specifications and realization

The ADA package (ideal structure of a software component) houses these two entities well distinct (usually in two files). Package declarations on the one hand and package body on the other hand are the labels of these two entities (respectively spec and production). The spec part (not quite specifications but more surely a contract) only presents the declarations (data and sub-programs). The body of the package will realize, meanwhile, the contract proposed by the spec. Brand new entity (subroutine or package) relying on an already specified package announce this addiction with. The compiler then only refers to the part spec to control the syntax of the new entity. The coding of the realization can be deferred. This separation encourages prototyping without thinking about implementation and this development technique is very important. In the teaching of computing this process helps to force students to think before coding and it's the language (and the compiler) that gives teachers valuable help for this educational challenge. ADA provides novices with solid foundations that these will be able to transgress or use in other languages but with knowledge of be deferred. This separation encourages prototyping without thinking about implementation and this development technique is very important. In the teaching of computing this process helps to force students to think before coding and it's the language (and the compiler) that gives teachers valuable help for this educational challenge. ADA provides novices with solid foundations that these will be able to transgress or use in other languages but with knowledge of cause (and not out of ignorance). For example in the definition of subroutines the scope and direction of information exchanged is very clear. The passage of arguments for the procedures is specified in the prototyping. (Mentions In, Out, or In Out). Note that an ADA function remains a function (it accepts parameters in input and provides a single output result), for a novice, these basic notions appear very clearly. The impacts on the modification of the parameters during the use of an external procedure or function are equally clear.

D. Genericity

In ADA, these parameters (called of genericity) are as complex as desired. The parameters range from very traditional (constant or variable) through the types, subroutines and up to packages themselves generic! This profound degree of abstraction is absolutely remarkable. In ADA, the implementation of the genericity (declaration, instantiation and use) is very simple and elegant (so easy to teach). Packages generic ADA are compiled with authority without waiting for them to be instantiated which is not the case of C++ templates. This authoritative compilation validates the generic contract and to ensure that any instance respecting the contract will compile and will work as expected. Genericity allows and facilitates reuse and is even the safest technique to reuse reliably.

E. Exceptions

The exceptions are present in the language from ADA83. This concept is obviously essential in programming and allows to take into account the "anomalies" during the course of an application. ADA implementation of exceptions (declaration, initiation and treatment) seem to us of great ease and therefore very nice to teach. ADA95 has significantly improved this baggage and allows deeper treatments (a little less simple however to apply). In the same way, we point out a didactic property of importance namely the possibility of put in place, in the code, assertions.

F. Modular approach

This concept belongs to Object Oriented Design (OOD) techniques well illustrated with ADA83. A priori, when we stay at this stage of conception (and it is very often enough in many developments) it is not necessary to the "true" object. That is, it is often unnecessary to provide structures that to be extended by derivation (thus to make the design by analogy). However, if this is the case, ADA95 has an answer to make classes and objects.

G. Classes and objects

To make classes and therefore objects just take the concept of encapsulation, seen with the packages, and declare the first data structure (root) with the name tagged. Clearly any type 'tagged (or rather labeled) "is likely to be derived by extension and this inheritance characterizes the class structure. We can intelligently mix this design technique with the use of the hierarchies of packages seen above allowing, thus, even more flexibility and elegance in developments. Note, however, that the legacy multiple is not expected, indeed the designers of the language did not find useful to add a specific construct for multiple inheritance because too complex for a reduced use. On the other hand, conjunction "derivation and genericity" makes it possible to solve the cases of "mixing inheritance 'much less rare.

VI. STRENGHTS OF ADA

We are already talking about the software crisis and today, the problem is recurrent and even more worrying: development cost exceeded or difficult to predict, deadlines not respected, delivery not according to specifications, programs too greedy, unreliable, often impossible changes, etc. Let us review, briefly, some criteria or properties that must satisfy a consistent application and quality. We present in what follows the strengths of ADA language meeting the stated objectives.

a) Reusability: it is the ability of a software to be taken over, partly or even entirely, to develop new applications. We then talk about components software like the components that are reused in electronics.

b) Extensibility: it is the ease of adaptation of a software to the changes of specifications. Evolution of the data structure or adding features are desirable. This involves quick and reliable changes allowing a safe adaptive maintenance.

c) Portability: it is the possibility for a software product not to depend on a hardware environment, neither a system nor a particular compiler is particularly important for digital applications. Portability makes easier transfer of a hardware configuration and / or software system to another.

d) Testability: it is the implementation of aggressive processes whose purpose is to find errors in software. This phase of software development is important but often neglected or sloppy. This step is prepared before the implementation because we build test plans before coding (during the design stages).

e) Maintainability: it is the ability of a software to be modified elegantly, quickly, without fundamentally questioning the structure already specified or the existing applications.

f) Readability: it is the property of a code accessibility and understanding by more developers. The verbosity of a language sometimes decried can become a quality. As anecdote we could show the traditional "Hello World" to non-specialists, in different languages, The ADA version is the most readable (even compared to Pascal).

g) The ease of certification and validation: it is the ability of software to be able to be associated with properties proving that it meets its specifications, that it ends correctly or that it does not lock up in situations of load saturation or lack of resources. The existence of standardized language and verification possibilities helps to meet this goal.

VII. CONCLUSION

ADA is a design language as much as a programming language. ADA is designed to be read by ADA programmers and programmers not knowing ADA. From the point of view of the software engineers, in addition to being a programming language, ADA can be used as a communication language for some aspects of the needs and for some aspects of the design. With its embodiment of modern software engineering principles ADA is an excellent teaching language for both introductory and advanced computer science courses, and it has been the subject of significant university research especially in the area of real-time technologies. In our future work, we will plan to consider a case study in ADA showing an empirical study about advantages of ADA for software engineering.

REFERENCES

[1] M. Ben-Ari, ADA for Software Engineers, Weizmann Institute of Science, 2005.

[2] G. Booch and D. Bryan, Software Engineering with ADA, 3rd Edition, Addison-Wesley Professional, 1993.

[3] A. Wearing, Software Engineering, ADA and metrics, LNCS volume 603, 2005.

[4] D. Feneuille , "Teaching ADA-Choose a language: between the tendant and the reasonable", Version 3,2, 2005.

[5] S. F. Zeigler , "Comapring Development Costs of C and ADA", Rational Software Corporation, 1995.

Supercomputer Calculation of Gas Flow in Metal Microchannel Using Multiscale QGD-MD Approach

Viktoriia Podryga[1,2] and Sergey Polyakov[1,3]
[1] Keldysh Institute of Applied Mathematics RAS, Moscow, Russia
[2] Moscow Automobile and Road Construction State Technical University, Moscow, Russia
[3] National Research Nuclear University MEPhI, Moscow, Russia
e-mail: pvictoria@list.ru, polyakov@imamod.ru

***Abstract*–An important factor in modern development are promising nanotechnologies. One of the most popular areas of research in this field is modeling the nonlinear gas-dynamic processes in micro- and nanochannels. This problem is relevant for many applications on introducing and using the nanotechnology in various industries. A feature of mathematical problems in this area is the simultaneous study of processes at many scales, including micro- and nanoscales. In this paper, technology of the supercomputer realization of multiscale two-level approach to modeling the gas flow in microchannel is presented. The approach is based on combining the models of continuum mechanics and the Newton's dynamics for single particles. Two scale levels are considered: macroscopic and microscopic. The quasigasdynamic equations system is used as a mathematical model at the macrolevel. The molecular dynamics method is used as a mathematical model at microlevel. Numerical implementation of approach is based on the method of splitting into physical processes. The quasigasdynamic equations are solved by finite volume method on grids of different types. The Newton's equations of motion are solved by Verlet integration in each cell of grid independently or in groups of connected cells. Within the framework of common methodology, the four classes of algorithms and methods of their parallelization are offered. Parallelization technology is based on the principles of geometric parallelism and efficient partitioning the computational domain. Special dynamic algorithm is used for load balancing the computational units. The approach testing was made by the example of the nitrogen flow in the nickel microchannel. Obtained results confirmed the high efficiency of the developed methodology.**

Keywords-multiscale mathematical models; parallel algorithms; multiscale computing; gas dynamics

I. INTRODUCTION

Modern computer technology allows modeling very large technical systems and complex physical processes at the level of detailing that was previously not available. In computer models of past years, the lack of detail was often compensated by introducing the correction coefficients in the model that reflected the data obtained experimentally. This approach is still being applied, but with the development of massively parallel computing systems, it becomes possible to get rid of many limitations inherent in simplified models and perform direct predictive modeling of a large set of interacting nonlinear and multiscale processes. The foregoing is relevant to the study of complex gas-dynamic processes in technical micro- and nanosystems, developed with the aim of introducing the nanotechnology in industry. A feature of mathematical problems in this area is the simultaneous study of processes on many scales, including micro- and nanoscale. One of the modern and actively developing approaches to solving such problems is a multiscale approach that combines the methods of continuum mechanics and particle methods. This combination allows you to replace an expensive and difficult realized physical experiment with computer calculations.

In the paper, the problem of gas flow through a microchannel is considered as an example. A multiscale approach [1][2] is used for modeling the process, which has two levels of detail related to the dimensions of the specific geometry of the problem (tens of mean free paths of gas molecules and more) and the distance between interacting particles (on the order of 1 nm). The implementation of the approach is based on splitting by physical processes. At the macrolevel of detail, a description of the flow of gas media occurs. At the microlevel, the interactions are calculated for: 1) gas molecules among themselves (forming the equation of state, determining transport coefficients); 2) gas molecules and atoms of solid surfaces (describing phenomena in boundary layers). The system of QuasiGasDynamic (QGD) [3] equations is used as the macrolevel model, the Molecular Dynamics (MD) [4] method is used as the microlevel model.

Modeling of tasks with many scales should occur according to certain rules. In the approach used, these rules also apply. The MD calculations can be carried out in a direct way, combining QGD and MD in one implementation, and indirectly, by accumulating a corresponding database, calculated in advance. It is also possible to use partially the MD database and partial direct MD modeling in conjunction with the QGD calculations. As a result, computational technology contains four main classes of algorithms.

The main goal of the work is to describe the details of algorithms in which the QGD and MD models are used directly, alternating at each step, and the results of calculations for these algorithms and analysis of the calculated data obtained will also be presented.

This paper is organized as follows. Section II describes the state of the art. Section III states the problem and the mathematical model. Section IV describes what methods and computing algorithms are used in the research. Section V presents the results of the current research.

II. STATE OF ART

The computing complexity of modeling the gas flows in microchannels is associated with the violation of continuity hypothesis in some parts of the computational domain. The physics for functioning of the similar systems is usually described by whole hierarchy of mathematical models up to the atomic level. The difference in the scales of the computational domain and near-surface interaction of the gas with the metal lead to the necessity to take into account the relief and the properties of the microchannel at the molecular level. As a result, the mathematical model of the research flow can not be fully formulated within the framework of the macroscopic approach.

The way to overcome the problem of boundary processes is molecular modeling of flow-wall interactions [5][6]. In the proposed approach, a joint solution of the gas-metal problem taking into account the wall structure is carried out within the framework of direct MD simulation. Previously, the structure of the walls was not taken into account due to the complexity of the calculations and the lack of computing power.

The way to overcome the problem of discontinuity is using a multiscale approach [7]-[12]. Multiscale approaches have become popular, but existing combinations have many limitations on the type of problems, the size of systems, on taking into account the real boundary conditions, and so on. Most often within the framework of the multiscale approach, the Navier-Stokes equations with a continuous model of the boundary layer are used without taking into account the real structure of the walls. In the proposed approach, there is a combination of two models (QGD, MD) and various methods of this combination (4 classes of algorithms) are presented, and a database calculated by the first class of algorithms is also created. Such an integrated approach did not exist before.

Why and when it is necessary to choose the proposed approach: when precision calculation is needed; when the simulated process is not represented enough and a detailed picture of what is happening is necessary; there is computing power to apply the approach.

Advantages of the developed approach are the possibility of calculations from the first principles; the ability to vary the different parameters of the technique in order to obtain acceptable accuracy results within a reasonable time.

The motivation for a particular study of this work is to show that in reality a continuous boundary layer model can not give an accurate picture of the flow, since all important factors are not known, especially in the case of microflows. In this situation, algorithms of class 4 or direct MD modeling can give an adequate result to reality.

III. STATEMENT OF THE PROBLEM

The mathematical model includes two components corresponding to the scale levels.

At the macroscopic level, the QGD equations are used. In the case of a pure gas of one kind, the system of QGD equations in the three-dimensional case in a form invariant with respect to the coordinate system in dimensional variables, together with the equations of state is written as:

$$\frac{\partial \rho}{\partial t} + \operatorname{div} \mathbf{W}^{(\rho)} = 0, \quad \frac{\partial E}{\partial t} + \operatorname{div} \mathbf{W}^{(E)} = 0,$$
$$\frac{\partial (\rho u_k)}{\partial t} + \operatorname{div} \mathbf{W}^{(\rho u_k)} = 0, \; k = x, y, z, \tag{1}$$

$$E = \frac{1}{2}\rho|\mathbf{u}|^2 + \rho\varepsilon, \;\; \varepsilon = c_V T, \; p = Z\rho\Re T. \tag{2}$$

Here $\rho = mn$ is the mass density (m is the mass of molecule of gas, n is the concentration), T is the temperature and $\mathbf{u}$ is the macroscopic velocity. Other parameters: p is the partial pressure of gas; E and ε are the total energy density and internal energy. Variables $Z = Z(T,\rho)$, $c_V = c_V(T)$ and $\Re = k_B / m$ are the compressibility coefficient, specific heat capacity and individual gas constant (k_B is the Boltzmann constant); vectors $\mathbf{W}^{(\rho)}$, $\mathbf{W}^{(\rho u_k)}$, $\mathbf{W}^{(E)}$ coincide, up to sign, with the fluxes of mass density, momentum density of the corresponding components, and energy density.

The system of equations (1)-(2) is closed by the corresponding initial and boundary conditions. The initial conditions are taken in accordance with the equilibrium state of the gas medium in the absence of interaction with external factors. The boundary conditions for the QGD equations on the microchannel walls can be specified by determining the fluxes of mass density, momentum density and energy density across the boundary using Newton's conditions, or by the normal components of them near the walls by the MD method. On the free surfaces of the computational domain, the so-called "soft" boundary conditions [3] are given.

Near the walls, the particles (atoms or molecules) that make up the material of the walls and are potentially capable of detaching from the microchannel surface should be added to the consideration. The evolution of the investigated system of particles is described by Newton's equations [4]. The equations system describing the motion of particles of l kind (gas or metal) has the following form:

$$m_l \frac{d\mathbf{v}_{l,i}}{dt} = \mathbf{F}_{l,i}, \quad \frac{d\mathbf{r}_{l,i}}{dt} = \mathbf{v}_{l,i}, \quad i = 1,...,N_l, \;\; l = a,b, \tag{3}$$

where i is the particle number, l is the particle type (a – molecules of gas, b – atoms of metal in the microchannel), N_l is the total number of particles of type l, m_l is the mass of particle, $\mathbf{r}_{l,i} = (r_{x,l,i}, r_{y,l,i}, r_{z,l,i})$ and $\mathbf{v}_{l,i} = (v_{x,l,i}, v_{y,l,i}, v_{z,l,i})$ are the position vector and the velocity vector of the i-th particle of type l, $\mathbf{F}_{l,i} = (F_{x,l,i}, F_{y,l,i}, F_{z,l,i})$ is the resultant force acting on this particle.

The forces include the component of i-th particle interaction with the surrounding particles and the component responsible for external action:

$$\mathbf{F}_{l,i} = -\nabla_{\mathbf{r}_{l,i}} U + \mathbf{F}^{ext}_{l,i}, \quad i = 1,...,N_l, \;\; l = a,b. \tag{4}$$

Here, $\mathbf{F}_{l,i}^{ext}$ is the force of interaction with the environment, U is the total potential energy and it depends on choosing the interaction potential of molecules. The potential energy of the system is represented as a function that depends on the coordinates of considered particles and describes the interaction between the particles of the system.

The initial conditions at the microlevel are determined by the equilibrium or quasiequilibrium thermodynamic state of the particle system at a given temperature, pressure, and average momentum. The boundary conditions at the molecular level depend on the simulated situation.

In the presented technique, there is a choice between the accuracy of the result and arithmetic complexity in combination with a large amount of computation. The compromise is to get the solution with the required accuracy in the minimum time. What parameters can we control: the size of the grid cells at the macrolevel. If the size is large, then QGD is considered fast, the MD is considered very slow; if the size is small, then a statistics for MD calculations is not very representative. In addition, there is a technique for allocating a virtual volume within a cell (see [2]). Also, the database, accumulated from the first principles, makes it possible to reduce the amount of computation in those flow zones where there are no strongly nonequilibrium processes. In particular, most of the metal can be frozen.

A set of benchmarking tests was carried out. For example, the calculations of kinetic coefficients were carried out according to the algorithms of class 1 [13], calculations of gas flows by algorithms 2-4 were carried out in [14][15].

IV. Computing Algorithms

The calculation of the macroparameters according to the QGD equations (1) is carried out using an explicit on time grid numerical algorithm, which is based on the finite volume method on grids of arbitrary type [16][17]. For the convenience of solving the problem in areas of complex geometry, the hybrid block meshes consisting of cells of various shapes and sizes can be used.

In the presented variant of computational technology, a hybrid spatial grid is introduced in the computational domain at the macrolevel. All parameters of gas components (density, pressure, temperature, velocity vector components, etc.) refer to the mass centers of the cells. Flux variables refer to the faces centers of the cells. Spatial approximations of the basic terms of the QGD equations are performed by standard methods (see, for example, [18][19]). The computing scheme on time is chosen explicit and two-stage (predictor-corrector) and is integrated with the variable step.

The system of MD equations (3), (4) is used in additional calculations independently, or as a subgrid algorithm applied within each control volume. To integrate the equations of motion (3), (4), the Verlet integration [20] is used.

To carry out a correct calculation of the QGD, the model is supplemented by real gas equations of state, transport coefficients and other accompanying parameters (enthalpies, average mean free paths, etc.), as well as real boundary conditions. Calculation of these dependencies, coefficients, and conditions is made using MD methods.

Modeling of problems on the basis of the multiscale approach under consideration with two levels of detail is carried out with the help of special algorithms that in general, depending on the degree of microlevel use, are divided into four classes [15].

Algorithms of class 1 suggest the study of the properties of gas medium and the properties of solid surfaces with which the gas medium contacts in technical applications. As a numerical implementation of the approach in this case, the Velocity Verlet scheme acts. With the help of 1 class algorithms, a DataBase of Molecular dynamic Calculations (DBMC) is accumulated for the properties of gases and solid materials, which can be used in the framework of other algorithms.

Algorithms of class 2 assume the solution of problems only at macrolevel based on QGD system of equations. In this case, the properties of the gas (the equations of state by pressure and energy, the kinetic coefficients such as viscosity and thermal conductivity, the parameters of the boundary conditions) are determined from the above-mentioned DBMC accumulated in advance for the desired temperature and pressure range.

Algorithms of class 3 imply the simultaneous use of QGD equations in the calculations and equations of Newtonian mechanics for molecules of a gaseous medium. Algorithms of class 3 are realized within the framework of the method of splitting into physical processes. It is assumed here that in the gaseous medium and on its boundaries it is possible to confine ourselves to a local consideration of the processes of the gases and gases with a solid wall.

Algorithms of class 4 also imply the simultaneous use in the calculation of QGD equations and equations of Newtonian mechanics for molecules of the gaseous medium and atoms of the surface layer of the wall. The difference of this case from the previous one is that in some areas of the medium (usually at the boundary and in the zones of a strong drop of the gas parameters), molecular dynamics calculations are carried out continuously without going to the macrolevel. In the same areas, the principle of locality of molecular interactions is not used, that is, in the general case, the algorithms of class 4 are nonlocal at the molecular level.

Direct MD calculation in the framework of algorithms of 3 and 4 classes seems to be the most justified, since it allows to coordinate the interaction processes at micro- and macrolevels. Also, a direct MD calculation can be performed for a specific set of physical conditions that are not present in the DBMC and appear in it as a result of this calculation.

In this work, the algorithms of class 4 are used for calculation the gas flow in microchannel. The resulting grid equations in the framework of the algorithms of class 4 at the predictor stage are solved not on the whole grid, but on its subset.

In algorithms of class 4, some of the cells are permanently assigned to molecular computations (produced in parallel with the QGD computations at each time step using (1)) and are not considered at the macroscopic level. As a rule, these are grid boundary cells. In some cases, internal cells are added to them, where highly nonequilibrium processes occur, characterized by large gradients of gas-dynamic parameters. Denote the set of all such cells as Ω_B (QGD equations in these cells are not used). The remaining cells of the grid will be denoted by Ω_V (in these cells, both QGD and MD calculations are realized). As a result, the grid is represented as a union of two disjoint sets: $\Omega_V \mathrm{U} \Omega_B$. The transition to the MD calculations in the cells of the set Ω_B is carried out once at the beginning of the general calculation. In cells from the set Ω_V the transition to MD calculations is performed at each step in time.

The corrector stage includes the use of MD calculations and is associated with obtaining corrective values of the main gas-dynamic parameters. In algorithms of class 4, this correction is used only in cells of the set Ω_V .

Before the calculation begins, a grid is constructed that is split into sets of cells Ω_V and Ω_B . Then in the cells of the set Ω_V , the equilibrium state of the macrosystem is set; in the cells of the set Ω_B , the equilibrium state of the microsystem, corresponding to the equilibrium state of the macrosystem, is given.

Then, at each step in time, a two-stage procedure is carried out. A two-level calculation is carried out in the cells of the set Ω_V , presupposing first the solution of the QGD equations, and then the correction of the obtained gas dynamic characteristics by means of MD calculations. In the cells of the set Ω_B , a one-level two-stage calculation is performed on the basis of the equations of molecular dynamics.

At the first stage, gas-dynamic variables are calculated in the cells of the set Ω_V according to the QGD equations. Variables are transferred to the MD unit to recalculate the parameters of the conditions at the boundaries of the sets Ω_V and Ω_B . In the cells of the set Ω_B , the evolution of the boundary microsystems is calculated, the data of which will then form the parameters of the conditions on the boundaries of the sets Ω_B and Ω_V .

At the second stage, in cell sets Ω_V and Ω_B the direct calculations are made, which allow obtaining all gas-dynamic variables at the macrolevel taking into account all physical processes.

The calculation step is completed by testing the breakdown criterion, which consists in determining the relative time derivatives of the mass density and the energy density of the gas.

Parallel implementation of algorithms of classes 1-4 is considered in detail in [15] and earlier works. Here, however, it should be noted that the parallel decomposition at the macrolevel is based on the method of static decomposition of the calculated grid into microdomains. Such a partitioning, even with large configurations of computers, is deliberately redundant. It allows to equalize the load of processors and/or special calculators at various stages of calculations by "transferring" a part of microdomains from one calculator to another. In the implementation of MD calculations, in addition to geometric decomposition, the particle partitioning and dynamic load balancing are used.

The developed approach can be generalized and applied to different types of flows, but additional calibration calculations and the addition of a database for specific gases and metals are needed. The algorithm itself will not change.

V. Results and Disscussion

In this section, we will briefly present the results of testing the developed modeling technology. For this, we have chosen the problem of the nitrogen flow in a thin microchannel with a nickel coating of the inner walls. The scheme of the computational experiment consisted in calculating, on the basis of the algorithm of class 4, the interaction of a gas with a real crystal lattice of nickel. For simplicity, we chose a channel of rectangular shape, in the middle section of which the gas moves with supersonic speed (Mach is 14), and on the periphery the gas is strongly retarded by the wall. In this case, we took into account the effect of nitrogen adsorption on the nickel surface and heat exchange of the gas with the wall. The calculated region in one of the transverse directions (y) was considered extended and periodic boundary conditions were used along it. This approximation made it possible to reduce the amount of computation and take the following dimensions of the computational domain: $L_x = 3051\,nm$, $L_y = 101.7\,nm$, $L_z = 636\,nm$ (See Figure 1). Within this region, two boundary layers were identified, in which the interaction of the metal atoms of the walls and gas molecules was calculated by the MD method. The magnitude of these layers along the z coordinate was $L_{z1} = 86\,nm$. In the remaining middle layer with thickness of $L_{z2} = L_z - 2L_{z1}$ the gas flow was calculated on the basis of the QGD model. As a result, in the boundary layers, the total number of metal and gas atoms was approximately 488 million particles. In the middle part, a Cartesian mesh measuring 305x10x46 was used. With this size of the QGD grid, the computation takes up no more than 3% of the total computation. Therefore, the general time characteristics of the developed algorithm were analyzed below.

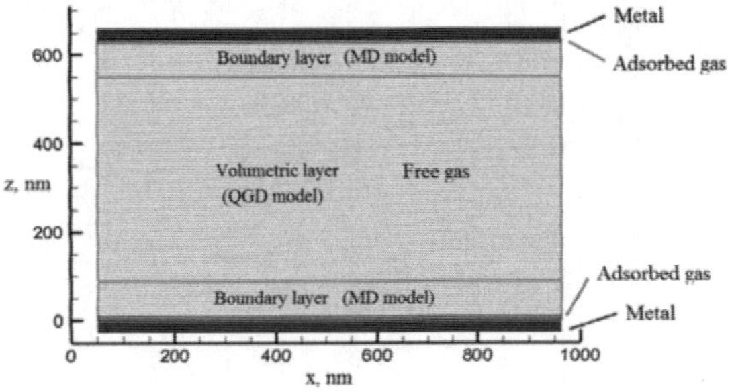

Figure 1. Computational domain. Section $y = 0$.

Test calculations of the flow in the microchannel of the indicated geometry were carried out on two computer systems with central and vector processors (see Table 1). The results of the acceleration and efficiency testing are presented in Figures 2 and 3.

TABLE 1. PARAMETERS OF USED COMPUTER SYSTEMS

Name	Node num-ber	Inter-connect type	Proc. type	Peak perfor-mance, TFlops	Proc. per node	Cores /Threads per proc.	Memo-ry per node, Gb
K60	78	Infini Band FDR	Intel Xeon E5-2690 v4	74,2	2	14/2	256
K48	16	Omni Path	Intel Xeon Phi 7250	48,7	1	68/4	96

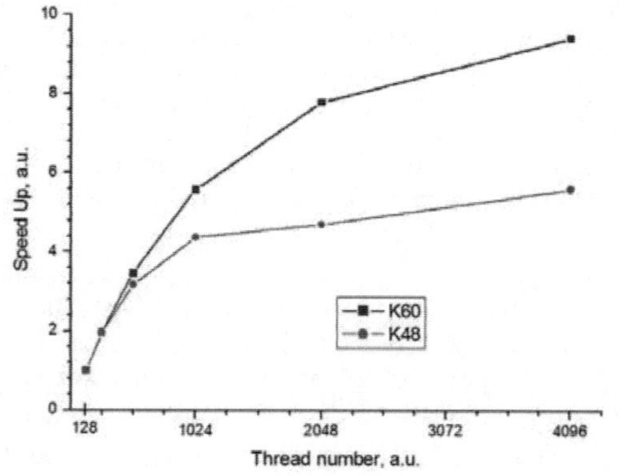

Figure 2. Speed up for the K60 and K48 systems.

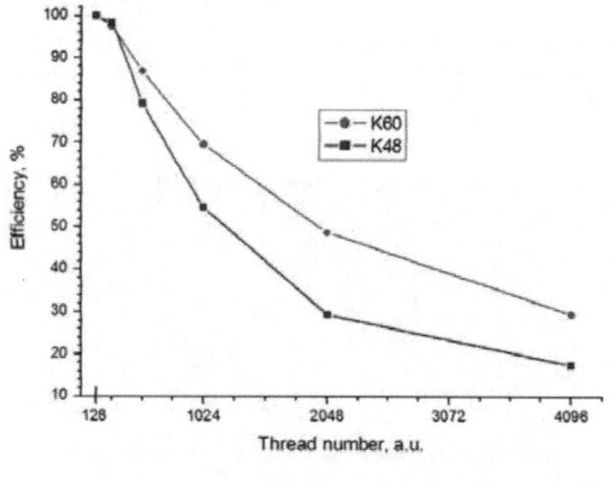

Figure 3. Efficiency of parallelization for the K60 and K48 systems.

Let us briefly discuss the results obtained. On the whole, it follows from the calculations carried out that the developed numerical approach and its parallel implementation make it possible to solve the chosen class of problems. A large amount of calculations in the MD block allows us to use rather large configurations of computer systems. However, the effective use of these systems lies in the ways of optimizing both the source algorithm and the developed code. In the case of using the CPU, the concurrency resource is not exhausted and the efficiency of the generated code is quite high. When using VPU of the specified type, there are 2 problems: 1) the cores of these processors are 10-15 times weaker than the CPU cores; 2) the fast VPU memory has a relatively small amount. As a result, in order to get the maximum effect from the VPU, you need to take order of magnitude larger configurations (in this example, containing about 160 nodes or more).

We also give some data on the simulated process. In accordance with the boundary value problem, the evolution of the jet is associated with the dissipative processes of the channel walls. They cause the jet to broaden with time, the flow rate decreases, the energy of the stream is transferred to the walls. This is illustrated by the distribution of the Mach number (Figure 4).

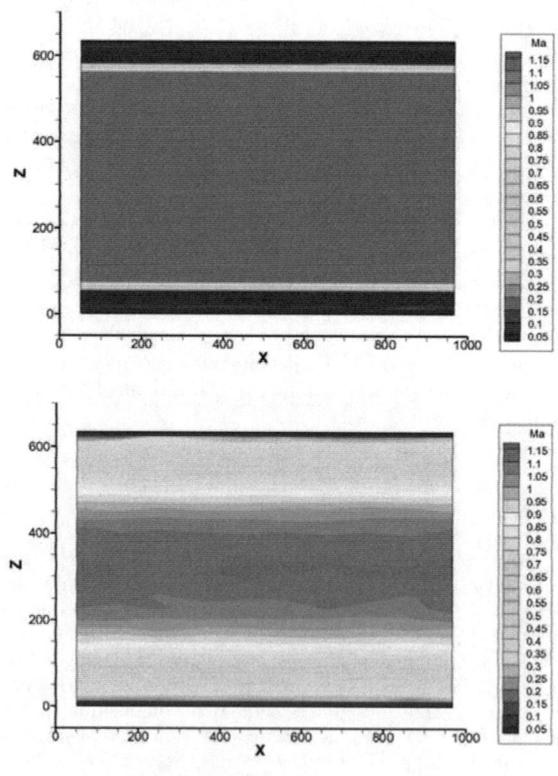

Figure 4: Initial (top) and steady state (bottom) distributions of Mach number averaged on y-coordinate.

VI. Conclusion and Further Work

The presented approach, computational algorithms and their program implementations work and allow specifying the flow parameters in the required place with the required accuracy.

The results are presented; they show the difference in performance between different computing systems when calculating the same problem. It should be noted that it is not possible to perform the calculation of one problem on one fixed computer system by other methods with the same or higher accuracy. Knowing the results of calculations for this approach, it is possible to form a QGD model or a Navier-Stokes model with a boundary layer and obtain the same result with the same accuracy in less time. However, "blindly" this can not be done.

The prospects of this work lie in further optimizing the code and adapting it to new generations of CPU, VPU and GPU and carrying out of detailed numerical experiments.

Future work involves expanding the database and analyzing the flows of various gases and liquids, as well as multiphase flows.

Acknowledgment

This work was supported by the Program of the Presidium of the Russian Academy of Sciences No. 26.

References

[1] V. O. Podryga, "Multiscale approach to computation of three-dimensional gas mixture flows in engineering microchannels," Doklady Mathematics, vol. 94, no. 1, 2016, pp. 458-460.

[2] V. O. Podryga and S. V. Polyakov, "Parallel realization of multiscale approach for gas microflows calculating," Numerical Methods and Programming, vol. 17, no. 2, 2016, pp. 147-165 [in Russian].

[3] T. G. Elizarova, Quasi-Gas Dynamic Equations. Berlin, Heidelberg: Springer, 2009.

[4] J. M. Haile, Molecular Dynamics Simulations. Elementary Methods. New York: John Wiley & Sons, Inc., 1992.

[5] V. Ya. Rudyak, A. A. Belkin, V. V. Egorov, and D. A. Ivanov, "Modeling of flows in nanocannels by the molecular dynamics method," Nanosystems: Physics, Chemistry, Mathematics, vol. 2, no. 4, 2011, pp. 100-112 [in Russian].

[6] V. L. Kovalev and A. N. Yakunchikov, "Accommodation coefficients for molecular hydrogen on a graphite surface," Fluid Dynamics, vol. 45, no. 6, 2010, pp. 975-981.

[7] V. A. Titarev, "Numerical method for computing two-dimensional unsteady rarefied gas flows in arbitrarily shaped domains," Comput. Math. Math. Phys., vol. 49, no. 7, 2009, pp. 1197-1211.

[8] M. K. Borg, D. A. Lockerby, and J. M. Reese, "A hybrid molecular–continuum method for unsteady compressible multiscale flows," J. Fluid Mech., vol. 768, 2015, pp. 388-414.

[9] K. Morinishi, "Numerical simulation for gas microflows using Boltzmann equation," Computers and Fluids, vol. 35, is. 8-9, 2006, pp. 978-985.

[10] A. Patronis and D. A. Lockerby, "Multiscale simulation of non–isothermal microchannel gas flows," J. Comput. Phys., vol. 270, 2014, pp. 532-543.

[11] S. Y. Docherty, M. K. Borg, D. A. Lockerby, and J. M. Reese, "Multiscale simulation of heat transfer in a rarefied gas," Int. J. Heat and Fluid Flow, vol. 50, 2014, pp. 114-125.

[12] A. Alexiadis, D. A. Lockerby, M. K. Borg, and J. M. Reese, "A Laplacian-based algorithm for non-isothermal atomistic-continuum hybrid simulation of micro and nano-flows," Comput. Methods Appl. Mech. Eng., vol. 264, 2013, pp. 81-94.

[13] V. O. Podryga, "Calculation of kinetic coefficients for real gases on example of nitrogen," Lecture Notes in Computer Science, vol. 10187, 2017, pp. 542-549.

[14] V. O. Podryga, Yu. N. Karamzin, T. A. Kudryashova, and S. V. Polyakov, "Multiscale simulation of three–dimensional unsteady gas flows in microchannels of technical systems," Proc. of the VII European Congress on Computational Methods in Applied Sciences and Engineering (ECCOMAS Congress 2016), Crete Island, Greece, 5–10 June 2016, vol. 2, pp. 2331-2345.

[15] V. O. Podryga and S. V. Polyakov, Multiscale Modeling of Gas Jet Outflow to Vacuum. Preprint No. 81. Moscow: Publishing of Keldysh Institute of Applied Mathematics, 2016 [In Russian].

[16] R. Eymard, T. R. Gallouet, and R. Herbin, "The finite volume method," in Handbook of Numerical Analysis, vol. 7, P. G. Ciarlet and J. L. Lions, Eds. Amsterdam: North Holland Publishing Company, 2000, pp. 713-1020.

[17] R. Li, Zh. Chen, and W. Wu, Generalized Difference Methods for Differential Equations. Numerical analysis of finite volume methods. New York: Marcel Dekker Inc., 2000.

[18] I. V. Popov and I. V. Friazinov, Method of Adaptive Artificial Viscosity of the Numerical Solution of the Gas Dynamics Equations. Moscow: KRASAND, 2015 [In Russian].

[19] W. Gautschi, Numerical Analysis, 2nd ed. New York: Springer / Birkhäuser, 2012.

[20] L. Verlet, "Computer «experiments» on classical fluids. I. Thermodynamical properties of Lennard-Jones molecules," Phys. Rev., vol. 159, 1967, pp. 98-103.

An Enumerative Variability Modelling Tool for Constructing Whole Software Product Families

Chen Qian and Kung-Kiu Lau

School of Computer Science
The University of Manchester
Kilburn Building, Oxford Road, Manchester, United Kingdom, M13 9PL
Email: chen.qian, kung-kiu.lau@manchester.ac.uk

Abstract—**Constructing a product family requires the formulation in problem space of a domain model (including a variability model) and its implementation in solution space. Current Software Product Line Engineering tools mostly aim to build an 'assembly line' for deriving one product at a time by assembling domain artefacts according to the variability model. Therefore, those tools support enumerative variability in problem space, but parametric variability in solution space. In this paper, we present a tool to model and implement enumerative variability in both spaces, and hence construct a whole product family in one go.**

Keywords–Enumerative Variability; Product Family Engineering; Web-based Tool.

I. Introduction

Current Software Product Line Engineering (SPLE) tools, e.g., pure::variants [1], AHEAD [2] and Clafer [3], construct a product family by using an 'assembly line' (product line). In the domain engineering phase, SPLE tools (i) construct a variability model in the problem space, and (ii) model and implement domain artefacts in the solution space, that can be used to assemble individual products. In the application engineering phase, SPLE tools assemble one product at a time from the domain artefacts in the solution space [4]. By contrast, we have defined an approach that constructs a whole product family in one go [5].

Existing SPLE tools usually define a feature model to specify variability in the domain engineering phase, and use a configuration model to specify a particular product variant in the application engineering phase. A feature model defines *enumerative variability*, as it includes all valid variants. A configuration model defines *parametric variability*, as it is parameterised on the presence/absence of features in a single product.

By contrast, we use enumerative variability in both the problem space and the solution space [5]. In Section II, we briefly introduce our product family engineering approach with the underlying component model. In Section III, we present a web-based tool that supports every step in our approach. In Section IV, we use an example to show how to construct a product family and derive products from the family by using our tool. Finally, in Section V, we finish our paper by conclusion of our work and discussion of the future work.

II. Overview of Our Approach

Starting from a feature model, we model and implement the enumerative variability defined by the feature model. Our approach is component-based, i.e., it follows a component model [6], [7]. We define a whole product family as a composition of variants of sets of components, as illustrated in Figure 1.

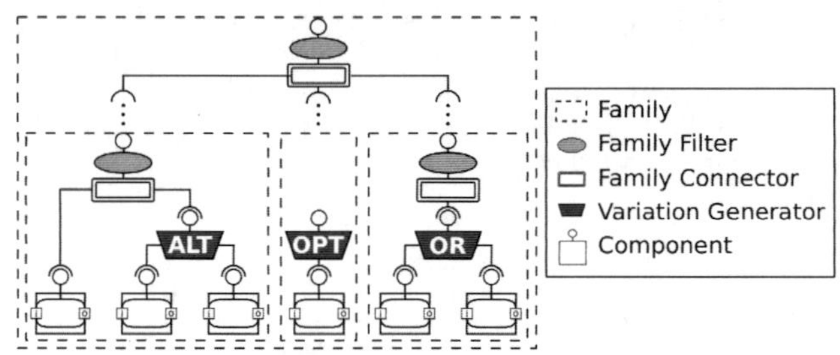

Figure 1. Component model: Levels of composition.

We proceed in three main stages, modelling and implementing (i) features, (ii) variation points, and (iii) product variants, respectively. Firstly, we construct components (atomic or composite) as the implementations of leaf features in the feature model. Notably, the abstract features aggregate behaviour corresponding to leaf features. A component is a software unit with a *provided service* (a lollipop in its interface) but no required services. Such a component is called an *encapsulated component* [7]. Then we apply *variation generators*, which model variation points in the feature model, viz. *optional*, *alternative* and *or* (respectively OPT, ALT and OR in Figure 1), and therefore generate sets of components as variations of the input set of components. So at the next level of composition, we apply *family composition connectors*. Each of them yields a set of product variants, i.e., a (sub)family of products, in the form of Cartesian product of its input sets, and composes components in each element of the Cartesian product using the corresponding component composition connector.

In our component model, the composition operators are algebraic, i.e., composite components are the same type as their sub-components, and composition is therefore strictly hierarchical. This important property enables us to model and implement the elements of a feature model (features, variation points, product variants) level by level.

Constraints in the feature model as well as feature interaction are dealt with by filters in family composition connectors. Invalid products are immediately removed from the Cartesian product of component sets produced by a family composition connector. We can also create new components for interacting features, and use them to replace original ones if feature

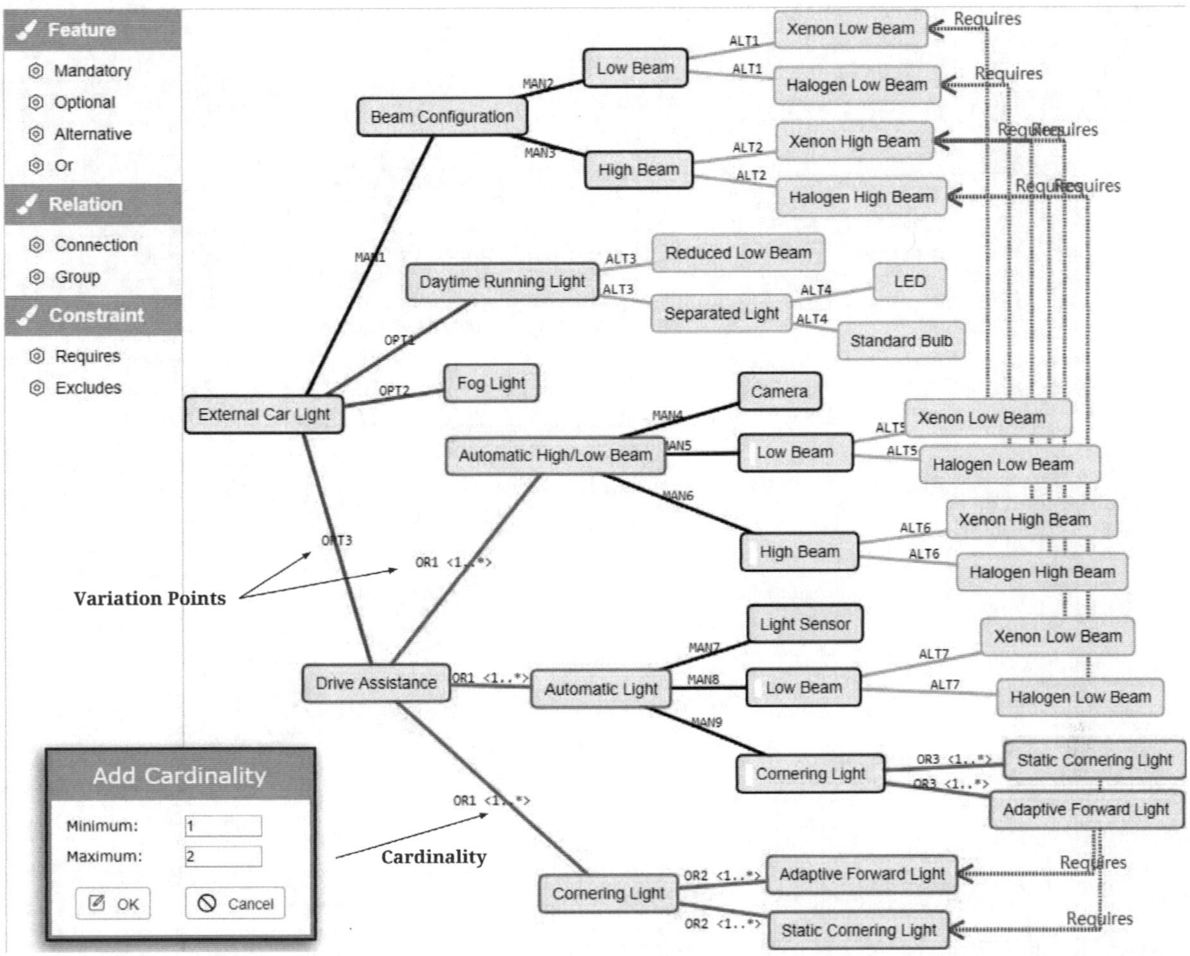

(a) Feature model.

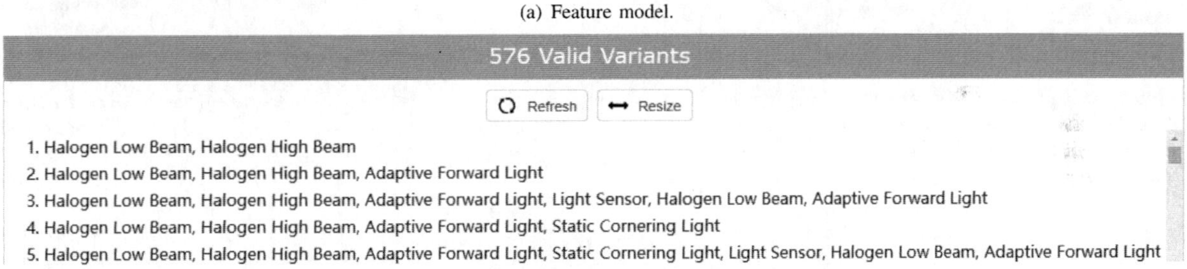

(b) All 576 valid variants.

Figure 2. Canvas for constructing feature model.

interactions occur in a product. The interaction rules are set up in the family filters, which are bound with every family composition connector, as shown in Figure 1.

III. The Tool

Our tool is a web-based graphical tool that implements our component model [8]. The GUI is realised using HTML5[9] and CSS3 [10], whereas the functionality is implemented using JavaScript [11]. In particular, we adopt the latest edition of ECMAScript as JavaScript specification since its significant new syntax, including classes and modules, supports complex applications. Additionally, we import jQuery [12], the most widely deployed JavaScript library, to improve code quality and enhance system extensibility. Our tool also offers a client-side repository called IndexedDB [13], which is a NoSQL database for massive amounts of structured data, as shown on the right side of Figure 3 (and Figure 4). For the purpose of user-friendliness, all building blocks, including constraints and interaction, can be easily added through buttons and dialogue boxes, as seen in Figures. 2-5.

The tool provides a workbench with functionalities that support the stages of our approach. Here, we describe these functionalities and illustrate them with the construction of a whole product family with 576 valid variants. The example is a family of *External Car Lights* (ECL) systems, which is adapted from an industrial example provided by *pure-systems*

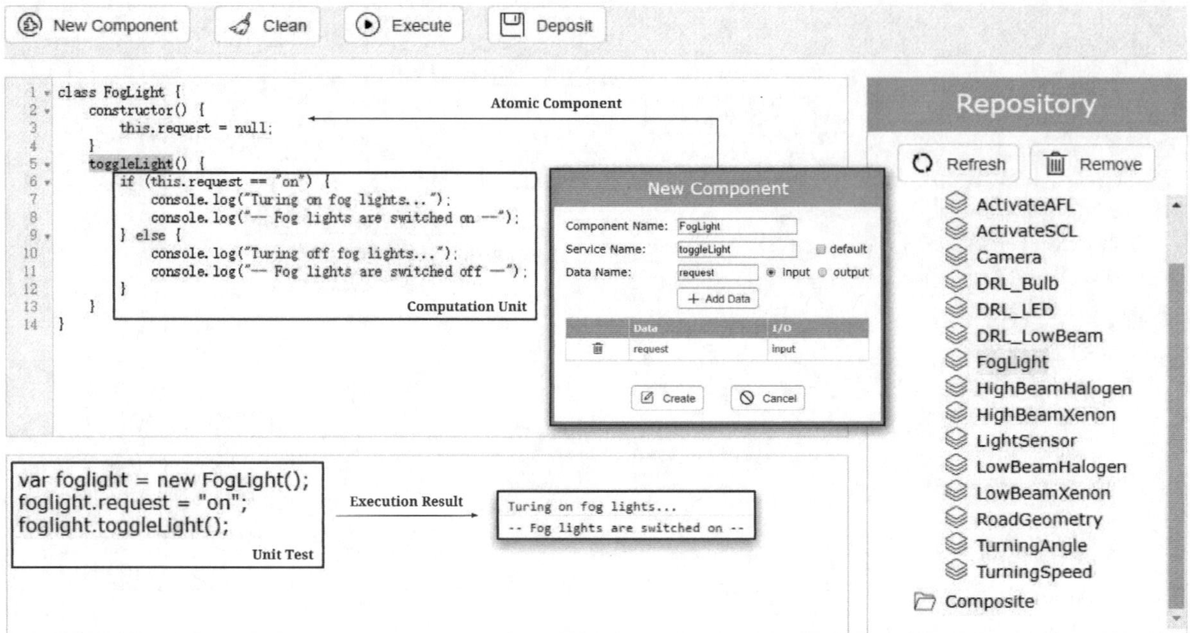

(a) Atomic component.

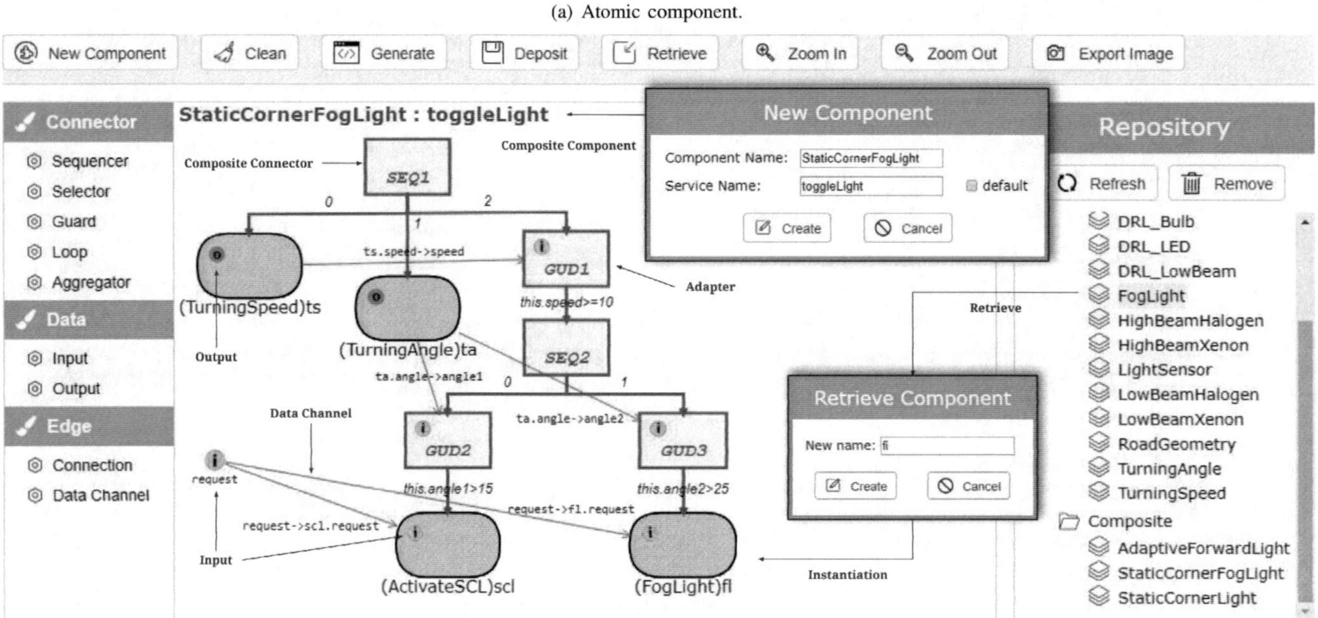

(b) Composite component.

Figure 3. Canvases for constructing components for leaf features.

GmbH. The requirement of ECL family is demonstrated in Section IV. Figure 2(a) shows the feature model that contains all 576 valid product variants enumerated in Figure 2(b).

A. Component Construction

Figure 3 shows the canvases provided by our tool for constructing components for leaf features. After a component is created, it should be deposited in a repository, and therefore can be retrieved for further construction.

Figure 3(a) depicts the construction and deposition, of an atomic component, `FogLight`, which is the implementation of leaf feature FOG LIGHT. By simply clicking the 'New Component' button, we can define the component name, service name, input data and output data in a dialogue box, which automatically generates an implementation template for the computation unit. Additionally, we can immediately test the component as soon as the computation unit has been implemented, and examine the result through browser console.

Figure 3(b) illustrates the construction of a composite component, `StaticCornerFogLight`. According to requirements, it implements the feature interaction caused by STATIC CORNERING LIGHT and FOG LIGHT. A composite com-

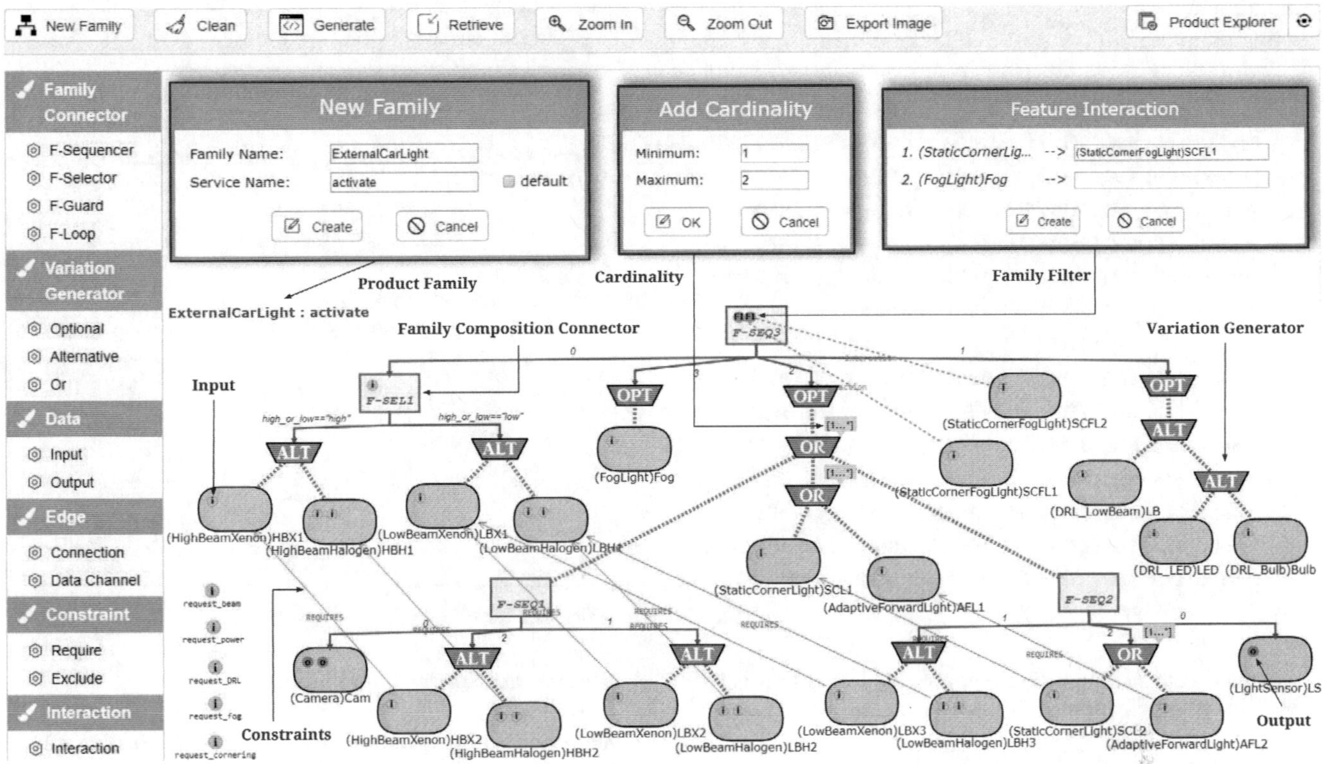

Figure 4. Canvas for constructing a whole product family from a feature model.

ponent is defined by its name and service, and constructed by composing components (retrieved from repository) via predefined composition connectors and adaptors (on the left of Figure 3(b)). Composition connectors include *Sequencer* and *Selector*, which provide sequencing and branching respectively. Adapters include *Guard* and *Loop*, which offer gating and looping respectively. Components can also be aggregated into a façade component, i.e., one that contains the aggregated components, by an *aggregator* connector *AGG*. Aggregates are essential for implementing the *or* variation point.

B. Variants and Family Construction

Figure 4 shows the canvas for constructing a whole product family from the feature model. It is worth noting that we omit the repository and data channels for clarification. A product family is defined by its name and service, and constructed by composing components (retrieved from repository) via predefined variation generators and family composition connectors (on the left of Figure 4). Constraints, derived from the constraints in the feature model (Figure 2(a)), as well as feature interaction, are defined as rules in a family composition connector filter. For example, if interacting features `StaticCornerLight` and `FogLight` are selected together, the former will be replaced by `StaticCornerFogLight` immediately.

C. Product Explorer

Figure 5 presents a useful feature of our tool, namely *Product Explorer*. It enumerates all valid products in the form of variability resulting from each variation generator at any level of nesting. For each product, by a simple click, the user can examine its structure and built-in components, and hence compare this product with the corresponding variant derived from the feature model. In this case, there are a total of 576 products in solution space, matching exactly the 576 variants enumerated in problem space in Figure 2(b). Figure 5 also shows the model structure of product No. 165.

Furthermore, any product can be executed and tested directly. A batch download link of all source code files is available.

IV. DEMONSTRATION ROADMAP

In this section, we will present how to construct a software product family step-by-step from scratch by our approach and tool.

Step 1: Construct Feature Model

An ECL system can control headlights (including LOW BEAM lights and HIGH BEAM lights), FOG LIGHTS and DAYTIME RUNNING LIGHT (including REDUCED LOW BEAM lamp, LED and STANDARD BULB). These lights can be switched on or off according to the driver's instructions. A beam is either Xenon or Halogen.

On the other hand, in some cases, an ECL system enables lights and signal devices by automatic detection. It provides a functionality called DRIVER ASSISTANCE, which supports AUTOMATIC LIGHT, AUTOMATIC HIGH/LOW BEAM and CORNERING LIGHT (including STATIC CORNERING LIGHT and ADAPTIVE FORWARD LIGHT).

Figure 2(a) shows the canvas for constructing the ECL feature model along with features, variation points and constraints. It defines an enumerative variability with a total of

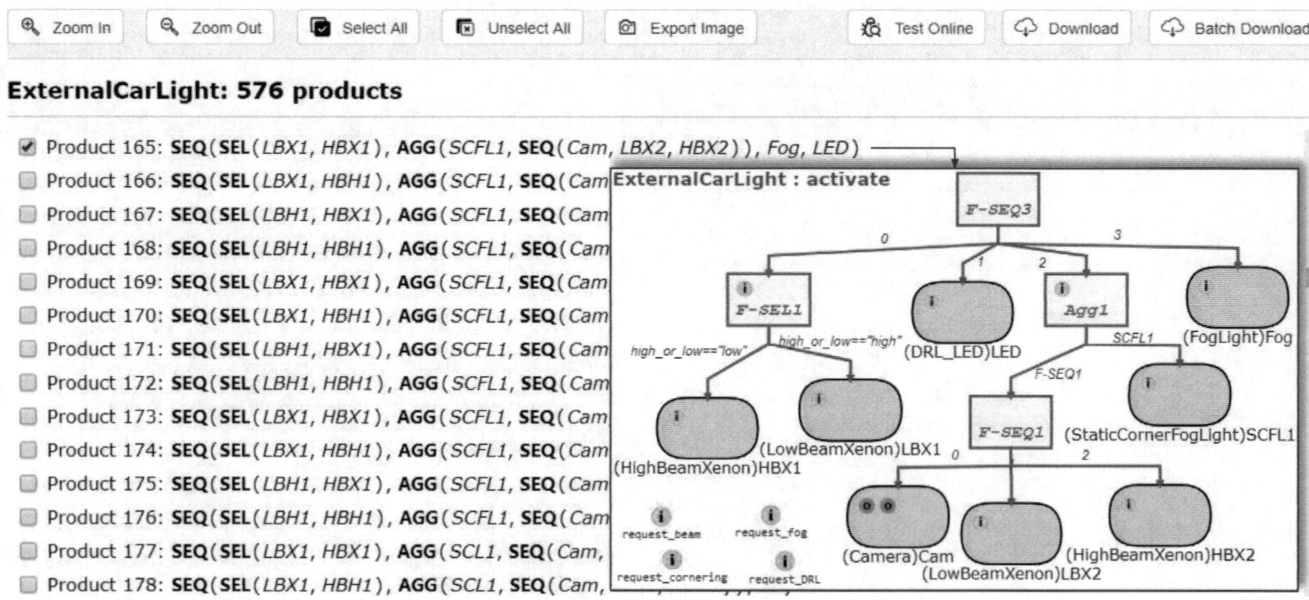

Figure 5. Product explorer and product No.165.

576 valid variants. Figure 2(b) shows all valid variants in terms of feature combinations.

Step 2: Construct Bottom Level Components

There are 20 leaf features in Figure 2(a), but some of them are reused. As a result, we construct 12 components (atomic or component) for them. In addition, we construct an optional component for feature interaction, as already stated in Section III-A. Once implemented, they are deposited for further construction. The repository in Figure 3 shows all the components, each of them can be tested directly, as illustrated in Figure 6.

Step 3: Apply Variation Generators

Now, we retrieve the pre-constructed components from repository. After instantiation, we have prepared 22 component instances for family construction, as shown in Figure 4. Then we apply the variation generators according to the feature model in Figure 2(a). For example, the OPT applied to *Fog* yields the set $\{\emptyset, \{Fog\}\}$; the ALT applied to *LED* and *Bulb* and gives the set $\{\{LED\}, \{Bulb\}\}$; and the OR applied to *AFL1* and *SCL1* generates the set $\{\{AFL1\}, \{SCL1\}, \{AFL1, SCL1\}\}$.

Step 4: Apply Family Composition Connectors

This step is to compose the variations into sub-families of the ECL family using family composition connectors. The choice of family composition connectors is a design decision, however it will not affect the total number of products in the (sub)family. For instance, in Figure 4, a family sequencer called *F-SEQ1* composes a sub-family, which is the implementation of abstract feature AUTOMATIC HIGH/LOW BEAM. The whole family is constructed when all sub-families have been constructed and composed. However, in order to filter out the invalid products, we need to add constraints between component instances, which are mapped onto the constraints we defined in Figure 2(a).

Step 4: Establish Interaction Rules

In Figure 4, we show a family filter for setting out interaction rules. It has been exemplified in Section III. The interaction will be displayed in the nearest family composition connector that composes the components involved. We add necessary data channels to define data flows. The final whole product family is shown in Figure 4.

Step 5: Test Products

All the products in the family are fully formed and executable, so they can be directly tested. Figure 6 shows the generated source code, testing code and result of product 165. This concludes the demonstration.

V. CONCLUSION AND FUTURE WORK

Our tool is a complete re-implementation of an earlier version presented in [14]. We have re-defined the underlying component model, added new capabilities including feature interaction, and used a different technology stack.

Compared to current SPLE tools, which use parametric variability to configure one product at a time in solution space, our tool offers a new possibility of constructing the whole family in one go, by using enumerative variability in solution space. Although, from a customer's point of view, constructing all products at once may seem like overkill, our approach/tool can be adopted by current SPLE techniques in application engineering, since our approach can provide all the necessary domain artefacts. For example, for the ECL family, our tool can generate an annotative code base using pure::variants notations. This code base can be correctly used in pure::variants for application engineering (Figure 7).

Finally, our tool will facilitate product line testing [15]. So far, our tool only provides a workbench for domain unit testing, i.e., testing components and products. However, it does not support domain integration testing and domain system testing [16]. Therefore, the further development of our tool includes (1) automatic comparison of variability specified in

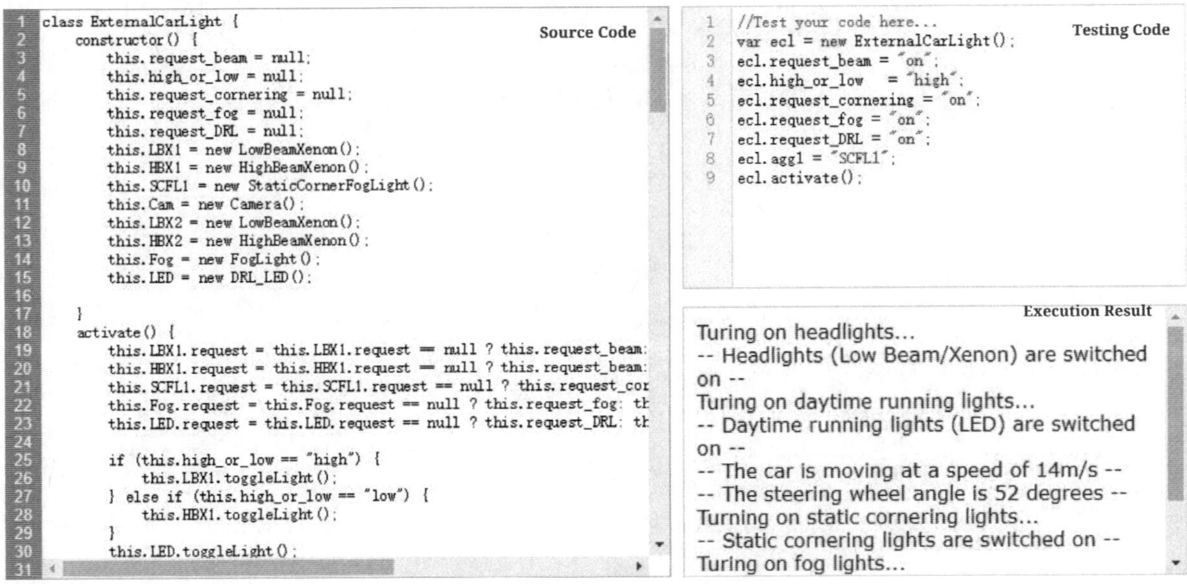

Figure 6. Product/Component testing.

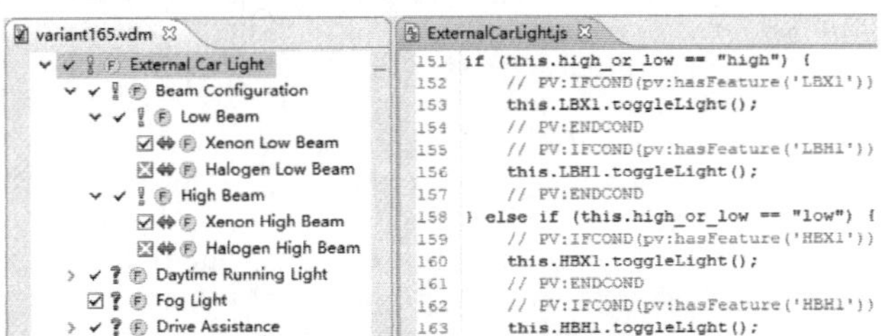

Figure 7. Generating annotative code base for pure::variants.

the problem space (Figure 2(b)) and implemented in the solution space (Figure 5), (2) the validity of every data channel, (3) generation of featured statecharts to examine behaviour at family level [17], [18].

REFERENCES

[1] D. Beuche, "Modeling and building software product lines with pure::variants," in Proceedings of the 16th International Software Product Line Conference-Volume 2. ACM, 2012, pp. 255–255.

[2] D. Batory, "A tutorial on feature oriented programming and the ahead tool suite," Generative and Transformational Techniques in Software Engineering, 2006, pp. 3–35.

[3] M. Antkiewicz, K. Bąk, A. Murashkin, R. Olaechea, J. H. J. Liang, and K. Czarnecki, "Clafer tools for product line engineering," in Proceedings of the 17th International Software Product Line Conference co-located workshops. ACM, 2013, pp. 130–135.

[4] K. Berg, J. Bishop, and D. Muthig, "Tracing software product line variability: From problem to solution space," 2005, pp. 182–191.

[5] C. Qian and K.-K. Lau, "Enumerative variability in software product families," in Computational Science and Computational Intelligence (CSCI), 2017 International Conference on. IEEE, 2017, pp. 957–962.

[6] K.-K. Lau and Z. Wang, "Software component models," IEEE Transactions on Software Engineering, vol. 33, no. 10, October 2007, pp. 709–724.

[7] K.-K. Lau and S. di Cola, An Introduction to Component-based Software Development. World Scientific, 2017.

[8] C. Qian, "Enumerative Variability Modelling Tool," http://www.cs.man.ac.uk/~qianc?EVMT, 2018, [Online; accessed 1-July-2018].

[9] G. Anthes, "HTML5 leads a web revolution," Communications of the ACM, vol. 55, no. 7, 2012, pp. 16–17.

[10] T. Celik and F. Rivoal, "CSS basic user interface module level 3 (CSS3 UI)," 2012.

[11] D. Flanagan, JavaScript: the definitive guide. O'Reilly Media, Inc., 2006.

[12] D. S. McFarland, JavaScript & jQuery: the missing manual. O'Reilly Media, Inc., 2011.

[13] S. Kimak and J. Ellman, "The role of html5 indexeddb, the past, present and future," in Internet Technology and Secured Transactions (ICITST), 2015 10th International Conference for. IEEE, 2015, pp. 379–383.

[14] S. di Cola, K.-K. Lau, C. Tran, and C. Qian, "An MDE tool for defining software product families with explicit variation points," in Proceedings of the 19th International Conference on Software Product Line. ACM, 2015, pp. 355–360.

[15] T. Thüm, S. Apel, C. Kästner, I. Schaefer, and G. Saake, "Analysis strategies for software product lines: A classification and survey," Software Engineering and Management, 2015.

[16] L. Jin-Hua, L. Qiong, and L. Jing, "The w-model for testing software product lines," in Computer Science and Computational Technology, 2008. ISCSCT'08. International Symposium on, vol. 1. IEEE, 2008, pp. 690–693.

[17] V. H. Fragal, A. Simao, and M. R. Mousavi, "Validated test models for software product lines: Featured finite state machines," in International Workshop on Formal Aspects of Component Software. Springer, 2016, pp. 210–227.

[18] A. Classen, P. Heymans, P.-Y. Schobbens, A. Legay, and J.-F. Raskin, "Model checking lots of systems: efficient verification of temporal properties in software product lines," in Proceedings of the 32nd ACM/IEEE International Conference on Software Engineering-Volume 1. ACM, 2010, pp. 335–344.

Feature-Oriented Component-Based Development of Software Product Families: A Case Study

Chen Qian and Kung-Kiu Lau

School of Computer Science
The University of Manchester
Kilburn Building, Oxford Road, Manchester, United Kingdom, M13 9PL
Email: chen.qian,kung-kiu.lau@manchester.ac.uk

***Abstract—Feature-Oriented Software Development* (FOSD) is widely used in *Software Product Line Engineering* (SPLE). FOSD constructs product families by incremental feature implementations. In this paper, we introduce a feature-oriented component-based approach, which implements features as an encapsulated components for further family modelling. A case study of elevator systems is also presented to describe the use of our approach.**

Keywords–SPLE; FOSD; CBD; Enumerative variability.

I. Introduction

Software Product Line Engineering (SPLE) traditionally proceeds in two phases: domain engineering and (ii) application engineering [1]. In the domain engineering phase, existing SPLE approaches (i) usually use a *feature model* to specify variability, and (ii) from these, identifies and implements domain artefacts, e.g., a code base [2]. In the application engineering phase, SPLE (i) creates product configurations, and (ii) assembles one product at a time from the domain artefacts based on its configuration [3].

The key abstraction of *Feature-Oriented Software Development* (FOSD) is a *feature*, which represents a logical unit of behaviour specified by a set of functional requirements [4]. FOSD aims at constructing software product families by incremental feature implementations [5]. Thus, variability can be traced from features directly to the domain artefacts, which promises the manageability and maintainability of product families.

In this paper, we present a feature-oriented approach to construct product families in a component-based manner, i.e., following a component model [6]. In [7], we elaborated the principles of our component model and discussed the feasibility of using it in SPLE. Hence, this paper discusses the concrete details. In Section II, we show the essential background knowledge and related work. In Section III, we present a case study to exemplify how to construct a software product family step-by-step from scratch by our approach and tool. Finally, in Section IV, we finish the paper by conclusion of our work and discussion of the future work.

II. Background and Related Work

The essence of FOSD is to model and implement variable domain artefacts, and each of them must be mapped onto a non-mandatory feature. In general, three main categories of variability mechanisms are adopted in FOSD approaches and tools [8]: (i) *annotative*, e.g., CIDE [2], FORM's macro language [9] (ii) *compositional*, e.g., AHEAD [10], FeatureC++ [11] and (iii) *transformational*, e.g., Δ-MontiArc [12], Delta-Oriented Programming (DOP) [13].

Annotative approaches usually build a single, superimposed model, namely 150% model, to represent all product variants. The variable features are implemented as code fragments with annotations, i.e., boolean feature expressions. Subsequently, in order to generate a product, code fragments corresponding to unselected features have to be removed according to the product configuration. By comparison, compositional and transformational approaches develop code fragments isolated from the base programs. Compositional approaches add the fragments correlating with the selected features to the base program for product generation. In regard to transformational approaches, fragments are not only added to the base model, but also modified the existing code under some circumstances.

There are two kinds of variability in current FOSD approaches, as known as negative and positive variability [14]. The former is adopted by annotative approaches, whereas the latter is used by compositional approaches. But both of them are used in transformational approaches. However, no matter negative or positive, we consider such a variability as a *parametric variability*, due to it is parameterised on the presence or absence of features in a single product. Thus, SPLE approaches using parametric variability can only generate one product at a time. On contrary, *enumerative variability* includes all valid variants directly [7]. For example, in the problem space, feature model defines enumerative variability, while a configuration model defines parametric variability. In this paper, our approach construct enumerative variability in the solution space, which results in a whole product family and therefore all products can be generated in one go.

Another area where our approach could bring advantages is feature mapping. The early work on SPLE, such as FODA [15], did not represent features explicitly, instead build n-to-m mappings between features and domain artefacts, which causes severe tangling and scattering in the code base eventually. Hence, the construction of product families are infeasible. FOSD have made a great progress by bringing a distinguishing property that aims at 1-to-n feature mappings. However, it becomes obvious that the ideal mapping is 1-to-1 [16], but it is difficult to be achieved in current FOSD approaches, mostly because of the cross-cutting concern of features. Our approach is capable to build 1-to-1 mappings between features and components. In this paper, we show how to deal with the cross-cutting problem in the case study.

Regarding to the outstanding maintainability and reusability, *component-based development* (CBD) is another paradigm that seems suitable for SPLE. But earlier researches certified that constructing product families only using CBD is barely feasible, due to features often do not align well with the decomposition imposed by component models [5]. Some researches [17], [18] try to integrate CBD and FOSD in order to obtain both their advantages in SPLE, but problems still occurs. In this paper, our approach adopts a state-of-the-art component model that partners FOSD very well.

III. A CASE STUDY

We have developed a web-based graphical tool that implements our component model and constructs product families [19]. The graphical user interface (GUI) is realised using *HTML5* and *CSS3*, whereas the functionality is implemented using JavaScript. In particular, we adopt the latest edition of *ECMAScript* as *JavaScript* specification since its significant new syntax, including classes and modules, supports complex applications. Additionally, we import *jQuery*, the most widely deployed JavaScript library, to improve code quality and enhance system extensibility. For the purpose of user-friendliness, all building blocks, including constraints and interaction, can be easily added through buttons and dialogue boxes.

In this section, we use an example of the elevator product family, which originates from [20], developed by Feature-Oriented Programming (FOP) in *FeatureIDE* [21]. The elevator contains a control logic mode that can be either `Sabbath` or `FIFO`, and an optional feature called `Service`. In `Sabbath` mode, the elevator reaches all levels periodically without user input, whereas in `FIFO` mode, the elevator moves to specific floors in turns according to the requests. The `Service` is special, it allows authorised persons to send the elevator to the lowest floor. Notably, `Service` is a *cross-cutting feature*, as its implementation scatters across other features' (`Sabbath` and `FIFO`) implementations. Consequently, the behaviour of `Service` can be triggered at any time, and on any mode, during elevator running period.

We will implement the elevator family in our tool, by extending it with the 3 features one at a time. Notably, for the clarification, we omit data channels in the figures in this paper. The design and implementation process is identical to the original example. Therefore, we can evaluate our approach based on the scientific control.

A. Adding Feature "Sabbath" to the Elevator Product Line

We add `Sabbath` as an optional child feature of the root, as shown in Figure 1. Then we need to implement a component for it. It is worth noting the underlying component model is already described in [6] and [7].

According to the requirement analysis of `Sabbath`, we can identify 3 behaviours behind it. Figure 2 shows the *composite component* composed by several *atomic components* and *composition connectors*. For example, *MovingUp* controls the elevator to move one floor up and returns the next direction, while *MovingDown* makes the opposite move. Contrariwise, *Flooring* leaves the elevator in the current floor. The *selector*

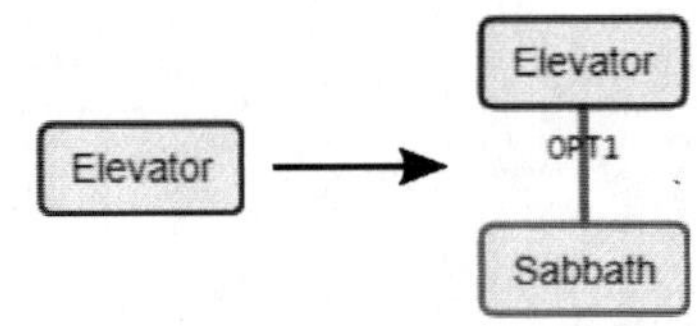

Figure 1. Adding `Sabbath` to the feature model.

SELs define branching depending on selection conditions, whereas the *sequencer SEQ* defines sequencing sequentially. As a result, the elevator changes direction when it reaches bottom floor and top floor.

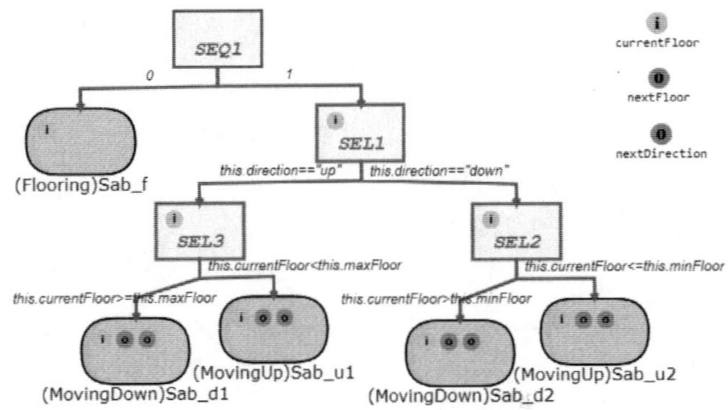

Figure 2. Component *Sabbath*.

After all, the elevator moves one floor up or down for each execution of `Sabbath`. In order to keep the elevator running, we only need to apply an *adaptor*, called *loop*, to repeat the control to this component (not discussed in detail here). Figure 3 shows the transition systems of the `Sabbath` component within the elevator product, which gives us a clear vision of the behaviour. So far no cross-cutting occurs, due to only one product exists.

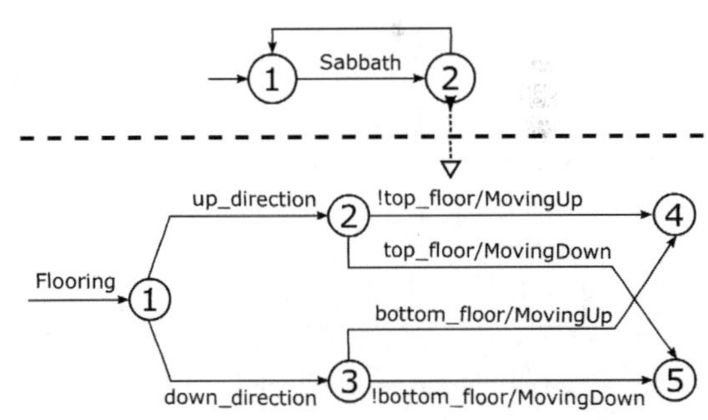

Figure 3. Transition systems of Elevator and *Sabbath*.

B. Adding Feature "Service" to the Elevator Product Line

Now, we add `Service` feature to the elevator product family. As this feature has no functional dependencies with `Sabbath`, we put it under the root. In addition, `Service` feature is not always required by every product, thus we set it optional. Figure 4 shows the change of the feature model.

We can reuse two components implemented before: *MovingDown* and *Flooring*. But in order to construct *Service* component, we need to implement another, namely *StopService*, which allows the authorised persons to deactivate the

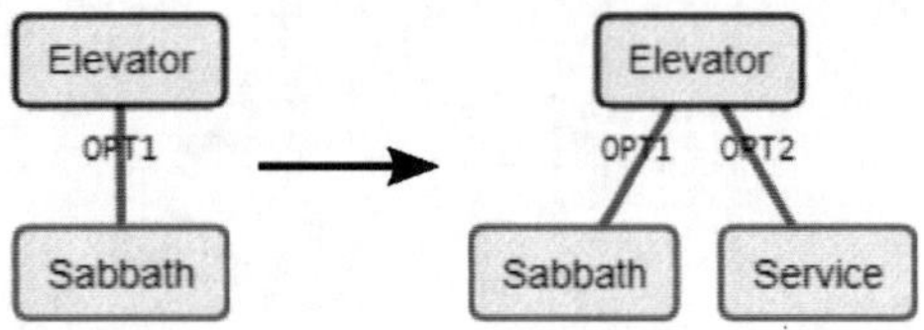

Figure 4. Adding `Service` to the feature model.

`Service` functionality after the elevator reaches the bottom floor. Figure 5 shows the construction of *Service* component.

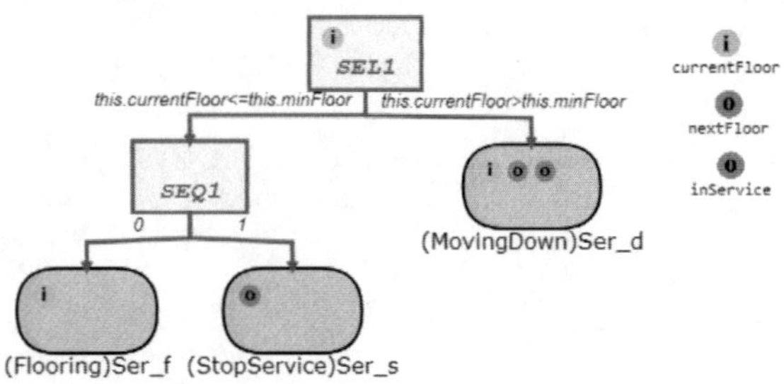

Figure 5. Component *Service*.

Next, we need to apply *variation generator*s to the components, which are mapped onto the variation points specified in the feature model (Figure 4). A variation generator generates multiple variants: it takes (a set of) sets of components as input and produces (a set of) permuted sets of components, i.e., variants. We have implemented variation generators for the full range of standard variation points, viz. *optional*, *alternative* and *or* (respectively OPT, ALT and OR. Notably, the components are algebraic and hierarchical at this level, which means the variation generator can be nested.

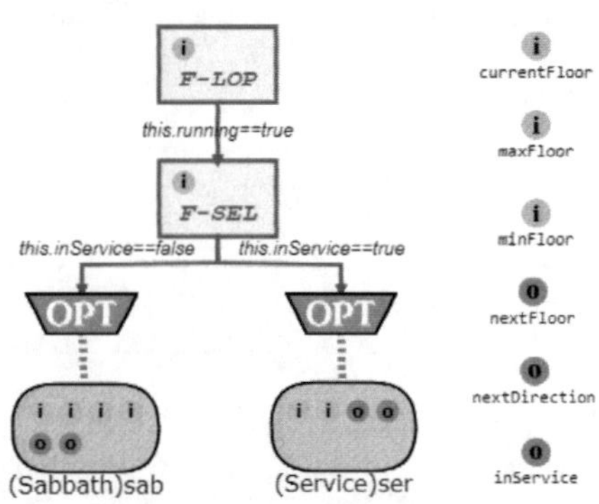

Figure 6. Elevator product family with *Service*.

At the next level of composition in our component model, family composition takes place, by means of family composition operators, also defined as connectors. A family composition operator is applied to multiple input component sets to yield a set of product variants, i.e., a (sub)family of products. These operators are defined in terms of the component composition operators: a family composition connector forms the Cartesian product of its input sets, and composes components in each element of the Cartesian product using the corresponding component composition connector. For example, in Figure 6, the family composition connector *F-SEL* applies the corresponding component composition connector *SEL* to components in each element of the Cartesian product, as well as the *F-LOP* indicates *LOP* (loop). The result of a family composition is thus also a family, so this level of composition is also algebraic.

The choice of family composition connectors is a design decision that only depends on the functional requirements, however it will not affect the total number of products in the (sub)families. Figure 6 shows the elevator family with two optional features. Derived from the family model in Figure 6, Figure 7 shows a *featured transition system* (FTS) [22] of the family, which depicts the cross-cutting feature `Service` takes part in family behaviour, e.g., 1-2-3-1 workflow.

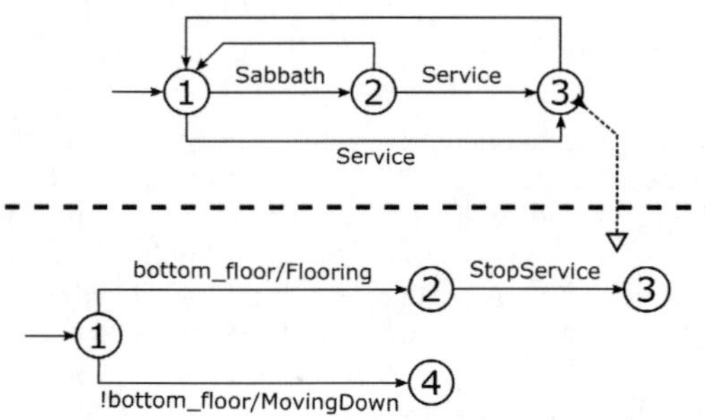

Figure 7. FTS of Elevator and *Service*.

At present, the elevator family generates 3 products, as shown in the *product explorer* in Figure 8. The product explorer enumerates all valid products in the form of variability resulting from each variation generator at any level of nesting. For each product, the user can examine its structure and built-in components, and hence compare this product with the corresponding variant derived from the feature model.

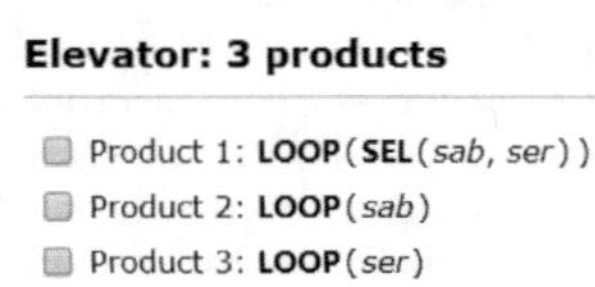

Figure 8. Product explorer (3 products).

C. Adding Feature "FIFO" to the Elevator Product Line

`FIFO` (first in, first out) is another control logic of the elevator. As the name suggests, if more than one floor requests exist, the oldest request is handled first, i.e., the elevator directly move to the required floor. By contrast with the feature `Service`, `FIFO` is an alternative to the already existing `Sabbath` mode. Therefore, we reform the feature model by adding features and modifying variation points, as Figure 9 shows.

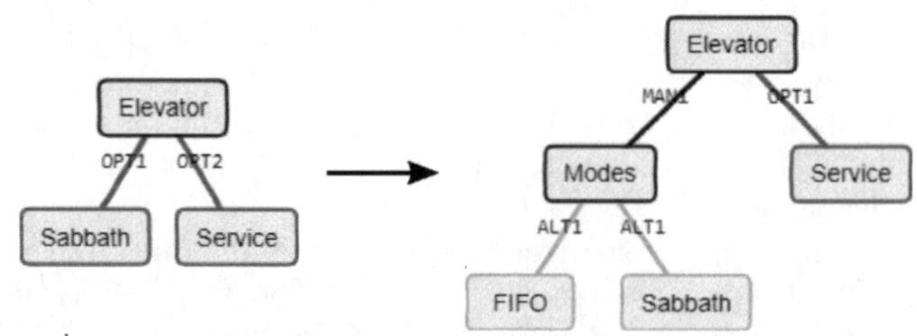

Figure 9. Adding `FIFO` to the feature model.

Likewise, we implement a component *FIFO* for feature `FIFO`. Figure 10 shows the architecture of the component, which is a composition of four sub-components. Two of them are newly prepared: *FloorQueue* and *RemoveRequest*. The former appends an incoming floor request to the end of the request queue, while the latter removes the first floor request from the queue.

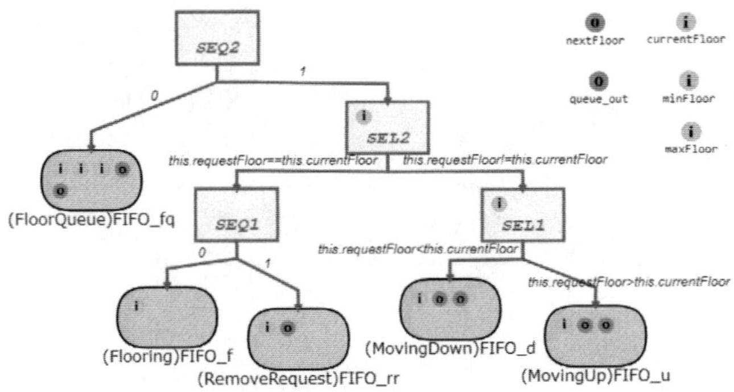

Figure 10. Component *FIFO*.

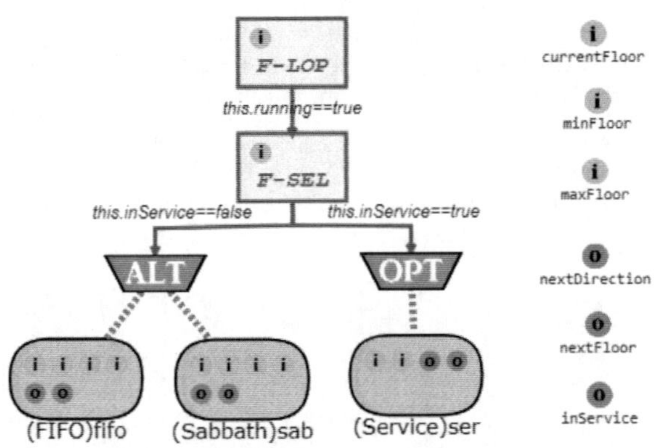

Figure 11. Elevator product family with *FIFO*.

After all leaf features are realised, now we can construct the new elevator product family. Since we have already presented *variation generators* and *family composition connectors* in Section III-B, the details of family construction are no longer described here. Figure 11 shows the latest elevator product family, which contains 4 valid products. The behaviour of the family is illustrated in Figure 12, in which we can see `Service` remains cross-cutting relationships with both `FIFO` and `Sabbath`. Finally, the products are enumerated in the product explorer in Figure 13.

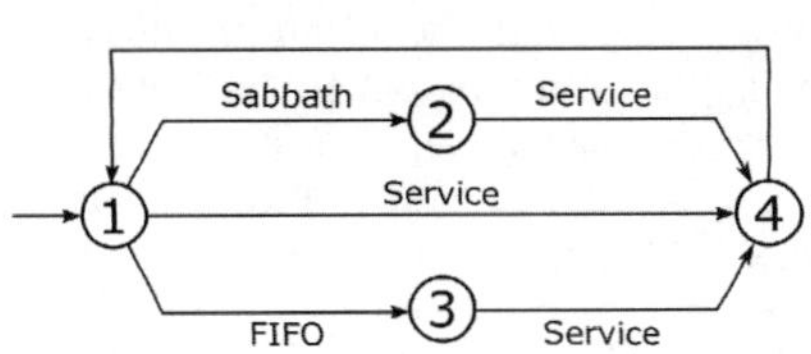

Figure 12. FTS of Elevator family.

D. Testing Elevator Product Line

Software product family testing comprises two related testing activities: domain testing and application testing. The former refers to domain engineering, whereas the latter refers to application engineering. Figure 14 depicts a V-model that describes the stages of domain engineering [23]. It involves 3

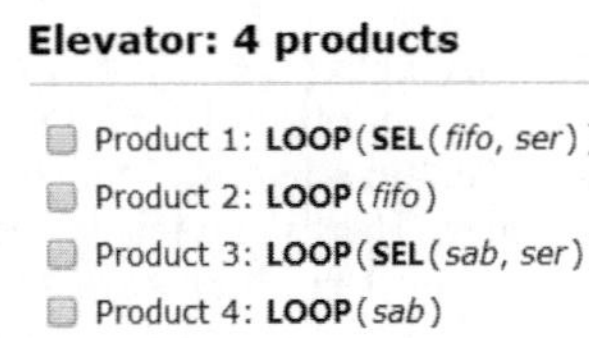

Figure 13. Product explorer (4 products).

different testing types, each of which tests a product line at a specific level.

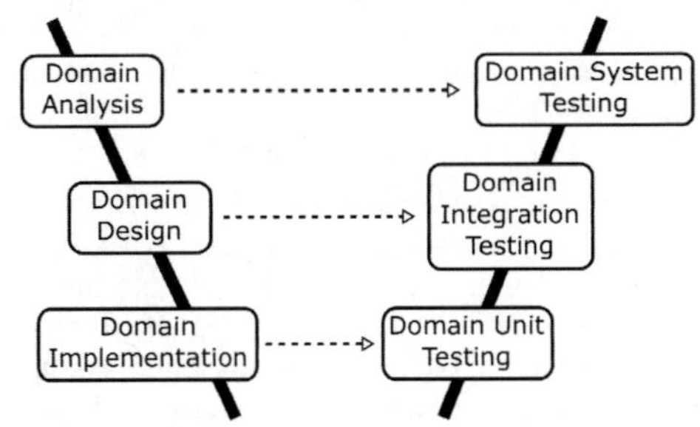

Figure 14. The V-Model for domain engineering.

Domain unit testing is easy to be operated for a feature-oriented architecture constructed in a component-based manner. In our approach, every component can be invoked via a *provided service*, which is a piece of behaviour (an input-output function) implemented by its methods. Therefore, the components, no matter atomic or composite, can be tested by the traditional techniques, e.g., structural testing. Our tool provides a workbench that all components can be executed directly. For example, we test component *MovingUp* within a simulation that controls an elevator to move from fifth floor to seventh floor. The result is demonstrated in Figure 15.

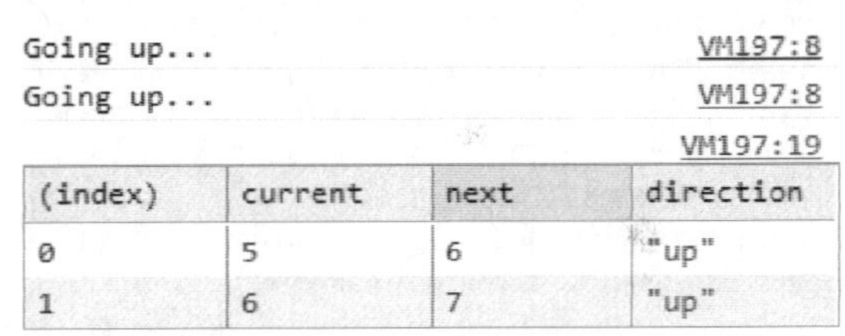
Going up... VM197:8
Going up... VM197:8
VM197:19

(index)	current	next	direction
0	5	6	"up"
1	6	7	"up"

Figure 15. Unit testing result of *MovingUp*.

Domain integration testing focuses on the testing of combinations of components. For most SPLE approaches, variability handling is a huge challenge in the integration testing phase, due to it heavily influences the components and their interactions [24]. Briefly, a variation point in the feature model may be modelled by multiple variation points scattered across a number of components, which results in too many component interactions for exhaustive testing. However, our approach may copes with the problem.

Firstly, the variability in family model is embodied by variation generators, which achieve a 1-to-1 mapping onto variation points in feature model, as well as the 1-to-1 feature mappings refers to the components. As we introduced earlier, the variability is *enumerative* in the final product family architecture. Notably, the product family architecture is isomorphic to the feature model. Thus, mismatched variability caused by invalid component interactions can be easily spotted in product explorer. For example, in Figure 11, if we misplace an OR variation generator on the top of *FIFO* and *Sabbath* instead of ALT variation generator, then we can observe 5 products in the product explorer. That is obviously incorrect due to the feature model only gives 4 product variants in total.

Secondly, the component model adopted in our approach exposes a provided service, but no required service. Such components are known as *encapsulated components* [6]. There are no coupling between encapsulated components, i.e., they do not call others. Instead, they are invoked by composition connectors. Thereby, we do not need to worry about the faulty component compounds, i.e., the incorrect bound interfaces. Moreover, as we mentioned earlier, the level of family composition is algebraic, as it generates a set of encapsulated components, which can be tested directly.

In conclusion, the distinguished property of our component model makes domain integration testing convenient and crystal, especially for the software product families of non-trivial size. All we have to do is examining the 1-to-1 mappings between (i) (leaf) features and components, (ii) variation points and variation generators. The correctness of behaviours between components will be tested at the next level.

Domain system testing evaluate all products' compliance with their requirements. It becomes obvious that verifying the behaviour of each product individually is difficult due to an exponential number of combinations of assets is unmanageable [25]. Since by our approach, the control flows are clearly coordinated by exogenous connectors and the components are directly mapped onto features, every family model can derive a family-based functional model that describes the combined behaviour of an entire family, such as FTS [22] or *Featured Finite State Machine* (FFSM) [26]. In this section, we have generated FTS diagrams for different elevator families in Figure 7 and Figure 12. The FTS describes the overall behaviour of family, and hence the behaviours of every product within the family. For example, if we misplace a *F-SEQ* (family sequencer) instead of *F-SEL* (family selector) in the family model in Figure 11, then the derived FTS would not show the 1-4 workflow as in Figure 12. Therefore, we can detect the problems in family composition, due to the FTS does not describe the required behaviour.

Family-based functional model can help us to verify the behaviour of component interactions, but it is not straightforward to validate the execution results. However, we cannot order test executions for every single product. Thus, we should execute a test case in the whole product family, i.e., all configurations of the family, without actually generating a concrete product. In that case, a product line testing method, called *Variability-Aware Testing* [27], is perfect for our family model. The key step of variability-aware testing is to extract an abstract syntax tree (AST) with explicit variability. In our approach, the final family model has a tree structure with enumerative variability, so it provides a seamless migration to the testing model. The testing model of the elevator example is demonstrated in Figure 16 (not discussed in detail here because of the limited space).

E. Product Generation

In Section II, we have presented that our approach construct enumerative variability in the solution space. In other words, all valid products are defined during composition. Unlike

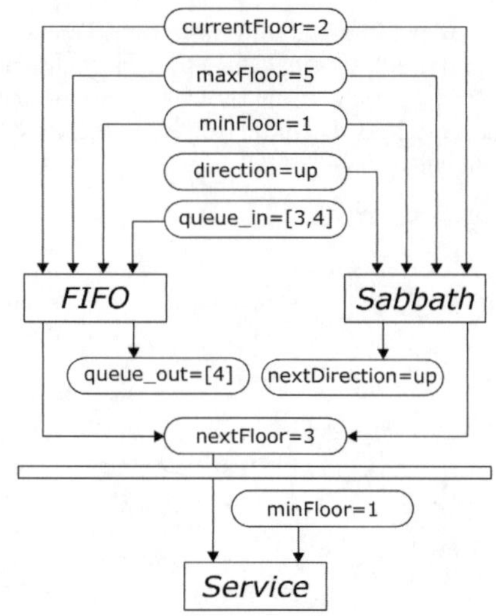

Figure 16. Variability-aware testing of Elevator.

conventional FOSD approaches, we can 'pick up' any number of products from the product explorer in one go, instead of one product at a time via configuration.

Here, to exemplify, we choose product No.3 from the product explorer in Figure 13. Figure 17(a) shows the product architecture, which is executable, and Figure 17(b) expresses partial execution result.

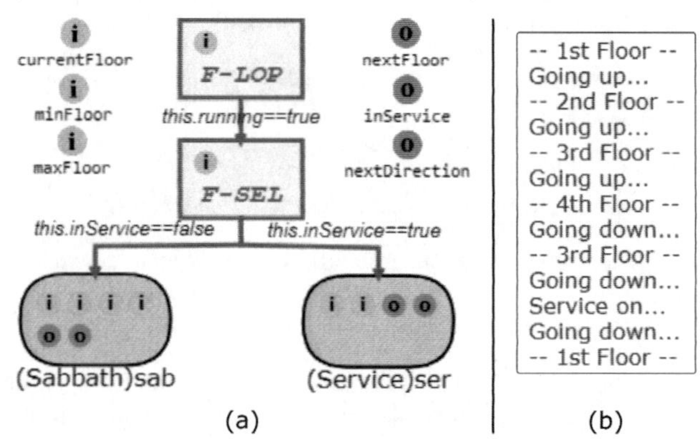

Figure 17. Product 3.

IV. Conclusion and Future Work

By comparison with the original elevator family implementation in [20], our implementation has many merits. For example, the original example is realised by FOP, in which every feature is mapped onto multiple code fragments scattering cross three classes. Each feature cannot be tested in isolation. Simply put, our approach provides better maintainability, manageability and testability because of the explicit 1-to-1 feature mappings. However, our family model only realises behaviour in the family. Contrariwise, in [20], FOP can define user interface for simulation, because as a low-level programming language, FOP can overwrite any code directly.

To provide step-by-step instructions of how to use our approach for family construction, we choose a small example for the simplicity. But our approach can be used for product families of non-trivial size. Besides the functions shown in

Section III, our tool can deal with cross-tree constraints (e.g., '*require*', '*exclude*') among features, and among components. Our tool can also set cardinalities to narrow down massive families. Moreover, our tool can handle feature interaction problem, which becomes the most significant challenge in SPLE [28], by importing extra off-the-shelf components during composition. As a matter of fact, we have successfully constructed product families for industrial cases, i.e., consisting of dozens of features and hundreds of products. In future, we plan to present these results of our research.

According to [29], in the real world, many organisations adopt product families using three techniques: *proactive*, *reactive* and *extractive*. A proactive approach implies that a product family is modelled from scratch. In contrast, a reactive approach begins with a small, easy to handle product family, which can be incrementally extended with new features and artefacts. An extractive approach starts with a portfolio of existing products and gradually refactors them to construct a product family. At present, it is apparent that our work is proactive. However, recent researches [30], [31] in reverse engineering suggest that our work also has potential to support reactive and extractive techniques.

References

[1] K. Pohl, G. Böckle, and F. J. van Der Linden, Software Product Line Engineering: Foundations, Principles and Techniques. Springer Science & Business Media, 2005.

[2] C. Kästner, S. Trujillo, and S. Apel, "Visualizing software product line variabilities in source code." in SPLC (2), 2008, pp. 303–312.

[3] K. Berg, J. Bishop, and D. Muthig, "Tracing software product line variability: From problem to solution space," 2005, pp. 182–191.

[4] J. Bosch, Design and use of software architectures: adopting and evolving a product-line approach. Pearson Education, 2000.

[5] S. Apel and C. Kästner, "An overview of feature-oriented software development." Journal of Object Technology, vol. 8, no. 5, 2009, pp. 49–84.

[6] K.-K. Lau and S. di Cola, An Introduction to Component-based Software Development. World Scientific, 2017.

[7] C. Qian and K.-K. Lau, "Enumerative variability in software product families," in Computational Science and Computational Intelligence (CSCI), 2017 International Conference on. IEEE, 2017, pp. 957–962.

[8] A.-L. Lamprecht, S. Naujokat, and I. Schaefer, "Variability management beyond feature models," Computer, vol. 46, no. 11, 2013, pp. 48–54.

[9] K. C. Kang, J. Lee, and P. Donohoe, "Feature-Oriented Product Line Engineering," IEEE software, vol. 19, no. 4, 2002, pp. 58–65.

[10] D. Batory, J. Sarvela, and A. Rauschmayer, "Scaling step-wise refinement," IEEE Trans. Software Eng., vol. 30, no. 6, 2004, pp. 355–371.

[11] S. Apel, T. Leich, M. Rosenmüller, and G. Saake, "FeatureC++: on the symbiosis of feature-oriented and aspect-oriented programming," in Generative Programming and Component Engineering. Springer, 2005, pp. 125–140.

[12] A. Haber, T. Kutz, H. Rendel, B. Rumpe, and I. Schaefer, "Delta-oriented architectural variability using MontiCore," in Proceedings of the 5th European Conference on Software Architecture: Companion Volume. ACM, 2011, p. 6.

[13] I. Schaefer, L. Bettini, V. Bono, F. Damiani, and N. Tanzarella, "Delta-oriented programming of software product lines," in Software Product Lines: Going Beyond. Springer, 2010, pp. 77–91.

[14] I. Schaefer, "Variability modelling for model-driven development of software product lines." VaMoS, vol. 10, 2010, pp. 85–92.

[15] K. Kang, S. Cohen, J. Hess, W. Novak, and A. Peterson, "Feature-oriented domain analysis (FODA) feasibility study," Software Engineering Institute, Carnegie-Mellon University, Tech. Rep. CMU/SEI-90-TR-021, 1990.

[16] C. Kästner and S. Apel, "Feature-oriented software development," in Generative and Transformational Techniques in Software Engineering IV. Springer, 2013, pp. 346–382.

[17] W. Zhang, H. Mei, H. Zhao, and J. Yang, "Transformation from CIM to PIM: A feature-oriented component-based approach," in International Conference on Model Driven Engineering Languages and Systems. Springer, 2005, pp. 248–263.

[18] P. Trinidad, A. R. Cortés, J. Peña, and D. Benavides, "Mapping feature models onto component models to build dynamic software product lines." in SPLC (2), 2007, pp. 51–56.

[19] C. Qian, "Enumerative Variability Modelling Tool," http://www.cs.man.ac.uk/~qianc?EVMT, 2018, [Online; accessed 1-July-2018].

[20] J. Meinicke et al., "Developing an elevator with feature-oriented programming," in Mastering Software Variability with FeatureIDE. Springer, 2017, pp. 155–171.

[21] C. Kastner, T. Thum, G. Saake, J. Feigenspan, T. Leich, F. Wielgorz, and S. Apel, "FeatureIDE: A tool framework for feature-oriented software development," in Proceedings of 31st ICSE. IEEE, 2009, pp. 611–614.

[22] A. Classen, P. Heymans, P.-Y. Schobbens, A. Legay, and J.-F. Raskin, "Model checking lots of systems: efficient verification of temporal properties in software product lines," in Proceedings of the 32nd ACM/IEEE International Conference on Software Engineering-Volume 1. ACM, 2010, pp. 335–344.

[23] J. Lee, S. Kang, and D. Lee, "A survey on software product line testing," in Proceedings of the 16th International Software Product Line Conference-Volume 1. ACM, 2012, pp. 31–40.

[24] L. Jin-Hua, L. Qiong, and L. Jing, "The w-model for testing software product lines," in Computer Science and Computational Technology, 2008. ISCSCT'08. International Symposium on, vol. 1. IEEE, 2008, pp. 690–693.

[25] T. Thüm, S. Apel, C. Kästner, I. Schaefer, and G. Saake, "Analysis strategies for software product lines: A classification and survey," Software Engineering and Management 2015. Gesellschaft fr Informatik e.V., 2015, pp. 57–58.

[26] V. H. Fragal, A. Simao, and M. R. Mousavi, "Validated test models for software product lines: Featured finite state machines," in International Workshop on Formal Aspects of Component Software. Springer, 2016, pp. 210–227.

[27] C. Kästner et al., "Toward variability-aware testing," in Proceedings of the 4th International Workshop on Feature-Oriented Software Development. ACM, 2012, pp. 1–8.

[28] M. Calder, M. Kolberg, E. H. Magill, and S. Reiff-Marganiec, "Feature interaction: a critical review and considered forecast," Computer Networks, vol. 41, no. 1, 2003, pp. 115–141.

[29] C. Krueger, "Easing the transition to software mass customization," in Software Product-Family Engineering. Springer, 2002, pp. 282–293.

[30] R. Arshad and K.-K. Lau, "Extracting executable architecture from legacy code using static reverse engineering," in Proceedings of 12th International Conference on Software Engineering Advances. IARIA, 2017, pp. 55–59.

[31] R. Arshad and K.-K. Lau, "Reverse engineering encapsulated components from object-oriented legacy code," in Proceedings of The 30th International Conference on Software Engineering and Knowledge Engineering. KSI Research Inc., July 2018, pp. 572–577.